Don't Blame Us

Politics and Society in Twentieth-Century America

William Chafe, Gary Gerstle, Linda Gordon, and Julian Zelizer, editors

Recent titles in the series

Don't Blame Us

Suburban

Liberals

and the

Transformation

of the

Democratic

Party

Lily Geismer

Princeton University Press
Princeton and Oxford

Library of Congress Cataloging-in-Publication Data

Geismer, Lily.
    Don't blame us : suburban liberals and the transformation of the Democratic party /
Lily Geismer.
        pages cm. — (Politics and society in twentieth-century America)
    Includes bibliographical references and index.
    ISBN 978-0-691-15723-8 (hardback)
    1. Democratic Party (U.S.)—History—20th century. 2. Liberalism—United States—
History—20th century. 3. Suburbs—Political aspects—United States. I. Title.
    JK2316.G34 2014
    324.273609'04—dc23   2014021096

British Library Cataloging-in-Publication Data is available

This book has been composed in Sabon Next LT Pro and Helvetica Neue LT Std

Printed on acid-free paper. ∞

Printed in the United States of America

10 9 8 7 6 5 4 3 2 1

to Mom, Dad, and Sarah

Contents

Illustrations and Maps

Acknowledgments

Perhaps the greatest joy of finishing this book is being able to thank all the institutions that supported and shaped me, and the people who helped with everything from the foundational ideas and arguments to the missing commas. I am first and foremost grateful to the staff at a number of archives and special collections departments, including the Arthur and Elizabeth Schlesinger Library, the Healey Library at the University of Massachusetts Boston, the Massachusetts State Archives, the State Library of Massachusetts, the Seeley G. Mudd Manuscript Library at Princeton University, the Concord Free Public Library, and countless local libraries around Boston. I owe particular gratitude to Northeastern University's Archives and Special Collections department and, especially, Michelle Romero for maintaining a terrific and accessible collection, and all their help as I finished this project remotely. I am also extremely appreciative of cartographer David Dies, who masterfully contributed maps that went far beyond my expectations of what was possible. I thank Will Frank and Caitlin Parker for their assistance as well. This project received generous financial support from a number of different institutions, including the Arthur and Elizabeth Schlesinger Library, the Institute for Research on Women and Gender at the University of Michigan, the Rackham Graduate School at the University of Michigan, the Miller Center for Public Affairs at the University of Virginia, the Andrew W. Mellon Foundation, the American Council of Learned Societies, and the Dean of Faculty's Office at Claremont McKenna College.

Claremont McKenna College has been a wonderful place to transition this project into a book. I am appreciative of deans Gregory Hess and Nicholas Warner for their commitment to my scholarly development, and Cindi Guimond and Bridgette Stokes as well. All my colleagues in the Claremont McKenna College history department have provided substantial support and encouragement. I am especially thankful to Diana Selig for her various forms of mentorship and humanity. Heather Ferguson, Niklas Frykman, Seth Lobis, Ellen Rentz, Raquel Vega-Duran, and Tamara Venit-Shelton have offered a great deal of camaraderie and advice. I am also grateful to the students at the Claremont Colleges whose curiosity and enthusiasm has stimulated me.

I am deeply indebted to my series editor, Julian Zelizer, who saw the potential in the project at an early stage, and has provided invaluable and immediate advice despite his own busy schedule. At Princeton University Press, Chuck Myers, Eric Crahan, Eric Henney, Leslie Grundfest, and Cindy

Milstein all patiently and skillfully guided the book through various stages of its evolution. I owe particular thanks to the press for assigning terrific reviewers. Joe Crespino and David Freund both took the time and care to offer feedback that helped me sharpen my analysis, strengthen the narrative, and see the project in new and important ways.

One of the most exciting and rewarding parts of this process has been the opportunity to meet and receive feedback from several scholars who I greatly admire. I am especially thankful to Jennifer Burns, Brent Cebul, Lizabeth Cohen, Deborah Dash Moore, Matthew Delmont, Kevin Kruse, David Levitus, Eileen Luhr, Margaret O'Mara, Suleiman Osman, Tom Sugrue, Bryant Simon, Peter Siskind, and Leah Wright-Rigueur for providing important chapter readings, sharing ideas, and offering suggestions and counsel. I was fortunate to serve as a fellow at the Miller Center of Public Affairs, which has given me a vibrant network, and connected me with Brian Balogh and my "dream mentor," Nancy MacLean. Meg Jacobs has offered essential advice, perspective, and reassurance at the most critical stages. When I moved to Boston to do research, Bruce Schulman generously embraced me as one of his own, and even after I left the city, has remained a crucial source of guidance. I also thank Bruce for introducing me to my "de facto" graduate school cohort, including David Atkinson and Kate Jewell, and especially Anne Blaschke and Kathryn Cramer Brownell. In Los Angeles, Becky Nicolaides has gone above and beyond to help me. The questions and suggestions from the members of the Boston University American Political History Seminar, Miller Center fellows, Princeton University American Political History Seminar, and Los Angeles History & Metro Studies Group as well as the audience at several conference presentations have undoubtedly strengthened this project. I owe a particular debt to the members of the Metropolitan History Workshop at the University of Michigan who participated in a reading of the entire manuscript, and collectively offered careful and incisive comments, which helped to sharpen the project substantially.

I have had many wonderful teachers throughout my academic career. At Brown University, I learned a great deal from Kenneth Sacks, Michael Vorenberg, and the late John Thomas, who all instilled and enriched my love of history. The University of Michigan History Department offered an unrivaled academic community. I am especially grateful to Penny Von Eschen, Mary Kelley, Jesse Hoffnung-Garskof, and Geoff Eley, who all were instrumental in my intellectual development and expanded my understanding of the possibilities of historical analysis. In addition, Matthew Countryman and Anthony Chen both provided a great deal of advice and alternative perspectives. Since my first semester of graduate school, I have benefited from the multifaceted support and guidance of Gina Morantz-

Sanchez, and I remain in awe and appreciation of her academic and personal generosity.

I am still not sure how I lucked out to have Matt Lassiter as my adviser. My appreciation for how generous with his time, energy, and insights Matt has been toward me for over a decade has only grown since becoming a faculty member myself. He has patiently engaged with my ideas—big and small, good and bad—and provided countless close readings of drafts, including an indispensable reading of the entire manuscript when things were down to the wire. I can say without a doubt that he has improved this project immeasurably, and his advice and model have pushed me to be a far better scholar and teacher.

I have also been fortunate for the chance to collaborate with a fabulous group of University of Michigan graduate students, including Aaron Cavin, Tamar Carroll, Nathan Connolly, Andrew Highsmith, Drew Meyers, Molly Michelmore, Josh Mound, Minayo Nasiali, Andrew Needham, and Dale Winling. Lauren Hirshberg and Laura Ferguson have remained invaluable sources of kindness and compassion. Clay Howard has read many, many drafts and talked me down from more than one ledge. This project and I have benefited greatly from his thoughts, humor, and friendship.

There are many drawbacks to the geographic uncertainty of academia, but one of the greatest parts of working on this project has been the opportunity it has given me to live nearer to and see many of my good friends and family. Whether in New York or Ann Arbor, Boston or Los Angeles—or in several of these places—Carolyn Bachman, Kristin Heitmann, Emily Janney Elliott, Anne Purdy, Mike Rothman, Emily Blumberg, Elizabeth Ryan, Leanne Hartmann, Molly Moeser, Paul Ramirez, Taylor Reilly, Sai Samant, Jonah Lehrer, and Sarah Liebowitz have been wonderful roommates, travel companions, and readers, and our conversations over the years have all shaped the project. I also owe much thanks to Meg Ostrum, Karen Roubicek, the Geoffroy family, Laurie Goldberger, Leslie Kogod, Marc Levitt, and Janet Mendelsohn. Mirra Levitt and Sarah Petrie were sources of academic and personal guidance long before we all wrote our senior theses together. Since then, they have remained an inextricable part of my own history, and I am grateful to them for their unflagging friendship and support. I thank Michael Kaufman for making the process of finishing the book a lot less painful.

My late grandmothers, Ruth Dangel and Barbara Geismer, long offered a sense of optimism and unwavering encouragement for all my pursuits. My sister, Sarah Geismer, has provided intellectual curiosity, enthusiasm, and giggles throughout my life, but especially in Los Angeles. My mom Susie Dangel's wellspring of energy, creativity, and devotion has both inspired and sustained me. I have benefited greatly from her insights and knowledge about Boston. The editing skills and advice of my dad, Alan Geismer, throughout my academic career has made me a much better writer and improved the prose of this book. He has encouraged me to set the highest standards, but is always the first person to express his confidence in me. This book would not have been possible without the understanding and unconditional support of my family, and I dedicate it to them with all my love and appreciation.

Abbreviations

ADA	Americans for Democratic Action
AFSC	American Friends Service Committee
ATP	Association of Technical Professionals
BPS	Boston Public Schools
BSC	Boston School Committee
BTPR	Boston Transportation Planning Review
CBT	Citizens for Balanced Transportation
CCF	Cabot, Cabot & Forbes
CHOC	Concord Home Owning Corporation
CLT	Citizens for Limited Taxation
CORE	Congress of Racial Equality
CPP	Citizens for Participation Politics
CPPAX	Citizens for Participation in Political Action
DLC	Democratic Leadership Council
DNR	Department of Natural Resources
DPW	Massachusetts Department of Public Works
ERA	Equal Rights Amendment
ET	Employment and Training Choices
FHPC	Fair Housing Practices Committee
GBC	Greater Boston Committee on the Transportation Crisis
GCSW	Governor's Commission on the Status of Women
HAC	Housing Appeals Committee
HUD	Housing and Urban Development
LCRC	Lexington Civil Rights Committee
MCAD	Massachusetts Commission Against Discrimination
MCFL	Massachusetts Citizens for Life
METCO	Metropolitan Council for Educational Opportunity
MFFHER	Massachusetts Federation for Fair Housing and Equal Rights
MHFA	Massachusetts Housing Finance Agency
MHTC	Massachusetts High Technology Council
MIT	Massachusetts Institute of Technology
MORAL	Massachusetts Organization for Repeal of Abortion Laws
MPP	Metropolitan Planning Project
NAACP	National Association for the Advancement of Colored People
NCDF	Newton Community Development Foundation
NEPA	National Environmental Policy Act
NOW	National Organization for Women
NLUCA	Newton Land Use and Civic Association

PAX	Massachusetts Political Action for Peace
ROAR	Restore Our Alienated Rights
ROUTE	Residents Opposed to the Urban Traffic Encouragement
SBPA	Swamp Brook Preservation Association
SVT	Sudbury Valley Trustees
VOW	Voice of Women–New England
WEP	Work Experience Program

Don't Blame Us

Introduction

In 1972, Democratic candidate George McGovern captured only Massachusetts in the presidential election. This crushing defeat cemented the reputation of the state as the unrivaled bastion of American liberalism. The outbreak of the infamous busing crisis just a few years later, however, gave the state's capital, Boston, the dubious and contradictory status as the "Little Rock of the North" and "most racist city in America."[1] Massachusetts earned national notoriety once again in 1988 with the resounding defeat of Democratic presidential candidate and Bay State governor Michael Dukakis, which seemed to confirm the view that "Massachusetts liberals" were out of touch with the rest of the country. The 1972 electoral map, violence of the Boston busing crisis, and the Dukakis presidential bid have become signposts of the exceptionalism of Massachusetts, failure of New Deal/Great Society liberalism, and decline of the Democratic Party.

This book counters those conventional narratives of exceptionalism and decline by examining the liberal residents who lived and worked along the high-tech corridor of the Route 128 highway outside Boston. Dispelling the widely held view that the rise of the New Right and the Reagan revolution led to the demise of liberalism, *Don't Blame Us* demonstrates the reorientation of modern liberalism and the Democratic Party away from their roots in the labor union halls of northern cities, and toward white-collar suburbanites in the postindustrial metropolitan periphery. The individualist, meritocratic, suburban-centered priorities of liberal, knowledge-oriented professionals embody the rise of postwar metropolitan growth, inequality, and economic restructuring, and contributed directly to the transformation of liberalism itself. The stories of the political activism by residents in the Route 128 area link these larger processes to local politics, reinforcing the key role of the suburbs in shaping party politics, public policy, and structural and racial inequality. The grassroots mobilization for the liberal causes of civil rights, environmentalism, peace, and feminism simultaneously challenges the scholarly assessments that have focused primarily on the reactionary, republican, and Sunbelt-centered dimensions of suburban politics. Connecting political culture and activism in the Boston suburbs to larger national political developments, *Don't Blame Us* shows that liberals did not prioritize "posteconomic issues" such as race, gender, foreign policy, and environmentalism, and become less responsive to the economy and workers in the 1970s and 1980s.[2] Rather, in supporting these issues, liberalism and the national Democratic Party increasingly came to reflect the materialist concerns of suburban knowledge workers rather than autoworkers.

1

The growth of liberal politics and support for the Democratic Party in postindustrial, high-tech enclaves across the country proves that Massachusetts holds an influential, but not exceptional, position in national politics. Engineers, tech executives, scientists, lawyers, and academics in the suburbs of New York, Philadelphia, northern Virginia, Atlanta, Chicago, Seattle, and Los Angeles, the college towns of Ann Arbor, Madison, Austin, and Boulder, and regions like the Research Triangle and Silicon Valley shared similar political priorities. This agenda combined economic and cultural issues, including a commitment to equality through support of affirmative action, pro-choice policies, concern about the environment and urban sprawl, and promotion of high-tech industry.

These priorities contributed to the increased support of knowledge workers in high-tech suburbs for the Democratic Party in national elections. Marking a trend that began with McGovern's candidacy, in 1988 a majority of professionals supported Dukakis in the presidential election. This pattern steadily grew over the next twenty years, and by 2012, Barack Obama earned the support of an overwhelming number of knowledge workers, particularly those with a postcollege education. Suburban knowledge workers tended to be less party loyal at the state level, which illustrates the complexity of both electoral patterns and the definition of liberal politics. In Massachusetts and other heavily suburbanized states, such as Connecticut, New York, New Jersey, and California, white-collar professionals consistently elected governors who promoted a blend of government reform, lower taxes, and socially liberal policies from both parties, helping to perpetuate a strand of moderate republicanism. Liberals in the Route 128 corridor, therefore, are equally important to understanding national political realignment and postwar suburban politics as New Right strongholds in the South and West.[3] Although a small portion of the electorate and an even smaller percentage of the national population, this group of people has come to hold a tremendous amount of political power at the national, state, and local levels.[4]

The suburban liberals along Route 128 also symbolize the larger economic and occupational reorganization of the nation after World War II that Daniel Bell famously deemed the "coming of the post-industrial society."[5] As soon as Bell coined the term, a reporter contended, "Probably no institution can claim to satisfy Bell's definition more completely than M.I.T."[6] The Cold War and other postwar imperatives led the federal government to significantly increase its funding of scientific-based research projects at universities. Boston and especially the Massachusetts Institute of Technology (MIT) benefited from an enormous windfall of defense dollars. The money spawned new innovation and led to an explosion of technology and electronics companies in office parks and labs along the ring of the Route 128 highway.[7] The rise of the high-tech industry propelled the

Figure I.1 Members of the technology industry unveiling the new sign heralding Route 128 as "America's Technology Highway" in 1982. These signs appeared on the side of the roadway to signal and promote Route 128's long-standing position at the forefront of the Information Age. Courtesy of the *Boston Globe* and United Press International.

migration of engineers, scientists, academics, and other knowledge professionals to move to the affluent suburbs clustered along Route 128.

In the early 1960s, real estate executive Daniel Wheeler offered a reporter a driving tour of the office parks spread along Route 128 that his company Cabot, Cabot & Forbes (CCF) had been instrumental in developing. Speeding by the exits to the suburbs of Lexington, Concord, and Lincoln, Wheeler declared, "Scientists and engineers are the main thing here." He described the towns as "quiet leafy places with good public schools, and scientists with young children like to live in them. They favor them because of their history—Paul Revere and so on."[8] Wheeler's depiction encapsulated the distinct set of polarities of history and modernity, tradition and progress, typicality and distinctiveness that animated the political culture of the Route 128 communities and the sensibility of the people who moved and lived there. Wheeler's comments also capture the meritocratic commitment to education, a desire for high quality of life and superior municipal services that defined most residents' priorities. The desire to live in proximity to the commuter roadway in a community with good schools and other amenities was not the exclusive domain of self-described liberals. Conservative, moderate, and apolitical people also sought out these areas, which created key tensions over local and national issues.

The communities of Lexington, Concord, Lincoln, Newton, and Brookline were by no means the only liberal suburban places in the Boston area or the country. Yet in this particular set of suburbs, the convergence of postwar demographic patterns with their specific histories and identities as spaces of tolerance, beauty, and open-mindedness created an especially fertile context for the emergence of liberal politics. As affluent families with ties to universities and Route 128 companies sought out communities that had certain cultural, social, and political markers of open-mindedness and a commitment to education, it further emboldened the distinctive reputation of this group of suburbs and made them ever more attractive to a particular type of liberal homebuyer. Attorney Julian Soshnick, for instance, explained that he settled in Lexington because he believed the "wall-to-wall Ph.D.'s, and the doctors and the lawyers" made it "a very nice, sensitive, caring community." Fellow Lexington resident and grassroots activist Bonnie Jones similarly observed that "like-minded folks tend to move into the same communities."9

The clustering of "like-minded people" in Lexington and other Route 128 suburbs catalyzed grassroots political activity for a range of liberal causes. Residents like Soshnick and Jones got involved in the fair housing movement in the late 1950s and early 1960s. These efforts led to the formation of the Metropolitan Council for Educational Opportunity (METCO) in 1966, a voluntary one-way integration program that transported African American students from Boston into the predominantly white suburban school systems. Suburban activists along Route 128 organized local open space and environmental movements, participated in peace and antiwar movements in the 1960s (formulating the idea for the Vietnam Moratorium in 1969), feminist and reproductive rights campaigns in the early 1970s, and mobilized for liberal politicians such as Eugene McCarthy and Father Robert Drinan. These activists displayed a consistent ability to work effectively within the formal channels of the political system, especially at the state level. The federal government and national organizations embraced many of the laws, policies, and initiatives first launched by grassroots suburban activists in Massachusetts, including fair housing, school integration, inclusionary zoning, open space and growth controls laws, the Vietnam Moratorium, and single-issue advocacy for abortion rights.

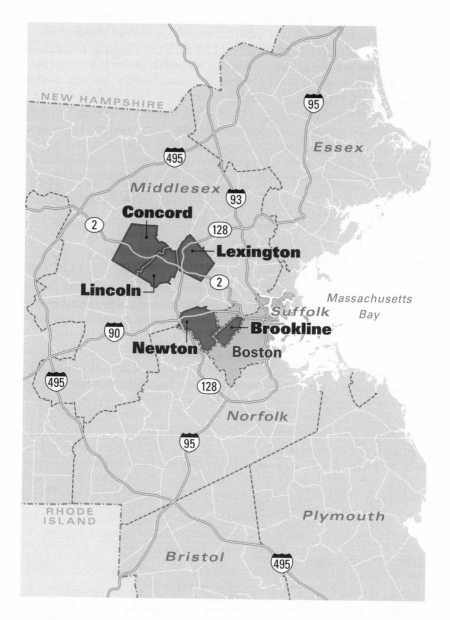

Figure I.2 Metropolitan Boston and the Route 128 area. The five suburbs that compromise the basis of this study are shaded, and the map also highlights the major commuter highways of Route 128 and Route 2.

This set of causes reflected the class identity and consumer-based, merito-cratic priorities of the affluent suburbanites who spearheaded and champi-oned them. Each element of suburban liberals' lives—from their homes in affluent suburbs like Lexington or Concord, jobs at research and develop-ment (R & D) labs along Route 128, and the roadway itself, to the educational opportunities for their children and the open spaces they enjoyed—emerged from the extensive array of federal policies produced by the pro-growth agenda of New Deal liberalism and the Cold War military-industrial complex. In turn, many suburban liberals sought to use their identities, privileges, ex-pertise, and social networks to shape policy through politics and legislation. Looking at how and why suburban liberals had success with some campaigns more than others underlines the broader structural and political forces that gave rise to yet also constrained their philosophy and actions.

Suburban liberals achieved the greatest victories in campaigns that pro-posed individualist solutions to rights-related issues, required limited finan-cial sacrifice, and offered tangible quality-of-life benefits. These campaigns included fair housing, voluntary integration, environmentalism, peace poli-tics, and feminism. Issues that challenged structural inequalities and threat-ened residents' property values and the entitlements of homeownership met greater resistance and far less success in the Route 128 suburbs. The limita-tions of this suburban liberal vision predicated on individualist solutions and middle-class privilege became most pronounced when the nation's economic climate shifted following the 1973 recession. The large cutbacks in defense spending hit the Route 128 area particularly hard, and fears about job security and a sharp rise in local property taxes buoyed by inflation brought many of the limits and challenges of suburban liberalism into sharp focus. Fierce bat-tles emerged over the construction of small affordable housing developments, expansion of involvement in the METCO program, and a statewide cap on local property taxes in the same suburbs that had been most vocal in their support of fair housing and environmentalism, and had turned out in large numbers for McGovern and against the Vietnam War. These fights revealed the internal and external limits and constraints of suburban liberalism.

Suburban Liberalism

Despite their important role in national politics and the economy, com-mentators and scholars have long struggled to find a term that accurately portrays the political consciousness of these highly educated professionals who supported a liberal agenda, and figure out where they fit into tradi-tional class, political, and geographic schema.[10] In the 1970s, the broad term "New Class" emerged, and since then critics and defenders have for-mulated a series of variations on that label, ranging from "professional-managerial class," "professional middle class," "knowledge class," "educated class," "knowledge worker," and "creative class," to "liberal elite," "latte liberal," "bobo," "neoliberal," and "Atari Democrats."[11] Each phrase captures a certain aspect of the professional identity, class standing, and political outlook of this constituency. Yet most of the white-collar professionals living in high-tech suburbs like the Route 128 area rarely used the words in this lexicon to self-identify. Instead, these residents often adopted the label "suburban liberal," which combined their explicit geographic, ideological, and political sensibilities and implicit racial and class identities.

The terms "suburban" and "liberal" have each been difficult to define satisfactorily. Scholars have long debated the proper mechanisms of how to determine what makes a space or person suburban, using a series of overlapping and competing measures, such as geography, the built environment, density, transportation networks, racial and economic characteristics, familial arrangements, cultural sensibility, ideology, and politics.[12] Liberal has proven an even more elusive term, whose meaning has shifted across the twentieth century depending on the context, scale, and especially who is invoking it. Liberal has described growth and regulation, free markets and economic justice, racial equality and racial privilege, and hawkish foreign policy and pacifism.[13] Critics and defenders often invoke the word liberal less to connote a unified set of values but as a term of opposition to mean "not radical," and especially "not conservative."[14]

Putting suburban and liberal together does not resolve many of these problems of capacious and contradictory terminology. Suburban liberal suggests a particular geographic location and political sensibility, but the term is neither spatially fixed nor static. Homeowners in the college towns of Cambridge, Boulder, Austin, and Palo Alto and the gentrified enclaves of Brooklyn, Chicago, and Seattle shared many of the same class and political priorities and politics, but did not deem their communities or themselves "suburban." The term suburban liberal is therefore as useful for the categories that it does not explicitly signal as those that it does. The label intimates but does not identify a partisan affiliation with the Democratic Party. Moreover, suburban liberal suggests a white middle-class identity, but neither word on its own is an explicit marker of race or class.[15] Suburban liberal thereby naturalizes the forms of systemic inequality and privilege embedded in both the meaning and the class and racial status of the people who embody the label. The terms suburban and liberal also each represent the ideals and values of individualism, yet suburban liberal itself is a category of shared identity. Thus, suburban liberalism reflects an ideology and politics of individualism that obscures the structures and forms of privileges and entitlements that link the people who ascribe to it together.

Less than a completely stable and consistent identity or ideology, it is more useful to consider suburban liberals and suburban liberalism the product of a set of interrelated historical processes. These processes and the relationship between them have their roots in the early twentieth century and the rise of urbanization, corporate capitalism, and progressive reform and flourished during the New Deal. Changes in the economy and the explosive growth of US cities led to the expansion of corporate institutions, and gave rise to both modern professions such as medicine, law, and engineering and a new emphasis on expertise and technocratic skill. The progressive movement's visions of government reform, which advocated for qualified elites to solve the problems of unregulated capitalism and social disorder, made technocratic expertise, science, and rationality a fundamental part of twentieth-century liberalism.[16] The New Deal further elevated this managerial ideology and the importance of using scientific expertise to solve the problems of social, economic, and racial inequality. In doing so, the New Deal agenda placed technocratic ideas and people at the heart of the mechanisms of government and ideals of liberalism.[17]

The Cold War not only vastly expanded the scope of the federal government but also fueled the rise of professional sectors, particularly in the sciences, and contributed to making "knowledge workers" the fastest-growing occupational sector in the decades after World War II.[18] The commitment of such knowledge-oriented fields to the ideals of hard work, intelligence, and skill elevated meritocratic individualism and accomplishment as ever more core values of twentieth-century liberalism. In the early 1970s, Daniel Bell observed that the "professional," who provided "not raw muscle power or energy, but information," had become the central figure in the postindustrial economic and social order, and predicted that "eventually the entire complex of prestige and status will be rooted in the intellectual and scientific communities."[19] Barbara Ehrenreich and John Ehrenreich similarly contended that for the new postindustrial professional class, education and knowledge had supplanted property and capital as the primary markers of identity and social status.[20]

This conceptualization of the significance of education, nevertheless, elided the importance of suburbanization as another key development to emerge from the New Deal, which played an equally critical role in shaping the nation, economy, and political outlook and identity of the new professional class. As part of its effort to create economic security and opportunity and stabilize market forces, New Deal and postwar bureaucrats developed a vast range of public policies—from mortgage initiatives, tax incentives, consumer credit, and subsidies for home building, to road construction, and urban disinvestment—to encourage single-family homeownership for whites outside central cities.[21] The same forces and policies of postwar suburbanization also produced systemic residential segregation by race and class that largely prevented minorities from gaining the privileges of homeownership.[22] Yet as several scholars have powerfully proven, the state-mediated real estate market fortified by the ideals of postwar liberalism and popular cul-

ture popularized a "free market" discourse that encouraged white suburbanites to understand their decisions about where to live as individual choices
and rights, and not see how such actions perpetuated forms of racial and
economic privilege and inequality.[23] The directives and incentives of state-
sponsored suburbanization simultaneously prompted homeowners to adopt
a more market or consumer-minded attitude toward government services—
from federal tax policy to local public schools—that further fostered an individualist outlook.[24] The set of policies that took shape at all levels of government magnified the privileging of individual self-interest over collective
obligation in postwar liberal ideology and institutions.[25]

The increasing popularity of psychology in the 1940s and 1950s accentuated this focus on individualism, injecting a new emphasis and vocabulary
of the self and therapeutic ethos into the politics of postwar liberalism.[26]
Psychoanalytic theories became especially important to liberal ideas about
race and racism during the postwar period, and reinforced the idea that
racism was the product of personal prejudice and moral deficiencies, rather
than public policy or the directives of the market. Thus, postwar liberals
demonstrated a renewed commitment to working within the political system to solve the problems of racial inequality, but tended to advocate for
civil rights policies that created "equal opportunity" and "individual rights,"
rather than those that focused on eradicating the structural underpinnings
of racial segregation and economic inequity.[27] Thomas Sugrue has powerfully shown how the quests of African Americans to fulfill their right to
housing and jobs came into direct conflict with the expectation of white
homeowners that the state would protect the privileges of property ownership, and revealed the fissures structured into the New Deal coalition.[28]
Suburban liberals came to embody and extend both aspects of this dual
definition of rights consciousness. As their attitudes toward fair housing,
school integration, and affirmative action demonstrate, this duality structured their political priorities before and after the so-called crisis of liberalism in the late 1960s.

This set of historical developments—from the rise of expertise and meritocracy, to homeownership, the focus on the self, and the popularity of racial
liberalism—converged to intensify the commitment to individualism within
liberalism as well as define the key parts of the worldview, political affiliations,
and voting patterns of suburban liberals. The Democratic Party never experienced a "golden age" of unity and equality, and was always rife with forms of
exclusion. Yet the increased emphasis on individualism after World War II did
mark a deviation from the forms of collective politics—particularly unionization—that defined the party's agenda for much of its history.[29] The dedication
to ideals of individual meritocracy rooted in knowledge work and suburban
residency did more than prevent the forging of coalitions across racial, economic, and spatial lines, or even the development of class consciousness

among white suburban professionals.[30] These individualist values submerged the ways in which many of the policies that suburban liberals benefited from fortified structures of economic and racial inequality. This multifaceted form of "class-blindness" had a profound impact on public policy, party politics, and the metropolitan landscape, and contributed to the continuation of, changes in, and constraints on liberalism since the end of World War II.

The "Problem" of Liberalism

Suburban liberals in the Route 128 area have stood at the intersection of the political, economic, and spatial reorganizations that occurred in the United States since 1945, but they have been largely left out of the traditional frameworks of twentieth-century political and urban history. Scholars have revitalized the field of political history by applying the ideas from urban studies to central questions about electoral realignment and the persistence of racial segregation.[31] Yet many of these works have rested on a geographically overdetermined narrative exaggerating the importance of the election of Ronald Reagan in 1980, and a binary relationship between the decline of the New Deal coalition in the industrial centers of the Rust Belt North and Midwest, on the one hand, and the conservative ascendance in the suburbs of the Sunbelt South and West, on the other.

In his seminal 1994 essay "The Problem of American Conservatism," Alan Brinkley accused historians of a political prejudice by overlooking conservatives.[32] Efforts to correct this prejudice led to a generation worth of scholarship reinforcing a story of inexorable liberal decline. Yet even before Brinkley's essay appeared, a declension narrative posed a "problem" for the study of twentieth-century liberalism. The earliest accounts of postwar politics argued that the "excesses" of 1960s' liberalism led to the "unraveling" of the New Deal coalition. The development of the "rise and fall of the New Deal Order" argument complicated that narrative and offered key insights into changes in the political economy fostered by New Deal policy. But the "rise and fall" framework focused primarily on the experiences of white male union members in the blue-collar neighborhoods of the Rust Belt, thereby wedding the travails of liberalism to the "Reagan Democrats."[33]

A counternarrative of postwar politics has examined the mobilization of the New Right in places like Orange County, California.[34] Lisa McGirr's *Suburban Warriors* and other works also demonstrate the importance of using grassroots methodology to address national political developments, and helped move conservatism from the "orphan in historical scholarship" to its increasingly favored child.[35] Many of these works, however, have treated the growth of the New Right and suburbanization as interchangeable processes, taking elements of suburban development and culture more broadly—such as the rise of the military-industrial complex, massive migration, federally subsidized entitlements, exclusionary zoning, and racial homogeneity—and attribute them solely to Sunbelt conservatism. In doing so, this analysis has obfuscated not only the alternative political constituencies that exist in suburban settings but also the ways in which a similar set of factors created the context for liberal activism and voting patterns.

There are undoubtedly differences between many of the suburbs in the "red" strongholds like Cobb County outside Atlanta, Hamilton County outside Cincinnati, Phoenix, Colorado Springs, and parts of Southern California versus the "blue" Northeast and Pacific Northwest. These differences derive from their respective histories, migration patterns, religious cultures, and particular forms of corporate and military investment. Yet concentrating only on these regionally based reputations and differences has obscured the fact that there are liberal and conservative suburban professionals everywhere. Many engineers in Orange County campaigned with the same fervor for McGovern that their colleagues had for Barry Goldwater a decade earlier. Housewives outside Miami fought as hard for gay rights as Anita Bryant and her supporters stood against it, and scores of suburbanites in Atlanta and Houston remained committed to school integration. At the same time, there were many conservatives in bastions of liberalism like the suburbs along Route 128. Robert Welch, founder of the John Birch Society, lived in the Boston suburb of Belmont. And as this study documents, there were many homeowners in Newton who held strong against affordable housing and busing, committed tax revolters in Concord, and opponents to the legalization of abortion in Lexington.[36]

More important, looking solely at these regional distinctions has prevented scholars from recognizing the factors that transcend both regional and partisan divisions and that are symptomatic of a larger suburban political ethos predicated on low taxes, high property values, quality education, and the security and safety of children. This set of priorities influenced conservatism *and* liberalism as well as their relationship to one another.[37] Expanding the definition of and issues that fall under the rubric of suburban politics to include causes and concerns like environmentalism, peace, and feminism not only reinforces how national issues contributed to the development of grassroots activism and political identity formation in the suburbs. It also shows how the quests to preserve open space, oppose the Vietnam War, and advance abortion rights collided and interacted with the bread-and-butter suburban priorities of homeownership, taxes, and education, and heightened the forms of inequality embedded within both the metropolitan landscape and campaigns for progressive causes. Looking at how this set of issues are inextricably intertwined at the grassroots level does not just expand understandings of modern liberalism and suburban politics but also widens the analytic boundaries of both political and urban history.

Political and urban historians have often drawn too rigid a binary between cultural and economic issues, which has obscured the ways in which average suburban residents fused their material and cultural priorities. The new literature on evangelical Christians, especially those residing in the suburbs, has illustrated convincingly the processes through which faith and free market principles became fundamentally intertwined in the worldview of evangelicals at the individual level and the platform of policies of the Republican Party at the national level.[38] This connecting of cultural and economic priorities was not exclusive to evangelical conservatives or the Republican Party. Affluent suburbanites in the Route 128 area gained specific material benefits and rights from the adoption of policies related to racial diversity, environmentalism, reproductive freedom, and national security. Likewise, liberal political ideals often dictated pocketbook decisions such as in which community to purchase a home and where to send a child to school.

The campaigns that liberals spearheaded and supported underscore that the politics of family was by no means the sole domain of social conservatives of the religious Right. Liberal residents in the Route 128 area forged alternative definitions of family values that relied on a language of defending and protecting their children. But these concerns manifested less in standing against abortion, gay rights, and sex education, and more in advocating for fair housing, voluntary integration, peace, and environmentalism in order to protect their families from the dangers of nuclear war, pollution, and sprawl and to prepare their children for the demands of a diverse and competitive global society. Individualist and rights-based programs like METCO that advocated for one-way busing and did not threaten property values or inconvenience white children, therefore, were not posteconomic or postmaterialist but directly complemented the material priorities of suburban liberals as well as their forms of political activism.

Political Activism and Party Politics in Massachusetts

Liberal activism in the Route 128 area illuminates several key factors about the nature of suburban politics and the relationship between national developments and the particularities of political patterns in Massachusetts. Suburban liberals in Boston were extremely effective at grassroots mobilization to secure the passage of landmark legislation in a variety of arenas, especially at the state level. This success derived in part from the fact that many of the campaign leaders used their professional and class status, expertise, and personal ties to build support at the grassroots level and pressure politicians and policymakers, which was particularly important in Massachusetts with its small size and the heavy concentration of its population around Boston. These campaigns underscore that on the left, right, or in the center, a small group of well-organized affluent suburbanites can have a tremendous amount of impact on local, state, and national politics and policy.[39] The record of legislative victories is equally notable since committed liberal activists in the Route 128 area were always the minority in their towns. Many of the most dedicated activists, like Bonnie Jones of Lexington, Newton's Jerome Grossman, Anita Greenbaum, and Rhona Shoul, and Concord's Paul Counihan were involved in and moved between campaigns around several different issues. These connections helped to tie the tactics and issues closer together.

Suburban activists along Route 128 proved equally effective at navigating the political culture of their own communities, adopting a strategy that couched issues to align with and complement the privileges and priorities of suburban residency. Such strategies enabled activists to earn support for potentially controversial issues such as voluntary integration or opposition to the Vietnam War among more moderate neighbors, and channel that support through the political process. This pragmatic approach, however, often foreclosed the possibility of subsequent reform and restricted the possibility of more comprehensive change.[40] These tactics also made it difficult for suburban liberals to create coalitions across racial, economic, and spatial lines.

The limited ability of suburban liberals in the Boston area to forge alliances with other traditionally Democratic constituencies like union members, African Americans, and urban ethnic party regulars underscores the relationship between metropolitan fragmentation and the splintering of the New Deal coalition in the postwar era, especially as it coincided with the historical patterns of Massachusetts politics. The vast majority of suburban professionals worked in settings such as research labs, universities, and corporate law firms, which were nonunionized, and lived in communities with negligible rates of union membership. Issues related to organized labor rarely penetrated the daily concerns or lives of even those residents who might have had an abstract commitment to union causes. Similar spatial structures imposed barriers on suburban liberal alliances with minority activists. White suburban liberals worked with African American organizations to address specific issues such as fair housing legislation, the formation of the METCO program, and the campaign to stop the construction of the Inner Belt highway, but certain ideological and practical considerations made such coalitions difficult to maintain permanently. The persistence of racial segregation in white-collar occupations and suburban neighborhoods meant that the majority of white Route 128 residents had rare sustained contact with African Americans and did not confront the realities of systemic racial inequality in their daily lives. Many suburbanites had never traveled into the low-income and predominantly minority parts of Boston like Roxbury, and some rarely went into the city at all. These forms of limited contact contributed to the direction and agenda of suburban liberal activism. Thus, suburban liberals might have voted in similar ways as labor and minority groups in national elections, and worked with civil rights organizations or unions to support a particular candidate or cause, but it did not mean that these types of collaboration led to sustained and meaningful coalitions.

The particularities of Massachusetts politics further shaped liberal coalitions, strategies, and voting patterns in the Boston suburbs. Dating back to the nineteenth century, the tension between the Boston Brahmin elite and working-class white ethnic groups, especially the Irish, structured the political culture of Massachusetts.[41] By the early twentieth century, partisan loyalties had divided neatly along ethnic, class, and spatial lines. Upper- and middle-class "Yankees" in the suburbs and rural parts of the state aligned with the Republican Party, and working-class ethnic groups in Boston and the state's other industrial areas joined the Democratic Party, which was led by colorful and corrupt figures such as John "Honey Fitz" Fitzgerald and James Michael Curley.[42] From the 1930s through the postwar era, many parts of Boston remained some of the most consistently Democratic wards in the nation, with Republicans regularly losing by margins of five to one.[43] More than identifying with the values of Franklin Delano Roosevelt or the New Deal, most urban, Catholic, blue-collar voters followed the model of the archetypal "Al Smith Democrats."[44] The rise of suburbanization and growing power of postindustrial professionals upset the balance of these long-entrenched voting patterns, and led to growing gains for the Democratic Party in the suburbs of Boston in national elections.[45] After 1960, Democratic candidates consistently won the presidential contests in Massachusetts, but it did not indicate an across-the-board realignment of Massachusetts or the disappearance of the Republican Party in state politics.[46]

These patterns demonstrate many of the problems of using the red state/blue state framework to understand national political polarization or suburban politics, especially when interpreting historical events.[47] Throughout the decades after World War II, the state Democratic Party continued to boast a long rap sheet of patronage, bribery, and other illegal activities, which alienated and angered a large contingent of suburban professionals, and inspired them to adhere to a split-ticket voting pattern.[48] "I am not entirely sure whether I am a Republican or Democrat," Henry B. Cabot, a resident of suburban Dover and member of one of the state's most prominent families, explained in a letter to a friend in the mid-1950s. "I am a Republican in Massachusetts state politics, but I usually vote Democratic in national elections."[49] Affluent suburban professionals like Cabot helped keep alive the state's tradition of liberal Republicanism, and led the state to elect a series of governors from Christian Herter and John Volpe to Francis Sargent, and later William Weld and Mitt Romney.[50] The traditional factions in the state Democratic Party remained strong as well, which meant that suburban liberal activists often worked outside the formal mechanisms of the parties, and mobilized around particular issues and candidates instead. The assumption of Massachusetts' bluest of the blue identity, derived from its returns in recent presidential elections, has produced a distorted view of the state's liberal distinctiveness both in the present and past, concealing a more complex history and reality.

Don't Blame Me, I'm From Massachusetts

The popularity of the blue state identity represents the most updated version of long mythology of Massachusetts exceptionalism. Dating back to the Puritans' christening of Boston as "the city on a hill" and claims that the city was the "birthplace of liberty" during the American Revolution and extending to the recent invocations of the "Massachusetts liberal" label, residents have frequently adopted various elements of the state's history and even appropriated criticism as a means to distinguish themselves from the rest of the nation. By reducing the state's politics to the 1972 election, and emphasizing the ways that Massachusetts stood outside and above the rest of the nation, this discourse also makes exceptional the persistence of racial segregation in metropolitan Boston, the state's role in the tax revolt, its strong tradition of moderate Republican politicians, and deep and long-standing ties to the military-industrial complex. Understanding what issues and events this discourse has magnified and what it has concealed as it coincided with structural forces, grassroots activism, and electoral politics constitutes one of the main objectives of this study.[51]

Don't Blame Us consists of a community study focused on the five Route 128 suburbs of Brookline, Concord, Lexington, Lincoln, and Newton. The argument is organized around ten chronologically thematic chapters arranged in two parts. Part I begins by exploring in more detail the structural and culture forces that produced both the political culture of the Route 128 suburbs and the suburban liberal worldview of many residents. Chapter 1 also shows how these developments established the foundations for a variety of forms of grassroots liberal activism, which the rest of part I examines. With chapters devoted to fair housing, voluntary integration, open space and environmental politics, and peace and antiwar activism, it looks at how these movements fortified Massachusetts' reputation as a "bastion of liberalism" and certain forms of exclusivity and inequality.

Part II investigates the continuities and changes in suburban liberal politics as residents in the Route 128 area confronted and adapted to new economic and political realities, including the scaling back of defense spending, the recession and rise of inflation, changing family structures, busing crisis, the rise of the pro-family movement, and the Reagan revolution in the 1970s and 1980s. It returns to many of the issues, spaces, and figures discussed in part I. Following an examination of the McGovern campaign in 1972, the subsequent chapter concentrates on a series of conflicts over affordable housing that took shape during the late 1960s and early 1970s that pitted traditionally liberal causes like civil rights and environmentalism against each other. Chapter 8 places the debates over voluntary integration within the context of Boston busing crisis and the national recession. Chapter 9 looks at the growth of suburban feminism as a means to consider the persistence of certain elements of suburban liberal activism and ideology in this changed political and economic climate.

The final chapter explores both Dukakis's career from the early 1970s to his presidential bid and the state's economic turnaround, dubbed the "Massachusetts Miracle," which made the high-tech industry and skilled professionals ever more central to the state's economy and politics, and the Democratic Party. Despite Dukakis's loss, his platform of abortion rights, affirmative action, the environment, and other quality-of-life concerns coupled with an emphasis on using market incentives to stimulate high-tech growth had a deep impact. Dukakis's platform influenced the set of policies and approach adopted by the Democratic Leadership Council (DLC) and its leader, Bill Clinton, in their efforts to appeal to suburban voters and move the party closer toward the center. This agenda continued to disproportionately benefit postindustrial professionals, while also perpetuating forms of racial and economic inequality within metropolitan Boston and in the Democratic Party's priorities.

In the aftermath of the 1972 election, a bumper sticker began appearing on cars along Route 128 declaring "Don't Blame Me, I'm From Massachusetts." While the slogan, from which this book draws its title, clearly referenced the state's sole support of McGovern, its underlying meaning is equally important to understanding the larger dynamics of Massachusetts, suburban, and liberal politics. The individualist, exceptionalist, and progressive meanings embedded in that seemingly unapologetic statement illustrate both the possibilities and limits of suburban liberalism. Rather than celebrating or blaming suburban liberals, it is more important to understand the broader structural and political forces that both gave rise to and constrained their particular form of politics and worldview. Suburban liberals and Massachusetts both need to be understood less for the reasons that they proudly stood against the national tide, and more for what they represent about American politics and society over the last fifty years.

Part I Suburban Activism

1

No Ordinary Suburbs

Political scientist Robert C. Wood began his influential 1959 critique of suburban political ideology, *Suburbia: Its People and Their Politics*, with a disclaimer. The MIT professor and Lincoln resident deflected accusations that it might be hypocritical that he chose "to live in a place I criticize so strongly." Wood contended that the town where he lived was by no means the typical suburb that his book criticized. "Lincoln is undoubtedly an anachronism and it is probably obstructive to the larger purposes of the Boston region," conceded the leading expert in urban affairs and later undersecretary for the US Department of Housing and Urban Development (HUD) in the Johnson administration. "But it is a pleasant and hospitable anachronism and while it exists I am quite happy to indict myself."[1] Fellow Lincoln resident, book editor, and nature writer Paul Brooks used similar language in reluctantly admitting that "the town would have to be called a suburb" after World War II, but only "by accident of geography and economics."[2]

As white upper-middle class professionals with ties to MIT and Harvard, Wood and Brooks embodied the demographic profile and outlook of many of the new residents who moved into single-family homes in the predominantly white, affluent neighborhoods of Lincoln and its surrounding communities in the postwar era. Homeowners in Lincoln and its counterparts shared a view of their communities as distinct from the typical mass-produced postwar suburbs like Levittown or Lakewood, and saw themselves as being different from the average conformist, homogeneous, or ordinary suburbanite criticized by C. Wright Mills, William Whyte, and Wood himself, and represented on television shows like *Leave It to Beaver* and *Father Knows Best*. Owning a home in Lexington, Concord, Lincoln, Brookline, and Newton became a powerful marker of residents' socioeconomic status and political values, and assumed a set of cultural, social, and political meanings tied to a sense of distinctiveness. The Newton Chamber of Commerce deployed this self-image in a late 1960s' promotional campaign to attract a particular type of newcomer, proclaiming that the "descriptive terms and phrases that characterize Newton just don't apply to other places." Newton is "no ordinary suburb," with citizens as "socially responsible as they are affluent."[3] It was, in fact, Newton's level of affluence more than the ethos of its residents that it made it least "ordinary," and positioned it and its corollaries as some of the wealthiest and most exclusive suburbs in the state and nation.

The archipelago of communities of Brookline, Concord, Lexington, Lincoln, and Newton and their residents were therefore in many ways far from "anachronistic," "exceptional," or "accidental." The Route 128 area and residents like Wood and his cohort literally and figuratively embodied the deliberate processes of postwar suburban growth and land control, and the major trends in postwar society. These developments included the rise of the postindustrial knowledge and university-oriented economy, the federal government's investment in defense research and weapons buildup, the baby boom, and patterns of economic and racial segregation.

These structural processes, policies, and national trends intersected with the particular history, geography, and reputation of the Boston area to produce the set of juxtapositions—between history and progress, tradition and technology, open-mindedness and exclusivity, meritocracy and equality—that characterized the physical landscape and political culture of the Route 128 suburbs and the political ideology of many of their residents.

Homeowners' view of themselves in rural Lincoln and cosmopolitan Newton fueled grassroots activism on a range of liberal issues. This sense of individual and collective distinctiveness simultaneously made many residents see themselves as separate from, and not responsible for, many of the consequences of suburban growth and the forms of inequality and segregation that suburban development fortified. Exploring the structural and cultural forces that produced the identity and ideology shared by Wood, Brooks, and many of their knowledge-worker neighbors sheds light on the dimensions of this worldview, and its multifaceted and wide-reaching consequences.

The Hub of the Universe

The construction of the Route 128 highway in the 1950s reinvigorated the ethos of distinctiveness in Boston and the rich history of Massachusetts. The city served as the site for many of the key events of the American Revolution. Just across the Charles River in Cambridge stand the ivy-lined walls of Harvard University, while ten to fifteen miles westward along the route of Paul Revere's famous ride sit the towns of Lexington and Concord, first founded around 1640. Further north lies the city of Lowell, whose textile factories were the birthplace of the nation's Industrial Revolution and the famous former whaling port of New Bedford is to the south. Beginning in the nineteenth century, boosters labeled Boston the "hub of the universe," an appellation that captures both the city's central economic and cultural standing and elevated sense of itself. Route 128 revised the meaning of the slogan, as it transformed the Boston area into a major hub of the science and technology universe, and pushed the city's economic and labor centers to its suburban ring.

The high-tech white-collar workers who emerged around Route 128 in the postwar decades represented a major change from the nineteenth century, when Boston had served as an industrial center with a heavily unionized workforce. By 1840, nearly two-thirds of the nation's textile industries operated in Massachusetts, and between 1850 and 1900 metropolitan Boston shifted from a small merchant city of 200,000 inhabitants into a metropolis of more than 1 million people.[4] The rise of industrialization in Boston and its surrounding communities coupled with the region's location on the Atlantic Ocean made Massachusetts a favorable destination for Italian and Jewish immigrants and union activity.[5] Between 1880 and 1920, Massachusetts experienced a large number of strikes and lockouts, including the great Lawrence strike of 1912 and Boston police strike of 1920.[6] Yet by the early 1920s, the Massachusetts textile and manufacturing industry began a long period of decline, and trade union rates followed suit. Over the decade, the Massachusetts industrial labor force shrunk from 695,00 to 481,000. World War II momentarily buoyed industrial production, but after the war the state experienced a string of major textile factory closures. Companies moved south, and the total factory employment dropped in Massachusetts by 9 percent between 1947 and 1955.[7] This loss of manufacturing jobs coupled with the Cold War suppression of labor activism contributed to the continued drop in the state's unionization rate.[8]

The postwar growth of the technology and science sector offered a much-needed infusion into the sagging Massachusetts economy. Since its founding in 1860, MIT had served as a source of scientific and technological innovation for the federal government, but its role magnified during World War II when the university became "the nation's unofficial center for wartime research."[9] MIT received the main contracts for several of the government's largest defense projects, including the development of radar and microwave technology. At the beginning of the Cold War, the bond between the university and Pentagon tightened.[10] Throughout the postwar era, MIT boasted the largest defense research budget of any university, with neighbor Harvard following close behind in third place. With full funding by the federal government in 1954, MIT opened Lincoln Laboratory in Lexington near the Hanscom Air Force Base, which employed nearly 4,000 people.[11] The development of the Semi-Automatic Ground Environment (SAGE) system at Lincoln Lab represented the largest R & D initiative since the Manhattan Project and led to many key advances in computer innovation.[12] Numerous researchers used the ideas first incubated at Lincoln and other MIT labs as launching points for lucrative private companies.[13] An internal report in the 1960s revealed that just 3 MIT academic departments and 4 laboratories had created 129 companies during the postwar decades. The rapid growth of industry connected to the university proved to one observer that "M.I.T. is Boston's greatest asset."[14] "MIT has spawned more spin-off companies than any other single institution in the country," Susan Rosegrant and David Lampe later remarked.[15]

Most of these spin-offs moved to the research parks along Route 128. Transportation developers in the late 1940s had primarily intended for Route 128 to ease commuting into Boston and vacation travel north to New Hampshire and Maine and south to Cape Cod by connecting a collection of existing roadways. Skeptics initially deemed Route 128 "the road to nowhere" because of its semicircular shape.[16] A key intervention, however, changed the fate of the highway and gave it several more affirmative nicknames, such as the "magic semi-circle," "golden horseshoe," and "ideas road."[17] Gerald Blakely, son of an MIT professor, and an executive at the real estate investment and development company Cabot, Cabot & Forbes (CCF), recognized that the construction of Route 128 opened up new opportunities for research parks that would be ideal for the burgeoning technology industry emerging from MIT, where there was little room for physical expansion.[18] Even before the Route 128 ribbon-cutting ceremony, CCF executives not only lobbied suburban municipalities to rezone land by the unfinished highway for commercial development but also approached Cambridge- and Boston-based technology firms and labs about relocating to these new sites. The company opened its first research park in the suburb of Needham in the early 1950s, and over the next decade CCF developed several others along the perimeter roadway.

The names of the corporations filling the modernist structures along Route 128 sounded as if they came from sci-fi novels. Companies such as Digital, Itek, Trans-Sonics, MITRE, Tracerlab, Dynametrics, Bose, AVCO, High Voltage, and Wang Laboratories positioned Route 128 as the "biggest and fastest growing science-based complex in the U.S."[19] Aware of its client base in the knowledge industry, CCF designed the parks to resemble college campuses with low, detached structures and pastoral landscaping surrounded by trees.[20] By 1967, the number of companies located on or near the highway rose to 729, and collectively employed 66,701 people in manufacturing plants and R & D departments.[21] In addition to several start-ups, established companies like Polaroid shifted their headquarters to land along the highway in Waltham, and national companies such as RCA, Sylvania, and General Electric also opened up corporate branches, labs, and manufacturing plants on or near Route 128.[22] A profusion of other companies and laboratories appeared at sites removed from the actual highway, but the name Route 128, according to the *New York Times*, came to "symbolize the technological boom in the Greater Boston area."[23]

Many observers cited "Yankee ingenuity" as the key ingredient in the rise of this new industry, obscuring the pivotal role of Cold War federal investment in the expansion.[24] During the 1950s, Massachusetts firms and laboratories rivaled "Sunbelt centers" like Orange County, California, and received more than six billion dollars in US Department of Defense contracts. This funding increased annually by one billion dollars throughout the 1960s.[25] By 1962, the federal government accounted for fully half the sales of Route 128 industry, and Massachusetts ranked third nationally behind California and New York in Pentagon spending.[26] In the 1950s Raytheon, the state's largest beneficiary of defense spending, opened twenty-five additional plants that employed thirty-six thousand people within a thirty-five-mile radius of downtown Boston as well as a large new headquarters along Route 128 in Lexington.[27]

Route 128 boosters confidently believed that the rise of the technology industry would provide the answer to the area's economic problems. Industry advocates optimistically predicted that the new companies would seamlessly replace the shuttered manufacturing and textile factories as the main staple of the Massachusetts economy.[28] In 1961, a study sponsored by a Boston bank even proposed that Raytheon's Hawk missile rather than the textile spindle serve as the symbol of the local economy.[29] Much of the new industry along Route 128 demanded highly skilled nonunionized labor, thereby excluding large sectors of the existing population from new employment opportunities. With few exceptions, the office parks along Route 128 lacked access to adequate public transportation, and likewise most transit schedules served suburban commuters going into the city instead of the reverse. Automobile ownership was virtually a prerequisite, which precluded many poor people in the city from seeking or obtaining employment in the new companies.[30] Corporate decentralization ultimately obscured many of the unsolved negative consequences of deindustrialization even as it intensified the patterns of economic and racial segregation in metropolitan Boston, which the simultaneous process of mass suburbanization further exacerbated.

Route 128: The Road to Segregation

By the 1970s, Route 128 had earned the labels as both "America's Technology Highway" and the "Road to Segregation," each of which connote the array of federal polices and important larger processes of postwar development that led a government commission to dub the area a "bellwether for certain national trends in suburban growth."[31] The titles confirm metropolitan Boston's long-standing history as the pacesetter for national patterns of suburbanization, which contributed to the area's particular spatial, racial, and cultural evolution.

In the nineteenth century, Boston spawned the nation's earliest streetcar suburbs, including Dorchester and Roxbury.[32] In the decade following the Civil War, the city annexed and engulfed the towns, doubling its size and population.[33] This trend of consolidation abruptly ended in 1873, when the town of Brookline, which sat adjacent to Boston, became the first municipality in the country to vote to oppose annexation and remain a separate entity. Brookline's action set off a chain reaction in other communities throughout Boston and the nation that would have profound consequences. For Boston in particular, it meant that upper-class communities sharing as many as two or three borders with the city remained separate entities and exempt from the burdens of urbanization, which established new and long-lasting patterns of racial and class segmentation in the metropolitan area.[34] This decision set Brookline and Roxbury on different trajectories. By the mid-twentieth century, Roxbury contained some of the poorest parts of the city, while separate Brookline with its stately Victorian homes upheld its identity and reputation as "the wealthiest town in the world."[35]

The increasing popularity of the automobile and the building of new roadways in the first decades of the twentieth century quickened the pace of metropolitan development in Boston, while extending the pattern of suburbanization and resistance to annexation to include previously rural towns like Belmont, Concord, Lexington, and Wellesley.[36] Developers and home-owners often placed formal restrictive covenants in residential deeds preventing houses from being sold to racial or ethnic minorities, or used more informal gentlemen's agreements, which served largely the same function. These practices ensured that residents in the towns remained overwhelmingly Protestant, white, and affluent.[37] Like many early suburbs in Boston and throughout the nation, Brookline and Newton did retain pockets of laborers and domestic servants, many of them Irish Catholic immigrants, while the more rural Concord, Lexington, and Lincoln still had clusters of farmers into the twentieth century, creating clear socioeconomic divides within the communities.[38]

Many of the Boston area's wealthier towns during the interwar period exacerbated these divisive patterns by adopting rigid zoning and municipal planning laws to preserve both their physical characteristics and economic exclusivity. By the late 1930s, towns like Weston had implemented a set of lot-size minimums, thereby safeguarding against commercial development as well as new working-class and nonwhite residents.[39] When a developer challenged the town of Needham's zoning code in 1942, the Massachusetts Supreme Judicial Court upheld local zoning power, affirming the benefits of minimum one-acre plots to prevent the "overcrowding of land" and protect the "public welfare." The decision established an important state and national precedent as suburban municipalities throughout the country used the ruling as justification to adopt an extremely subjective definition of the "public welfare."[40]

The federal government's spending priorities after World War II dramatically intensified suburban development and racial and economic segregation in metropolitan Boston. Between 1950 and 1957, the federal government and private developers invested four hundred million dollars in home construction throughout Boston's suburban ring.[41] Funding from the 1956 Federal Highway Act led directly to the construction of several new expressways, which made commuting exponentially easier for people who worked downtown to live in the suburbs. It further channeled homes, businesses, shopping, and people from the city center to its margins.[42] By the end of the 1950s, suburban residents outnumbered urban dwellers two to one, and fully 80 percent of metropolitan Boston's white population had dispersed through the city's outer ring.[43]

While the metropolitan area population as a whole grew 17.6 percent between 1940 and 1960, Boston itself lost 13 percent of its population, most of them white.[44] A generation of upwardly mobile Irish Catholics, Italians, and Jews with roots in the city's ethnic neighborhoods participated in this movement. Relying on the maps generated by the Home Owners Loan Corporation, local banks classified many of Boston's older neighborhoods and former streetcar suburbs, such as South Boston, Charlestown, Dorchester, and Roxbury, as "depressed" and "blighted," and refused to grant mortgages in these communities. Like in other metropolitan areas around the country, this policy of redlining effectively forced veterans with GI Bill loans and other individuals with government-underwritten mortgages to purchase single-family detached homes outside the city.[45] The out-migration coincided with and partially inspired the city's aggressive urban renewal program, which demolished many ethnic neighborhoods, including the largely immigrant West End. The combination of these forces led the remaining white residents in places like Charlestown, South Boston, and Hyde Park to be poorer than two decades before, demonstrate a heightened sense of neighborhood allegiance, populist resentment of the government, and to distrust of newcomers, especially any new nonwhite neighbors.[46]

The forces of suburban growth and urban redevelopment even more effectively constricted the region's nonwhite population, especially African Americans, to particular neighborhoods within the city's boundaries. Boston had contained a small black population since the eighteenth century, and while the community had established important educational, social, cultural, and religious institutions, it had never reached the scale of other northern urban centers. Following World War II, however, the city experienced a surge in African American migrants. Although not nearing the majority of other northern metropolitan areas like Chicago, Cleveland, or

Detroit, the influx made African Americans an increasing presence in Boston. Until 1960, Boston's black population remained 9 percent of the city's population, or sixty-three thousand residents, and then increased to a hundred thousand by 1965.[47] The deliberately discriminatory policies of the Federal Housing Administration, Boston Housing Authority, and urban renewal agencies combined with mass suburbanization left African Americans across the economic spectrum largely concentrated in increasingly overcrowded neighborhoods.[48] By the early 1960s, 80 percent of the city's African American population remained largely confined to fifteen contiguous census tracts in the South End, Roxbury, and North Dorchester.[49] While it is difficult to fully calculate the percentage prior to the 1970 census, metropolitan Boston's small Latino and Asian populations experienced similar patterns of residential segregation.[50]

The construction of Route 128 and attendant business growth rapidly intensified the patterns of suburban migration and racial and economic segregation already under way along Boston's ring. Many scientific firms and other companies sought to open headquarters in the communities, recognizing, as a CCF executive explained, that places like Lexington made "a good address on their letterhead."[51] Many of the workers also sought to live along the roadway, and as developers began to subdivide former estates and farms into multiple plots, the populations of Lexington and Lincoln more than doubled, and Concord and Newton's populations rose substantially. All these municipalities nonetheless remained overwhelmingly white and upper middle class. The dual pressures from industry and new families caused anxiety among local officials, and zoning assumed greater salience as a means to control land development and population flows.[52] In the mid-1950s, Lexington and Concord revised their respective zoning codes to establish one-acre-plot minimums, limit new construction to single-family detached homes, and prevent almost all commercial and industrial developments. Lincoln went further in order to remain a "country town" by setting an eighty-thousand-square-foot (roughly two acres) minimum and preventing all commercial enterprises.[53] Several other affluent communities followed suit.[54]

The establishment of local historic preservation ordinances coupled with new state legislation gave town officials further power to preserve the historical integrity of their community and erected another barrier to certain kinds of construction.[55] Paul Brooks and his wife, Susan, who lived in an old farmhouse on a sixteen-acre plot of land in Lincoln, celebrated how the town's rigid housing code prevented "jerry-built 'Colonials' and 'Capes' (that no colonist or cape would be caught dead in)" that might have created a "rural slum."[56] Yet as such policies preserved the sense of colonial "charm," they raised the cost and value of homes, also restricting the subset of the population that could only afford the type of houses the Brooks's derided from moving to Lincoln.

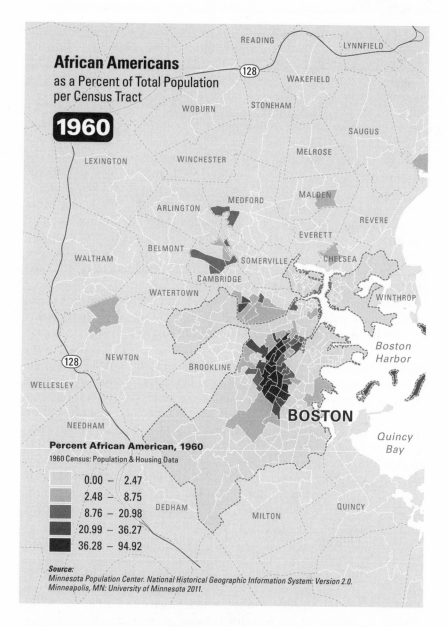

African Americans
as a Percent of Total Population
per Census Tract

1960

READING
LYNNFIELD
128 WAKEFIELD
WOBURN STONEHAM
SAUGUS
MELROSE
LEXINGTON WINCHESTER
MALDEN
MEDFORD
ARLINGTON REVERE
EVERETT
BELMONT
WALTHAM SOMERVILLE CHELSEA
CAMBRIDGE
WATERTOWN WINTHROP

*Boston
Harbor*

128 NEWTON
BROOKLINE
WELLESLEY

BOSTON

NEEDHAM
*Quincy
Bay*

Percent African American, 1960
1960 Census: Population & Housing Data

| 0.00 – 2.47 |
| 2.48 – 8.75 |
| 8.76 – 20.98 |
| 20.99 – 36.27 |
| 36.28 – 94.92 |

DEDHAM QUINCY
MILTON

Source:
Minnesota Population Center. National Historical Geographic Information System: Version 2.0.
Minneapolis, MN: University of Minnesota 2011.

Figure 1.1 Distribution of African American population in metropolitan Boston, 1960, by census tract. The forces of mass suburbanization and systemic housing segregation led to the heavy concentration of the area's African American population in Boston. As the darkly shaded area shows, by 1960, fifteen contiguous census tracts in the Boston neighborhoods of the South End, Roxbury, and North Dorchester contained over 80 percent of the area's African American population. *Source*: US Census Bureau, *Census of Population and Housing, 1960* (Washington, DC: US Census Bureau, 1960).

In the more developed and denser communities closer to the city, large-lot zoning proved more difficult to implement, but planning ordinances continued to intensify existing forms of socioeconomic inequality. Newton officials concerned about overdevelopment limited the construction of nondetached units and required single-family homes on sizable lots in many of the suburb's wealthier neighborhoods. By the 1960 census, 70.5 percent of the homes in Newton were one unit, 74.3 percent were built prior to 1939, and 85.7 percent were valued above fifteen thousand dollars.[57] Brookline, which even more clearly embodied the characteristics of an inner-ring suburb, had little nondeveloped land and was actually the only one of this set of towns to lose population after World War II. It also contained a large diversity of housing stock, with both a sizable number of apartments and rental units as well as large nineteenth-century Victorian and colonial revival mansions, which remained some of the most expensive homes in the state. In 1958, the Brookline Town Planning Board took assertive steps to limit the development of multifamily, high-density structures and "conserve" its "'suburban' character."[58]

Zoning codes established key economic and social distinctions even among municipalities that sat adjacent to one another. *New Yorker* writer Christopher Rand, who toured the Route 128 area in the early 1960s, marveled how "the Road passes through twenty towns, which is like passing through twenty different countries where zoning is concerned."[59] These differences became inscribed in the physical landscape. Weston and Lincoln prevented industry, and restricted commercial enterprise to plant nurseries and farm stands. Nearby Framingham took a different approach, and became a mecca for shopping centers and strip malls that lured customers from the surrounding towns.[60] The city of Waltham, situated between Newton, Lincoln, Lexington, and Weston, contained sixty-four firms in industrial parks and other locations directly along or adjacent to Route 128. On Lexington's northern border, Burlington added fifty new companies during the decade. Commercial enterprise comprised fully 60.6 percent of Burlington's real estate, but due to deals between the companies and town officials, it only amounted to 25 percent of the taxable property, placing a tremendous burden on municipal services.[61]

State tax policy compounded this socioeconomic hierarchy. Unlike the federal government and most other states, Massachusetts did not tax residents on a progressive scale. Instead, Massachusetts used a flat rate, which limited the amount of revenue that the state government could generate, and hence the amount of aid and services it could provide. Municipalities therefore relied heavily on local property taxes to pay for public services such as education, public works, recreation, and medical aid, giving Massachusetts one of the highest property tax rates in the nation throughout the postwar era.[62] The dependence on property tax to finance local education and town services and the increased demand for housing made it more economical for low-density towns to remove land from the market entirely rather than risk an increase in the number of families that could not share the tax burden. By allowing only large-lot zoning and limited industry, towns like Lincoln, Lexington, and Concord had smaller school enrollments and less demand for police, fire, and road maintenance, and were thus able to offer better services at lower rates. Just the opposite occurred in Boston, Burlington, and Waltham.[63]

Residents in Lincoln, Concord, and Newton frequently celebrated their land use measures and building codes as signs of their foresight and commitment to historic preservation. This attitude combined the promotion of proper planning and expertise of the Progressive era with the technocratic and meritocratic ethos of postwar liberalism. Paul Brooks proudly explained that the resistance to the forces of urban sprawl in Lincoln evolved from the town's desire "to shape its future rather than passively allowing the future to shape it." Lincoln's "long history of public service" and "present state of awareness," as Brooks described, came together to produce "self-respecting and far-sighted" planning policies.[64] The Newton Chamber of Commerce touted a similar set of ideals to outline how "planning underlies everything," and occurred in "an orderly and efficient basis" with "no helter-skelter growth." This approach, it claimed, had led to a community that was both "attractive to the eye" yet "sophisticated and in complete touch with the world."[65]

The US Civil Rights Commission came to a different interpretation of the land use policies of towns like Lincoln and Newton. In its 1975 study *Route 128: Boston's Road to Segregation*, the commission found that in such affluent suburbs, "planning succeeded almost too well," since "they were beautiful, although their beauty was paid for, in part, by the ugliness of others." The restriction of industry and a diverse housing stock made "the distribution of resources within the suburbs themselves unequal."[66] Despite clear forward thinking, local planners in places like Lincoln and Newton throughout the postwar era focused little or no attention on how the decisions to adopt minimum-acre zoning and restrict commercial enterprise would impact metropolitan Boston, particularly the growing problems of racial and economic inequality. Professional planning consultants hired by Lincoln instead justified the town's low-density land use policy by suggesting "different parts of a metropolitan region should be expected to serve different purposes, peculiar to the physical conditions and potentialities of the particular area."[67] The Civil Rights Commission, however, condemned the lack of "serious consideration given to the ramifications of one community's actions upon its neighbors or upon the suburban belt as a whole." It rebuked the "naïve amazement" of local residents at the accusation that their local zoning ordinances and other measures played a role in

Table 1.1 Selected Demographic Features of the Route 128 Suburbs as Compared to Boston

Town	Brookline	Newton	Lexington	Concord	Lincoln	Boston
Size	6.63 sq. miles	18.2 sq. miles	16.64 sq. miles	25.9 sq. miles	14.56 sq. miles	48.28 sq. miles
Distance from Boston	4.4 miles	11 miles	11 miles	19 miles	13 miles	N/A
Population, 1950	57,589	81,994	17,335	8,623	2,427	801,444
Population, 1960	54,044	92,384	27,691	12,517	5,613	697,197
Percent of population white, 1960	99%	99%	99.5%	99.3%	97.4%	90.2%
Percent of population, African American, 1960	0.3%	1%	0.3%	0.5%	1.9%	9.1%
Median income per family, 1960	$8,380	$9,008	$9,043	$8,392	N/A	$5,747
Number of engineers, 1960	511	1,686	766	307	102	2,707
Number of engineers per 1,000 population	8	18	27	25	27	3

metropolitan Boston's persistent problems of racial and economic segregation.[68] The commission perhaps overlooked residents like Robert Wood, who in *Suburbia* conceded that Lincoln's land use pattern "was probably obstructive to the larger purposes of the Boston region." Yet his statement of wanting to enjoy its "very pleasant and hospitable" environment "while it exists" intimated recognition that there was little he as an individual could do to change these patterns.[69]

The end result of this deliberate land use agenda enabled many white affluent professionals to see their towns as exceptional and themselves as exempted from many of the consequences and ideology of mass suburbanization. Brooks, Wood, and their contemporaries would frequently celebrate how the distinctiveness of Lincoln's landscape of rolling fields and absence of commercial development made the town along with its residents different from the typical "cookie cutter" and "gridiron development of flimsy houses and postage stamp lawns" that represented the "drift . . . toward suburban sameness and tameness."[70] The historical valences of the Route 128 suburbs further enhanced the notion that the communities offered residents oases of progressive values and alternatives to the homogeneity of postwar life. The Battle Green located in the center of Lexington served as a constant reminder of the community's revolutionary roots. Similarly, the homesteads of Ralph Waldo Emerson, Henry David Thoreau, and Louisa May Alcott infused Concord with a commitment to transcendentalist ideas and aesthetics.[71] Brookline residents built their postwar identity around the town's proximity to Boston, which gave them a "cosmopolitan spirit," and made them more enlightened than people in the area's more western and isolated suburbs.[72] This image, however, obscured the structural consequences of Brookline's continued pattern of political separateness from Boston.

Not the Country-Club Set

The arrival of new knowledge-based professionals who moved to the Route 128 suburbs also enhanced the notion that these communities and their residents were distinctive and excused from accusations of conformity and parochialism. Many of these newcomers moved into a series of newly constructed modernist "colonies" deliberately designed to counter the atomizing and artificial quality of the prototypical postwar suburban neighborhood. The enclaves aligned with local zoning and building codes, and represented a mixture of progress, expertise, and technology with tradition, history, nature, community, and exclusivity that embodied the values of the towns in which they appeared. The developments helped attract knowledge professionals who wanted to avoid the typical suburban tract house and live in a more experimental home. "Within the town we were sometimes seen as the radicals, the intruders," Pat Sterling, the wife of a Raytheon engineer and an early resident of the Conantum development in Concord, later declared. "Our community of new PhDs definitely were not the country-club set."[73] Her comment captures how many newcomers felt a sense of distinctive identity even from the town in which they lived. People like Sterling would always remain one small faction of "radical" local residents who resided side by side with more conventional community members. Yet by the early 1960s, both the modernist homes and newcomers who lived in them had integrated into and contributed to reshaping the social and political culture and reputation of Route 128 suburbs like Concord.[74]

The modernist trend began in 1938 when Walter Gropius, renowned architect and newly appointed dean of the Harvard School of Architecture, sought to adapt the Bauhaus style to the New England landscape, climate, and building tradition in the design of his own house, built on a former apple orchard in Lincoln.[75] Gropius's design inspired other well-known architects affiliated with Harvard to seek out plots in Lincoln and neighboring towns as "laboratories" to similarly explore the relationship between modernist principles and the natural environment. A few architects recognized that such homes were unattainable for the vast majority of even upper-middle-class professionals and began to conceive of a more affordable solution for entire neighborhoods.

By the late 1960s, Lexington had nine such modern subdivisions, including the Six Moon Hill, which members of Gropius's firm, The Architects Collaborative, designed for their own families and that of several friends from Harvard in the medical and science fields. The Architects Collaborative experimented with how design mechanisms could foster community and cooperation.[76] Peacock Farms was another Lexington cluster whose "sleek" and "flexible" design also explicitly sought to avoid the trappings of conformity in order to appeal to scientists and engineers who worked at nearby "atomic and missile research centers."[77] An advertisement for the firm's Five Fields development promised "imaginative site planning," "expert engineering," and a setting "ideal for children," with "common land" designed by architects "internationally known for their contemporary design" in "Historic Lexington" at a "moderate purchase price."[78] Herb and Ruth Weiss purchased a home at Five Fields after Herb, who was an engineer at MIT, received a postcard through the MIT interoffice mail inviting him to hear Gropius speak about the new project at Harvard's Memorial Hall. Ruth recalled, "He spoke about line and form and function. I'd never heard these words used architecturally before. It appealed immediately."[79]

The largest of these developments, Concord's Conantum, where Pat Sterling lived, evolved from MIT economics professor Rupert McLurin's desire to create an "affordable utopia" that would be an "antidote to postwar tract developments like Levittown."[80] He enlisted the help of fellow MIT faculty member Carl Koch, an architect and innovator of prefabricated homes committed to constructing attractive, high-quality homes affordably and efficiently.[81] Koch's design for a hundred chalet-style homes on the two-hundred-acre plot coupled the latest technological advancements and expertise drawn from the MIT labs with an appreciation for local history and the environment, including a large amount of open and shared space in order for residents to feel in harmony with both nature and their neighbors. McLurin also used the university mail services to promote the project, sending postcards to Harvard and MIT faculty that promised not simply "a house" but also "a community" just twenty-two minutes from Harvard Square.[82] Koch, who both designed the houses and moved into one of them, described the early inhabitants of Conantum as "a few maverick social scientists, a brace of psychiatrists, mathematicians," but running "heavily to engineers."[83] In fact, almost all of the initial buyers had a connection to MIT or Harvard as alumni, faculty members, or employees at Lincoln Laboratory.[84] These ties made Conantum residents not "radical" but actually consistent with the profile of the new residents in the Route 128 suburbs, further solidifying the connections of the towns to both area universities and the science and electronics industry.

Cambridge had served as a college town since the seventeenth century, but following World War II the Boston metropolitan area boasted one of the densest concentrations of academic institutions anywhere in the world with more than sixty colleges and universities, including Harvard, MIT, Boston College, Boston University, Northeastern University, Tufts University, Wellesley College, and the recently founded Brandeis University. This amalgamation had a reverberating impact on the surrounding area.[85] Many people who had attended college or graduate school in metropolitan Boston decided to stay, and others moved to work at area universities.[86] While some academics and other knowledge workers opted to reside in Cambridge or the gentrifying Boston neighborhoods, drawn to the "magnetism" of the old buildings and cosmopolitan culture, many more found the rents too high, air too smoggy, traffic too enraging, and schools too inadequate, and instead chose to migrate to the attractive suburbs along Route 128.

Occupations often dictated suburban settlement patterns. Brookline and Newton's proximity to Boston provided them with a larger degree of lawyers and doctors, given their easier access to downtown firms and hospitals. Lexington, Concord, and Lincoln's location along the interchange of Route 128 and Route 2 meant a higher concentration there of scientists and engineers.[87] In contrast to the employee profiles of companies in Orange County and Silicon Valley, where most workers had moved to California from other parts of the country, the majority of Route 128 engineers and executives "were from New England, many had attended local educational institutions and their identities were already defined by familial and ethnic ties."[88]

By 1960, the greater Boston area had 25,500 engineers, 6,900 scientists, 1,334 engineering professors, and 11,000 students majoring in some type of science—and most of these students hoped to stay in the Boston area after graduation.[89] The Massachusetts Chamber of Commerce claimed that metropolitan Boston had the largest concentration of skilled professionals and technical personnel of "any metropolitan area in the free world."[90] Many of these "bright" and "innovative" engineers favored the research environment of places like Lincoln Laboratory and its spin-offs. One employee explained that the people who worked at Lincoln "wouldn't be there if they wanted to work for a large corporation" and instead sought out an opportunity to be at the "forefront of technology."[91] Even for those engineers and scientists employed in the research branches of larger corporations, the lab setting fostered seemingly contradictory sets of values: rationality and creativity, hard work and innovation, competition and collaboration, individualism and teamwork. The engineers usually reflected a professional ethos of science-based training predicated on the meritocratic ideal of acquiring and maintaining the skills and specialization necessary to excel at difficult, rewarding work. "I'm a professional! In a way that makes you different," one Route 128 engineer declared. "No one can take your skills away."[92] The emphasis on the importance of education and merit carried over to life outside work as well.

True Believers

The influx of "new PhDs" and their families infused the Route 128 suburbs with an achievement-focused sensibility, and made education a core component of their culture and exclusivity. The promise of high-quality public education often informed both the home-purchasing decisions and political ideology of the professionals who moved to these communities in the decades after World War II. Unlike other older suburbs such as Belmont, which traditionally underemphasized public education and often attracted families that sent their children to private or parochial schools, Brookline, Concord, Lexington, and Newton all had reputations as "education oriented" and a tradition of excellent public schools that dated back to the nineteenth century.[93] Journalist Peter Schrag, who used Newton as a case study of an outstanding suburban system for a book about public schools across the United States, asserted that in that community, "education is a religion, and almost everyone is a true believer."[94] Jackie Davison later contended that she and her husband had liked living in Boston, but chose to purchase a home in Lexington in 1954 because it had a school system that "was interesting, challenging and would be worth the move to the suburbs."[95] MIT professor Noam Chomsky, who moved to Lexington a decade later, similarly commented, "We had young kids and we were looking for good schools and the usual thing [so] we made the move."[96] Davison and Chomsky shared the attitude typical of many new families. Between 1951 and 1959, Lexington gained about a thousand residents per year with a 100 percent increase in school enrollments.[97]

The majority of the new families that decided to buy a home in towns like Lexington and Newton possessed the ability and willingness to expend additional tax dollars to ensure that their children received a first-rate education. A survey of Concord residents conducted in the late 1950s revealed that residents had high academic expectations of the schools, and saw them as the most important municipal service and most in need of expansion, and were overwhelmingly willing to support changes and funding that would provide the "best possible" education for their children.[98] Residents in neighboring towns echoed these sentiments. Between 1946 and 1960, the cost per pupil in Newton increased from $194 to $476.[99] Schrag estimated that a home in Newton cost at least $6,000 more than a comparable house in another community because of the cost of maintaining the school system.[100] By the mid-1960s, school financing became by far the largest municipal budget item in all the Route 128 suburbs.[101]

The new population of educated parents injected schools and school politics with not just a surging population of students and tax dollars but also an enhanced accentuation on academic excellence that further increased the quality of education and desirability of each town. Dubbing Newton a "university pipeline," Schrag noted that in Newton, like most upper-middle-class suburbs "a good deal of parental ambition, especially regarding admission to the eastern colleges," fueled "a large part of the passion" in education.[102] The Newton School Committee and its counterparts in the Route 128 communities included engineers, lawyers, professors, and former teachers who were alumni from esteemed institutions, such as Harvard, Princeton, Dartmouth, and Mount Holyoke, and prone to quoting James B. Conant or David Riesman during meetings.[103]

Many of the professionals also became invested in the day-to-day workings of the schools. Carl Koch later recalled that many Concord "mothers who had gone to Smith and Vassar and places like that joined the PTA, and took the school by a storm. Test scores went up."[104] Concord developed a high school computer mathematics course dubbed "Mathematics for the Modern World" by enlisting the help of engineers, mathematicians, and physicists from the town and Lincoln Laboratory, and arranging field trips to the lab and other Route 128 industries that applied mathematical concepts.[105] Lexington incorporated presentations by resident architects, bankers, book editors, chemists, geologists, and engineers into its curriculum as a way, according to one teacher, "to get people interested in the schools, and that's the best way to get better schools."[106]

The nickname "university pipeline" gained additional meaning as suburban administrators and teachers developed close relationships with education scholars at area universities, often consulting faculty members at Harvard and other institutions on pedagogy and curricular ideas. Professors from Harvard, Brandeis, and Boston University frequently used Newton and Brookline classrooms as laboratories for experimenting with cutting-edge ideas—not just elevating the quality of the curriculum, but also attracting top teachers exhilarated at trying out the latest techniques and theories.[107] Ties to area institutions also placed the towns on the receiving end of many foundation and government grants, further enhancing the quality of the curricula. Charles E. Brown, the superintendent of the Newton schools, worked aggressively to secure outside funds from the federal government and private organizations like the Ford Foundation for efforts to create innovative curriculum. By the mid-1960s, Newton had received over a half-million dollars from thirty-five private institutions, and worked with thirty different colleges and universities.[108]

The combination of committed parents, unparalleled resources, and direct ties to universities secured the school systems in Newton, Brookline, Lexington, Concord, and Lincoln top spots on the lists of the best, most innovative schools in the state and country.[109] The national attention and praise reassured local residents that they were not merely "apathetic" suburbanites who lived in towns with "ordinary" schools.[110] Instead of offering the bland, basic, and rote learning to children that provoked panic following the launch of Sputnik in 1957, local school officials and parents prided themselves on their trailblazing instruction that prepared students for the demands of the postindustrial, technical, cosmopolitan, and diverse world they would enter.

The shared commitment to education enhanced both the progressive ideals and socioeconomic exclusivity of the Route 128 communities. The considerable costs of and personal investment in public education bolstered the fiscally minded attitude of many residents toward local and state services and politics. The schools also reflected and reinforced the meritocratic ethos among the set of achievement-oriented professionals who moved to the communities. Similar to the land control agenda that led to the implementation of exclusionary zoning codes, residents often saw local educational policies in terms of hard work, expertise, and forward thinking, not the simultaneous ways that the initiatives produced forms of inequity. At the same time that Newton was garnering national praise, less than ten miles away in Boston the quality of public education was slowly deteriorating, with test scores dropping, college matriculation dwindling, and rates of racial segregation rising. Although these trends affected all Boston children, a disproportionate impact fell on the nonwhite population. The schools in Roxbury, North Dorchester, and the South End were overcrowded and had outdated textbooks, and many of the buildings violated health and safety codes.

Residents in Newton, Concord, or Lexington in the late 1950s and early 1960s rarely discussed how economic mechanisms positioned their community's schools over others, or how the loss of their tax dollars and gains of federal funding and expert consultants might have an impact on public education in the city of Boston. Concern for their own children's education and future did drive many residents to become involved in peace, civil rights, and environmental causes. The schools and supportive activities like the PTA served as a site for liberally oriented residents to meet each other, and they frequently used the connections they made through educational activities to expand the membership and volunteer networks for key political and social campaigns.[111]

The Social World of the Suburbs

The schools and PTAs joined with other local well-established religious, social, cultural, and political institutions to provide the foundation for various forms of grassroots liberal activism. A 1950 booklet distributed to new Lexington homeowners featured a long list of church groups, benevolent societies, civic organizations, and sporting clubs that predated the wave of postwar migrants.[112] These affinity groups supplied recently relocated married couples to Lexington and elsewhere a way to forge community, gain a sense of belonging, and meet people who shared their socioeconomic characteristics and political outlook.[113] Through these interactions and activities, the families of professors, engineers, and other white-collar professionals altered the religious, social, and political makeup of the Route 128 suburbs, making them increasingly liberal.

Religious institutions in particular served as a central component of residents' identity and social world, and became an important way to meet like-minded individuals. In the postwar period, many local churches increasingly sponsored secular activities during the week, such as dances and card games. David Riesman observed in 1957 that in many postwar suburbs, the "church, like the high school and the country club, has become a center for the family as a social and civic unit."[114] The array of different activities became so extensive and secular at Hancock Congregational Church in Lexington, for instance, that residents jokingly renamed the religious institution "the Hancock Country Club."[115] In the late 1940s, a young engineer and his wife organized a group of fellow congregants at the Hancock Church to study scripture and discuss its message for modern times. By the early 1960s, the church boasted ten groups of dedicated parishioners and their friends who met at one another's houses for religious study.[116] Dozens of similar groups became popular in the surrounding area in the postwar era.

Many new residents had moved from other parts of New England, and were more attracted to the less doctrinal denominations of their youth, largely in the Mainline and Congregationalist traditions, or those that more closely aligned with their liberal political outlook.[117] Unitarian churches especially flourished after World War II in the Route 128 area. The Unitarians had taken over the former Puritan parishes in places like Concord and Lexington beginning in the nineteenth century. These religious ties and values deepened the towns' physical and ideological connections to Harvard, a center of the religion. The Unitarian merger with the Universalist Church in 1961 made the religion particularly appealing to the postwar generation of Route 128 transplants, specifically those steeped in the values of New England's leading universities.[118] Unitarian Universalism's academic roots coupled with its emphasis on rationality, progress, and faith in science also directly complemented the professional worldview of this cohort of new residents.[119] Reverend Dana McLean Greeley, a Lexington native, first president of the American Unitarian Association, and later pastor at the First Parish Church in Concord, explicitly declared, "Religion and science should not be rivals; they should be partners."[120] Unitarian Universalism's inclusive values served as a middle ground for many married couples raised in different religious traditions as well and made it popular with many newcomers.[121] In addition to well-established Protestant institutions, in the postwar era the Route 128 suburbs included a wide diversity of religious options, which further encouraged interfaith collaboration. Newton's population of 40 percent Catholic, 36 percent Protestant, and 22 percent Jewish residents by the late 1950s gave the suburb a reputation for religious diversity.[122]

The rising Jewish population in Newton represented the broader national postwar "exodus" of Jews and institutions toward the suburbs.[123] Levels of religious commitment dictated the suburban settlement patterns of many Jewish families in the Boston area. Most observant families opted to live in Newton or Brookline, both of which had large concentrations of Jewish residents, synagogues, religious schools, and kosher grocery stores, necessary for those who kept kosher and observed the Sabbath.[124] Less observant Jews frequently chose to live in communities such as Lexington or Concord that had a tradition of progressive values, but not necessarily a well-established Jewish community or institutions.[125] The patterns of Catholic worship also highlighted several larger spatial and political trends. Most area suburbs had contained small enclaves of Catholics since the nineteenth century, and most had at least one Catholic Church by the turn of twentieth century. After World War II these parishes grew significantly. Belying the often-repeated suggestion that Catholics either remained in cities to stay by their parishes or commuted back into the city on Sunday, the suburbs of Boston experienced a flood of new church construction in the fifteen years following World War II. Between 1944 and 1959, the Archdiocese of Boston approved the building of seventy-five new churches, the majority of which, it proudly declared, were "in small historic communities in the midst of which no church steeple bore the cross."[126]

In Lexington, the Catholic Church membership patterns revealed a spectrum of worship practices and politics. Many liberal-leaning newcomers gravitated to St. Brigid's Church, which sat just off the Battle Green and preached a message that combined the community's revolutionary tradition with the values of the Jesuit order. More devout and doctrinal Catholics in Lexington tended to go to the Church of the Sacred Heart in East Lexington. One resident succinctly reduced the distinction between St. Brigid's and Sacred Heart "to the liberals versus the conservatives."[127] This type of dichotomous split replicated throughout suburban Boston and showed how religious institutions helped to cluster ideologically like-minded people—a prerequisite for grassroots mobilization around social and political causes.

Many new suburban residents developed personal and political connections through their involvement in organized religion, and the institutions often served as springboards for political action. For instance, Norma McGavern-Norland recalled that growing up in New York City, "I had never been involved even with a church before." But upon moving to Lexington and encouraged by a local Unitarian minister, she decided that participating in the church would be a good way to meet people, perform organized community service, and it "might be fun."[128] The positive experiences of church participation inspired her to get involved in the League of Women Voters and later several other liberal causes and groups. McGavern-Norland's example reflected a common trend among suburban residents who got involved in forms of grassroots activism, particularly among female participants. Most women who moved to the Route 128 suburbs in the 1950s did not hold salaried jobs but instead engaged in full-time parenting and other traditional household duties. Many women had college degrees from elite schools, and looked for ways to continue their education and intellectual engagement. "I and a lot of other people who became my friends all had young children around the age of my children," McGavern-Norland later observed. "We were all united by child care and interest in what was going on in the world. I suppose we gravitated to the same organizations because we cared for the same things."[129]

The League of Women Voters served as a major magnet for female activism and the launching point for later forms of political participation. Several Boston suburbs had existing chapters by the 1930s, but in the postwar period, broader demographic shifts led to a flourishing of the organization, and Massachusetts emerged as the largest state chapter in the country.[130] Louise Haldeman explained that when she moved to Lexington, she answered an

Table 1.2 Electoral Percentages in Selected Elections for the Route 128 Suburbs and Boston, 1952–64

Municipality	1952 presidential election	1952 governors election	1960 presidential election	1960 governor election	1964 presidential race
Boston	Eisenhower (R) 39 Stevenson (D) 58	Herter (R) 31 Dever (D) 65	Nixon (R) 25 Kennedy (D) 73	Volpe (R) 38 Ward (D) 55	Goldwater (R) 13 Johnson (D) 83
Brookline	Eisenhower (R) 59 Stevenson (D) 39	Herter (R) 59 Dever (D) 36	Nixon (R) 48 Kennedy (D) 51	Volpe (R) 64 Ward (D) 31	Goldwater (R) 18 Johnson (D) 79
Newton	Eisenhower (R) 67 Stevenson (D) 31	Herter (R) 65 Dever (D) 33	Nixon (R) 48 Kennedy (D) 51	Volpe (R) 67 Ward (D) 30	Goldwater (R) 22 Johnson (D) 76
Lexington	Eisenhower (R) 76 Stevenson (D) 22	Herter (R) 73 Dever (D) 25	Nixon (R) 57 Kennedy (D) 41	Volpe (R) 71 Ward (D) 20	Goldwater (R) 31 Johnson (D) 66
Concord	Eisenhower (R) 74 Stevenson (D) 25	Herter (R) 72 Dever (D) 27	Nixon (R) 59 Kennedy (D) 40	Volpe (R) 72 Ward (D) 26	Goldwater (R) 33 Johnson (D) 64
Lincoln	Eisenhower (R) 75 Stevenson (D) 23	Herter (R) 76 Dever (D) 22	Nixon (R) 63 Kennedy (D) 36	Volpe (R) 79 Ward (D) 17	Goldwater (R) 33 Johnson (D) 61

advertisement from the League in the local newspaper because she found herself "a young mother with a baby at home and needed some intellectual companionship."[131] Davison described the League as a "starting point for many of us."[132] The League's focus on studying key local and state issues and presenting of facts in a dispassionate, objective tone offered educated women a way to continue their intellectual pursuits, widen their knowledge base, and participate in various levels of government.[133] It also served, Davison remarked, as "a good way to get to know our town."[134] Through such efforts, many suburban women came to learn much about the inner workings of governmental and policy processes, which they applied to other grassroots liberal campaigns.

The League's strict policy of nonpartisanship actually sparked many women to become more active in party politics, especially in the Democratic Party, and contributed to larger changes in Route 128 voting patterns. Davison was a registered Republican when she moved to Lexington, but through the League of Women Voters, she made friends who inspired her to switch parties. "It was interesting to meet some Democrats for the first time in my life and learn that they had ideas," Davison later explained. "They had the issues that were the most appealing. So I left the ranks of my childhood and became . . . a born-again Democrat."[135] Davison's conversion narrative provides a synecdoche for the realignment of Lexington and the Route 128 suburbs, which became increasingly Democratic in presidential elections with the influx of new residents in the decade after World War II.

Although Adlai Stevenson did not capture any of the Route 128 communities in either of his presidential bids, his campaigns also proved particularly important for symbolizing and propelling this shift.[136] Stevenson's rational and moral brand of progressive politics found widespread appeal among suburban professionals, including Republican and independent voters.[137] Marion Coletta helped mobilize the local Volunteers for Stevenson campaign in Lexington. She recalled the experience of how she and a group of "very educated" young women "who had just graduated from Radcliffe or something" went door-to-door in the "very Republican, really Republican" town. As to her older Republican neighbors, she observed, "They were kind of surprised to find that we weren't all dirty and from the slums. I guess they thought only people from the slums were Democrats." Colletta explained that although she and the other women did not succeed in swaying the vote toward Stevenson, "the men, then, wanted to join us," and eventually "we really changed the thinking of the town in those days" and "finally got the town to be more Democratic than Republican."[138] By 1964, Lexington and the other Route 128 communities had begun to consistently tip the voting scales toward the Democratic Party in presidential elections, invigorating residents' collective sense that the communities were both liberal and distinct from the typical suburb.

Voting patterns offered but one indication of the impact of the resettlement of white-collar technocrats and educated housewives and their families to the engineering labs and tree-lined streets off Route 128. This migration set the parameters for many of the political developments and debates that would take place over the next thirty years. The movement established the foundations for grassroots activism on fair housing, school integration, environmentalism, peace, and the campaigns of several political candidates. Liberal initiatives like the fair housing movement and METCO program simultaneously codified the ethos of individual meritocracy and provided Route 128 residents with further ways of maintaining their sense of difference from the typical conservative and conformist suburbanite. This attitude of distinctiveness also exacerbated patterns and problems of racial and spatial inequality, as the battles over housing, school desegregation, and property taxes in the 1970s would bring into sharp relief.

2

Good Neighbors

During the same week as the March on Washington, on August 31, 1963, thirty protesters stormed on to the Lexington Battle Green, the site of the famous "shot heard round the world" and mythical birthplace of the American Revolution. Singing "We Shall Overcome," the group, predominantly made up of well-dressed white women, marched beneath the iconic statue of John Parker, the leader of the Minutemen and a symbol of the suburb's prominent past. Walking the picket line, they carried homemade signs with messages emblazoned such as "Birthplace of American Liberty??" "Jim Crow Must Go," and "Lexington Live Up to Your Name."[1] The protest intended to draw attention to the case of the African American Parker family. A local real estate developer had allegedly discriminated against Foreign Service Officer James Parker, who sought to rent a cottage in Lexington. Upsetting both Boston and Lexington's sense of distinctiveness, the protesters distributed leaflets to curious onlookers that declared, "There *is* discrimination in the North! It exists in Lexington too!"[2]

The protest became front-page news in Boston's major papers and exposed the vibrancy of fair housing activism, which had emerged within Lexington and other affluent suburbs along the Route 128 highway in the early 1960s. Interpreting residential segregation largely as a locally rooted problem, the network of fair housing groups took grassroots action to raise tolerance for residential integration and help individual African American families find homes in their communities. These white middle-class suburbanites also joined a broader coalition in metropolitan Boston to place the issue at the forefront of the local civil rights agenda in the early 1960s and ensure that Massachusetts had the most extensive fair housing laws in the nation by 1963.[3]

By the mid-1960s, the group's umbrella organization, the Massachusetts Federation of Fair Housing Committees, came to include thirty-five hundred members in thirty-seven communities and comprised the largest and most organized network of a national suburban-based movement, stretching from New York, New Jersey, and Chicago, to Seattle, San Francisco, and Los Angeles. Historians of civil rights and suburban politics have traditionally focused on the fights of white suburban residents *against* rather than *for* fair housing legislation and integrated communities. The campaign for the passage of Proposition 14 in California in 1964 and Martin Luther King Jr.'s 1966 march in Chicago have become well-worn examples of white backlash to residential integration outside the South.[4] The efforts of the movement, however, show underappreciated and important linkages between grass-roots suburban activism and the creation of state laws aimed at combating residential discrimination. In fact, by the time Congress passed the 1968 Fair Housing Act, Massachusetts was one of more than twenty-two states in the North and West with long-standing and wider-reaching laws on the books.[5] The movement illustrated the power that white suburbanites could wield in the political system. It established a model and infrastructure for other forms of liberal activism, ranging from voluntary integration and antiwar activism, to environmentalism and feminism. The movement's ideas about individualism and equal opportunity also proved extremely influential to later suburban liberal campaigns in the Route 128 area in the 1960s and beyond.

The fact that mobilization around the issues of housing and property emerged as one of the first and most active forms of political action in the Route 128 area showed the extent to which notions of homeownership converged with racial liberal principles to structure the political ideas and worldview of liberal suburbanites in the postwar era. The political imperatives of postwar suburbanization promoted the powerful message that property ownership offered a means of opportunity and advancement in American society along with the meritocratic ideal that anyone with means deserved to have the right to live where they choose. Liberal religious organizations and social scientists concurrently promoted the principles of racial liberalism, suggesting that legislation and organizing strategies focusing on individual rights and equal opportunity offered the best means to eradicate legal segregation. The combination of these goals channeled fair housing activism away from seeing or addressing many of the interlocking causes of residential discrimination, such as the federal policies that buttressed discriminatory lending practices and local exclusionary land use policies.

The fair housing movement created the grassroots support and legal means to fight racial discrimination through methods that simultaneously revealed the serious limits of suburban activists to solve the problems of systemic inequality. The agendas and policies of the fair housing movement grounded in the ideals of equal opportunity and meritocratic individualism led to the creation of pathbreaking new laws and a new outpouring of support for the cause. The movement, nevertheless, succeeded in helping only a handful of primarily middle-class African Americans, like the Parker family that had sparked the Lexington protest, move into affluent communities. While the results did have symbolic importance, they did little to alleviate the housing problems of the majority of Boston's African American population or patterns of systemic residential segregation.[6] Thus, the fair housing movement contributed to liberal ideals and modes of activism and perpetuated larger patterns of residential and class inequality.

The Emergence of Fair Housing Activism

The momentum for the Massachusetts fair housing movement and its dual goals of promoting "interracial understanding" and assisting individual African Americans to purchase homes in the suburbs emerged from the interplay of the larger national open housing campaign with the localized concerns about metropolitan Boston's segregated housing market.[7] In the 1950s, the National Committee Against Discrimination in Housing (NCDH) along with religious organizations like the American Friends Service Committee (AFSC) helped to popularize the issue of housing integration.[8] Combining the moral language of religion with social scientific evidence, the cause drew inspiration from Gunnar Myrdal's influential 1944 work *An American Dilemma*. Perhaps the clearest articulation of the principles of racial liberalism, Myrdal's work promoted the idea that personal prejudice and moral deficiencies, not state-sponsored policy, produced racism. Thus, the best way to eradicate discrimination came through changing the "hearts and minds" of individuals.[9]

Myrdal's hypothesis served as a template for the open housing movement's agenda. By the late 1950s, the NCDH and AFSC made a more concerted effort to spread the open housing cause at the local level, and this enterprise met with its greatest success in the Boston area.[10] The New England Regional Office of the AFSC created a Community Relations Committee to work on race relations and housing discrimination in the suburbs, and it proved particularly important in fostering the growth of the fair housing movement in metropolitan Boston. The AFSC hired a paid staff person to work with religious leaders from other denominations in the suburbs to "spark" interest in the cause.[11] Members and observers usually emphasized the "indigenous," "spontaneous," and "grassroots" origins of the suburban fair housing groups, and while these adjectives were not misnomers, religious institutions undoubtedly sped their pace of development.[12] One Boston reporter described "religious leaders of all three major faiths" as the "driving force behind" the housing movement.[13]

The Route 128 area contained a large number of religious institutions committed to tolerance and social justice, making it especially fertile ground for the rapid spread of fair housing activism. The tenets of the faiths popular in the Route 128 suburbs connected with the emphasis on individualism and individual rights in the movement and postwar liberalism as a whole. In the 1950s, many ministers and rabbis had begun to focus more on the therapeutic dimensions of religious life, and several started to engage with psychoanalytic theories of self and community.[14] This attention on psychological and personal development would have important implications for the development of fair housing activism, particularly as clergy increasingly combined therapeutic and individualist messages with those about the significance of racial and religious tolerance and equality. National Jewish and Christian antidiscrimination organizations had been circulating social scientific theories about racial equality, which suburban religious leaders at liberally leaning Unitarian churches, Quaker meetinghouses, and synagogues incorporated into their sermons and activities.

Fueled by a tradition of cross-denominational collaboration, the suburbs all had well-established interfaith networks by the late 1950s. The clergy frequently met and were in regular dialogue, and encouraged their parishioners to do the same. In places like Brookline and Newton, members of Catholic, Protestant, and Jewish congregations came together for weekly informal discussions on issues such as civil rights and other liberal concerns, which proved important to the spread of fair housing activism.[15] In the mid-1950s, churches and synagogues throughout the Route 128 suburbs, propelled by the AFSC's outreach efforts, began to sponsor events where African American families told their stories about the difficulties they confronted in Boston's housing market to congregants.[16]

These individual experiences reflected the more systemic problems of housing segregation in the Boston area, especially the policies and practices that denied African Americans access to the suburbs. Following industry guidelines to prevent panic selling and other fluctuations in the housing market, real estate agents in the Boston area refused to show prospective African American buyers homes in the suburbs. For most African Americans across the economic spectrum, the housing search was largely confined to the limited housing stock in the former streetcar suburbs of Roxbury and Dorchester. Many sellers and landlords took advantage of the fact that African Americans had few options by greatly overcharging for sales or rent, and it was extremely difficult and expensive to obtain mortgages or home repairs.[17] Boston's urban renewal program compounded the problem since it removed a significant portion of housing units from the market. Urban renewal also increased hostility toward outsiders in many of the city's lower-income white neighborhoods, which made them unwelcome to prospective African American buyers and sellers.

Massachusetts actually had the largest number of antidiscrimination statutes in the nation by the late 1950s. The Massachusetts response to the crisis of racial discrimination in housing first emerged in the immediate aftermath of World War II as state officials reacted to fears that racism violated the American creed and marked a potential weakness in the arena of foreign affairs.[18] In 1950, the legislature expanded the scope and jurisdiction of the state's Fair Employment Practices Commission to include oversight of discrimination in public housing and public accommodations, and changed the agency's name to the Massachusetts Commission Against Discrimination (MCAD).[19] As the decade unfolded, both the agency and local civil rights activists increasingly understood the need to extend the reach of state power beyond only public housing and into the private housing market. Throughout the 1950s, the local chapters of the National Association for the Advancement of Colored People (NAACP) and Urban League had made the issue of housing, both public and private, central to their efforts to create legal remedies to segregation.[20]

In 1957, the NAACP, Urban League, and American Jewish Congress sponsored legislation to include publicly financed private housing within the antidiscriminatory laws and enforcement powers of MCAD. The Fair Housing Practices Law, signed into state law on June 7, 1957, enlarged MCAD's jurisdiction to include private housing for any person buying or renting a house under FHA or Veterans Affairs programs, urban renewal, or redevelopment projects.[21] Since almost 80 percent of the housing purchased in the state had some assistance from the FHA, the law had bold intentions and constituted a clear effort by Massachusetts to create accountability for the discriminatory actions of the federal government. The legislature did not apply the statute retroactively, however, and MCAD received almost no complaints in its first years of existence because almost no housing in the entire state fell within its jurisdiction. The stories of the African American families that testified to concerned suburbanites in the late 1950s therefore underscored the ineffectiveness of the new fair housing laws.

The narratives offered by African Americans at churches and other venues about both the kinds of hardships they experienced purchasing property and the clear inadequacy of the existing laws shocked audience members. Many suburban residents were themselves recent homebuyers, and the stories forced them to confront the privileges that their skin color had afforded them in the real estate market. After hearing one such account of an African American family at his Unitarian Church, Natick accountant Robert Brainerd decided to form a local fair housing committee. Brainerd and the committee aimed to use their own privileges and advantages as white suburbanites to help individual African American families like the one whose story they had heard gain access to the local real estate market as well as educate their friends and neighbors.[22] By 1960 the idea for such committees had spread to eighteen communities, and in 1961 the groups formed the Greater Boston Federation of Fair Housing Committees in order coordinate activities and establish a united front.[23] The creation of the Federation lent the issue of fair housing the structure of an organized movement, which would prove important as its members aimed to expand their activities and gain more legitimacy.

Good Neighbors

In *Couples*, John Updike's salacious story of marriage and adultery set in the fictionalized suburb of Tarbox north of Boston in 1962, Irene Saltz, the wife of an engineer at one of the firms along Route 128, tries to recruit the members of her social circle to join the town's Fair Housing Committee. One scene at a cocktail party captures an exchange over the issue:

"They should have the protection of the law like everybody else," Frank said, . . . "I don't approve of discriminatory legislation and that's what the Massachusetts Fair Housing Bill is. It deprives the homeowner of his right to choose. The constitution, my dear Irene, tries to guarantee equality of *opportunity*, not equality of status."
Irene said, "Status and opportunity are inseparable."
"Can't we shut them up?" Eddie Constantine asked.
"It's sex for Irene," Carol told him.[24]

Updike dismissed fair housing activism as little more than cocktail banter, and another indication of the ennui of Tarbox residents and their belief that they could not impact society. This sentiment actually went against the vast majority of the real-life suburbanites who participated in the movement. The scene from *Couples*, nevertheless, does accurately portray many features of the fair housing movement, especially how the early leaders built their ranks, their commitment to the goals of implanting interracial understanding among their neighbors, assisting individual African Americans to purchase homes in their communities, and promoting the importance of state fair housing legislation.

The fair housing movement's early members reflected the demographic profile and gender dynamics of the newcomers to the Route 128 suburbs— consisting of a large contingent of male scientists, engineers, academics, lawyers, and business executives and educated female housewives. The Lexington committee's board of directors, for instance, included Harry Petschek, an astrophysicist and then president of the AVCO Corporation, David Reiner, an MIT-employed engineer, and Ephraim Weiss, a physicist. In addition, lawyers like Soshnick and Albert Sacks of Belmont, who would later become the dean of Harvard Law School, and other academics like social psychologist William Ryan of Brookline and sociologist Milton Rubin of Newton, also served as leaders in their local committees. Real-life Irenes such as Barbara Petschek of Lexington, Sadelle Sacks of Belmont, and Phyllis Ryan of Brookline served as central figures in the fair housing movement, and played a major role in its popularity and growth in the affluent Route 128 communities.[25] Like Saltz, the suburbanites often relied on their social contacts and networks to build the movement, recruiting fellow co-workers, neighbors, school parents, church and synagogue members, and League of Women Voters participants through events such as coffee klatches, cocktail parties, and informal individual discussions.

The recruitment strategy and early activities connected with the fair housing movement's belief that segregation was "essentially a community problem," and the "long-run solution" would be when a "neighbor convinces another" that discrimination was "morally and legally wrong."[26] A *Boston Herald* article about the rising movement described how the leaders had decided "that they wanted to do more than just 'feel guilty' about the discrimination suffered by Negroes" by ending it "not in distant Alabama but in their own backyard."[27] This commitment to working "in their own backyard" demonstrated the participants' recognition that racial discrimination was not just a southern problem but operated in the northern suburbs as well. Yet the movement's emphasis on the specific issue of housing rather than the broader civil rights cause simultaneously implied that unlike the more systemic problems of southern white supremacy, residential segregation represented the last and only barrier to racial integration and equality.

The focus on "housing practices" also bore the legacy of New Deal liberalism and its commitment to homeownership as well as the civil rights movement across the North, which had begun to raise public awareness about the problems of discrimination in housing and tactics such as panic selling and racial steering.[28] The movement developed forms of individual action to change these discriminatory patterns, seeking to work within rather than alter the parameters established by the suburban housing market. The groups had intimate understanding of the role that property values played in shaping the political subjectivity of suburban residents, and their earliest efforts involved convincing their fellow residents that a black neighbor did not create real estate value declines. The Brookline Fair Housing Practices Committee (FHPC) published a series of articles in the local newspaper that incorporated information from a variety of academic studies to show that panic selling, not racial integration, caused a decline in property values.[29] In neighboring Newton, the FHPC marshaled a local sociologist, lawyer, and group of housewives to conduct a study—later published as a scholarly article in the *Journal of Intergroup Relations*—proving black families moving into all-white neighborhoods in Newton did not affect property values.[30] Fair housing committees also sponsored many talks by a variety of government officials, politicians, community activists, and academics, including leading experts on intergroup relations such as Gordon Allport who were affiliated with area institutions.[31] Several groups even tried to suggest that integrated housing would enhance property values in an effort to fuse the priorities of middle-class homeowners with the basic theoretical findings of intergroup relations scholarship.[32]

The movement aimed to use individual action to change real estate market patterns by circumventing the practice of racial steering. Members used their personal contacts to gain promises from homeowners and real estate brokers that they would sell homes on a nondiscriminatory basis and convinced some residents to list their houses directly with their local committee.[33] In addition, the organization took over the AFSC's "Clearing House," setting up an office in the lobby of Freedom House, a social services agency in Roxbury to help African American families find homes. Members worked closely with potential African American buyers or lessees accompanying them to look at available housing options, and serve as advocates, negotiators, and mediators in the purchase or rental process. Some suburban volunteers devoted long hours and full weekends to helping a single African American family find housing in their community, and one committee collectively invested four hundred hours assisting one prospective buyer.[34]

The efforts of the committees to find housing for potential African American buyers produced a disturbing cartography of residential segregation in suburban Boston. While developers were luring white families with promises of attractive homes and FHA-backed mortgages, many of the prospective buyers who enlisted the help of the fair housing groups had experienced protracted struggles finding housing in the suburbs, including overt racial prejudice from landlords and tenants. For instance, Newton native Samuel Turner, a teacher in its public schools who had earned the title "Outstanding Young Man in Newton," found a home in that community only through the assistance of the local committee after a twelve-month search.[35] In Belmont, the committee went into action after an African American Harvard dean's attempt to move into a particularly exclusive neighborhood created a surge of protest. Committee members worked to reassure residents that he would not tarnish the prestige of the area or valuation of its property and only wanted to raise his family in a neighborhood "suited to his intellectual and financial position."[36]

The dean represented the typical buyer who secured a home through the assistance of the fair housing movement. A report conducted by an organization closely affiliated with the movement discovered "out-of-state families are more successful than any other group" in finding housing, and most of the "homeseekers in this group are professionals in the scientific industries."[37] It shocked Federation activists to learn how few African Americans in Roxbury had heard of their organization, and even when they did know about the committees, they did not believe that they could provide them with effective assistance.[38] Yet it is not surprising that most African Americans were skeptical of the movement, or that the beneficiaries of the committee's strategies were almost exclusively white-collar professionals and academics with ties to Route 128 industry who had recently relocated to the Boston area for professional purposes. These factors represented deeper problems of racial and residential segregation that surpassed what the movement could address. The federal government systematically denied African Americans the federally subsidized mortgages available to white borrowers, and thus the only people who could purchase homes available through the fair housing committees were ones who could pay for the home in cash.[39] Thus, the number of African Americans who wanted to move into suburban areas and could afford to do so actually represented a very small percentage of the city's black population.

In addition, many of the communities most "open" to residential integration and with the most active fair housing committees also had some of the metropolitan area's most expensive housing stock. The Federation compiled long lists of single-family houses in the Boston area available to nonwhite buyers, but these homes were in places like Lexington or Concord and usually fell within the relatively unaffordable sixteen to twenty thousand dollar price range.[40] Between 1961 and 1963, the Federation and its offshoot Fair Housing, Inc. secured housing placements for slightly more than one hundred people spread out among over a dozen suburbs, punctuating the breadth, but lack of depth of its efforts.[41] The Federation did concede in October 1962 that its success rate was "not staggeringly high." Still, the operators of the Clearing House contended that each placement secured represented "a genuine contribution to integration, often occurring in all white areas," and that they had kept in touch with many of the families and "almost all" had made "a happy adjustment," speaking "glowingly of neighbors bringing chocolate cakes, rounds of cocktail parties and teas."[42] The Federation also noted that the fact that four African American families had purchased homes in Newton without the help of the Clearing House demonstrated the success of the education wing of the local committees.[43]

The mismatch between available houses and potential beneficiaries reveals the very specific way that members of the groups understood the broad idea of fair housing. In their mission statements and promotional literature, the groups frequently adopted the expansive terms and ideas of "equal opportunity" and "freedom of choice" in narrow, class-specific ways.[44] Robert Feldmesser of the Concord FHPC clarified about the effort to encourage residents to put their homes for sale on an "open market." "Many people thought it meant definitely selling to a Negro family which would also be a form of discrimination," Feldmesser explained, but, in fact, it meant that "you are willing to allow who can afford to buy, an equal chance at getting the house." The statement reveals how even many of the suburanites who vocally opposed residential discrimination had absorbed and replicated the discourses about the "free market" that had created many of the very factors the movement aimed to fight.[45]

The discourse of choice and opportunity also reflected a distinctly white middle-class understanding of racial integration that promoted meritocratic

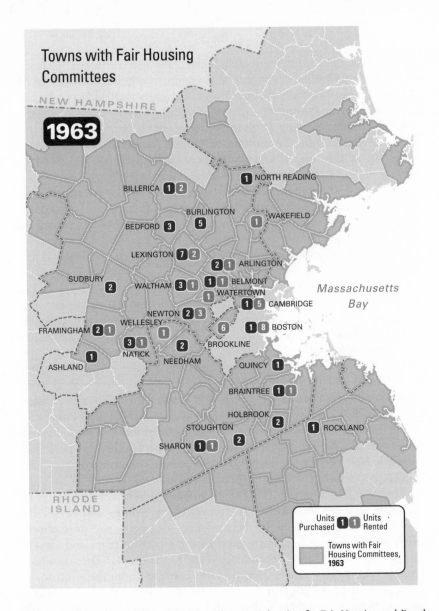

Figure 2.1 Towns with chapters of the Massachusetts Federation for Fair Housing and Equal Rights along with the number of housing rentals and purchases that the organization helped to secure for African American families between April 1962 and August 1964. Only the names of those communities with placements secured by the fair housing committees are included. The map shows the geographic breadth of the movement, but the limited of number of housing placements it secured. *Sources*: Sadelle Sacks, "An Open Door to Integrated Housing in Metropolitan Boston," 1966, Freedom House Inc. Records, Archives and Special Collections Department, Northeastern University, Boston; Fair Housing, Inc., "Annual Housing Report, April 1962–March 1963," Lexington Civil Rights Committee Collection, Cary Memorial Library, Lexington, MA; Fair Housing, Inc., "Annual Housing Report, Sept. 1963–Aug. 1964," Papers of Phyllis M. Ryan, Special Collections, Northeastern University Library, Boston.

principles and normalized class exclusion as a natural feature of the suburban landscape.[46] In a flyer titled "An Invitation to Act for Democracy," the
Belmont FHPC explicitly declared that it was not "seeking to induce a member of any race, religion, or ethnic group to move to Belmont" but rather to
provide "the same freedom of choice" to minorities as have "members of
majority groups with essentially the same needs, resources and capacities."[47]
The fair housing committees also frequently qualified the people they
sought to help with designations such as "good character" and even "financially qualified."[48] The Belmont FHPC's flyer outlined a cognitive map of
the metropolitan region by affirming its goal as "maintaining and improving the high standards of attractive well-kept homes, fine schools and local
enterprises" in Belmont and not to create new "slums and ghettos" in the
town.[49] While the group clearly aimed this point at skeptics fearful about
their declining property values, its choice of imagery exposed the ways in
which this strategy of promoting racial integration rested on an explicit language and ideology of class difference and individual advancement.[50]

The movement's "Good Neighbor for Fair Housing" campaign further
highlights the individualist and class-based dimensions of the mission and
grassroots tactics. The Brookline committee first launched this door-to-door
effort in the winter of 1962, asking residents to sign a pledge that it defined
as "a simple concrete way ... to show broad community support for the principle of Fair Housing." The idea quickly spread to the towns of Arlington,
Belmont, Lexington, and Wellesley. The three-point contract began with a
sweeping articulation of the racial liberal principle "that all people regardless of race, religion, or national origin should have equal opportunity for
housing." Moving to the more concrete, the pledge made the signers promise
to rent or sell the property they owned or managed without regard to race,
religion, or national origin, and encourage their neighbors to join with them
to achieve an integrated neighborhood.[51] The campaign embodied the basic
tenets of postwar racial liberalism in both its implicit focus on creating
equality of opportunity and confidence that changing the hearts and minds
of individuals offered the surest route to ending racial discrimination.

Although promoting a seemingly simple promise, a Brookline campaign
poster best illustrates the initiative's complex web of meanings. Drawn by a
member of the local committee, the poster featured two identical single-
family homes in stick-figure form. In the forefront of the picture, two stick-
figured men talked while leaning on push mowers, behind them two
women spoke to each other from inside the respective houses, and off in the
distance (or conceivably the backyard) two small girls held hands. The pair
of smiling families exactly mirrored each other except that the artist had
colored in the faces of the family on the right to mark their race.[52] The message of a Lexington Civil Rights Committee (LCRC) flyer touting its goal to
"make possible for every one of Lexington's neighbors to view a prospective

Figure 2.2 Good Neighbor for Fair Housing poster drawn by a member of the Brookline Fair Housing Practices Committee as part of the organization's 1962 campaign to get local residents to sign a Good Neighbor pledge promising not to discriminate. The drawing captures the commitment of the campaign and fair housing movement to the ideals of racial liberalism, normative notions of family, and class-specific interpretations of equality. Courtesy: Papers of Phyllis M. Ryan, Special Collections, Northeastern University Library, Boston.

neighbor not as a Negro, but as a doctor, engineer, or businessman" could have provided the poster's accompanying text.[53] This image and text shows how the fair housing groups adhered to both a color-blind definition of equality explicitly grounded in notions of class difference and traditional gender roles. This designation built on and reified the family-centered ideology and traditional gender norms of postwar suburbia.[54] The visual and rhetorical emphasis on domesticity also implicitly contained the racialized, class-coded message to reassure less committed neighbors that the fair housing committees did not aim to recruit dangerous and deviant single black "bachelors" or welfare mothers with a large number of children into the suburbs, and instead sought safe and stable middle-class families.[55] The mission statement of many of the groups articulated the common goal of making their communities open to "families" of all races, nationalities, and religions, and the groups usually referred to the prospective homeowners they aimed to help in terms of familial units. Thus, the movement and its iconography implicitly suggested that the concept of a "good neighbor" ran in two directions.

In total, the campaign gathered four thousand signatures across five communities in the Route 128 area in the span of two months, and in doing so helped to promote the reputations of these communities as strongholds of liberalism. The LCRC's twelve-week drive had the most favorable response, garnering the signatures of 1,540 residents.[56] Once the drive concluded, LCRC members Irene Blum and Dee Zobel conducted an analysis of the basic demographics of the signers broken down by location, gender, and profession.[57] The detailed study demonstrated community-wide support for the pledge, but revealed a disproportionately high response on certain streets where particularly active committee members lived. Using information from the town directory, Blum and Zobel reported that 802 men and 738 women had signed the document, representing a spectrum of white-collar vocations. While housewives represented more than one-third of the total signers, engineers constituted "the most predominant profession by far," with teachers, doctors, physicists, chemists, business executives, and lab workers following behind.[58] Never losing an opportunity to make an allusion to the town's historic importance, a local reporter observed that this enthusiastic response to the campaign proved that the "birthplace of American liberty" continued to be "its most ardent champion."[59] Similarly, Brookline committee members convinced fourth-fifths of the town residents canvased to sign the petition, thus boasting what one member characterized as "a better than 80% batting average."[60]

The *Boston Globe* and *Boston Herald* each featured editorials on the campaign and cited the canvasing as an important effort "to implement basic American principles" and attack the "citadel of prejudice in the North." The *Globe* noted that the drive proved the "enormous reservoir of good will" in Boston's suburbs as well as the ways in which individuals had the power to affect and change public opinion.[61] It also gained strong endorsements from both local and national politicians. US congressman Lawrence Curtis patriotically proclaimed the Brookline group as acting "in our country's best interest in seeking to eliminate discrimination in housing," and a few months later Representative Benjamin Smith read a copy of the Lexington committee's pledge on the floor of the US House.[62]

The campaign received wide-ranging support, revealing that indifference to issues of race and civil rights among suburbanites in the North was by no means a given. The Good Neighbor campaign proved extremely popular largely because it provided a relatively easy way in these largely affluent communities for residents, even those not formally affiliated with their local fair housing group, to demonstrate their commitment to the cause of ending housing discrimination and to liberalism more broadly. The limits of this commitment and approach became patently clear in a story out of Lexington just a few months after the campaign's conclusion. A distressed women wrote to the LCRC to complain about how her efforts to sell her house to a black family failed after her neighbor, who had signed the pledge, blocked the transaction.[63] This story confirms Thomas Sugrue's observation that in "wealthy suburban circles" in the 1960s, "collecting signatures on pro-housing integration petitions proved to be easy," but "creating integrated housing markets in the suburbs proved to be much harder."[64]

Many of the leaders of the movement had reached a similar conclusion, recognizing the metropolitan and economic dimensions of the problem of residential discrimination.[65] Sadelle Sacks, who ran the Clearing House in Roxbury, and other members of the organization who volunteered there gained a more direct, personal understanding of the various factors that had prevented most African Americans from gaining access to the suburbs. Sacks and others continually stressed that the organization should be exerting less energy on promoting tolerance and more on increasing the availability of decent low- and middle-income housing in both the city and suburbs. Internal discussion among leaders often revealed disagreement about their interpretation of the movement's purpose and goals. People like Ephraim Weiss and Father Thomas McLeod of Lexington believed that having individual neighbors convince one another that discrimination was "'legally and morally wrong" offered the most effective means to overcome the problem.[66] But other activists, such as sociologist Bill Ryan and his wife, Phyllis, of Brookline, saw an individual approach like the one adopted in the Good Neighbor campaign as only the first step toward addressing more structural problems. "We always keep in mind that our strategic target is the *community* and that we are aiming for SOCIAL change, not individual change," the Ryans warned their fellow Federation members in the fall of 1961. "The problems of fair housing [are] ... largely economic in nature," and "we must concern ourselves with low rent housing, public housing, city housing."[67] The Federation's efforts to work more directly within the formal channels of government aimed to address both concerns. Yet the movement's contribution to the campaigns for the passage of fair housing legislation would reproduce several of the same strengths and weaknesses of the Good Neighbor campaign and the fair housing movement's other projects.

Fair Housing Law

The Massachusetts fair housing movement's advancement of legal and political solutions provides three critical insights into the tactics of this brand of activism and suburban liberalism more broadly. First, it highlights members' faith in the formal mechanisms of the law to eradicate the societal problems of racial segregation and effectiveness at working within the formal channels of government. Second, it shows the ways in which the fair housing movement, especially attorneys, successfully harnessed and applied the professional expertise of its members to create laws and policies that upheld a vision of equality centered around equal opportunity and individual rights. Third, it reveals the successes and limits of the coalitions that suburbanites forged with local civil rights groups, and the ways that the fair housing movement both contributed to and constrained the achievements of the black freedom struggle in Boston.

The entrance of members from the fair housing movements into the fight for more robust fair housing laws and aggressive state oversight of the private housing market in 1959 helped the ongoing campaign achieve new success.[68] The members' contribution to the larger cause illuminated the effectiveness of the fair housing movement in harnessing both its members' existing organizational infrastructure and status as educated, upper-middle class, white suburbanites to gain the support of members of the legislature and influence legal change. Members of the fair housing committees wrote articles for the local newspapers, placed cards on cars in various suburban town centers, and distributed colorfully illustrated pamphlets throughout their communities alerting residents about the need for the enhancement and better enforcement of state housing laws.[69] In addition, the local committees launched letter-writing campaigns and staged organized visits to the State House to pressure representatives, and individual members repeatedly testified at committee hearings, often using personal anecdotes from their grassroots experiences assisting prospective African American buyers to find homes in their communities.[70] The local fair housing committees often encouraged prospective buyers or renters to file charges with MCAD, thus supplying many of the cases that came before the commission in the late 1950s and early 1960s.

The actions helped to gradually expand the percentage of the targeted housing as well as enforcement and awareness of the new statutes. William Ryan observed that the committees contributed to the "climate of opinion" among Massachusetts politicians such that they were "required to damn discrimination with as much fervor as a Minnesota politician is required to damn margarine," and that "big-city Democrats" and "Yankee Republicans" sought to "outdo each other in speaking out for Fair Housing."[71] While the change in attitude led to revised statutes, the new laws only applied to developments with ten or more contiguous units and apartment buildings with three or more units, and still did not cover conventionally financed or single-family homes. The improved laws therefore covered only about 15 percent of the housing in the state, 180 of Massachusetts' 351 cities, and virtually none of the housing stock in places like Newton and Lexington with the most active fair housing groups.[72] MCAD, moreover, quickly recognized that the housing market usually moved faster than the processes of administrative agencies. In many cases, by the time the commission made a finding of the existence of discrimination, the property in question had already been rented or sold. The Federation members set out to use their legal expertise and lobbying acumen in order to correct this substantial loophole, thereby bringing the organization into closer physical and ideological collaboration and conflict with other civil rights organizations like the Congress of Racial Equality (CORE) trying to eliminate residential discrimination in metropolitan Boston, but covered different geographies.

CORE

In the fall of 1958, at the same moment that the fair housing committees in Boston held their first coffee klatches, quintessential postwar liberal Arthur Schlesinger Jr. responded to an inquiry from James Robinson of the national chapter of CORE about the possibility of opening a chapter of the organization in the Bay State. The Harvard historian and future Kennedy staffer, citing MCAD and the suburban housing committees, answered, "While conditions are far from perfect here, I would suppose that CORE activities might be more urgently needed in other parts of the country."[73] While Schlesinger's reply represents one strand of postwar, northern white liberal thinking about race, the individuals who opted to ignore his counsel represent another. The group's mission to draw attention to issues of racial inequality and enforce the implementation of fair housing laws put it at the center the cases of residential discrimination in the Boston area, especially in places that lacked an active fair housing committee.

A group of white Cambridge residents had initially contacted the national CORE office in the spring of 1958 about the possibility of reviving the area's long-dormant chapter. Perplexed by reports of discrimination against black home seekers in its community, the group believed that CORE's biracial and nonviolent philosophy would offer the best means to confront these problems. The first meeting, held in December 1958, attracted seventeen participants, who largely mirrored the racial, class, and political affiliations of the suburban fair housing committees. The founding members of Boston CORE also shared with their suburban counterparts both a commitment to the broad ideals of equality and the vision of an integrated society.[74] CORE began to develop strategies that would challenge individual discriminatory practices while at the same time drawing attention to the larger cause. The activities resembled some of the work of the suburban housing committees, but assumed more of a direct action approach and style. Boston's chapter pioneered a formula of testing realtors by sending in white teams to apply for the same unit denied to an African American family. Once they established the existence of clear discriminatory practices, members sought to negotiate with the developer or owner to seek fair treatment, and if these efforts failed, they then filed formal charges with MCAD.[75] The technique provided a relatively simple way of determining whether black and white families received equal treatment. It also proved a form of activism where white middle-class volunteers could be particularly effective.

CORE continued to develop these tactics during the next year, coordinating more than fifty cases of racial testing in apartment buildings and new housing developments throughout the metropolitan area. In the summer of 1960, the organization staged its boldest endeavor. Ulysses Marshall, a black electrical contractor, asserted that the Woodvale development in Danvers repeatedly discriminated against him over a two-year period and eventually decided to file a complaint with MCAD. Marshall's lawyer, Edward A. Barshak, contacted the Greater Boston CORE to supply further evidence for the case using its testing and direct action techniques. During two tests, real estate agents at the large suburban housing development literally ran away from the black testers trying to obtain applications. In response, CORE members staged a series of sit-ins in one of the model homes, successfully shutting down the developer's business activities for multiple days.[76] Ten CORE members returned to the site to picket the Woodvale office with provocative messages such as "Democracy Begins at Home" and slyly inverted the development's sylvan name: "Woodvale Tries to Be Whitevale."[77] These theatrical tactics gained national press attention, and, coupled with evidence from the tests, motivated MCAD to take action. MCAD issued a cease-and-desist order in which it found Woodvale's builders and owners guilty of discrimination.[78] The activities proved the effectiveness of direct action to not only shape public opinion but also ensure compliance with the legal process.

The successful strategies of testing and pickets further distinguished CORE from other local civil rights organizations, especially the Federation. While both groups sought to challenge discriminatory practices and create integrated housing in the suburbs, they did not just develop diverging

tactics but also covered different geographies. Many of CORE's projects occurred in middle-class communities like Danvers and Waltham that lacked
active fair housing communities. The reason that CORE's activity centered
on these particular places was less to fill in the gaps in the Federation's activities, and more because these communities contained the type of housing that fell under the jurisdiction of the 1959 law. The chapter's tactics made
it a leader in combating housing discrimination not only in the Boston area
but also among other CORE affiliates. By 1961, Boston surpassed New York
City as the most active and effective chapter in the arena of housing, and
earned the notice and praise of the parent office. Executive Secretary Robinson lauded the Woodvale situation as the "first really different thing which
CORE has done in the field of housing."[79] And James Farmer, the eminent
national chair, suggested that the housing tactics of the Boston chapter provided a valuable blueprint for how to establish roots in local communities
and "viable" groups in the North.[80]

The 1962 legal case *Massachusetts Commission Against Discrimination v.
Colangelo* showcased both CORE's strategy and successful coalition with
the suburban fair housing groups.[81] In 1960, Maurice Fowler, a single African American member of the Air Force, sought a "garden-type" apartment
at the Glenmeadow development in Waltham, but real estate developer A.
J. Colangelo turned him down on the basis of his "bachelor status."[82] Fowler's lawyer, Barshak, a member of the Brookline FHPC, contacted CORE,
which discovered that many white "bachelors" lived at Glenmeadow and
the owner also offered apartments to two white CORE testers. This fact
pattern almost duplicated that of the Woodvale case, underscoring the similarities in the types of residential discrimination that occurred in Greater
Boston and the cases that CORE pursued. As with Marshall, Barshak filed a
complaint on behalf of Fowler with MCAD, and at the final hearing CORE
presented overwhelming testimony and evidence that convinced the commission not just to rule in Fowler's favor but to require that the real estate
developer pay damages. After a series of appeals, Colangelo and the rental
agent appealed to the state Supreme Judicial Court to challenge MCAD's
order and the constitutionality of the 1959 law on the grounds that they
had been denied due process, protection of private property, and freedom of
association.

The case attracted the attention and participation of many members of
the fair housing movement who saw it as the ideal opportunity to both
apply their professional knowledge to social activism and test the constitu-
tionality of the state's housing laws.[83] Harvard Law School professor Albert
Sacks, whose wife, Sadelle, was a leader in the Federation and the Belmont
FHPC, along with Assistant Attorney General Gerald Berlin, represented
MCAD and together wrote the Brief for the Petitioner.[84] The Fair Housing
Federation also officially joined with the American Jewish Congress, NAACP,

and four other civil liberties and religious groups to submit a joint amici curiae brief written chiefly by Laurence S. Locke and Norman Landstrom, two of the central figures in the fair housing movement. Covering a wide range of issues, the petitioners and amici curiae briefs combined structural evidence and broad appeals into a convincing, nuanced argument about the need for legal action in the area of housing.[85]

The petitioners and amici curiae relied most heavily on a report, presented in the appendix to the state's brief, officially titled "Statistical Study of Housing Discrimination against Negroes in the Commonwealth of Massachusetts" by Helen Kistin. In this remarkable study that included thirty-four pages of text and nineteen tables, Kistin drew on twenty years of census data to illustrate the problem of residential discrimination in stark statistical terms. Her report showed that racial segregation had increased between 1950 and 1960, and that the majority of black families in Boston lived in substandard housing at disproportionately high rents. The study and briefs together created a stark portrait of the economic, spatial, demographic upheaval of the 1950s, which as Landstrom and Locke stressed, had made the Boston area a "dramatic" example of "the national trend towards development of a central city with its 'black core' in a ring of 'lily-white suburbs.'"[86]

Despite this careful attention to the dynamics of structural racism, the lawyers opted to couch their respective and collective arguments in the racially liberal language of individual rights and moral wrongs. Reflecting their commitment to the basic tenets of racial liberal ideology, the petitioners emphasized the psychological damage of racial discrimination on its victims. In an emotional appeal that borrowed directly from both Myrdal and the *Brown v. Board of Education* decision, Sacks and Berlin contended that housing discrimination had "ramifications beyond bricks and mortar and beyond not just the hearts and minds of men of all races and nationalities, and to their modes of living together in one society."[87] This reasoning proved persuasive, and on May 16, 1962, the Massachusetts Supreme Judicial Court upheld the constitutionality of the statute prohibiting discrimination in private housing, declaring "neither property rights nor contract rights are absolute; for the government cannot exist if the citizen may at will use his property to the detriment of his fellows, or exercise his freedom of contract to work them harm."[88]

The decision established important local and national precedent. The successful outcome of the case validated the efforts of the fair housing movement, and reinforced the ways in which grassroots actors and activity could use the law to create meaningful change.[89] The court case also provided the legal justification for the Massachusetts legislature to expand the parameters of the existing fair housing law to cover all private property. In the spring of 1963, the state legislature passed a new act that outlawed discrimination on the basis of "race, creed, color or country of origin" in the sale or rental of all private housing, with the sole exception of a two-apartment house if the owner occupied one of the apartments as their home.[90] The revised law, which passed with little opposition, solidified the state's claim to have the strongest antidiscrimination laws in the nation. When California residents voted overwhelmingly to overturn their state fair housing law the following year, it only further enforced Massachusetts' progressive identity.[91]

The new fair housing law, however, not only bolstered the state's position at the vanguard of liberalism but also perpetuated the suburban movement's racial liberal ideology. The law represented a symbolically significant step in codifying into law the opposition to explicit discrimination. Yet Updike's fictionalized Frank misunderstood its intent and scope when he stated that the law tried to give "equality of status," not "equality of *opportunity*," and denied "the homeowner of his right to choose." In fact, the law took no affirmative steps to create equality of status and did not even contain a measure to legally enforce the Good Neighbor for Fair Housing pledges.[92] Since it only addressed discrimination in rental and sales, like the movement from which it emerged, it offered little assistance to the majority of African Americans who could not afford housing outside segregated neighborhoods.[93] The case of discrimination that led to the protest on the Lexington Battle Green highlighted the impact and limits of the 1963 law in particular and suburban fair housing activism in general.

"Lexington, Live Up to Your Name"

On August 27, 1963, James Parker and his wife Odessa had gone to Lexington in response to an advertisement for a cottage for rent. Parker, a Foreign Service Officer who had previously served in Liberia, Algeria, and Spain, was about to begin a year in the African Studies Program at Boston University, and he and his wife wanted to find a home in a town with good public schools in which to enroll their two young children. When they arrived for the showing in Lexington, the cottage's owner, Mark Moore Jr., a local real estate developer, whose advertisements in the local newspaper promised homes "for the discriminating buyer" without a hint of irony, expressed visible surprise.[94] Using the excuse that another couple had already made an offer on the rental, Moore told the Parkers that the house was not available. Frustrated, the Parkers boarded a plane back to Washington. The previous spring, members of the LCRC had received training in the racial testing strategies pioneered by CORE, and when Barbara Petschek, who along with her astronomer husband Harry, was active in the suburban civil rights group, learned of the Moore and Parker interaction, she recognized that it offered an ideal chance to experiment with these new skills. Petschek and fellow LCRC member Julian Soshnick, a state assistant attorney general, contacted the developer posing as interested buyers. After Moore informed the couple that they could move in starting in September, Soshnick unmasked his true identity and interrogated Moore on his discriminatory rejection of the Parkers. Moore apparently explained that he had "nothing against" the Parkers, but had recently invested four hundred thousand dollars in a prospective subdivision on the same property and feared that if he rented "to a Negro," he would lose his money.[95] Soshnick filed an official complaint with MCAD the next day, and simultaneously Parker contacted the Boston Chapter of CORE and alerted it of his case.

CORE immediately announced that it would stage a series of demonstrations on the Lexington Battle Green to spotlight Parker's case and promote compliance with the Fair Housing Law. Several LCRC members decided to join in the protests.[96] The picketing duplicated the strategies of nonviolent direct action that CORE had skillfully deployed in its previous housing protests around Boston's metropolitan region, only the organizers chose the location of the Battle Green, appropriating the site's symbolic and historic associations with freedom, equality, and democracy. The placards that the protesters carried made explicit references to the town's revolutionary tradition with messages such as "Birthplace of American Liberty??" and "Lexington, Live Up to Your Name," at once invoking and questioning the community's exceptionalist reputation.

As with most CORE and fair housing movement activities, white middle-class women comprised the majority of the protesters on the Battle Green. Marching along the green's edge on the late summer morning, most of the women sported modest dresses or skirts, dress shoes, and coiffed hair.[97] Some of the female protesters pushed baby carriages while others had small children in tow, drawing on the strong political and social associations of white motherhood.[98] These depictions helped draw a sympathetic reaction from many community members. Liz Collins, for instance, declared her "deep concern" that such drastic action was necessary to make Parker "a fellow resident."[99] The tactics also elicited significant media attention. The *Boston Globe* made the picketing front-page news in a prominent above-the-fold location. Over the caption "Peaceful Protest beside Minuteman Statue," a photograph depicted two white women in the foreground walking side by side and holding a sign that read "Jim Crow Must Go" with the Minuteman statue hovering in the immediate background.[100]

The press couched the coverage of the Parker family in the discourses of middle-class respectability and domestic ideals as well. The *Globe* discussed Parker's biography as a World War II veteran, civil servant, and devoted father, his wife's role as president of the American Women's Club in Barcelona, and the stellar academic record of their children.[101] The Parkers' own comments upheld and even reified the fair housing movement's implicit

Figure 2.3 Members of the CORE and the LCRC march on September 5, 1963 at the Lexington Battle Green to protest a case of housing discrimination against African American James Parker. The marchers stand below a statue carrying signs declaring "Freedom. Let it Begin Here" and "Birthplace of American Liberty?" It was one of two protests that the organizations held on the Battle Green in response to the case. Images like this one appeared on the front page of several local newspapers. Photo by Williams Smith. Courtesy of the *Boston Herald* from the *Boston Herald-Traveler* Photo Morgue, Special Collections, Boston Public Library.

image of what a "good neighbor" looked like.[102] In newspaper interviews, Parker presented himself as a apolitical concerned parent who desired to move to Lexington because of the "town's reputation for having an outstanding school system."[103] He stated that he would not move to Massachusetts at all if he had to live in Roxbury and send his children to the Boston Public Schools. Parker also relied on his out-of-state, expatriate status as a means to profess innocence of the realities of American racial and class structures. He explained, "We've been away for so long that I was not psychologically prepared for it. If I had been assigned to the Deep South and this had happened, it wouldn't have been such a shock."[104] Like the CORE protesters' use of the Jim Crow analogy, the comments reflected both a critique and invocation of Massachusetts exceptionalism. Noting that he was "surprised that the incident had happened in New England," Parker amplified that regional difference by an appeal to a sense of northern morality and social consciousness.[105] His perspective both upheld and challenged the notions that the Bay State was more tolerant and enlightened than the Deep South.

The public nature of the Parker controversy, coupled with political pressure at both the state and local level, led MCAD to schedule an expedited conciliation session.[106] The commission found "probable cause of discrimination" by Moore, and the Parkers quickly settled into their new home in time for the first day of school.[107] This rapid resolution exposed the widespread effectiveness of the new state law and protest strategy—both of which came directly from the hard work of the fair housing movement. Lexington residents Arlene and Michael Morrison publicly applauded that the case "could not have been brought to such a swift and acceptable decision if the tremendous pressures of the picket lines had not been invoked."[108] The dedication of CORE and the Federation in advocating for the Parker family undoubtedly deserved praise. The case, nevertheless, punctuated the fact that the fair housing law and movement more broadly were really only effective in challenging overt discrimination against individual middle-class African Americans, and helping the same constituency move into affluent suburbs. The grassroots and legal tactics of the fair housing groups had little impact in changing the racial demographics of these communities. The Federation frequently cited Lexington as a success story because the active committee there had boosted the number of nonwhite families in the town to just over forty out of more than twenty-seven thousand residents.[109] The gap between the goals and reality of the fair housing movement's effectiveness contributed to undoing the coalition forged between the Federation and members of the larger Boston freedom struggle and forced both to reassess their respective goals.

By the end of 1963, CORE made a sharp move away from its own definition of fair housing to emphasize improving the housing conditions of lower-income African Americans in Boston. Paralleling the shift in strategy of its national umbrella organization, the Boston group launched a campaign "to remedy housing blight."[110] Between 1964 and 1965, CORE sent inspection teams into buildings to canvas for health and safety violations, staged a successful monthlong rent strike to force landlords to make necessary repairs, organized pickets of tenants to protest the suburban homes of landlords, led the press and local and state politicians on walking tours of Roxbury's housing stock, and pressured city officials to intensify the enforcement of building codes.[111] This shift in attention placed the group in closer concert with the needs of Boston's black population, but it made the possibility of meaningful collaboration with the suburban fair housing groups increasingly remote. Many of the more committed suburban fair housing activists, such as the Ryans, also followed suit, leaving the Federation in order to get involved in campaigns that more directly targeted the structures of racial and residential segregation.[112]

From Fair Housing to Civil Rights

Beginning in late 1963, the majority of Federation members decided to shift their focus as well, widening their interests and activities beyond housing alone toward other civil rights issues. In order to reflect this revised agenda and strategy, the leaders also voted to officially change the name of the organization to the Massachusetts Federation for Fair Housing and Equal Rights (MFFHER). The decision to add the words "equal rights" to its name marked the Federation's effort to acknowledge the "inseparability of housing problems from those of education and employment."[113] Between 1963 and 1965, most of the local chapters widened their interests and activities to other civil rights issues, and many of them became actively involved in the growing controversy over integrating the Boston Public Schools. The majority of committees also took on new names to reflect this expanded range of interest, with the Brookline Fair Housing Practices Committee now calling itself the Brookline Civil Rights Committee, and the Newton group changing to the Newton Committee for Fair Housing and Equal Rights.[114] The attention to the civil rights cause at the national level motivated this expansion in focus and attracted many members to the local groups as well. In 1964 and 1965, all the committees experienced a spike in membership and the LCRC became the largest in the area, reaching over a thousand members by February 1965.[115]

Despite their new names and rapidly growing memberships the Federation and local committees still struggled to define their purpose. In the spring of 1964, incoming Federation president Roy Brown delivered a speech titled "What We Are and Where We Are," encouraging the group to embrace rather than shun its unique geographic and ideological position. He insisted that "the Federation's strength lies in the unique grass roots character of its constituent committees," and made a convincing case that "No other civil rights group is so favorably situated to speak for and to the essentially white suburban areas of greater Boston."[116] Recognizing one area where this grassroots structure and suburban base could be particularly beneficial, the Federation began to broaden its legislative agenda and lobbying role. The grassroots and suburban infrastructure of the Federation provided a unique advantage in its legislative pursuits. Most of the thirty-five hundred largely white, middle-class suburban members spread throughout about thirty-seven communities maintained only a nominal affiliation to the organization, which highlighted the key distinction in most liberally oriented suburbs between committed activists and the majority of the residents in the towns where they lived. Yet invoking the numerical strength and dispersed geography of its membership gave the Federation a powerful lobbying device and, in particular, leverage in building coalitions of suburban politicians to pass certain pieces of legislation. The leaders also marshaled the organizational structures of the local chapters frequently to pressure their state and national representatives through letter-writing campaigns and visits to the State House. By the mid-1960s, the Federation had become one of the most powerful and effective advocates in the state for laws related to housing and other civil rights issues. Furthermore, the Federation served as an important training ground for suburban liberal activism on a variety of other causes, from opposition to the Vietnam War to feminism.

The movement's complex legacy is most evident in the fact that by 1970, Massachusetts had some of the most progressive state laws devoted to challenging housing discrimination, but metropolitan Boston remained roughly as racially and economically segregated as it was a decade earlier.[117] In suburbs with the most active fair housing committees like Lexington and Newton, the population was still over 98 percent white.[118] The results underscore that even a movement of three thousand well-organized, confident suburbanites who had the ability to get laws passed could not alter the structures and priorities of the federally subsidized real estate market, lending practices of banks, racial steering, consistent disinvestment in cities, coupled with urban renewal, and entrenched land use patterns of suburban municipalities that had produced systemic residential segregation by race and class.

The fair housing movement's combination of localized and legal tactics did succeed in transforming the notion that African Americans should have the opportunity to live anywhere from a fringe into a mainstream belief over the course of the 1960s—an important shift and no small feat. The small number of middle-class black professionals and their families scattered throughout the Boston suburbs reinforced the meritocratic ideal that everyone had the "opportunity" to overcome the structures of segregation.[119]

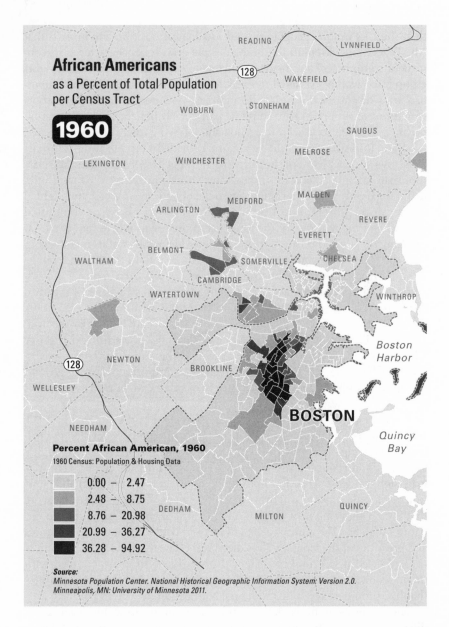

African Americans
as a Percent of Total Population
per Census Tract

1960

READING
LYNNFIELD
128
WAKEFIELD
WOBURN
STONEHAM
SAUGUS
MELROSE
LEXINGTON
WINCHESTER
MALDEN
MEDFORD
ARLINGTON
REVERE
EVERETT
BELMONT
WALTHAM
SOMERVILLE
CHELSEA
CAMBRIDGE
WATERTOWN
WINTHROP

Boston Harbor

128
NEWTON
BROOKLINE
WELLESLEY
BOSTON

NEEDHAM
Quincy Bay

Percent African American, 1960
1960 Census: Population & Housing Data

	0.00 – 2.47
	2.48 – 8.75
	8.76 – 20.98
	20.99 – 36.27
	36.28 – 94.92

DEDHAM
MILTON
QUINCY

Source:
Minnesota Population Center. National Historical Geographic Information System: Version 2.0.
Minneapolis, MN: University of Minnesota 2011.

Figure 2.4 Distribution of African American population in metropolitan Boston, 1960 and 1970, by census tract. These two maps show how little change occurred to the patterns of residential segregation in the Boston area between 1960 and 1970 despite the concerted efforts of the fair housing movement and the passage of state and federal fair housing laws aimed to combat residential discrimination. Source: *US Census Bureau Census of Population and Housing, 1960* (Washington, DC: US Census Bureau, 1960); US Census Bureau, *Census of Population and Housing, 1970* (Washington, DC: US Census Bureau, 1970).

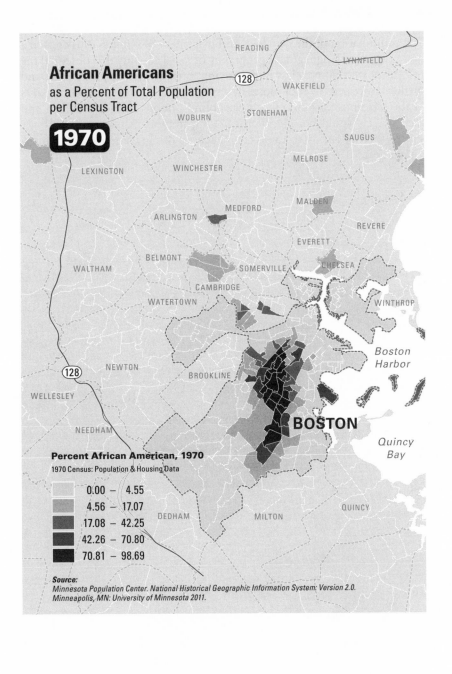

African Americans
as a Percent of Total Population
per Census Tract

1970

READING
LYNNFIELD
128
WAKEFIELD
WOBURN
STONEHAM
SAUGUS
MELROSE
LEXINGTON
WINCHESTER
MEDFORD
MALDEN
ARLINGTON
REVERE
EVERETT
BELMONT
WALTHAM
SOMERVILLE
CHELSEA
CAMBRIDGE
WATERTOWN
WINTHROP
Boston
Harbor
NEWTON
128
BROOKLINE
WELLESLEY
NEEDHAM
BOSTON
Quincy
Bay

Percent African American, 1970
1970 Census: Population & Housing Data

	0.00 – 4.55
	4.56 – 17.07
	17.08 – 42.25
	42.26 – 70.80
	70.81 – 98.69

DEDHAM
MILTON
QUINCY

Source:
Minnesota Population Center. National Historical Geographic Information System: Version 2.0.
Minneapolis, MN: University of Minnesota 2011.

The combination of the new laws and placement of families thus created a new class-blind language and geography of racial equality that obscured the role of socioeconomic class in producing forms of systemic inequality and further concealed the root causes of segregation. The power and constraints of the fair housing movement's class-blind notions of individualism and meritocracy would become ever more apparent as members increasingly shifted their attention to the issues of school desegregation and voluntary integration.

3

A Multiracial World

On a Saturday afternoon in the spring of 1969, the Neileys hosted the family of one of their daughters' classmates at their Lincoln home, set on a backdrop of two acres of woods with a tennis court and horse-filled barn. Seven-year-old Rhonda Williams played Monopoly with the three Neiley daughters, while their parents chatted over sherry in the glass-enclosed living room of the large modernist home.[1] The Williams family lived in the Roxbury section of Boston, not Lincoln, and Rhonda was one of fifty African American students who took the bus each day from Boston to Lincoln as part of the Metropolitan Council for Educational Opportunity (METCO). Beginning in 1966, the voluntary integration program transported black students from Boston into predominantly white and affluent suburban school systems throughout the metropolitan ring in an initiative fully underwritten financially by the Commonwealth of Massachusetts.

Despite the fact that Rhonda had to get on the bus early each morning and ride almost an hour from Roxbury to Lincoln, her parents had decided to enroll her in METCO because they believed it would provide her with a better education than she would receive in the severely segregated, inadequate Boston Public Schools (BPS). The Neileys served as Rhonda's host family in the suburbs, which led to several social get-togethers between the two families at the Neileys' spacious home. The experiences of playing with Rhonda in and out of school had instilled in seven-year-old Susan Neiley the belief that "it's what's inside that counts." Her ten-year-old sister, Lisa, similarly stated, "Everyone's the same inside except for pigment, so everybody should be treated equal." Mrs. Howard Stoudt, Lincoln resident and parent of another of Rhonda's suburban friends, declared of METCO's purpose, "I think that all of us feel we are preparing these children for a multiracial society."[2]

The scene of the white suburban and black urban families socializing served as a counterpoint to the protracted, violent battle that occurred over busing in Boston a few years later. It also almost brought to life the poster of the fair housing movement's Good Neighbor campaign: black and white stick-figure families standing side by side. This symbolism was not surprising since METCO evolved directly from the ideology and organizational infrastructure of the suburban fair housing movement. These roots directly influenced METCO's commitment to equal opportunity and changing individual attitudes through one-on-one interaction.

Beginning in 1964, many of the white suburban members of the Massachusetts Federation for Fair Housing and Equal Rights (MFFHER) expanded the strategies they had developed to fight against residential discrimination and conjoined with the black-led effort to confront systemic school segregation in Boston. The Federation became involved in the efforts to boycott BPS and then spearheaded the lobbying campaign that led to passage of the Racial Imbalance Act in 1965. The legislation, which withheld state funds to districts that did not eliminate majority black schools, made Massachusetts the first state to take action against racial imbalance. Following that success, the Federation worked in coalition with members of the black community to coordinate the establishment of METCO. The program's structure and goals fused racial liberal principles with the social science and legal backgrounds of many of the suburban organizers, who were deeply committed to using expertise to solve social problems.

The Neiley family's enthusiastic endorsement of the program challenges the typical discussions of white suburban attitudes toward school integration, especially remedies that involved busing. This support highlights the fact that many of METCO's most salient features, particularly its limited size, voluntary commitment, and state government funding, actually complemented the political agenda of most upper-middle-class homeowners in the Route 128 suburbs and their counterparts in other parts of the nation. METCO represented one of the most imaginative, far-reaching voluntary integration schemes in the United States and, like the fair housing movement, provided benefits and opportunities to a small number of African American children. Yet also similar to the fair housing movement, METCO's success was due in part that it did not create any significant financial or personal hardship for participation on the part of white suburbanites. The one-way busing program appealed directly to the worldview of many liberal-leaning suburbanites, who supported racial and educational equality in principle, but not routes to achieving those goals that could potentially increase local tax rates or have a potentially negative impact on the education of their own children.

METCO's dynamics reinforced the ideological and financial premium that many suburban professionals placed on education. The program's emphasis on education as a means of advancement served as a crucial point of overlap between the white suburbanites like the Neileys and African American participants like the Williams, but the white and black groups had divergent interpretations of the idea. Recognizing Route 128 suburban residents' commitment to providing the best and most cutting-edge instruction for their children, METCO's advocates frequently touted the specific educational benefits of the program for white middle-class children by preparing them to operate in a multiracial world. The program's proponents emphasized that white middle-class youths needed to understand the realities of the larger world in order to achieve future success. This consumer-oriented claim about the value of diversity presaged a key rationale for affirmative action policies. Scholars like Nancy MacLean and Thomas Sugrue have led the way in demonstrating how affirmative action policies emerged "from below" primarily due to the efforts of African American, Latino, and feminist grassroots activists. Few scholars have examined the constitutive role that white middle-class suburban liberals played in shaping the ideas and backing for affirmative action.[3]

The diversity argument proved crucial to gaining support for METCO in the suburbs. In the process, though, the claims helped to marginalize from public consciousness or debate the structural dynamics that created school segregation and racial inequity. The argument also concealed that it was not an abiding commitment to integration or diversity that primarily motivated black families like the Williams to enroll their children in METCO but a desire to circumvent the interlocking forms of inequality that prevented their children from achieving adequate education. While METCO offered a rare example of interracial and urban-suburban cooperation, its focus on collective benefits rather than collective responsibility had wide-ranging consequences. Tracing the development of METCO offers an important case study of the trade-offs suburban liberal activists made in their quests to achieve social justice. The organizers' pragmatic approach ensured the acceptance of the program in the suburbs and paved the way for later support of diversity claims about the value of affirmative action. This strategy, nevertheless, fortified the consumer-based and individualist dimensions of the Route 128 political culture. It ultimately made community members more resistant to grappling with the systemic and historical circumstances that necessitated programs like METCO and affirmative action in the first place.

Stayout for Freedom

The long commitment of the Boston School Committee (BSC) to the romantic ideal and policy of "the neighborhood school" clearly favored some city areas over others. The schools in the neighborhoods of Roxbury, North Dorchester, and the South End, where roughly half the black population of Boston resided, were overwhelmingly nonwhite and overcrowded. Officials had not built new school buildings in these neighborhoods in over thirty years, and most of the existing ones violated health and safety codes. In contrast, the BSC spent an average of a hundred dollars more per pupil on its white students and provided white children with a more advanced curriculum and more experienced teachers.[4]

Beginning in the 1950s, a group of African American parents along with the Boston chapter of the NAACP came together to challenge these overtly discriminatory practices. Roxbury mother Ruth Batson, who would become one of the main leaders for Boston's African American community and later the director of METCO, led the effort.[5] In the late spring of 1963, Batson, Paul Parks, and the other members of the NAACP education subcommittee began a series of particularly tense exchanges with the notoriously intransigent, all-white BSC chaired by longtime integration opponent Louise Day Hicks. The subcommittee submitted a long list of requests to the BSC, the majority of which addressed problems of educational resources. The group also demanded "an immediate public acknowledgement of the existence of de facto segregation in the Boston school system."[6] The BSC had cautiously agreed to study most of the requests, but the majority of the members staunchly refused to publicly recognize the existence of "de facto" segregation, and thus the school board and civil rights community of Boston reached what journalist J. Anthony Lukas called "an impasse over two small Latin words."[7]

The stalemate provoked allies of the NAACP to stage a school boycott in order to dramatize "the intolerable conditions" of "de facto segregation" and literally expose the thirteen Boston schools with "predominately Negro pupil enrollment."[8] On June 18, 1963, 8,260 junior and senior high school pupils (about 30 percent of the total secondary population) participated in "Stay Out for Freedom," and one-third of the three thousand African American students who opted out of class instead attended "Freedom Schools."[9] Noel Day and Reverend James Breeden, the central organizers of the Stay-out, who had been college roommates at Dartmouth, crafted the curriculum, with classes devoted to "Negro history," the rights and responsibilities of American citizenship, and the meanings of nonviolence and civil rights.[10] The Freedom Schools and larger Stayout proved successful ways to draw attention to the problem of school segregation, and the tactics established an important precedent for civil rights groups throughout the country. Similar protests rippled throughout the North and West during the next year, using the Boston Stayout as a model. Indeed, the Mississippi Summer Project the following year borrowed many of the Stayout's materials in its own network of forty-one Freedom Schools.[11]

The Stayout might have brought the issue of educational inequality into the local and national spotlight, but it did not persuade the BSC to officially compromise its position. In the November BSC election, Hicks won 68.8 percent of the vote and the NAACP-backed candidate lost. It seemed that the comparisons to George Wallace and other southern segregationists helped rather than hurt the incumbents. Thus, as BSC members began to fully understand the potential political benefits of racial antagonism, it only strengthened their unwillingness to negotiate and indicated to Boston's civil rights community that the fight remained very much on.

The members of the MFFHER had watched these events unfold in Boston from a removed yet concerned position. The fair housing activists remained unsure about how exactly their suburban-based membership could intervene. In the winter of 1964, the Federation found the ideal opportunity when Day and Breeden decided to plan a second Stayout. If the June event had dramatized segregation through empty classrooms, the winter version sought to make its case by creating integrated ones. Breeden believed "the presence of thousands of white and black children learning" would "demonstrate the promise of what our public schools could be."[12] The members of the fair housing movement provided Day and Breeden with willing white participants in this symbolic action by recruiting student participants, adult chaperones, and teachers. Cheered by the tide of support, Thomas Atkins, NAACP executive secretary, told a group of suburbanites, "I only wish some of you still lived in town!"[13]

A thousand white youths from more than twenty suburbs came into the city on February 26, 1964, to show "people we care," as one Wellesley eighth grader stated, "and that we feel there is a problem being ignored."[14] Katherine Ashbrook, a high school senior from Weston, explained that she wanted "to learn more about the conditions and the problems in Roxbury from Roxbury students."[15] The suburbanites mingled with the 20,571 Boston students who had opted to stay out as well. Roughly ten thousand of Boston's black student population attended Freedom Schools at thirty-four churches, social centers, and neighborhood houses in Roxbury, the South End, and Dorchester.[16] The "educationally and culturally enriching" alternative curriculum included discussions of the "psychological effects of segregated education," "the Negro's contribution to American history," the issue of teenage unemployment, and "college scholarship opportunities."[17] The program also included chances for singing "freedom songs" and socializing, which hit a literal and figurative high note when a Harvard student picked up his banjo and led about a thousand students gathered at the Saint Mark Center in an impromptu sing-along of "We Shall Overcome." For most of the white and black children, the event marked both their initial exposure to most of this information and their first time learning in an integrated setting. Sociologist and fair housing activist William Ryan later described watching as the children listened intently "as if they were trying to gulp and chew a lifetime of learning in one day."[18]

The major newspapers in Boston made the Stayout front-page news with images of rows of attentive white and black children sitting side by side, putting in visual and printed form the civil rights activists' case about the value and necessity of integration. The suburban students represented only one-tenth of the participants in Freedom Schools and one-twentieth of the Stayout, yet they received a disproportionate amount of the press coverage, particularly in the *Boston Globe*, which had a wide circulation throughout

the city's suburban ring. The presence of white middle-class children assured a quick way to elicit media attention and suburban sympathy, and
reporters never failed to mention that most of the white children came
from "well-to-do families."[19] These descriptions and the overall media attention reflect the effectiveness of the Stayout in using suburban students to
gain support for the school integration cause among Massachusetts residents and politicians.[20]

The overall outcome of the Stayout significantly pleased Boston civil
rights activists. The NAACP's Atkins hailed the boycott as "100 per cent
successful"; Day called it "a great day"; and Breeden dubbed it a "resounding
success."[21] These words of praise, however, did little to move the obdurate
Boston school officials' sympathies. Superintendent William Ohrenberger
publicly denounced the event as a "Pyrrhic victory," and Hicks as usual went
even further, calling it "a tremendous failure."[22] Although the Stayout had
failed to persuade the BSC, the project did have important short- and long-
term impacts. By galvanizing state officials, civil rights activists in Roxbury,
and concerned suburbanites in the cul-de-sacs of Boston's outer ring, the
events served to not only strengthen the channels of interracial and metropolitan cooperation but also quicken the pace of legislative activity.

The Racial Imbalance Act

The most immediate response to the protests emerged from the State
House. The day after the Stayout, Governor Endicott Peabody announced
plans to establish a blue-ribbon advisory committee to study the problem
of "racial imbalance." The distinguished appointees included four university
presidents, prominent Boston businessmen, and religious leaders like Car-
dinal Richard Cushing and Lucy Benson, president of the Massachusetts
League of Women Voters. State Commissioner of Education Owen Kiernan
served as the chair. The task force announced its first findings in the summer of 1964, uncovering the fact that African American students constituted the majority in fifty-five schools across the state and forty-five in Boston alone.[23] On April 8, 1965, the Kiernan Commission released its final
report, "Because It Is Right—Educationally," condemning this racial imbalance as harmful to both white and black children and "a serious conflict
with the American creed of equal opportunity." The commission recommended a law officially banning the practice.[24]

The BSC voted to reject the claims of the Kiernan Report within hours
of its release. Hicks reflexively dismissed the report as "pompous proclamations of the uninformed" and dubbed the Kiernan Committee "a band of
racial agitators, non-native to Boston, and a few college radicals who have
joined the conspiracy to tell the people of Boston how to run their schools

and their lives."[25] The report's release came just a month after the violence in Selma, Alabama, where a white mob had clubbed to death Reverend James Reeb, a white Unitarian minister from Lexington. For nearly a week, media coverage of Reeb's death ran next to news of Selma, which brought the confrontation on Pettus Bridge home for many Bay Staters and made Hicks's inflammatory remarks appear that much more bewildering. More than twenty thousand people attended a memorial service for the slain minister on the Boston Common. Speakers drew comparisons between the situation in Alabama to those "less bloody, but in the long run, no less destructive processes of injustice" occurring in Boston's public schools.[26] When King came to Boston on April 22, 1965, his visit further amplified the pressure on the BSC. At a rally on the Boston Common in front of a crowd of twenty-five thousand, King declared, "Boston must become a testing ground for the ideals of freedom."[27]

As the arguments and agendas of local and national civil rights movements intertwined, they created a powerful sense of urgency for solving the problem of racial segregation in Boston's public schools. Soon after, newly elected Republican governor John Volpe announced the need for "appropriate legislation" as "an important step in this particular issue and in putting the force of our state government behind the fight for equal rights."[28] In June 1965, the state's Board of Education submitted a pathbreaking bill to the Massachusetts legislature that prohibited racial imbalance in the state's public schools. Synthesizing the recommendations of the Kiernan Commission, the proposed act sought to empower the Massachusetts Board of Education to withhold state funds from any town that had not adopted a reasonable plan for eliminating racial imbalance. Beryl Cohen, a liberal state representative from Brookline, volunteered to sponsor the bill. In what one observer labeled "a case study in coalition politics," Cohen enlisted a group of citizens to help get the landmark legislation passed.[29] He first gathered a team of lawyers and civil rights activists, many from his own constituency, to essentially redraft the Board of Education's initial proposal.[30] Cohen then recruited Helene LeVine, the chair of the MFFHER's legislative committee, to help build support for the legislation in suburban communities and at the State House. LeVine and other Federation members readily embraced the challenge.

With opposition to the legislation predictably increasing among representatives of city districts, the Federation's response confirmed that its structure and strategy provided an effective way to provoke legislative change. To build support for the law, MFFHER leaders fine-tuned the lobbying formula they had crafted in earlier campaigns for fair housing laws. During the summer of 1965, members collaborated with representatives from several of Boston's civil rights organizations. Volunteers canvased the State House, demanding face-to-face meetings with state politicians. The Federation and local chapters supplemented these meetings with other grassroots tactics such as petitions and letter-writing campaigns. This support from concerned suburbanites in the almost forty communities with Federation affiliates demonstrated the geographic scope and political reach of the organization. These lobbying efforts successfully overpowered the opposition, and in August 1965, the bill eventually passed in the House and Senate.[31] In the aftermath of this hard-fought victory, many politicians, civil rights leaders, and media observers identified the suburban groups as the driving force behind the legislation.[32]

The Racial Imbalance Act made Massachusetts the first state to outlaw racial imbalance in its public schools.[33] Yet the actual statute had more rhetorical than enforcement power. The law classified a racially imbalanced school as one that had 50 percent black students. By defining imbalance in these terms, the law naturalized a white norm while conveniently ignoring the state's Asian and Latino populations.[34] It also exempted municipalities with large white populations, including every suburb of Boston, all of which had racially imbalanced schools in every sense except the law. As with the purportedly landmark fair housing law passed six years earlier, the communities and children of the Brookline, Newton, and Lexington activists who had been most enthusiastic in their lobbying efforts fell outside the new statute's jurisdiction. In addition, the law contained significant mechanisms to delay implementation since it gave school systems found in violation both the leeway to devise their own plans for remedy and the chance for judicial review. The provisions enabled Boston to avoid actually having to rectify the racial imbalance in its schools for over nine years. Thus, as praise for the law dwindled and the BSC sought to devise ways to evade it, both black activists and their white suburban supporters searched for alternative solutions to the increasingly untenable situation in the city's public schools.

A Suburban Education for Urban Children

The white participants in the February 1964 Stayout had returned home to their respective communities with a desire to extend the experiment of interracial education and their coalition beyond that single day. Residents in more than a dozen towns on or near Route 128 immediately established small summer programs based on the Stayout model, inviting inner-city children to their communities for a series of activities. The MFFHER proudly noted that the pictures of white and black children swimming and playing appeared in town newspapers throughout Boston's outer ring that summer, providing what it claimed was "dramatic evidence" that the "civil rights drive has spread from urban centers to the surrounding suburbs."[35] Citizens in several suburbs also petitioned their local school committees to admit black students from Boston, but each request was turned down.[36] These suburbanites did not give up. In November 1965, the Federation held a meeting of its members along with school superintendents and school committee members to discuss a more coordinated metropolitan approach to enabling black students to attend school in the suburbs.[37] By the winter of 1966, this idea evolved into METCO.

The formal proposal for METCO emerged from Brookline School Committee member Leon Trilling. An astrophysics and aeronautics professor at MIT, Trilling embodied many of the characteristics of the knowledge professionals who had migrated to the Route 128 area in the postwar era. The son of Jewish immigrants who had fled Poland in the 1930s, Trilling had come to the United States when he was sixteen, and received both his BA and PhD from the California Institute of Technology. He moved to the Boston area to work at MIT in the early 1950s and opted to settle in Brookline, enrolling his young children in the local school system. Learning about the severe discrimination in the BPS made him question his definition of equality of opportunity. Even though he was a Jewish immigrant, he had confronted no barriers in his own professional advancement and achievement. Trilling's view aligned with many knowledge-based professionals who believed education offered the best means for advancement and that the opportunities that flowed from merit should be available to everyone.[38] Trilling's concern led him first to join his local fair housing group and then to run for the Brookline School Committee, where he became a strong advocate for integrated education. Ruth Batson would later herald Trilling as the person "whose idea it was to conceive Metco" and praise how he "worked in a very quiet . . . very low profile, low key way to get this off the ground."[39]

Creating the proposal for what would become METCO, Trilling relied on two earlier models. First, he was inspired by a program developed in 1962 by the American Friends Service Committee (AFSC) to arrange for a few students from Prince Edward County, Virginia, where officials had closed the public schools to avoid compliance with court-ordered desegregation, to spend the academic year in Boston. The Virginia students who took part in the Boston–Prince Edward Exchange lived with host families and attended school in their districts.[40] Even after the yearlong experiment ended, Leslie "Skip" Griffins one of three students placed in Newton, had decided to complete his education at the suburb's high school, where he had an outstanding academic and athletic career, and eventually earned admission to Harvard. The success of the experiment had convinced Trilling that if the suburbs could offer spaces to students from Virginia, then they could provide for African American children with a far shorter commute.[41]

Trilling combined this exchange idea with a proposal by Boston Redevelopment Agency head Edward Logue. The nationally renowned urban planner had publicly denounced the recommendations of the Kiernan Report upon its release in April 1965 and decided to create an alternative remedy to the problem of school segregation that looked beyond the city's corporate limits and included the entire metropolitan region. Logue had no background in educational policy and instead drew on his urban redevelopment expertise to craft a proposal for a one-way busing of four thousand "imbalanced" fifth- through eighth-grade black students from Roxbury into the surrounding suburbs. He sought to "transport the children, but not the problem of racial imbalance." He therefore compiled a list of twenty-one towns to receive the "disadvantaged" youths that each lacked a significant black population, were within a half hour of the city, and had a per pupil expenditure that exceeded that of Boston. He recognized that this formula of "scatteration" would prevent overcrowding and keep the black student population in the towns well below the tipping point.[42] Logue, who had pioneered strategies of acquiring federal funding for urban redevelopment, suggested that money from the Federal Aid to Education Act or the Federal Poverty Program could cover the estimated five million dollars per year cost of his plan.[43] These funding ideas derived directly from his conviction that it was "essential to any enduring solution to the problem of racial imbalance," that it not affect the property tax base of either Boston or the participating towns. Logue acknowledged that many white parents who had encouraged their children to participate in the Stayout might be less "willing to practice at home the Civil Rights they bespeak elsewhere" and less enthused to underwrite these convictions with their property taxes.[44]

Overall, Logue's "scatteration plan" demonstrated his deep commitment to the basic tenets of postwar liberalism, especially its abiding faith in state power to solve problems of social inequality. Yet for the most part, Logue's metropolitan busing proposal sparked immediate controversy and denunciations. People ranging from Owen Kiernan and suburban school administrators to Louise Day Hicks denounced the proposal, deeming it not only a form of "forced busing" but also an example of downtown bureaucracy and social engineering at its worst.[45] The *Boston Globe* editorial page suggested that Logue "scatter his 'scatteration' ideas far enough that they get lost."[46] Several of the local MFFHER chapters took Logue's plan seriously, however, and established study groups to explore and debate his recommendations. Lexington resident Grace Sullivan, who had been involved in the Stayout, strongly supported Logue's idea and even publicly called it a "wonderful" way to end "the smug, snobbish days of the suburbs."[47]

In crafting the early blueprint for METCO, Trilling repackaged Logue's program and placed it in distinctly racially liberal and suburban terms. While Logue had pitched his program as the sole remedy to the issue of racial imbalance, Trilling presented his version as a "temporary" and "partial solution."[48] The MIT professor expanded the reach to include all grades, not just middle school, but his suggestion of "1 or 2 Negro children per class in any suburban school district" fell even further below the tipping point of each suburban classroom than Logue's design, and was more in line with the Boston–Prince Edward Exchange. Unlike the Logue's plan, Trilling did not offer a list of towns to receive the nonwhite students based on a complicated formula and sought to involve only those communities that wanted to participate.

Presenting the program as a "voluntary" means to create "equal opportunity," Trilling suggested that the plan be optional rather than compulsory. This voluntary element constituted his most important alteration of Logue's proposal and underscores a key difference in the strands of liberalism that each one presented. Although the metropolitan busing plan now appeared as a bottom-up, grassroots, and optional solution, Trilling clearly shared Logue's skepticism that few, if any, suburban communities would volunteer to financially underwrite the endeavor or that the notoriously difficult BSC would want to pick up the tab. Trilling, therefore, incorporated many of Logue's ideas about ways to secure federal, state, and philanthropic funding. Through these revisions, the concept of metropolitan busing cleverly no longer appeared a top-down program of government bureaucrats, but instead a spontaneous and grassroots reaction. The alterations made the idea palatable not only to white suburbanites but also to many African Americans in the inner city. Members of the black community had joined the clamors of opposition to Logue's scatteration idea and were especially resentful of the way it had depicted urban parents and their children as passive victims.[49] Trilling's revised version of the plan, however, appealed to many African American parents and civil rights leaders since it enabled them, like the suburban districts, to participate by choice rather than force.

In the Brookline High School auditorium on December 14, 1965, Trilling laid out his plan before an audience that included members of MFF-HER such as Astrid Haussler and Elizabeth Keil, leaders in the area civil rights community such as Ruth Batson and Paul Parks, and several Massachusetts Department of Education officials.[50] The presentation received a very favorable reaction. Furthermore, several members of the audience wanted to expand the proposal to include the possibilities of a two-way exchange and comprehensive metropolitan school system. A contingent of Lincoln residents had already been discussing the possibility of a project that could be the "groundwork for a metropolitan system of education" to offer all children in the area "the kind of public education now available only to children able and willing to apply a large proportion of their economic resources to public education."[51] While the majority of the gathering's sixty-five participants shared a sense that this could be the ultimate goal of the project, they recognized that such an undertaking was currently "impractical politically" and instead decided to pursue a "short-range" plan of one-way busing.[52]

Throughout the winter and spring of 1966, school officials, civil rights veterans, and grassroots suburban activists held evening meetings in empty MIT lecture halls and suburban school auditoriums in order to continue to formulate their plans. The organizers decided to formally name the project the Metropolitan Council for Educational Opportunity. The title succinctly captured both the urban-suburban dimensions of the endeavor as well as its emphasis on the racial, liberal, and meritocratic ideal of "equal opportunity." The organizers refined the specifics of the program, stating in its grant applications and official bylaws that it would bring two hundred nonwhite children with a range of academic abilities and economic backgrounds to a handful of districts in order to "develop and promote quality integrated education," "provide a meaningful educational experience for city and suburban children in relation to integrated learning," and create a "partial solution to the issue of de facto segregation."[53] The founding documents also addressed the long-term goal of creating a "vehicle for future related programs," including perhaps a full-scale metropolitan educational system in Boston.[54]

The formulation of the plans demonstrates the professional expertise of METCO's founders. The grant application's frequent emphasis that METCO would serve as a "model" of metropolitan education and "guidepost for the United States" underscores the scientific methodology by which many of the early organizers approached the idea. Physical scientists like Trilling and suburban school administrators like Charles Brown of Newton also had extensive experience with public and private grant applications, and knew what to accentuate in order to secure government funding. The drafters successfully convinced the US Department of Education to approve a two-year grant of $265,000 to cover the tuition and transportation costs of METCO under Title III of the 1965 Elementary and Secondary Education Act, which underwrote "innovative or exemplary ways of attacking persistent problems." Additionally, the project received a $100,000 check from the Carnegie Corporation to pay for staff salaries and office space. Soon after, Joseph Killory took a sabbatical from the Massachusetts Department of Education so that he could assume the position of executive director and Batson become associate director. The organization also established a board of directors, chaired by Trilling, which included school officials, civil rights activists, and many suburban veterans from the fair housing movement.[55]

MFFHER supplied METCO many of its initial board members as well as adroit lobbying skills, especially at the state level. Almost immediately after Trilling presented his idea, Federation members realized that the ambitious program needed state sanction and funding, since the federal and philanthropic money would be short term. Helene LeVine headed a committee to draft a bill to legally allow children to attend schools in cities or towns other than where they resided. The purpose of the legislation was not just to provide METCO with a sound legal basis but a source of future financial sub-

Figure 3.1 Ruth Batson and Leon Trilling testifying together before the US Civil Rights Commission, Boston hearings, October 1966. The image, taken a month after the launch of METCO, shows the partnership between Batson and Trilling, which was essential to making METCO operational, and the respect it earned from government officials, white suburbanites, and the African American community. Courtesy of the *Boston Herald* from the *Boston Herald-Traveler* Photo Morgue, Special Collections, Boston Public Library.

sidy, too.[56] Massachusetts senate majority leader Kevin Harrington submitted the bill to the Massachusetts legislature in December 1965, even before the organization had formally agreed on a name. An extension of the Racial Imbalance Act, this provision legally allowed children to attend schools in cities or towns other than where they resided and the Massachusetts Board of Education to financially support any program where one town adopted a plan to assist in the elimination of the racial imbalance of another town.[57] MFFHER lobbyists, with the help of State Representative Michael Dukakis of Brookline, an active member of his local fair housing committee, helped to ensure the bill's successful passage.[58] Reflecting on the role of MFFHER members in the lobbying as well as other key aspects of the program's development, Batson later observed, "I can honestly state that METCO would not have become a reality without their membership's resolve and determination."[59] The quest to get the fledgling program off the ground relied on the mutual determination of the Federation and Batson.

Getting the Buses Rolling

The efforts to put METCO in motion rested on a key division of labor along racial, spatial, and ideological lines between the largely white suburban board and predominantly African American staff. The board members played an especially instrumental role in convincing suburban towns to volunteer to accept Boston students. Batson assumed responsibility for performing the parallel task in order to get black Boston students to participate by appealing to their parents. The arguments that each set of organizers made to their respective communities and responses they received expose key differences in attitudes about METCO and its purpose between white and black participants, which became embedded into the structure of the entire program.

The case that METCO's white advocates made to enlist participating communities combined the individualist and therapeutic ideals of racial liberalism with the issues of low taxes, high property values, and quality education that represented the main planks of suburban political culture. The contentions underscore the distinctly consumer-based terms in which many Route 128 residents approached not just participation in the program but their attitude toward municipal services more broadly. The arguments also demonstrate the METCO advocates' astute ability to appeal to these values. The pitch stressed the facets of the program that Trilling had understood as essential to ensure that suburban municipalities would participate— the small size of the program, its voluntary nature, and how it would allow local school administrators to retain full control over the number of students each municipality accepted. Supporters put a particularly strong emphasis on the funding structure, explaining how the state and federal government would assume full financial responsibility. Proponents never mentioned any possibility that METCO could potentially serve as a model for a two-way program. In fact, in the notes he prepared for a public presentation to people from a variety of suburbs, Trilling crossed out a section where he planned to discuss how METCO could serve as a template for a metropolitan school district.[60]

A few residents in towns like Wellesley and Lexington publicly voiced concerns that the inclusion of "disadvantaged" students would weaken the academic standing of their currently "top-notch," nationally ranked school systems.[61] Boosters thereby went to extra lengths to prove that the program would do nothing to compromise the quality of education in the public schools. Addressing fears about the financial consequences of admitting African Americans students who might demand more resources, the promotional literature underlined that METCO would not lead to zero-sum funding and suburban children would not "receive fewer services such as counseling, remedial assistance, etc." Indeed, METCO's advocates recognized that it would not be enough just to highlight the opportunities the program offered to Boston students or point out in negative terms how the program would not increase the local tax rate.

Advocates, therefore, concentrated on the specific educational and social value that METCO offered to white middle-class students. Lexington resident Mrs. Thomas C. Schelling, wife of a prominent Harvard economist, argued that the program would offer "a broadening experience," and since "no burden will fall on our local tax rate," would actually enhance the return on local tax dollars.[62] Schelling's case aligned with that of many METCO boosters who suggested to members of their towns that the inclusion of a few African Americans in each suburban classroom would help to prepare white pupils to succeed in a diverse society. This rationale was notably absent in most of METCO's applications for funding from the federal government and Carnegie Corporation, even those drawn up by Charles Brown and other suburban school administrators. The case about the value of diversity, however, directly connected to the priorities of the cohort of knowledge professionals who resided in suburbs like Brookline, Newton, and Lexington, many of who had purchased their homes largely based on the reputation of the public school system and wanted to provide the best opportunities for their children. With little direct evidence to substantiate it, an early pamphlet challenged parents by forcefully contending, "Suburban children expect to work and learn with Negro youngsters."[63] Some early promoters went even further than this idealistic assertion to suggest that *not* participating in METCO would actually harm white suburban children.

In his case about why the suburb should participate, Superintendent Brown argued to the Newton School Committee that the admission of black pupils would aid in the education of local white children who were in fact "deprived" in the sense that "they have no realistic contact with other parts of our society."[64] Coming from a nationally respected administrator like Brown, these claims carried weight and offered an important counterbalance to METCO detractors. In addition to addressing the negative and confining effects of "racial imbalance for African-American students in Boston," the pamphlet that circulated among interested suburban districts bemoaned how "suburban white youngsters have been cut off from contact with young children of other races, to the detriment of the education and total development of members of both groups."[65] Such reasoning drew on new social scientific literature such as an influential multiyear study by a group of experts at Columbia Teachers College, resulting in articles and books with telling titles like "Are Children in the Suburbs Different?" and *The Shortchanged Children of Suburbia*. The study found that the lack of interaction with poor and minority children had damaging consequences for white suburban students and society as a whole.[66] Needham resident Jayne Burgess, who advocated for bringing METCO to her town, explained that she wanted to do so because she was "worried about the isolation of our children" and how the absence of black students in the schools was warping their worldview.[67]

The discursive shift of the terms disadvantage and deprivation from Boston children to white suburban ones also shifted the presentation of MET-CO's goals away from addressing many of the forces and factors that had created the problems of residential segregation and unequal resources. The emphasis now was toward both a cause and solution that were far more individualistic. Similarly, the argument advanced in materials distributed to interested communities that METCO offered suburban children "educational experiences which will better prepare them for life in a multi-racial world" also submerged the root causes of school segregation.[68] This forward-looking claim did not deny the existence and effect of racial and residential discrimination. As one later METCO pamphlet contended, "Simply because of where they happen to live, many urban and suburban children are not receiving . . . extremely desirable . . . integrated learning experiences," and were "not learning to live in our multi-racial world."[69] The argument did not dwell on the past, or the fact that it was neither "simple" nor circumstantial that white and black children did not live in the same or equivalent places. Instead, the case for METCO looked to a future where class differences and racial segregation had disappeared, and people of all races lived in the same towns, attended the same universities, and worked in the same professional environments.

The facets of the program that most suburban residents praised in endorsing their town's involvement in METCO were often the ones that least forced them to confront residential segregation and metropolitan fragmentation. Articulating his support for METCO, Lexington engineer Arthur Bryson Jr. stated that he favored how it was a "person-to-person" initiative as opposed to "impersonal programs like welfare, urban renewal and anti-poverty programs," which he did not approve of and believed to be ineffective.[70] Bryson's distinction obscured the many "impersonal" forms of government welfare—from mortgage subsidies to defense contracts—that had likely subsidized his lifestyle. Yet METCO's very success in securing suburban participation depended on not forcing residents like Bryson to acknowledge those facts.

The responses to METCO by Bryson and others offer insights into Route 128 residents' broader view of the relationship between their tax dollars and social programs. The persistent claim by proponents that METCO "would not cost suburban communities or Boston anything" did not entirely ring true.[71] As local resident and METCO supporter Elizabeth Weaver noted, "Since we pay state and federal taxes, Lexington citizens would certainly be paying for" the program. Further elucidating this position, Weaver noted that METCO would be funded not just by Lexington citizens but also by taxpayers in Selma, Alabama, and Houston, Texas, just as "all citizens of our country have built our roads, our schools, [and] have helped preserve our green areas."[72] Her comment implicitly suggested that like roads and conservation areas, participation in METCO would improve the quality of life in Lexington and other affluent suburbs. The willingness of suburban residents to support the use of federal, but not local funds, to pay for METCO, moreover, highlights an important distinction between conservatives who opposed all tax expenditures on civil rights and many moderates and liberals who did not object to using federal and state funds for "person-to-person" programs, yet who believed it was inappropriate to expend local tax dollars on such issues.

The METCO program's careful navigation of these ideas about federal and local funding combined with its emphasis on individual ideals played a critical role in solidifying support throughout the suburbs and across the partisan divide.[73] The push for METCO did confront some hostility in suburban communities, but most of the opposition occurred as "whispers at cocktail parties" rather than overt public statements, and none of these dissenters caused any town to forego participation in the program.[74] Newton and Brookline offered the largest numbers of places, with seventy-five and fifty seats, respectively, in a variety of grades. Lexington, Wellesley, Arlington, Braintree, and Lincoln followed behind, dividing the remaining hundred-plus seats between them.

The effort to get students to fill those spots fell to Ruth Batson. At first glance, Batson appeared an unlikely proponent of a suburban initiative since her commitment to alleviating the inadequacies in the BPS had been so long-standing that it had earned her the reputation as the "de facto lady."[75] Yet Batson's political outlook and activism resisted convenient categorization. The child of Garveyite parents and a lifelong resident of Roxbury, Batson was an early supporter of John F. Kennedy, the first black delegate from Massachusetts to the Democratic National Convention, and would later hold a variety of political appointments including a stint on the MCAD.[76] She combined a background in black nationalism, faith in the formal channels of political institutions, and personal concern about the education of her own children.[77]

Batson never believed that METCO supplied the sole answer to the problem of racial imbalance, but saw it as a significant and symbolic first step. "The day of the little red school is gone," she pragmatically contended. "Those who are still clinging to the concept of the neighborhood school are romanticizing. We've got to get decent facilities for all of Boston's children," even if it "means having them ride a bus or walk a distance."[78] She candidly acknowledged that transporting two hundred children to the suburbs would do nothing for the vast majority of African American students remaining in Boston. Still, she recognized that the program offered both

improved educational opportunities for the small number of children involved and a means to potentially publicly shame the BSC into addressing
the racial inequality of the city's schools.[79]

Batson became an extremely effective spokesperson for METCO, especially within the black community. She understood what aspects of the
program to accentuate in order to make METCO attractive to potentially
skeptical members of the city's African American population. In presentations at Roxbury churches and civic centers, Batson pitched METCO as a
temporary rather than permanent program with only a few years of funding and assured parents that the students would return to the city's public
schools "as soon as Boston 'straightens out.'"[80] Appealing to a sense of self-
determination, she stressed that since the program paid their tuition, the
black children would not be suburban "charity cases."[81] These arguments
about quality education and self-determination proved crucial in recruiting
prospective students. When a colleague at New York University later expressed interest in starting a similar program in the Westchester suburbs,
Trilling told his fellow physicist that bringing Batson on board was an "essential" ingredient to the program, particularly because she had "the full
confidence of the community."[82]

From the outset, many of the African American participants interpreted
the goals of METCO differently from their white allies, although both were
invested in quality education. Batson noted among prospective parents that
"there was very little mention of a desire for integration."[83] Many parents
understood that the particular value in METCO rested on the fact that it
offered children the superior educational resources of the suburbs. "Just
[her] going to school with whites isn't important at all to me," one mother
explained about why she wanted her to daughter to participate, "because
that won't get Betty into a good college."[84] The location preferences that
Boston parents had selected on their children's application further demonstrate that the majority of prospective parents sought inclusion in the program more for its quality educational opportunities than because of a commitment to integration.[85] Brookline, Newton, and Wellesley sat at the top
of most parents' preference lists because of their proximity to the city and
the national reputations of their respective school systems. Lexington, with
its historical reputation of tolerance and enlightenment, followed close behind. The applicants expressed more reticence about Lincoln since it was
one of the wealthiest towns in Massachusetts, a forty-five- to sixty-minute
bus ride from Boston's predominantly black neighborhoods, and the only
town involved that did not have even a single black resident. Yet if Lincoln
appeared too well heeled, many parents eschewed Arlington and Braintree
for not being "elite" enough, and these two towns represented the least popular choices.[86] Thus, just as the name Roxbury evoked a particular racial and
economic taxonomy of association for white suburban residents, the names

of the various suburbs had their own specific meanings in the minds of much of Boston's black community.[87] The cognitive cartography embedded in these preferences offers one indicator of the expectations that both white and black participants brought to METCO.

Batson and the METCO staff sought to match parental preferences, and create a "representative" cohort of 220 from the 600 applicants that had a balance of boys and girls, a range of economic backgrounds and family sizes, and a cross-section of the city's predominantly black neighborhoods.[88] In keeping with the restrictive definition of race in both the Racial Imbalance Act and METCO grant applications, the planners selected only African American children, with the exception of the sole white applicant they opted to accept.[89] Finally, they tried to admit students from a range of different academic achievement levels, although they decided to exclude any student with a serious learning disability, or other significant educational or disciplinary problems.[90] This final goal sought to assuage the concerns of many skeptical whites and blacks that the program enabled the suburbs to "steal" the best black students from Boston. In the late summer, the METCO staff sent out placement notifications, and on the first day of school in September 1966, the inaugural cohort of 220 students boarded the buses and set out for the suburbs.

Two Worlds

METCO received immediate praise from school principals, suburban and city parents, and state politicians, and instantly attracted a swell of interest from suburban towns wanting to get involved. The program soon had a wait-list of hundreds of Boston students hoping to participate.[91] METCO also garnered national attention, and become a model for programs in other cities such as the suburbs of Westchester County and Philadelphia that sought to implement similar solutions to the problems of school segregation.[92] Even early detractors shifted their position and supported continued involvement beyond the trial-run year.[93] Many champions, especially those in the suburbs, praised the program for how it mimicked the diversity of the real world. "The black urban child has gone to a vastly better educational setting in the suburbs," David Sargent of Wellesley asserted, "while the suburban white child has had a multi-racial experience that will prepare him for the multi-racial world."[94] Even Governor Volpe declared that the program protected "thousands of white and non-white students from the psychological and educational harms of segregated schools and classrooms" that did not represent the "multi-racial cosmopolitan and urban centered society."[95]

In its first three years of operation, METCO remained a small program, transporting just 386 students to fourteen communities, but the spring of

1968, in the words of Batson, "sharply changed the picture."[96] By that point, the state of Massachusetts had assumed the entire financial responsibility for the program and Batson had become executive director. Events like the assassination of Martin Luther King Jr. and release of the Kerner Commission Report sparked concern among many white liberal-leaning suburbanites, and they saw METCO as a tangible way to ease the nation's urban problems. In the span of two months, thirty-six towns voted to submit plans for involvement in METCO, and those already participating decided to increase their level of commitment. By June 1968, these suburban communities had officially offered a total of twelve hundred seats for children from Boston.[97]

Yet at the same time that many suburbanites praised the program as an answer to the nation's urban problems, racial tensions increased among the students, especially at the high school level.[98] Brookline superintendent Robert Sperber surmised, "It is not as simple as we once thought, just putting black and white kids together."[99] Trilling contended that the physical fights and many other tense verbal exchanges "might be a blessing in disguise." He declared that through these encounters, "blacks and whites gain a more realistic understanding of the problems, aspirations, and life-styles of each other."[100] Batson and other staff members who saw METCO's primary objective as providing improved educational opportunities for African American children worried that the conflicts might threaten the program's graduation rate and college matriculation, which they interpreted as the clearest indication of the program's success.[101] Staff members often emphasized the special responsibility and burden that the students had assumed by participating in the program as well as the chances it offered them.[102] The staff repeatedly stressed the motto, "Opportunity is the key word in the name" to the students, punctuating themes of community control and self-determination, not integration or diversity.

The host family component of METCO further reflected the differing visions of the program's purpose.[103] Since the program's inception, METCO organizers required suburban communities to match each child from Boston with the family of a student from their school, grade, and preferably class to serve as a suburban host. The fair housing activists had been particularly insistent on making it a requirement, envisioning that host families would provide Boston students "a second home" in the suburbs as "a place to go for lunch, or if he is ill, or he desires to become in a social way in the community," and would offer additional opportunities for one-on-one interaction.[104] The idea had certain practical purposes and did lead to chances for extracurricular socializing such as the playdate between Susan Neiley, Rhonda Williams, and their families. The host program proved particularly eye-opening for the parents involved. Many white parents described how the program represented the first times they had interacted with African

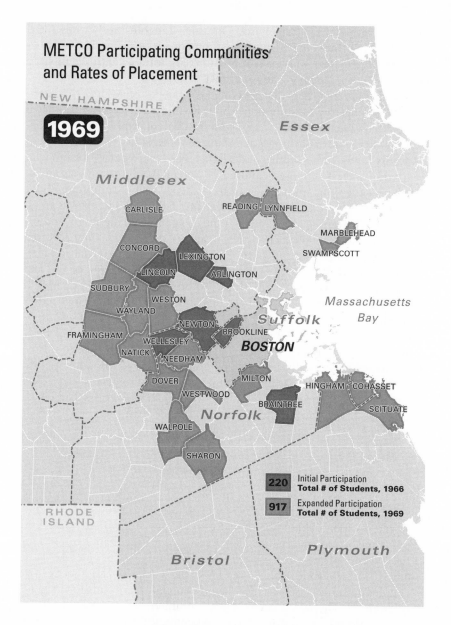

METCO Participating Communities
and Rates of Placement

1969

NEW HAMPSHIRE

Essex

Middlesex

CARLISLE   READING LYNNFIELD

                                   MARBLEHEAD
CONCORD
          LEXINGTON   SWAMPSCOTT
     LINCOLN
              ARLINGTON
SUDBURY
          WESTON   Massachusetts
  WAYLAND   Bay
                  NEWTON   Suffolk
FRAMINGHAM   BROOKLINE
          WELLESLEY   BOSTON
    NATICK
          NEEDHAM
     DOVER   MILTON
       WESTWOOD   HINGHAM COHASSET
                    BRAINTREE
                Norfolk   SCITUATE
  WALPOLE

     SHARON

RHODE | 220 | Initial Participation
ISLAND | | Total # of Students, 1966

                                | 917 | Expanded Participation
                                | | Total # of Students, 1969

                    Bristol   Plymouth

Figure 3.2 Initial participation in 1966 and expansion by 1969 of METCO. The map shows
METCO's growth from 220 students bused to 7 suburbs in its inaugural year of 1966 to 917 students bused to 27 participating suburbs in 1969. *Source*: Metropolitan Council for Educational
Opportunity, "1969 Annual Report," Records of the Metropolitan Council for Educational Opportunity, Special Collections, Northeastern University, Boston.

Americans other than their maids. One such Lincoln mother described how it "doesn't throw me anymore that someone is black," and how participating had made her and her family "more comfortable with the mixture now. And life is *interesting*—not so vanilla."[105]

Suburbanites reported that meeting the parents of METCO children helped challenge their assumptions about Roxbury, a place most had never visited. Mrs. Clarence Good, a Lexington host parent, explained that "when we sit in our comfortable homes and think about Roxbury, we don't think of a Roxbury home with a mother and a father who have regular jobs and who are terribly interested in their children."[106] Several Boston parents also mentioned how the program had helped to challenge their assumptions about affluent white suburbanites. Rhonda Williams' father, who worked as an estimator at a Roxbury plant, stated that the program had taught him and his children "to judge people by how they treat you." A *New York Times* reporter, who wrote about the host program as a rare example of interracial and metropolitan cooperation in the conflict-ridden urban landscape of the late 1960s, suggested that the relationships had brought parents and their children "the bare glimmer of a sense of one another as human beings rather than mystifying and frightening racial stereotypes," and sparked an "innocent vision beyond the color of the skin to the humanity underneath."[107]

Mrs. Howard Stoudt of Lincoln, who served as a paid part-time coordinator of the program locally and was the mother of one of Rhonda's friends, praised METCO for preparing all children for a "multi-racial society." She added, however, that the black children, more than white ones, had developed the ability to "live in the two worlds that do exist much earlier than their parents do."[108] Stoudt's observation captured an important element of the METCO experience. Even as white suburban parents and journalists enthusiastically endorsed it, some of the Boston students, especially at the high school level, began to challenge openly the ways in which the host family component specifically and the METCO program as a whole made them feel like guests in the suburbs and "thankful" to white students and their parents. "They should be thankful to us," one student attending Lexington High School maintained. "We're really educating them because a lot of the kids never saw a black kid before. They only saw people like Aunt Jemima." "The white kids here do not know the black kids," another Lexington student asserted, "because there aren't enough black kids to integrate the school."[109] The comment implicitly pointed out some of limits in METCO's one-way approach and the deliberate efforts to keep the number of students involved well below the tipping point.

METCO's use of one-way busing also meant that while the program placed a strong rhetorical emphasis on equality, in actuality the African American students bore much of the burden for participation. Students like Rhonda Williams had to attend school far away from their neighborhoods,

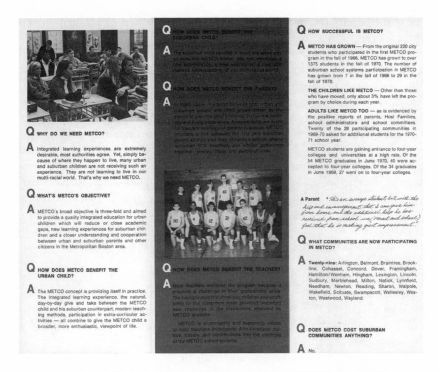

Figure 3.3 Part of a brochure titled "Questions & Answers About METCO" distributed by METCO in suburban communities in 1970. The brochure illustrated the ways in which METCO marketed itself to the suburbs by stressing the tangible benefits for suburban children and how the program did not require the outlay of local tax dollars. Courtesy of the Records of the Metropolitan Council for Educational Opportunity, Archives and Special Collection Departments, Northeastern University Libraries, Boston.

commuting by bus at least a half hour away to largely white, affluent suburbs. There, they were often the only African American student in the class, with only a handful of other METCO students in the entire school. This experience led many METCO students to feel like outsiders in both the suburbs and Boston's black community.[110] "It's a lonesome thing to be a Metco student," Bernice Bullock, who had attended Marblehead High, remarked. "Now that I'm at Boston University, I'm much happier."[111]

Many METCO participants experienced a sense of guilt that they had betrayed their neighborhoods in Boston and felt they should have stayed to help the fight to achieve educational equality there. Likewise, some students protested the inequity in resources between the city and suburbs. "I don't see why they (the suburban community) should have everything," one student stated. "I'm going to get a good education so that when I grow up, I can see that Roxbury has just as much as they do."[112] Robert C. Hayden, the executive director who replaced Batson on her resignation at the end of 1969, took these comments to heart. He made a deliberate effort to shift the program's definition of racial integration away from an individualist focus on the similarities between whites and blacks and toward an appreciation of racial, economic, and spatial differences.[113] In the late 1960s, Hayden oversaw the implementation of tutoring and psychological services at the central offices in Roxbury intended to address the unique educational and emotional demands of METCO students. The staff members also pressured suburban schools to implement more African American history and literature in the curricula and to recruit more black teachers.[114] Most suburban parents and school administrators readily embraced the multicultural materials, tutoring services, and teacher training as another way of broadening the education of white middle-class children. A white mother from the suburb of Needham succinctly asserted, "The schools would be worse without METCO."[115]

With this consumer-based attitude in mind, the organization adopted its new racial consciousness into a sellable attribute to suburban communities. A pamphlet titled "We Wish You Could Meet a METCO Boy and Girl" circulated to prospective communities and marketed the program's diversity. It promised that participation would give suburban children a "new appreciation, a new awareness, a new and realistic understanding of our multiracial world." The pamphlet claimed that "the backgrounds that inner-city children and youth bring to the classroom have provided important new resources."[116] The official literature did not mention the widespread sense of alienation among METCO students, and instead cited one young child from Boston's color-blind observation: "With your friends you can talk about everything. It doesn't matter whether you live in Wellesley or Boston."[117] This student's racial-liberal geography nevertheless consistently proved more of an aspiration than an actuality.

Conclusion

In the spring of 1972, Harvard sociologist David Armor released a report called "The Evidence on Busing" based on a study he had conducted on the METCO program in the late 1960s. The study, later published in the neoconservative publication *Public Interest*, suggested that METCO and similar racial integration programs did the reverse of their goals and actually reduced "opportunities for actual contact between the races."[118] The *Boston Globe* announced Armor's evidence in a front-page article with the headline "Busing Found to Have Backfired," creating immediate controversy as many activists, academics, and concerned citizens feared the report would undermine the protracted struggle to force the BSC to comply with the Racial Imbalance Act.[119] Thomas Pettigrew, another member of the Harvard sociology department, soon after published a sharp rebuttal to Armor's "evidence on busing," especially his use of a voluntary one-way program to draw broad conclusions about mandatory two-way integration.[120]

Pettigrew's defense of METCO inadvertently exposed the basic limits of the program. METCO had many obvious positive attributes. The program enhanced the opportunities of the small number of African American students who earned seats, altered the attitudes of many white children and their parents, and increased support for the value of diversity in many suburbs. In most districts, however, METCO students remained less than 1 percent of the total school population, thereby failing to reshape metropolitan patterns of racial or spatial inequality in any meaningful way. The program, moreover, never ushered in "national acceptance of public school integration," as one of its early flyers had touted as its "promise and challenge."[121] It did not create a comprehensive two-way busing system in metropolitan Boston, as a few of its most optimistic founders had initially hoped, and by the early 1970s, most of the early architects had abandoned hopes that it would be more than a small program.[122]

The design of the program and claims that the organizers used to sell it nonetheless proved crucial to getting suburban municipalities to voluntarily allow black to students to enroll in their schools. Without these features and arguments, METCO probably never would have become a reality at all. It is unrealistic to expect a small program to provide the solution to the structural problems of school segregation. The particular dynamics of the program and reasoning that its proponents used to promote it, however, meant that METCO did not force the vast majority of suburbanites to acknowledge the systemic problems that had produced school segregation and their own role in that process. Instead, by providing residents in the suburban municipalities that participated with a means to distinguish themselves as more open-minded than whites in the South or South Boston, it made them even less willing to consider more comprehensive solutions to the interrelated issues of residential segregation and educational inequity. The reaction to METCO in the Route 128 suburbs during the Boston busing crisis and the national recession in the mid-1970s makes this attitude and its consequence all too clear.

4

Grappling with Growth

On October 19, 1972, local resident Claire Ellis penned an impassioned plea to the *Concord Journal* in response to plans to expand a section of the Route 2 highway in the town. Ellis believed that widening the roadway threatened the measures Concord had taken throughout the postwar period to preserve its "country town atmosphere" and image as the incubator of American environmentalism. She asserted that if local residents had "wanted super highways or a main street emblazoned with lights until the wee hours we would have lived elsewhere." Ellis called on community members to use a bit of the "Yankee Ingenuity" that "Concord is famous for" and have the "guts and determination to stand up" and protest the "filling our little stretch of road with cement ramps" and "ripping out part of our town forest." "The rest of the country has ruined itself in the name of efficiency," Ellis implored. Thus, local residents had to draw on their Thoreauvian roots of protest and appreciation for nature to fight for "what makes Concord unique and special," and not "bow down to the coercion of being one part of this speed-crazed polluted world."[1]

Ellis and her allies eventually succeeded at stopping the expansion of the highway. The effort was part of a broader national suburban environmental movement committed to protecting open space that stretched from Concord, Westchester County, New York, Marin County, California, to the suburbs of Los Angeles.[2] During the decades after World War II, this movement redirected the ideology of postwar liberalism away from a growth-oriented vision and toward an emphasis on quality-of-life issues including a new appreciation of nature. White middle-class homeowners in Concord and several other affluent suburbs near the interchange of Route 128 and Route 2 actively resisted overdevelopment and sprawl through such tactics as minimum-acre zoning, private land trusts, and conservation commissions. This movement placed Massachusetts at the forefront of the emerging national effort to confront the consequences of sprawl, and directly influenced the passage of new state and federal legislation. It also helped to transform highways from serving as a symbol of postwar growth liberalism's success to a sign of its destructiveness.

In the late 1960s, Boston suburban open space activists joined the urban-based antihighway campaign, shifting it from a fight about housing displacement in the city into a metropolitan-wide movement about environmental protection. The coalition successfully convinced Governor Francis Sargent to declare the first-ever moratorium on highway construction and redirect the state's transportation policy toward mass transit. The campaign inspired similar shifts in the federal government's policy, permanently changing the parameters of transportation and environmental policy. The antihighway campaign offers a clear counterexample to the metropolitan and racial polarization that characterized the Boston busing crisis and many other key issues of the 1960s and 1970s.[3] The coalition illustrates how both proposed and realized roadways simultaneously fragmented and connected groups across racial, class, spatial, and political lines. As the momentum of the revolt shifted away from opposing highway construction in the city and toward the battle over expanding Route 2 and building a more comprehensive metropolitan rapid transit system in the suburbs, both the limits to the multifaceted transportation alliance and individualist tendencies of suburban residents became more evident.[4]

The issues of open space and environmental protection revealed the tension between the structural processes of growth that had produced Route 128 and its suburbs and the ideology of historical and liberal distinctiveness of many of the residents along its ring.[5] In her public plea, Ellis's claim of Concord as "unique and special" captured a key component of the reason that many residents had moved there or to surrounding towns.[6] This outlook propelled a genuine concern about the environmental degradation advanced by postwar suburbanization. Yet the localist measures that residents took to protect their communities elevated both a sense of their own distinctiveness and a focus on their own individual standard of living and quality of life, further obscuring an acknowledgment of their role in perpetuating many of the problems of environmental and social inequity.[7] The efforts to protect open space and grapple with growth made environmentalism a more important component of liberalism, especially in the suburbs, but it simultaneously further solidified the forms of localism and exclusivity at the center of the political culture and outlook of most residents in the Route 128 area.

Open Space

The construction of the Route 128 highway spawned both sprawl and the movement that aimed to address its effects. In the 1950s, rapid growth of industry and suburbanization along the roadway's ring stoked anxieties in the communities on or near the highway, particularly within affluent ones that prized their pastoral beauty and rural characteristics.[8] As a 1958 Lincoln planning document heralded, "The unique character of our town is dependent on one factor above all others: Open Space."[9] Lincoln and nearby towns like Concord, Lexington, and Wayland initially aimed to protect their open space through zoning ordinances, but soon felt the codes, even those setting large lot-size minimums, were insufficient. "Most people come to Lexington because they like among other things its rural atmosphere," and "30,000-sq-foot zoning" is simply not enough, resident and regional planning professor Roland Greeley decried, to "preserve the open-ness which we cherish."[10] Since zoning prevented growth rather than creating open space, lot-size minimums offered only a partial solution.[11] Thus, suburban residents like Greeley searched for a way to protect the pastoral charm and undeveloped land of their respective towns. Wayland native Allen H. Morgan was one such person.

Wayland sits twenty miles west of Boston on a reedy floodplain along the Sudbury River. Growing up prior to World War II, Morgan spent his childhood exploring the town's marshes and woodlands, which instilled his lifelong fascination with nature. When he returned to Wayland in the 1950s after college and the army, he found it fundamentally transformed. Sitting on the edge of the Massachusetts Turnpike and less than five miles from the newly constructed Route 128, the town became an ideal location for engineers and executives to live, and for corporations like Dow Chemical and Raytheon to construct R & D facilities. Atop the beloved landscape where he used to bird watch, Morgan was appalled to discover "subdivisions and shopping centers."[12] Morgan developed the idea of forming a private trust to purchase and preserve the town's natural habitats, and during the summer of 1953 gathered fellow nature-loving residents to establish the Sudbury Valley Trustees (SVT).[13] The founders envisioned that the trust would buy parts of the floodplain, and protect it both from encroaching development and state and federal taxes.[14] By 1958, five years after the SVT's founding, it had four hundred members and had placed more than four hundred acres of local marshland in the tax-exempt trust.

The SVT represented a departure from earlier conservationist efforts, which had focused primarily on exceptional tracts of forest, beach, or wilderness removed from urban life. In contrast, the SVT adopted as its guiding philosophy that "any natural land is worth saving" and concentrated on preserving the less sublime areas within the metropolitan ring.[15] The project also represented a deviation from many of the 1950s' treatises extolling suburbanization. Members of the group believed that vigorous open space protection, not unbridled growth, ensured white middle-class homeowners the high quality of life they deserved.[16] Like open space advocates at the national level, Morgan and his collaborators understood the private trust as a tactic to preserve land without upsetting the dynamics of the suburban real estate market.[17] The SVT's focus on property likewise reveals that many of the very forces that the movement aimed to ameliorate—especially the federally financed growth of suburban homeownership—also shaped its aims and tactics. The SVT contended the land in the trust would actually enhance local property values by both reducing the damage caused by annual flooding and adding to the pastoral aesthetic of the area. Similar to large-lot zoning, the members argued, the trust would also limit population, lessen the demand for municipal services, and reduce the overall local tax rate.[18] These claims would become a crucial component of local conservationists' success at marshaling the support of residents in the affluent Route 128 suburbs in the ensuing years, and prove both a strength and constraint on the movement's impact.

In the short term, the SVT inspired similar organizations throughout the state and nation, in places ranging from Lincoln and Concord, to Brandywine, Pennsylvania, to Westchester County, New York.[19] Lincoln and Concord had the most success in Massachusetts establishing their own private trusts based on the SVT model.[20] In its first two years, the Concord Land Conservation Trust fulfilled its mandate "to assist in and promote the preservation of the rural character of the Town" and "the establishment of sound conservational practices" by purchasing a large pond and a square mile of wetlands. Similarly, in its first decade of operation, the Lincoln Land Conservation Trust, chaired by Harvard physicist William B. Preston, employed tax-deductible land donations and easements across private property to create more than twelve miles of trails for walking, biking, and horseback riding surrounding the town's idyllic reservoir. The open space agenda of these private land acquisition organizations provided, in the words of historian Adam Rome, "a critical stage in the evolution of the modern environmental movement."[21]

Self-Help

The open space movement in the Route 128 suburbs, nevertheless, would not have reached the magnitude and success it did without the development of the Massachusetts Conservation Commission program and the assistance of the state and federal government. The commissions, like the land trusts, had roots in the open space impulses of white middle-class suburbanites. In the mid-1950s, a group of residents from the North Shore town of Ipswich secured the passage of state legislation to create official agencies consisting of a small group of unpaid and appointed local citizens whose responsibilities included advising authorities on proper natural resource protection policies and undertaking "action projects" such as open space acquisition to advance their community's conservation interests.[22] Over 275 cities and Massachusetts towns had established commissions by 1969, and inspired similar laws and agencies throughout the northeast, including in Connecticut, New Jersey, and New York.[23] Despite this wide reach, supporters and skeptics alike deemed the conservation commissions a "suburban-centered movement."[24]

The commission structure aligned most amenably with the political organization and ideological orientation of small and affluent communities that had already identified development as a threat to their core values. Department of Natural Resources (DNR) commissioner Charles H. W. Foster conceded that the commissions operated most successfully if the members represented "a scattering of professional backgrounds," noting that "legal, engineering, educational and public relations experience" were most useful.[25] A member of the Wayland commission observed that many board members consisted of transplanted engineers as well as "landscape architects, city planners, geographers, [and] cartographers," who provided their expertise and pragmatic sensibility to the effort.[26] Not surprisingly, the conservation commission idea received its earliest success in the towns along Route 128.

While this infrastructure played a crucial role in laying the base for the local commissions, state policy and financial assistance ultimately ensured the success of their open space goals. In 1960, the Massachusetts legislature approved the ambitious Self-Help Conservation Program, thus enabling the DNR to reimburse up to 50 percent of the local conservation commissions land acquisitions.[27] The pioneering policy made Massachusetts the first state in the nation to use financial incentives to fulfill conservation responsibilities.[28] The use of the word "self-help" in the title evoked a charged discourse laden more with conservative or therapeutic rather than conservation ideology. Yet this project offered one more example of the extensive reach of the state and federal government, and the many subsidies and entitlements they provided to white middle-class suburbanites in the postwar era. Critics would later deem such programs a form of "Ivy League Socialism," since the self-help initiative offered government intervention on behalf of the rich, not the poor, and federal assistance to the people most able to make land purchases on their own.[29]

Wealthier Route 128 suburbs had well-established conservation networks and the funds to cover the initial investment for state-subsidized acquisition programs, which was especially important since the program demanded that a community have a conservation commission to qualify. The self-help program thereby enhanced the open space priorities of places like Concord, where the town meeting annually allocated the maximum amount allowed by the state to participate in the initiative. Although the Concord commission spent $60,000 on open space purchases between 1959 and 1964, the state reimbursed the town $24,750.[30] By contrast, low-income and industry-heavy communities like Burlington and New Bedford were slow to establish commissions, and the city councils in these cash-strapped municipalities lacked the budget surplus to fund even a fraction of the costs for the conservation initiative.[31]

The federal subsidization of the self-help program only served to increase the inequalities between the conservation agendas of the suburbs and lower-income communities. In 1965, Congress passed the Land and Water Conservation Fund Act, which created a fund to help states develop water and land resources by providing 50 percent of the money. Massachusetts conservationists built on the momentum of the federal law in 1966 and persuaded the state legislature to increase the annual budget of the self-help program from $200,000 to $700,000.[32] The legislature also approved policy changes that enabled any commission that applied to a federal conservation, recreation, or open space program to then receive an additional 25 percent reimbursement from the state. This combined state and federal funding meant that local commissions could receive up to 75 percent reimbursement of the total acquisition costs. The federal budgetary windfall encouraged a more diverse range of communities to join, but the Route 128 suburbs continued to disproportionately benefit from the self-help program.[33] For instance, Lexington jockeyed the single-largest allocation, and Lincoln consistently received more state land acquisition funds than any other municipality in Massachusetts, which is particularly remarkable given the fact that the community had a population hovering between five and seven thousand residents.[34]

Other historic preservation and conservation activities of the state and federal government also significantly enhanced the open space agenda of the Route 128 suburbs. In the postwar decades, both the federal and state government continued their ambitious programs to preserve historic sites and wilderness areas.[35] During this period, Concord became a "regional center" of state and federal parks and lands. Within the 24.96-square-mile town lay state-owned Walden Pond and surrounding forest.[36] Just a few miles away sat the federally owned 750-acre Minuteman National Park, which the US Congress had created in 1959 in order to preserve the scene of the initial battles of the American Revolution.[37] The US Fish and Wildlife Service also established the Great Meadows National Wildlife Refuge, which protected 2,727 acres of marshland spread through six suburbs including Concord. Thus, despite the town's proximity to the major transportation and corporate nexus of Route 128 and Route 2, by the late 1960s over one-fourth of the total acreage of Concord had become state, federal, local, or privately owned conservation land. The local Natural Resources Commission would declare by 1972 that "Concord differs from most towns in that it is a precious national asset."[38]

The combination of these public and private, local and national land preservation initiatives certainly helped to make the landscape of Concord, Lincoln, and Lexington look physically unique from the mass-produced,

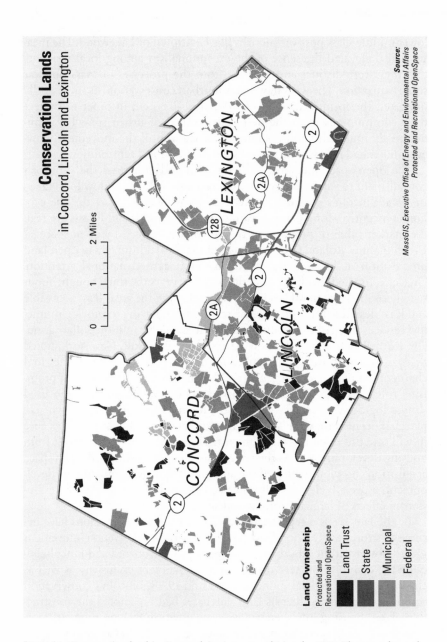

Source: MassGIS, Executive Office of Energy and Environmental Affairs Protected and Recreational OpenSpace

Conservation Lands in Concord, Lincoln and Lexington

2 Miles

0   1   2

LEXINGTON

128

2A

2

2A

2

LINCOLN

CONCORD

2

Land Ownership
Protected and
Recreational OpenSpace

Land Trust

State

Municipal

Federal

Figure 4.1 Conservation land in Concord, Lexington, and Lincoln, 2012. The map shows the extensive amount of land in these three suburban municipalities under protection by the federal, state, and local governments, or owned by a private conservation trust by 2012, which is particularly notable given the proximity of the communities to the commuter and high-tech corridor of Route 128. *Source*: Massachusetts Executive Office of Energy and Environmental Affairs, "Protected and Recreational Space," 2012, MassGIS.

lower-middle-class postwar suburbs like Levittown or Lakewood. The measures also elevated the sense of the exceptionalism among local residents that they were distinct and separate from the processes of mass postwar suburbanization. The ways in which suburban conservationists successfully navigated the formal channels of the political system in order to protect their communities from the destructive effects of urban sprawl was undoubtedly impressive and notable. Other features of the movement, however, illustrated many more typical suburban political sensibilities.

The open space measures both built on and enhanced the suburban commitment to superior services, high property values, and low local taxes. In 1965, Lincoln's planning board even more plainly asserted, "The economic incentives for a perpetuation of Lincoln's fields and forests are real: the market value of property in the Town is enhanced by open space."[39] Urban planner Roland Greeley's study of the fiscal advantages of open land preservation in his hometown of Lexington earned national attention. Greeley estimated that if over a period of a few years the town bought about two thousand acres of undeveloped land, selecting the areas least accessible and least desirable for residence, the savings from having to provide municipal services to these areas would amount to a quarter-million dollars annually. Ruth Rusch, a conservation activist from Peekskill, New York, noted that Lexington showed the significance of open space "to retain the rural charm of a suburban community" and "a sound financial investment promising future savings as well."[40] Concord's conservation commission used similar logic and language convince the town to acquire a ninety-two-acre parcel. It deemed the acquisition a "bargain" and "wise investment," because it "will save the Town costs of many town services which would result from housing development."[41] As the commission argument implied, open space acquisition consciously limited the amount of land available for new development, especially dense multiunit housing, and thus extended the exclusionary effects of large lot zoning policies.

By the late 1960s, a reporter noted, "Conservation commissions have become a strong arm of local government."[42] The conservation movement gained power within suburban municipalities like Concord and Lincoln because the commissions served as avenues to maintain exclusivity as well as channel state and federal money. By the mid-1970s, Lincoln's conservation commission estimated that its land purchases had preempted the construction of 250 housing lots, thereby saving the town money on municipal services that it could spend to "maintain good schools."[43] "In Concord today, or in Wayland or Lincoln or Sudbury," a National Wildlife Magazine reporter commented in the mid-1960s, "it is a rare conservation article that doesn't sail through virtually without opposition. The people here have demonstrated, to the surprise of many an onlooker, that taxpayers are willing to part with their dollars for the purchase of marginal lands, wetlands, and just plain swamps."[44]

Open space expenditures experienced little opposition from local residents in these towns partially because state and federal subsidies made land acquisitions a small fraction of their annual budgets and tax dollars.[45] Paul Brooks and Susan Brooks suggested that they and other Lincoln voters might have appeared "out of our minds" for overwhelmingly approving the $1.8 million purchase of five hundred acres of land, but because of the "secret" of federal and state assistance, the town only had to pay twenty-five cents on the dollar, which bonded over a fifteen-year period amounted to a dollar increase on the tax rate.[46] The ease with which land acquisition measures passed in places such as Lincoln and Concord defies the assumption about the reflexive fiscal conservatism and antigovernment sensibility of suburban residents. Rather, the support for open space purchases illustrates that the majority of citizens in the Route 128 suburbs, both Democrats and Republicans, and their counterparts in places like Westchester County and Marin County, did support local, state, and federal expenditures, and even small increases in their tax rates, especially when it would increase their own property values, municipal services, and overall quality of life.

Local conservation activists would often discuss the benefits of preserving "the natural attributes of a beautiful and historically important area" for the general public.[47] Yet several observers by the late 1960s had begun to raise concerns that the success of the open space movement had constructed literal and figurative barriers around suburban communities. The Massachusetts DNR clearly supported the push against urban development, but had started to worry that the conservation commissions also fostered "forms of ecological and political isolationism." Scholars such as Andrew Scheffey similarly wondered if the suburban-based conservation activities were "primarily a protectionist device" or could "meet the needs of an expanding metropolis."[48] As the suburban network joined in the effort to stop highway development, it revealed the possibilities and limits of this form of activism to protect the environment on a metropolitan scale.

People Before Highways

The battle to save Fowl Meadow, a four-hundred-acre wildlife preserve in the southern suburbs of Canton and Milton, thrust local conservationists in the late 1960s into an ongoing urban-based battle being waged to oppose the construction of a major highway in Boston. Fowl Meadow exemplified the type of open spaces that the conservation commissions clamored to protect, but the site conflicted with plans for the construction of the Southwest Expressway. The Master Highway Plan for Metropolitan Boston issued in 1948 served as the root of this controversy. The Massachusetts Department of Public Works (DPW) proposed an ambitious web of circumferential highways and radial roads that would become the basis of state transportation decisions for the next half century. As the linchpin of the plan, the architects envisioned an "Inner Belt" within the boundaries of Route 128 connecting Cambridge, Somerville, and Brookline with the Boston neighborhoods of Roxbury, Charlestown and the Fenway. Additionally, the Inner Belt would link seven radial routes including Route 2, I-93 North, I-95 North and South, and the Southeast Expressway, which would enable drivers to go around Boston without going through its center.[49]

By the end of the 1950s, federal funding enabled DPW officials to implement most of the plan, and the Inner Belt remained the biggest missing piece. The state sought to fill in that gap, but the Inner Belt plan threatened to cut through the heart of a series of lower-middle- and working-class neighborhoods.[50] In Cambridge, where the plan demanded the destruction of thirteen hundred housing units, residents decided to fight back to preserve the cohesiveness and socioeconomic diversity of their neighborhoods and have more of a say in local DPW projects. The protest spread to residents in neighborhoods throughout Boston whose homes the Inner Belt would also destroy. The opposition soon included African Americans from Roxbury, a racially and economically diverse group from the South End, working-class whites from Somerville and Jamaica Plain, and white upper-middle-class residents from a Brookline neighborhood that shared a border with Boston. With the help of several MIT-affiliated urban planners, this diverse group coalesced into the Greater Boston Committee on the Transportation Crisis (GBC). The GBC joined part of an informal network of citizens groups that spread across the nation in places like Baltimore, Nashville, Miami, Chicago, and San Francisco in the 1960s, all "revolting" against highway construction in the cities.[51] In Boston, the coalition shared the immediate goal of stopping the construction of any new projects within the circumference of Route 128, but eventually hoped to direct the metropolitan transportation system away from "its current over-emphasis on serving suburban auto-commuters at the expense of inner-city neighborhoods."[52] This twin agenda led the group to formulate a serious challenge to the pro-growth philosophy of officials at the city, state and federal levels.

The Boston antihighway activists made little headway convincing Governor John Volpe to halt the Inner Belt plans. As a former construction official, the first federal highway administrator during the Eisenhower administration, and the Massachusetts' Commissioner of Public Works in the 1950s, Volpe had a long history of pro-road politics. When Volpe accepted the position as the Secretary of Transportation under President Richard Nixon, however, the anti–Inner Belt movement had a crucial window of opportunity, and the GBC seized it in a rally called People Before Highways. On Saturday, January 25, 1969, two thousand people converged on Boston Common by the State House entrance to participate. Middle-aged Irish

Figure 4.2 Massachusetts governor Francis Sargent addressing the crowd at the People Before Highways rally on January 25, 1969. The protest, organized in opposition to the proposed construction of the Inner Belt, occurred just days into Sargent's tenure in office. The event marked the beginning of Sargent and the protesters working together, and represented a major turning in the direction of transportation policy in the state and nation. Courtesy of Associated Press Images. © 1970 The Associated Press.

Catholic housewives and young African American community organizers stood side by side, holding signs that read "Stop the Belt" and "Don't Belt Us," and many children clutched red balloons printed with the slogan "Homes Not Highways." The *Boston Globe* reported the rally radiated a "festive, almost carnival mood" and "ballgame atmosphere."[53] Governor Sargent, just two days into his term, eventually emerged from the State House. Appropriating the demonstration's theme, he declared, "Never, never will this administration make decisions that place people below concrete." At that, the crowd erupted in loud applause.[54]

Although the movement initially pitted the state government and grassroots movement against each other, following the People Before Highways rally, the grassroots coalition partnered with Sargent and his staff. The activists effectively capitalized on the unique personal ideology and leadership style of the new governor. Like his predecessor, Sargent was both a Republican and former DPW commissioner, but his pedigree and path to that position differed significantly from that of Volpe. Sargent had owned a sporting goods shop and commercial fishing business on Cape Cod, which led him first to the post as associate director of the DPW in charge of waterways and then head of the DPW. As commissioner, he had endorsed the Inner Belt, but his unusual résumé made him open to reconsideration.[55] Following the rally, Sargent made no official announcement about his decision regarding the fate of the Inner Belt. But in a series of speeches, he began calling for a "balanced transportation system" that would count highways as one form of transit among many other options and stating that he would not tolerate "the reckless ruin of environment."[56]

In the aftermath of the rally, the GBC also fine-tuned its tactics to move the state's transportation priorities away from roadway construction and toward a mass-transit-based policy for metropolitan Boston similar to what San Francisco activists had successfully established in their city. A shift toward mass transit, Boston activists argued, would prevent neighborhood destruction and displacement, decrease the air pollution created by automobiles, and increase employment opportunities for low-income people. The antihighway coalition began to work in closer alliance with suburban-based groups and causes, which would prove essential in the effort to change Sargent's mind and the direction of the Inner Belt project. In the summer of 1969, the GBC allied with the group of environmentalists trying to stop the DPW from routing the Southwest Expressway directly through the Fowl Meadow wildlife preserve.

Since the early 1960s, the conservation commissions, together with several environmental groups in the suburbs of Milton, Canton, Dedham, and Cohasset along the southern portion of Route 128, had sought to stop the plan.[57] Around the time of the State House rally, the groups had hired Guy Rosmarin, a young lawyer and political consultant from Brookline, to serve as their lobbyist to prevent the plans to route the expansion through the meadow. Rosmarin recognized that the suburban residents he represented were trying to fight "the route, not the road," but he convinced his clients that it might be a better tactic to oppose the whole plan instead of only the part slated to run through Fowl Meadow. Thus, the suburbanites joined in the GBC's effort to convince the governor to declare a stoppage of all highway construction and a complete restudy of the state's transportation policy.

The introduction of the suburban activists transformed the highway issue from a problem purely of neighborhood disruption in low-income areas into one of environmental destruction with truly metropolitan dimensions. The suburban conservationists also provided strategic value for the GBC and its broader attempt to alter the state's transportation policy. Sargent's aide Albert Kramer observed that when "their base had broadened beyond neighborhoods to conservation," it was "effective. They knew what they were doing" because the governor "instantly . . . relates to that."[58] In addition to gaining the governor's attention, the antihighway movement's newfound emphasis on the environmental implications of the Inner Belt drew the state's well-established conservation organizations into the cause, including the Massachusetts Audubon Society, the Massachusetts Forest and Park Association, the local conservation commissions, and private land trusts. The letters flooding the State House demanding a change in the plan confirmed the geographic reach of the grassroots conservation network as well as its effectiveness at pressuring state politicians. This outpouring proved Allen Morgan's declaration that the numerical strength of this movement surpassed either the Republican or Democratic Party and could serve as the "most powerful political force in the state."[59]

The leaders of the newly fortified campaign also recognized that in order to prove that the highway plan had detrimental social and environmental effects on the entire metropolitan area, they needed to create more participation from white suburban residents. The GBC made overtures and gained the support of the area's networks of suburban organizations, including the peace organization Citizens for Participation Politics (CPP), discussed in chapter 5, and the Massachusetts Federation for Fair Housing and Equal Rights (MFFHER), which both had significant knowledge of working within the formal channels of the political system. Culling the CPP and MFFHER memberships, activists launched "a suburban push" by arranging meetings in suburbs such as Concord, Brookline, Lexington, Wellesley, and Weston.[60] The organization urged its contacts that it was only "through joint political pressure from the city and suburbs that the governor will act."[61]

The campaign succeeded in gaining the support of suburban residents by emphasizing that altering the state's transportation policy would not just save inner-city neighborhoods and open spaces like Fowl Meadow but also could prevent urban sprawl and traffic. Adopting the antigrowth arguments of the open space movement, the GBC stressed that "new expressways encourage the present patterns of suburban sprawl which nullifies many of the features which drew people to the suburbs in the first place" as "quiet streets become busy connecting roads overnight; ugly and unplanned shopping centers bring noise and traffic."[62] Further linking the issues of conservation and social inequality, the GBC acknowledged that automobile-produced air pollution had detrimental consequences for both poor inner-city residents and affluent suburbanites. These types of assertions appealed to the environmental concerns and quality-of-life sensibilities of residents in the Route 128 suburbs, even those not officially affiliated with the fair housing or conservation groups. A group of Republican suburban commuters and downtown business elites orchestrated a meeting with Sargent to demonstrate "the wide spectrum of people" who favored "a fundamental reconsideration of the transportation dilemma."[63] Sargent responded to the well-heeled group, "I well understand the suburbanite's realization that a highway, which reduces his commuting time by five minutes, still may not be in his overall interest." "The lesson of the Sixties—that the corollary, and often destructive, effect of man's 'progress' is direct and pervasive—has come home to all citizens whether they live in the city or suburbia."[64] The antihighway campaign, in short, had led the former DPW official to question the basic tenets of growth liberalism.

The relentless pressure from the well-organized and wide-reaching anti-highway coalition eventually contributed to Sargent announcing on February 11, 1970 he had decided to "reverse the transportation policy of the Commonwealth."[65] He called for the creation of a new plan, based on the concept of balanced transportation, that would question not simply "where and how to build expressways" but whether to complete them at all. Sargent ordered a stop to all highway construction within Route 128, including work on the Southwest Expressway, Route 2, and the Inner Belt, until the release of his new program. "Four years ago I was the Commissioner of the Department of Public Works," Sargent candidly stated. "Then, nearly everyone was sure highways were the only answer to transportation problems for years to come. We were wrong." The last three words summarized the entire speech. The decision solidified the governor's popularity with voters throughout the state, but particularly liberal-leaning suburbanites in the Route 128 suburbs who would prove essential in Sargent's successful reelection the following November.[66]

The announcement put a hold on both the destruction of neighborhoods and open spaces like Fowl Meadow, thereby revealing the possibilities for changing policy when grassroots groups created broad alliances that transcended metropolitan lines and brought together a range of people and issues.[67] The effectiveness of the GBC directly depended on its combination of neighborhood activists and suburban professionals.[68] The expertise of white middle-class activists was particularly instrumental in helping the group forge a close working relationship with members of the governor's staff. These bonds became so close that following Sargent's announcement, several GBC members, including Rosmarin, decided to take positions within the administration as they believed they could contribute more to the cause by working within the system of government.[69] The shift also strengthened the ties between antihighway activists and State House officials, which in turn shaped the state's future transportation policies.

In order to transform the bullet points of his speech into a coherent policy, Sargent created the Boston Transportation Planning Review (BTPR) to evaluate whether there should be a permanent halt on highway construction within the Route 128 area. Sargent aimed for the $3.8 million study to be "open and broadly participatory" and attentive to "transportation, socio-economic and environmental values."[70] The seventy-five-person committee included representatives from state agencies, municipalities around metro-politan Boston, and groups such as the GBC, Boston Chamber of Commerce, and the Sierra Club and served as a model for transportation planning across the nation.[71] Throughout the restudy process, the region's network of environmental groups remained among the loudest lobbying forces, claiming the study's outcome as one of the "most significant environmental judgments made by a Massachusetts Governor in the latter half of the twentieth century."[72]

A series of new pieces of legislation and court decisions at the federal level enhanced this argument, and ensured that environmental concerns assumed new importance in the future of transportation policy. The announcement of the moratorium and creation of the BTPR coincided with a new epoch of environmental politics in the United States. In the late 1960s, the discontent about the environmental crisis exploded at the national level and significantly changed the terrain of both local and national environmental policy and politics. On April 22, 1970, almost twenty million people across the United States participated in Earth Day, which signified a major turning point in the popularization of environmental issues and created a favorable context for the passage of several important laws in quick succession. In addition to the Clean Air and Clean Water acts, Nixon signed into law the National Environmental Policy Act (NEPA), which one observer referred to as "the most sweeping environmental law ever enacted by a United States Congress."[73] The act had three provisions: first, it asserted environmental quality as a leading national priority; second, it established procedures for incorporating environmental concerns into federal agency decision making; and third, it created the President's Council on Environmental Quality (the precursor to the Environmental Protection Agency) to coordinate all federal environmental actions.[74]

The second provision of NEPA, Section 102, had the most direct effect on the highway controversy. It mandated that all federally funded projects prepare a detailed Environmental Impact Statement (EIS) that described the environmental effects of the action, identify any unavoidable harms, list any alternatives, and make all this information available to the public.[75] The broad law provided environmental officials a crucial mechanism with which to hold federal agencies accountable for the social, economic, and ecological consequences of their plans. The complex dimensions of these new federal laws and rulings and their role in establishing a new era of environmental activism came into sharp relief in the fight to prevent the expansion of Route 2 in Concord and Lincoln.

A Superhighway in Thoreau's Backyard

The plan for expanding Route 2 fell outside the official boundaries of the BTPR restudy, but the fight it spawned reveals how new federal policy and grassroots activism around environmental issues coupled with the influence of the urban-based antihighway movement altered both the debate about urban sprawl and transportation policy and invigorated the suburban open space agenda. Route 2 began in western Massachusetts and moved directly eastward, traversing through rural towns in the center of the state, and then the suburbs of Acton, Concord, Lincoln, and Lexington, and bisected Route 128, traveling through Belmont and Arlington before it ended in Cambridge. The highway served as the major commuter road for residents in the western suburbs to get to Cambridge and Boston, but it was built in the first half of the century and had struggled to absorb the increased traffic produced by postwar suburbanization. The 1948 Master Plan had first proposed significant expansion in order to make Route 2 an official expressway. While Sargent's moratorium stalled plans to extend Route 2 farther into Cambridge and link it to the Inner Belt, the DPW still sought to expand it in the other direction. Officials developed plans to partially relocate and widen an eleven-mile section between Acton and Lexington, doubling it from four to eight lanes, and adding a sixty-four-foot-wide median strip, overpasses, and a large cloverleaf. The DPW argued that the improvements would both increase the safety of the road and transform it into "the major freeway serving the northwest quadrant of the state."[76] The plan would have the most disruptive effects on the towns of Lincoln and Concord, where it would require the taking of over two hundred acres of protected open space.[77]

Lincoln and Concord citizens grew outraged at the prospect that a road comparable in size to Route 128 would slash through their communities and encroach on the conservation lands they had worked to preserve.[78] The recent passage of landmark federal environmental laws coupled with the success of the antihighway movement emboldened local residents to openly challenge the project and prove that residents were "simply not swallowing, in the 'old style' way, plans for huge highways."[79] Lincoln resident Gregory DeBarshye declared that while a decade earlier, the DPW might have had a "legitimate" case for the expansion, with the indefinite delay of the Inner Belt and growing recognition of the environmental impacts of roadway construction, those justifications were now "obsolete."[80] Likewise, a group of Concord residents acknowledged that the success of the GBC signaled "that the time is appropriate for local initiative to halt mindless construction of the highway."[81]

The opposition also reflected a heightened environmental awareness at the local level, which became particularly pronounced in Concord and Lincoln due to their self-identity as the places "where conservation began."[82] By the early 1970s, the local movement had expanded to a range of ecological concerns. Concord was one of the first communities in the nation to ban the use of DDT and had adopted other cutting-edge measures. "We are terribly keen on recycling," declared Marian Thornton, a mother of three who was known as the "the president of the dump."[83] This was a notable title since the Concord dump, which sat just across the street from Walden Pond, had become a hub of community activity where local politicians campaigned and Girl Scouts sold cookies. Observers could not help but notice the seeming irony of the strength of environmentalism in a community filled with so many scientists and engineers employed at major defense and technology firms. Yet for the residents it appeared less contradictory. Hugo Logemann, an engineer who had helped develop radar systems at MIT and who along with his wife was an avid nature lover, preferred not use his technological skill to kill bugs and mosquitoes. Instead, "if they bother us," he explained, "we go inside."[84] Residents like Logemann were less conciliatory toward highway construction.

Building on the existing conservation organizations and impulse, and influenced by the model and tactics of the GBC, Concord citizens quickly mobilized to oppose the expansion of Route 2. Two groups formed—Citizens for Balanced Transportation (CBT) and Residents Opposed to the Urban Traffic Encouragement (ROUTE)—and together launched a well-organized, aggressive campaign. In reference to this mobilization, one long-time resident declared that he "had never known the people of Concord to be so aroused and outspoken on an issue."[85] In just four days, the groups gathered twenty-five hundred signatures on a petition objecting to the DPW's plans. The grassroots groups largely concentrated on the ways in which the highway would disrupt the high standards of living and pastoral charm that Concord citizens had come to appreciate and expect. "It is time for all Concordians to take a hard look," ROUTE stated of its organizing philosophy, and "insist that the essential nature of the Town be preserved."[86] Linking older arguments about the value of open space with newer ones concerning the problems of highway construction, the CBT pointedly asserted that the highway expansion would significantly affect the "quality of life here in the future," encourage the "pressure to build more housing," create the "irreparable shrinkage of land in the Walden reservation, and other historic and recreational parts," and cause substantial "social and environmental effects."[87]

The success of the grassroots groups in bringing their arguments to bear on the transportation decisions of the state government reveals both the emphasis on citizen participation in new transportation and environmental policy and the power that suburban professionals could wield in the political system. The residents who led this campaign often presented themselves

as an "*ad hoc* citizens group" of amateurs, but the members had a high level
of professional expertise in law, business, and engineering, which clearly
helped in making state officials take their concerns and suggestions seriously.[88] "We write a lot of position papers, we circulate petitions, we write
letters," explained CBT leader and Harvard Business School professor Cyrus
Gibson of the campaign's strategies. "We tend to deal through channels" of
power rather than "push baby carriages in front of the bulldozers."[89] Between 1971 and 1972, local suburban activists met regularly with officials at
the State House and DPW, including Environment Secretary Foster, Transportation Secretary Alan Altshuler, Commissioner of Public Works Bruce
Campbell, and Governor Sargent and his close advisers.[90]

The outpouring of opposition forced the DPW to agree to several rounds
of redesigning the Route 2 expansion before they officially submitted the
EIS to the Federal Highway Administration. The redesign process con-
formed to the newly implemented NEPA guidelines and involved more
participation from local citizens and more attention to the ecological impact of the roadway, especially its effect on adjacent conservation lands and
water resources.[91] The DPW's official hearings on its draft impact statement
drew large turnouts of Concord and Lincoln residents, who asked pointed
questions of the bureaucrats and offered their own technical suggestions for
the redesign. The eventual design implemented for Route 2 through Concord and Lincoln bore the direct influence of this grassroots-based input.
The DPW abandoned the plans to add lanes and instead adopted a series of
smaller improvements.[92] The outcome showed that citizen opposition to
state-sponsored growth was particularly effective in communities that contained residents with backgrounds in science, engineering, law, and business. These citizens could point out specific nuanced deficiencies in the
design and had the resources to be persistent in fighting the bureaucracy of
the state and federal government. As the controversy finally subsided, however, it revealed that it was far more difficult to shift this type of activism
away from opposing highway construction toward support in earnest for
bringing mass transit into the suburbs.

A New Era in Transportation Policy

On November 30, 1972, just as the controversy over Route 2 began to wane,
Governor Sargent appeared on television to announce his momentous decision about the future of transportation policy in metropolitan Boston. He
declared that in order to "right the balance of transportation" policy, "future
investment must concentrate overwhelmingly on the improvement of public transportation." Sargent announced that he would permanently stop all
highway construction inside Route 128, including the Southwest Express-

way, and instead focus on increasing public transit in the areas that would have been served by the new roadways.[93] "I have borne in mind the impact these facilities would have on the social, economic and environmental fabric of the region," he stated, realizing that "the cost inevitably associated with these facilities would have exceeded their benefits." As the most obvious example of this cost-benefit analysis, Sargent cited the earlier plan to run an elevated highway directly through Fowl Meadow, indicating how much environmental concerns influenced his decision. Sargent canceled a billion dollars of expressway building. He received widespread praise both locally and nationally for a cutting-edge approach to recognizing the environmental concerns at the heart of transportation policy and for doing "what no other governor has dared to do."[94] An administrator for the Environmental Protection Agency even proclaimed, "Sargent is blocking downfield for us."[95]

Sargent would become a leader in the broader movement seeking the reform of the nation's transportation policy.[96] Following his landmark announcement, Sargent made several trips to Washington to advocate, first and foremost, for a change in the distribution of the federal road-building funds. Congress had established the Federal Highway Trust Fund in 1956 in order to ensure a reliable source of financial support for the construction and maintenance of the Interstate Highway System. The fund drew its money from a tax levied on gasoline purchases and stipulated that money cordoned off in the account could only be used for road construction. Sargent lobbied for the cause of freeing the four billion dollars per year in the fund from what one reporter dubbed its "straight jacket."[97] The governor's affiliation with the Republican Party and close ties to Secretary of Transportation Volpe made him crucial to convincing the Nixon administration to reassess its stance on the nation's transportation system.[98] Sargent stressed in these lobbying outings that "support for mass transportation is coming not only from intercity residents. It's coming from suburbanites as well"—an implicit reference to the Concord residents, who he proclaimed "write in support of balanced transportation, with a heavy emphasis on mass transit."[99] Members of the Nixon administration and Congress both proved "surprisingly receptive" to the argument, as did representatives from both political parties.[100] The *Congressional Quarterly* cited the effort to open the Federal Highway Trust Fund as one of the only areas where House members from suburban areas, regardless of party affiliation, voted in a decisive bloc.[101]

Congress eventually passed the Federal Highway Act of 1973, which offered an 80 percent federal match to state and local funds and authorized urban areas to divert their share of interstate highway funds toward the construction of mass transit facilities. The following year, the federal government enacted the National Mass Transportation Assistance Act approving the use of federal funds for transit-operating assistance. These new laws both validated Massachusetts' pioneering transportation policy, and included stipulations that offered the state much more flexibility and money in creating alternatives to highways. It also showed the consideration of the priorities of suburban constituencies, which in the case of towns along Route 2 would ultimately impede the effort to create a more environmentally sound and equitable mass transit system.

From Subway to Bikeway

The loosening of federal highway funds provided Massachusetts with the financial means to expand and improve the region's subway service. In the ensuing decade, the state began to replace the routes of the Master Plan with mass transit lines by rerouting the Orange Line and extending the Red Line southward to Braintree to partially mirror the abandoned Southwest corridor and northward past Harvard Square to Alewife Brook in place of a portion of the Inner Belt. The BTPR also proposed continuing the route of the Red Line past Alewife and through the western suburbs to a terminal near the interchange of Route 2 and Route 128. This extension, it argued, would both provide suburban residents an alternative form of travel into Boston and enhance access for inner-city residents to the employment opportunities in the many industries located along the high-tech corridor.[102] The BTPR suggested that the line follow the existing right-of-way of the Boston and Maine's railroad with stations in Arlington Center, Arlington Heights, and Lexington Center, ending at Route 128 in Lexington, just before Lincoln and Concord. The cities of Cambridge and Somerville supported the plan for the Red Line extension, but the citizens of Lexington and Arlington expressed more reticence. Many residents endorsed the idea of the expansion, yet raised concerns about having stations in their communities. Their stance led Secretary of Transportation Altshuler to observe that "every town that does accept a transit system wants it to keep on going. They want to terminal somewhere else."[103]

The response of Lexington and Arlington residents revealed that the term "quality of life" and goals of environmental protection were open to conflicting interpretations. A few residents believed, in the words of longtime liberal activist Nancy Earsy, that the project offered "Lexington's best opportunity to make a real commitment to ecological preservation and clean air."[104] Most residents who supported the project saw it less as a means to endorse ecological concerns and more to reduce the hassles of commuting by automobile or bus, thereby increasing their individual standard of living.[105] Several Lexington automobile commuters complained of paying a "high price in frazzled nerves," and one fed-up resident declared, "I have had it with traffic and better train service would ease my day considerably."[106] For many of their neighbors, nevertheless, the expansion of the mass transit system posed a threat to the privileges of suburban residency. A study of the Route 128 suburbs conducted in the mid-1970s concluded, "More than anything else suburban residents fear that if population continues to grow," then "the character of their communities will be lost."[107] The comments from local residents upheld this observation, voicing relentless concern that the Red Line project would destroy the "New England charm" of their "towns" and make them "automatically and inexorably become urbanized and citified."[108]

The parallels between the antisprawl arguments that residents used to oppose the Red Line and those that antihighway activists used to promote mass transit exposed the flexibility of environmentalist logic in the types of battles surrounding transportation and development. Lexington resident John Lahiff asserted that extending the Red Line would "have a detrimental effect on the environmental and especially population density of our town."[109] Herbert Meyer, a Lexington conservationist, pushed this contention even further, claiming that the plan would increase noise, air, and water pollution, and others suggested it would encourage sprawl and thereby deplete open spaces.[110] At least one Lexington resident aimed to point out the contradictions in this antigrowth discourse. Tom Forstmann warned that the pressures of suburban development would continue with or without the Red Line and saw the transit line as a means to actually control rather than encourage sprawl. "There is nothing charming about our congested and polluted roads," he maintained in order to support his contention that "the aims of providing transportation and limiting development" as "fundamentally compatible."[111] Fortsmann failed to persuade the majority of Arlington and Lexington residents of those connections.

Even more than the battles over open space and the highway extension, the reaction to mass transit made explicit the racial and class-based fears animating antigrowth politics. Although residents used words such as "charm" and "character," it was not simply the aesthetic beauty of their communities that they saw threatened but also their socioeconomic status and physical safety. A few people raised fears about "roving gangs on the transit system invading the calm of the suburban lifestyle" and increasing the incidence of crime.[112] More terrifying to many Lexington citizens than "roving gangs," however, was the prospect of low-income people moving into their community because of the subway. A sympathetic state representative summarized this attitude in noticeably racialized terms: "Wherever rapid transit has gone in other places, people would be fast to follow and many a rural area has become a rural jungle."[113] A study committee sponsored by the town of Lexington aimed to address this claim head-on. It declared: "Most of us are aware, although one does not hear it articulated very directly," of the concern that the "extension of rapid transit service will lead to an influx of lower income or lower class families to the town."[114] The study's authors nonetheless promised that due to the high property values, lack of existing apartments in Lexington, and established zoning policies, unless the town took deliberate action to encourage multiunit development, such an outcome would not occur. Instead, the increase in transit options, the study argued, would most likely make Lexington an even more desirable community and might actually raise local property values and make it even more economically exclusive.[115] Most residents remained skeptical. A group of residents in Arlington even formed an organization called the Arlington Red Line Action Movement (with the catchy acronym ALARM) to galvanize grassroots opposition to the proposal. The leaders included MIT economist Vincent A. Fulmer, who reduced the movement's goals to preserving "quality of life" and preventing "irreversible transformation" to the community's character.[116] Transportation official Fred Salvucci saw through this rhetoric, publicly accusing the group of using "racial fear and blatant mistruths" in the campaign against the proposal.[117]

The rationales that supporters of the proposal adopted about the metropolitan implications of bringing the mass transit line to Route 128 served only to inflame further resistance to the plan. The Lexington study committee concluded that the plan would have few negative effects on the town, but would provide assistance to the overall region, especially people who lived or worked along Route 128. This logic made some Lexington and Arlington citizens more insistent in their opposition. A resident from Arlington confronted head-on the arguments that the town must share responsibility for social and spatial inequality. "Arlington has contributed its share to the Metco experiment," H. H. Seward scoffed, but its "neighbors seem to feel that Arlington should take on even more of the burden."[118] A Lexington resident similarly lamented that the proposal would make the town a "sacrificial lamb on the altar of regional interests."[119]

A series of hearings and studies turned the debate around the Red Line extension into a five-year battle. The protracted process showed some of the limitations of the increased emphasis on community participation in environmental and transportation policy. Although the new procedures aimed to give residents a larger voice and more control over policies that affected their communities, in many suburban municipalities, it supplied residents with another means to delay or thwart action. In the case of the Red Line extension, this citizen participation effectively killed the project. Embracing the populist tenets of citizen participation, ALARM leader John F. Cusack enthusiastically remarked of this outcome, "It shows the people can beat the machine."[120] A state planner expressed far less exuberance. Peter Murphy mournfully observed, "You'll probably never see in your lifetime or mine a heavy rail commuter system to Route 128 in Lexington."[121]

Once suburban residents revolted against the plans, the Massachusetts Bay Transportation Authority had to determine a use for the right-of-way

Figure 4.3 A section of Minuteman Bikeway, which opened in 1992, running along eleven miles from Alewife Station in Cambridge, through Arlington, Lexington, and Bedford, following the proposed right-of-way for an extension of the Red Line. It became one of the most popular bike trails in the nation, but has had limited commuter benefits. *Source*: http://commons. wikimedia.org/wiki/File:Minuteman_Bikeway.jpg.

per a bankruptcy court ruling. The transportation authority eventually decided to accept a proposal from the communities of Lexington, Arlington, Bedford, and Cambridge to create a bikeway directly along the right-of-way.[122] The towns suggested that "the very attractive" and relatively inexpensive pathway would create little physical or environmental impact, provide commuter access from the suburbs to Boston, and increase accessibility to the town centers, schools, and historic sites of the communities it bisected.[123] The Minuteman Commuter Bikeway officially opened in 1992. The eleven-mile-long, twelve-foot-wide route now runs from Alewife Station—across bridges, alongside ponds and parks, and through the town centers of Arlington and Lexington, before ending in the rolling pastures of Bedford. It has become one of the most popular and notable rails-to-trails routes in the nation. Yet the path, which closely follows Paul Revere's historic ride, functions primarily as a space of "healthy recreation" for suburbanites and bike-owning residents of Cambridge and Boston looking to escape the congestion of the city, not as a major commuting artery.[124] If the pathway has limited commuter benefits for suburban residents, particularly because of unpredictable New England weather patterns, it is a woefully ineffective means for inner-city residents to reach the service sector jobs concentrated in the industrial parks and shopping malls along Route 128.

Although the bikeway was never intended to entirely replace the plans for the extension of the Red Line, it still reveals the choices and priorities of many residents in the Route 128 area. The route's natural beauty and recreational opportunities have become additional markers of the high quality of life of the suburbs along its path. The path has undoubtedly helped to inspire an appreciation for outdoor activity and nature in new generations of residents and their children. It has also increased the desirability and property values of homes that have easy access to its route while serving as another selling point for local realtors trying to lure a specific demographic of homebuyer to the area.[125] The Minuteman path ultimately offers these suburban communities many of the same assets of the conservation projects that it traverses: a means of maintaining open space, historic distinctiveness, exceptional quality of life, and socioeconomic exclusivity.

Conclusion

The conservation campaigns that took place in the towns along Route 128 in the 1950s and beyond reveal the complex ideas of localism and individualism at the heart of both suburban and liberal politics as well as their intersections. A commitment to improvement through government action propelled liberally minded suburban residents to advance environmental protection, just as they had supported fair housing and voluntary integration. Similar to these other causes, however, the environmental movement received the greatest suburban support for the components of its platform that promised to enhance the property values and standard of living of individual residents. People frequently couched both their decision to move to Concord or Lincoln and the set of stringent controls on growth and opposition to highway expansion or mass transit in their communities in a language of individual quality of life and choice. This language underscores just how few powerful voices in the postwar era made residents recognize how measures and forces like exclusionary zoning, tax entitlements, and the federal subsidization of corporate development along Route 128 had contributed to socioeconomic and environmental injustice.

While this language of quality and choice was seemingly individualistic and reflected a sense of distinctiveness, the ideology it represented, nevertheless, was part of a much larger and complex set of spatial, economic, and political structures. The issue and mechanisms of highway development connected suburban environmentalists to activists fighting against housing displacement in the inner city. Yet so too did residents' efforts to preserve the character and charm of their communities embody the shared racial and class privileges and power of affluent whites that the multipronged postwar growth agenda of the federal government had made possible. The environmental movement at the grassroots and national levels contributed to reorienting postwar liberalism's definition of quality of life from expanding economic and suburban growth, and toward an emphasis on amenities such as open space, clean air, and access to recreation. This challenge to ideas of growth did not make liberal politics and policy any less invested in economic forces but instead reflected the shared material benefits that white middle-class suburbanites in places like Concord received from open space and other forms of environmental protection.

The effort to protect open space and stop highway construction highlights the effectiveness of white suburban professionals to draw political attention to their concerns. It inspired at least rhetorical support for the environment to become a basic prerequisite for candidates from either party running for governor in Massachusetts as well as other states with a large, active, conservation-oriented suburban population, such as Connecticut, New Jersey, California, Oregon, and Washington. Likewise, national politicians increasingly started addressing the problems of sprawl, poor air quality, and traffic as a means to gain the support of citizens like those residing along Route 128.[126] The simultaneous emphasis on citizen participation in environmental politics and policy further empowered suburban residents in places like Concord, Lincoln, and Lexington to believe that they had power to change federal, state, and local policy, which as the movement to oppose the Vietnam War and the battles over affordable housing and METCO reveal, had multifaceted consequences.

5

Political Action for Peace

On October 15, 1969, forty thousand people joined a candlelight procession from the Washington Monument to the Capitol, twenty thousand businessmen attended an event on Wall Street, and more than a hundred thousand Massachusetts citizens converged on the Boston Common, all to participate in the Vietnam Moratorium.[1] Residents in over a hundred Boston suburbs joined cities and towns from North Newton, Kansas; Duluth, Iowa; Golden, Colorado; Cheyenne, Wyoming; and Thousand Oaks, California, staging events on their town greens and in other public spaces.[2] It was the vast majority of participants' first experience taking part in a public protest. President Richard Nixon's "been trying to pass off this whole thing as a student movement," Ellie Gelhar of Concord explained of her motivations for joining in. "I think when he sees the kind of people who are involved in this protest he may begin to realize that there is broadly based opposition to the war."[3] In total, more two million people in more than two hundred cities participated in the Vietnam Moratorium.

The idea for what became the largest civil demonstration in US history and arguably the most successful antiwar demonstration of the Vietnam era germinated not in a college dorm room but from a suburban father and business executive from Newton named Jerome Grossman. A balding, fifty-two-year-old envelope-manufacturing executive, he wore a suit and tie in public appearances and defied the image of the typical antiwar activist. Grossman told the press that if the event succeeded in convincing Nixon to withdraw troops from Vietnam, "I would be very happy to go back to the envelope business."[4] The comment conveniently elided the Newton resident's long activist career as chair of Massachusetts Political Action for Peace (PAX), which had placed him at the forefront of many of the major campaigns and issues of peace and progressive politics locally and nationally, and earned him titles such as "dean of the Massachusetts Peace movement" and "Number One Suburban Do-Gooder."[5] The moratorium marked almost a decade of activity for Grossman, PAX and their brand of suburban peace activism. Since the early 1960s, the suburbanites in the campaign had worked within the political system, especially the formal channels of electoral politics, to stop the construction and use of nuclear arms and US military intervention. From H. Stuart Hughes's 1962 senate race, the presidential

Figure 5.1 Newton resident Jerome Grossman, who conceived of the idea of the Vietnam Moratorium, on October 14, 1969, the night before the event, which would become the largest protest in US history. Grossman, president of PAX and the owner of the Massachusetts Envelope Company, carefully cultivated an image of himself as an ordinary businessman and suburban father. As he told the Associated Press, "I think that I would not be able to stand it if I lost a son in a war like this." Photo by Bill Chaplis. Courtesy of Associated Press Images. © 1969 The Associated Press.

campaign of McCarthy, opposition to the construction of antiballistic missiles (ABM), to the election of Robert Drinan to Congress in 1970, the movement had a direct impact on policy and politics at the state and national levels. As events like the moratorium reveal, peace and opposition to the Vietnam War constituted the arena where grassroots liberal activists proved most successful at galvanizing widespread suburban support.

Student activists in both the Boston area and across the nation played an essential and central role, but were not the sole driving force in the moratorium or antiwar effort.[6] Many of the engineers and knowledge workers who benefited from the Cold War economy, professionals like Grossman, and suburban housewives contributed in essential ways to the movement and merged peace and antiwar activism with fair housing, civil rights, and environmental politics as core pieces of the political culture of the Route 128 suburbs and agenda of the Democratic Party. The grassroots peace movement in Boston emerged during the same historical moment and from the same geography as the fair housing and open space causes, and shared many overlapping outlooks, tactics, and membership bases. Groups like PAX, and the issues of peace and opposition to the Vietnam War, reveal the broad scope of suburban politics.

The peace movement's campaigns, however, like the fair housing, METCO, and open space initiatives, also embodied and perpetuated the class-specific tactics and spatial constraints of suburban liberal politics.[7] By focusing attention and resources on activities like the moratorium in order to create more suburban support for its cause, this movement also increasingly excluded lower-income and racial minorities along with many of the issues that concerned them from its frame of focus. Unlike issues such as civil rights and environmentalism, peace also represented the cause around which suburban liberal activists explicitly worked within formal party politics, which both influenced the discussion about the Vietnam War and forged a new base for political candidates from the Democratic Party. These strategies, therefore, helped to not only solidify Massachusetts' reputation as the most liberal state in the nation but also channel peace politics and Democratic candidates toward the priorities and agenda of white knowledge professionals like those who lived and worked along the Route 128 ring.

By the time of the moratorium, the Route 128 suburbs had earned notice as "nerve centers" of the national movement to end the Vietnam War.[8] The outpouring of antiwar activity in places like Lexington and Newton initially appeared incongruous, given the fact that so many families in the area had some ties to the defense industry and that the majority of local scientists and engineers depended on military contracts for their livelihoods. The Vietnam War forced residents to grapple with the central role of defense spending in shaping the economy and labor market of the Route 128 area. The MIT scientists and Raytheon engineers who got involved in activities such as the McCarthy campaign and anti-ABM movement exposed their complex position about the dependency of their professions on defense spending. These attitudes challenge the assumption that residents of Cold War suburbs who worked in defense-related industries, regardless of partisan affiliation, were uniformly and reflexively supportive of national security issues.[9] The decision of some of this contingency to voice their opposition to the war through electoral politics underscores their faith in the liberal ideal of working within the system to create change, which would have a reverberating impact on the direction of liberalism, the Democratic Party, and the antiwar cause.

The Hughes Campaign

H. Stuart Hughes's campaign for the Senate in 1962 served, in the words of E. J. Dionne, as a "trial run for the antiwar movement."[10] The campaign brought together suburban residents and students committed to peace, nuclear disarmament, and other liberal causes. It demonstrated to them the possibilities of using the formal channels of politics to mobilize residents and raise attention to their cause. In the immediate decades after World War II, the combination of the Red Scare and broader postwar culture of consensus had muffled existing pacifist activity in metropolitan Boston, as elsewhere. By the mid-1950s, however, a small minority of residents began to articulate a new set of fears about the threat of the Cold War and potential harm of nuclear weapons and started to call for disarmament and an end to nuclear testing.

Grossman typified the family-centered yet global worldview of early peace activists in the Boston suburbs. Although he supported both Henry Wallace and the Progressive Party in the late 1940s, by the 1950s, he was living with his wife and three young children in the Waban neighborhood of Newton, serving as president of Mass Envelope, his family's stationery-manufacturing company, and spending much of his spare time with his own children and serving as a Little League coach and PTA member.[11] It was his "very-child oriented" perspective coupled with his predilection toward progressive politics that sparked his initial concern about the dangers of nuclear weapons.[12] In the mid-1950s, a friend brought Grossman to an AFSC meeting in Cambridge where he learned more about the power and danger of nuclear weapons. The information hardened Grossman's opposition to the Cold War and nuclear armament, and soon after, he joined the National Committee for a Sane Nuclear Policy (SANE), which was working for a nuclear test ban. He quickly saw this group's approach as too passive and insular and decided that peace activists should use "the political system to bring issues and ideas" to the public "because we can't reach them any other way."[13] The Boston area's small campus movement had reached a similar conclusion and was starting to search for a suitable candidate.

In the spring of 1962, a delegation of professors and students met with Hughes, urging him to run for the US Congress on a peace platform.[14] The grandson of former US Supreme Court Chief Justice Charles Evans Hughes, the Harvard history professor served with the Office of Strategic Services in World War II, worked at the Department of State, and authored six books including *An Approach to Peace*, which presented his views on the need for unilateral disarmament. Hughes agreed to run, but suggested that the Senate was a more appropriate forum for the experiment since the US Constitution gave it more of a role in foreign policy. The Senate also proved preferable since Republican George Lodge, the son of Henry Cabot Lodge, and Democrat Edward Kennedy, in his first run for public office, were already engaged in a highly publicized fight for the seat left open by President Kennedy.

The peace activists knew from the outset that victory in this race of political pedigrees was a long shot. Yet they saw the opportunity as a means to obtain a wide forum for peace issues, show the failures of the federal government's action on the subject, and get the attention of the president, who had a personal investment in the race.[15] Though a registered Democrat, Hughes ran as an independent in order to stay in the race beyond the primary and draw attention to the fact that there was "a lack of new thought in both major parties on foreign relations."[16] Hughes's campaign platform focused on issues of peace, including limiting the buildup of nuclear weapons by the United States, ending all nuclear testing, admitting China to the United Nations, and alleviating the dependency of the Massachusetts economy on military contracts through conversion to a peacetime economy. No candidate since Wallace in 1948, either locally or nationally, had provided this serious a critique of Cold War liberalism. Hughes's stance quickly gained the support of both peace-minded students and a number of suburban residents such as Grossman, who eventually became the campaign manager.

Massachusetts's election law required an independent candidate running for state office to collect 72,500 signatures before July.[17] Chester Hartman, a young urban planner also active in the fair housing movement who others deemed an "organizational genius," served as the mastermind of the ten-week petition drive, recruiting hundreds of volunteers.[18] Hartman picked local coordinators, assigned each town a signature quota, and prepared detailed instructions on how to canvas. The project became most effective, according to Hughes, "along the arc of educated, prosperous suburbia running through the near-urban Brookline and Cambridge through Newton, Lexington and Lincoln," where "liberal-minded middle-class housewives did most of the work."[19] In Brookline, a group of young mothers, who were "deeply concerned about the kind of world their children are going to grow up in," quickly collected 5,200 signatures, which constituted

16 percent of Brookline's voting population.[20] Like the Good Neighbors for Fair Housing campaign that also occurred in 1962 in the same communities, the effort punctuated the effectiveness of suburban liberals in building grassroots support for their causes. The signature drive faced more difficulty outside the Route 128 suburbs and so Hartman recruited students from Boston-area colleges to supplement the local efforts. During the week, the undergraduates would canvas Boston neighborhoods and housing developments, and on the weekend Hartman chartered buses for caravans to industrial cities like Worcester and Springfield and smaller towns across the state. The campaign eventually gathered 149,000 signatures from residents in 262 Bay State municipalities.[21]

The outbreak of the Cuban Missile Crisis just weeks before the election presented a major setback for the campaign. In line with his platform, Hughes widely distributed a plan for peaceful resolution that suggested Kennedy abandon unilateral action and "act calmly" through the United Nations.[22] The unpopular position made Hughes's chances of victory even more remote. In the general election, Edward Kennedy became one of youngest people ever to win a Senate seat. Hughes became notable in another sense as one of the few candidates in US political history to receive significantly more signatures to get on the ballot than actual votes in the election. Hughes won 2.3 percent of the vote (52,000 votes), doing best in affluent suburban precincts such as Lexington, Brookline, and Newton, as well as parts of Boston and Cambridge, where he had the most active local organizations. Hughes blamed his lack of support outside the suburbs on the media's overemphasis of his position on the Cuban Missile Crisis. Campaign workers privately noted that Hughes had difficulty connecting to blue-collar citizens, and only seemed comfortable with voters at suburban cocktail parties where the guests shared his economic and educational levels, which clearly was not the best campaign tactic to win a seat in the Senate.[23]

Many participants interpreted the success of the Hughes campaign less in terms of the votes tallied than the three thousand volunteers it attracted.[24] In the election's aftermath, the members of the Hughes campaign decided to direct the momentum from the effort into a more permanent organization. At the inaugural meeting at Weston's town hall, the ninety people present agreed to establish "a new political voice in Massachusetts" dedicated to ensuring that the "sentiment for peace is clearly heard at election time."[25] The group, which recruited fifteen hundred initial members largely from the lists compiled during the Hughes campaign, called itself PAX (the Latin word for peace) and elected Grossman as the chair.

In PAX's inaugural year, the federal government established a Partial Nuclear Test Ban Treaty, which President Kennedy signed with the Soviet Union over the summer. The group celebrated the signing of the treaty, and took indirect credit for the role that the Hughes campaign had played in alerting the public, politicians, and the president about the issue.[26] Although he believed the announcement was gratifying, Grossman feared that the group would simply become like "the tennis crowd, the drinking crowd, the church crowd, the P.T.A. crowd," or other suburban social groups, and needed to take steps to turn itself into an actual movement.[27] He believed that leaders of the peace movement at the state and national level had overlooked the power that "issue-centered, middle-class liberals in the North" could wield in the political system if they forged alliances with "Negroes, the unemployed, the slum dwellers, the poverty stricken, and other groups of embittered citizens."[28]

PAX sought to answer the call of its leader by creating a congressional campaign in 1964 that fused the constituencies and causes of peace and civil rights. In this effort, it selected Noel Day as its potential candidate to run as an independent in the Ninth Congressional District. The thirty-one-year-old African American activist and social worker ran the Saint Mark Social Center and had co-organized the School Stayouts in February 1964. In fact, it was through their participation in the Stayout that many of the suburban members of PAX had gotten to know Day and thought that he would be the ideal candidate for their experiment. For two reasons, the Ninth Congressional District served as a "symbolically ideal" site for the endeavor. First, the district comprised sixteen of the city's twenty-two wards, including the all-white, blue-collar precincts of South Boston as well as 97 percent of Boston's black population and the only significant concentration of racial minorities in Massachusetts. Second, Speaker of the US House of Representatives John McCormack had represented the Ninth Congressional District for thirty-six years and run unopposed in most of the past elections. For PAX, McCormack offered the "perfect symbol of entrenched political power," and the challenge could draw state and national attention to the problems of poverty and discrimination within the speaker's home district.[29]

The organizers boldly envisioned the campaign "as the prototype of a movement" to bring together "the economically insecure and disadvantaged," "the civil rights movement, the peace movement," and "the radical intellectuals" in order to reveal "the relatedness of their interests and to create a new base of political power."[30] PAX provided over half the funds for the campaign and much of the organizing energy. The group encouraged "car-loads of suburban men and women," to go door-to-door, providing them "with maps, voter lists and moral support."[31] The Massachusetts Federation for Fair Housing and Equal Rights (MFFHER) supplied the Day campaign with the mailing list of its more than three thousand members, and groups like the Lexington Civil Rights Committee brought Day to speak in the suburbs.[32] Despite this outpouring of support from suburbanites outside the district, the campaign floundered. The members of Boston's African American leadership failed to take Day's candidacy seriously. Leading African Americans interpreted the campaign as one run and financed by "white outsiders," and believed that the emphasis on peace issues gave it too much of a "middle-class flavor."[33] Day eventually received 7,440 votes, amounting to 5 percent of the overall total cast. PAX had not anticipated a win, but this poor showing exposed the difficulty of using the political system to build a diverse coalition around the issues of peace and civil rights and served as a challenge to the group's broader purpose.[34]

By the end of 1964, the US military presence in Vietnam quickly eclipsed and submerged these fundamental concerns and defined the future of PAX and the movement it represented. The escalation of the Vietnam War refocused the energy of PAX and the suburban peace movement, expanded its numerical ranks, and eventually gave it a more meaningful voice and presence within the sphere of electoral politics. PAX and its allies initially concentrated on inciting outrage to the war, especially in the suburbs. The related group Voice of Women–New England (VOW) proved especially important in that effort.

A group of suburban mothers founded VOW in 1961 to take local action against atmospheric testing and toward the goal of "a world without war"—an aim that represented a direct extension of their parenting responsibilities, especially their concern about providing the best future for their children.[35] A leading member, Rhona Shoul of Newton, had been politically active in college and then was a social worker, but after getting married had devoted her full energy to her family. Like Grossman, Shoul recognized the dangers that her young children confronted in a world of unnecessary militarization and decided to take action, joining the organization along with her close friend Louise Lown, who was the wife of the renowned cardiologist Bernard Lown, who would later win the Nobel Peace Prize.[36] VOW's early members also included Anita Greenbaum of Newton and many of the other members of the suburban fair housing movement who applied their activist experience to causes like the Hughes and Day campaigns as well as other peace and civil rights issues.[37]

VOW helped awaken opposition to the war within the suburbs, especially among women. Throughout the mid-1960s, the group became involved in a variety of activities including letter-writing campaigns, telephone chains, and an annual Flea Market for Peace to raise the necessary funds for members to attend the national protests in Washington against the war. VOW members also took part in protests closer to home, and along with the local chapter of the Women's International League for Peace and Freedom in 1966, began holding weekly silent hour-long vigils in the front of the Old State House in downtown Boston and on the Battle Green in Lexington.[38] As the war intensified, VOW members increasingly realized

Figure 5.2 "Stop the War" was a November 1967 picket held on the Lexington Battle Green by suburban residents to demonstrate their opposition to the escalation of the Vietnam War. Members of VOW and other peace organizations staged routine protests like this one throughout the Route 128 suburbs in the late 1960s against the Vietnam War. Photo by Urlike Welsch. Courtesy of the *Boston Herald* from the *Boston Herald-Traveler* Photo Morgue, Special Collections, Boston Public Library.

that the combination of their suburban image and social connections could provide both respectability and financial support to more radical causes. "We were comfortable middle-class women," Shoul later recalled. "If you've got these kinds of resources that a lot of people don't have, then you've got a responsibility to do something."[39]

VOW saw encouraging draft resistance as a main avenue through which members could assist the war effort. The group got involved in the case of Michael Ferber, a leader of the group New England Resistance who was arrested for burning his draft card and became a cause célèbre for radicals across the country.[40] The members persuaded school officials in Newton and Lexington to allow high school students to discuss their options and alternatives with draft counselors and, with a group of mothers from Roxbury, to extend some of these forms of draft counseling toward the black community.[41] The involvement in the draft resistance cause inspired Shoul and several other VOW members to encourage their own sons to become conscientious objectors.[42] Many members would also later engage in forms of tax refusal, withholding either all of their taxes, the projected sixty-nine cents per dollar that went to defense spending, or the 10 percent excise tax on their phone bills.[43] Although these actions clearly did not make a dent in the draft or the defense budget, they did help draw attention to the war's burden on American citizens and provided a symbolically powerful way for suburban residents to articulate their opposition to war. While the activities sponsored by VOW proved important in growing a large base of opposition to the war among residents of the Route 128 suburbs, many leaders of the peace cause believed it was electoral politics where white middle-class people could have the greatest impact.[44]

Grossman recalled learning about the Gulf of Tonkin invasion while standing outside Fenway Park protesting a speech by Barry Goldwater and saying to those around him, "Maybe we're picketing the wrong candidate.[45] By 1966, he and his collaborators had shifted their anger to the president, organizing a large demonstration when Lyndon Johnson came to speak in Boston. But they hoped to do more than simply picket. PAX took to heart the lessons from the failed Hughes and Day independent candidacies and realized that the group, which had grown from six thousand members in 1966 to over ten thousand by 1967, could be more effective by working within a formal political party.

As the 1968 election approached, Grossman saw a challenge to Johnson's hold on the presidency as a means for the grassroots group to direct popular opposition to the war into partisan political action. Grossman joined Allard Lowenstein and Curtis Gans of the Americans for Democratic Action (ADA) in their ongoing campaign to "Dump Johnson."[46] In August 1967, Grossman and his wife attended a dinner party where a fellow guest who was a close friend of Senator Eugene McCarthy of Minnesota asked Grossman what he thought about his chances for the presidency. Grossman responded enthusiastically, and the next day McCarthy himself phoned, asking him to come to Washington.[47] By January 1968, Grossman was commuting to Washington a few days a week to work for McCarthy as national director of administration, giving PAX early influence with the candidate and a great deal of oversight over the structure of the campaign locally and nationally.[48]

The national campaign organizers had planned to bypass the state's April primary, but Grossman and PAX persuaded the strategists that Massachusetts constituted "a hotbed of antiwar sentiment, with well-organized peace groups chomping at the bit to go work for a peace candidate."[49] Most journalists, both at the time and subsequently, focused on McCarthy's student supporters in Massachusetts. During the primary, however, Abigail McCarthy described her husband's constituency as "academia united with the mobile society of scientists, educators, technologists and the new post–World War II class."[50] The Massachusetts McCarthy campaign, led by Concord lawyer Paul Counihan, concentrated on targeting this constituency, building directly on infrastructure laid down by PAX and VOW.[51]

The McCarthy campaign offered many residents in the Route 128 suburbs, even those not previously involved in peace activism, a way to express their growing opposition to the war. Lexington's Bonnie Jones, active in both peace and civil rights causes, observed that most local liberals believed "in being part of the process, the so-called mainstream, and participating in it and trying to change it from within," and the McCarthy candidacy represented an effective means to do so. The campaign marked the first time that so many local liberals converged around a single issue. Jones explained that before the campaign in Lexington, "there were networks of people. The people I knew in town were active in similar political organizations—Civil Rights, Fair Housing—and they were sort of interlocked while other people in town got involved in the Democratic Town Committee, the League of Women Voters. The anti-war movement really bridged all of those in the suburbs."[52] The McCarthy campaign activities offered local residents a way to channel their frustration at the war and get involved in local social life incorporating seasoned politicos and political neophytes. One Lexington liberal activist later recalled, "People who I never think of as being active in politics got drawn [in]."[53]

Many of the McCarthy volunteers in Lexington and elsewhere engaged in defense work, which made the area's strong support for the avowed antiwar candidate that much more notable. Several observers remarked on the paradox of seeing "McCarthy for President" emblazoned on placards in the front yards of Lexington engineers and the bumper stickers of cars parked in the research parks along Route 128. For many of the residents with ties to the defense industry, however, this stance did not seem hypocritical. These scientists and engineers strongly opposed the Vietnam War because it was diverting federal research funds from other important projects.[54] Many of them were not uniformly opposed to war, but the Vietnam War specifically. Several engineers admitted to feeling like a "pawn" or "prostitute" having to work on projects they did not believe in, and some conceded it made them less ambitious and ineffective.[55] George Rathjens, an MIT professor, later sympathized with these scientists and engineers engaged in defense-related work. "They could go out and sell vacuum cleaners," he declared, "but if they wanted to use the skills they spent a lifetime acquiring, they didn't have much choice."[56] A few Route 128 professionals quit their jobs in protest of the war.[57] Yet many scientists and engineers instead opted to get involved in the McCarthy campaign and peace movement, which as sociologist Paula Leventman concluded, "made it possible for technical professionals to share community values and simultaneously absolve *themselves* of social responsibility."[58]

On April 30, 1968, McCarthy won the biggest number of votes in the history of the Massachusetts Democratic presidential primary—a higher tally than even Kennedy garnered in 1960.[59] Although McCarthy did not secure the national Democratic nomination, it revealed the processes of re-alignment among suburban professionals. In the general election, Hubert Humphrey did extremely well in the suburbs of Boston as well as in places like New York and Philadelphia that also boasted a large concentration of postindustrial professionals.[60] In the *Making of the President 1968*, Theodore White agreed that the voting patterns of "educated, technically trained elite" in the Northeast portended a new political trend challenging the older "rule of thumb" that all affluent suburban residents automatically supported Republican candidates.[61]

Grossman and his allies saw the McCarthy campaign as a major success in confirming the viability of working through the political system to achieve their goals. McCarthy's candidacy had not only issued a career-ending blow to Johnson but also placed antiwar issues at the center of the election and the Democratic Party's agenda. Likewise, the campaign had increased support and infrastructure for the opposition to Vietnam in the suburbs while demonstrating that "massive grassroots sentiment can be transformed into effective political action."[62] During the primaries, the press had dubbed the McCarthy style of campaigning, with its emphasis on grass-roots tactics and issues of social justice, as the "New Politics" in contrast to the "old politics" of the Democratic Party "Establishment."[63] This idea inspired the Massachusetts campaign leaders to take the new politics idea in both its name and practice when they formed Citizens for Participation Politics.[64] The organization embodied the direct influence of the McCarthy campaign and other suburban liberal groups like PAX and the MFFHER. While historian Allen Matusow later claimed that "being for McCarthy was the latest variety of suburban chic," CPP members and their allies remained committed to peace and political activism even after the campaign fell out of vogue.[65] CPP fortified the suburban peace movement and its dedication to operating within the formal channels of political power.

Hydrogen Bombs in Our Backyard

Soon after the 1968 presidential election, PAX and CPP mobilized a campaign to stop the construction of the ABM system. This effort ultimately redirected national defense policy, enhanced their shared cause, and provided a blueprint for subsequent action. The ABM issue dated back to the 1950s, when the Joint Chiefs of Staff first proposed a nuclear weapon shield. In 1967, Secretary of Defense Robert McNamara announced that the United States would proceed with plans for a thin ABM system called the Sentinel that would detect enemy missiles by means of radar and destroy them with thermonuclear warheads. Each of these warheads cost at least $1 million and would be a hundred times more powerful than the bomb dropped on Hiroshima. The plans called for fourteen ABM bases spread throughout the United States, with two in Massachusetts in the suburbs of Reading and North Andover, which were each about twenty miles north of Boston. Congress allocated the first appropriation for the project in the summer of 1968, and the military soon after broke ground on the 300-acre site in North Andover where it planned to place radar-tracking facilities, a power plant, military housing, and long-range Spartan missiles—160 acres of which sat on state forest land.[66] Many well-known scientists, including MIT provost Jerome Wiesner, had publicly spoken out against ABM construction, warning that such a shield could not stop a nuclear weapon. The issue proved more complicated, though, because Raytheon, the largest defense company on Route 128, had a sixty million dollar contract to build the missile site radars, and Lincoln Laboratory had supplied much of the research for the development of ABM technology.[67]

The members of Boston's suburban peace movement, long fearful about the threat of nuclear weapons and staunch advocates of disarmament, strongly opposed the ABM idea and by December 1968 turned their full attention to stopping it. CPP and PAX formed the ad hoc New England Citizens Committee on ABM with the goal of arousing widespread community concern in order to prevent the construction. The committee recognized that in the communities surrounding the proposed sites, including Andover, Lynnfield, Reading, and Wakefield, residents had voiced little opposition to either the Vietnam War or the ABM system, and voted consistently Republican.[68] The group, therefore, crafted a campaign strategy specifically to appeal to politically moderate local residents.

The campaign leaders developed an argument that combined the global threats of the ABM with more localized issues. Residents of Lynnfield, Wakefield, and North Reading received warnings that the site would affect their property values, water supply, flood control, public services, and television reception. For many citizens, these threats to property values and tax rates sparked more concern than potential nuclear radiation. Residents like Edward Kendrick of Wakefield and Beverly Bjorkman of Reading got involved in the anti-ABM effort because they feared the installation would force local officials to change their zoning laws to allow apartments for army employees.[69] Activists stimulated further opposition by emphasizing that the site in North Andover sat on Massachusetts conservation land and had already destroyed 90 acres of timber, which aroused the growing environmental consciousness of suburban citizens. By early February, 80 percent of those Reading residents polled opposed construction of the system, which was an exponential leap from just a few months before.[70] The grassroots opposition to the system spread beyond Reading and Lynnfield. Residents in several towns, with the assistance and guidance of PAX and CPP, formed their own local anti-ABM committees. The anti-ABM movement became particularly active in the northwestern suburbs along Route 128 such as Concord, Lexington, and Winchester, both because of their relative proximity to the site and the large number of scientists, engineers, and MIT professors and researchers who lived there.

The anti-ABM campaign coincided with growing opposition to the war among the scientific community, especially at MIT, which was transforming into a cauldron of debate about Vietnam among both students and faculty. Noam Chomsky, the well-known radical linguistics professor and Lexington resident, later observed that even though MIT was in many ways "more conservative than Harvard" and other area institutions, the "faculty peace movement activity almost always came out at MIT." Chomsky believed this outpouring was due in part to that "in the sciences, you just have to have independence and creativity, or you'll have nothing."[71] This emphasis on independence led many faculty members to come to their own positions on the war and other issues, even if they might be controversial or go against the interests of the university. The Vietnam War had brought into sharp focus MIT's inextricable ties to the Pentagon. By 1968, federal funds comprised $173.8 million of the university's $214 million budget, with $111 million from the Pentagon alone.[72] Leon Trilling represented the attitude of many faculty members who criticized the inflexibility of military contracts, which established external agendas and made scientific research too connected to the booms and busts of defense policy. In 1967, the METCO founder and aeronautics and astronautics professor circulated a memo to his department urging his colleagues to consider pursuing research for civilian goals instead.[73]

In late 1968, a group of faculty members had formed the Union of Concerned Scientists. The group's founding document asserted that the "misuse of scientific and technical knowledge presents a major threat to the existence of mankind" and issued a "call on scientists and engineers at MIT, and throughout the country, to unite for concerted action and leadership."[74] The members had implored their colleagues to "devise means for turning research applications away from the present emphasis on military technology" and "toward the solution of pressing environmental and social problems."[75] On March 4, 1969, the Union of Concerned Scientists coordinated a controversial nationwide strike or "research stoppage" of scientists to protest the government misuse of scientific knowledge in the war embodied by the ABM system. The roster of speakers included George McGovern and Harvard professor and Nobel laureate George Wald, who gave an impassioned speech against ABMs and nuclear weapons more broadly. Many of the professionals in the Route 128 area had ties to MIT, and it undoubtedly influenced their attitude toward the issue.

Since several residents worked at labs or companies that might have benefited financially from the ABM contract, the issue once again exposed the tension many of these people experienced between their professional responsibilities and political beliefs. "It's strange to work on something you hope will never be used," an engineer developing the ABM system declared. "If you decided to be an engineer, the only money is in working for the military."[76] The ABM issue, in particular, created a dilemma for engineers and scientists between the abstract sense of creating global security and their more immediate concerns about providing economic security for their families. The anti-ABM effort, like the McCarthy campaign, offered a means for engineers and scientists to voice opposition to the war and defense-spending decisions without having to quit their jobs in protest. The contributions of engineers and scientists to the anti-ABM campaign simultaneously supplied local groups with heightened scientific knowledge about the dangers of the system. The local committees combined this information with a discourse of taxes, property rights, and children in order to further provoke opposition. The committees circulated flyers with dire warnings such as "Missile Sites Near Concord" and "Hydrogen Bombs in Winchester's Backyard? The Pentagon Wants to Put Them There," and urged local residents to "let your voices be heard in Washington" and "remember it is your tax dollar at work."[77]

The Ad Hoc Committee and local groups also continued to work within the formal channels of government in order to prevent construction of the ABM system.[78] The letter-writing campaign and other forms of lobbying proved extremely powerful means of changing defense policy. Senators Kennedy and Brooke both responded to the demands by local citizens, and publicly expressed doubts about the efficacy of the Sentinel system. Kennedy deemed the proposal a "serious mistake" and "waste of money."[79] The entire Massachusetts Senate passed a resolution voicing grave concern and calling for the suspension of construction until there was a reevaluation.[80] All these officials expressly stated that they were responding to the "rising tide of public opinion."[81] By the time the US Congress put the issue to a vote, many previously uncommitted politicians in Massachusetts and other parts of the nation opposed further development of the ABM system.

Local interest in the ABM issue waned as a protracted debate over the system ensued in Congress. The United States eventually established an ABM treaty with the Soviet Union in 1972, in which both countries agreed to surrender the rights to protect populations and weapons through such systems.[82] Though it took years for representatives to terminate the project officially, by late 1969 the Pentagon permanently abandoned plans for the sites in Reading and North Andover. A year later, Governor Francis Sargent reached an agreement with the White House and Department of Defense to develop a state park on the former North Andover ABM site.[83] The Massachusetts Department of Natural Resources decided to transform the area already excavated to hold the missiles into a swimming pool. On announcing the plans, which the federal government agreed to subsidize partially, Sargent proclaimed, "The Commonwealth will be able to develop what has become an albatross around the neck of the Defense Department to a valuable addition to the State's park system."[84] The short- and long-term outcome ultimately provided a potent example of the possibilities of ordinary citizens to work for peace causes and change state and national policy.

Household Word

The anti-ABM campaign demonstrated to Massachusetts peace groups the political potential of galvanizing moderate suburban citizens and led directly to the idea of the Vietnam Moratorium.[85] In the spring of 1969, PAX met to discuss how to build on the grassroots model it had established in the McCarthy and ABM campaigns in order, in the words of Jane Webb, to "do something to turn people on—to take a symbolic act to dramatize the people's opposition to the war."[86] Business executive Betram Yaffee suggested that PAX prepare a mass demonstration six months in the future where Nixon would be handed an "ultimatum of some kind" to deliver on his campaign promise to end the war.[87] Jerome Grossman expanded on this idea, proposing a "deadline demonstration." He suggested that activists pick a day when to expect Nixon to withdraw troops, and if the administration did not do so, then people around the country would launch a one-day general strike to halt the wheels of commerce in protest of the war, similar to what the MIT scientists had sought to do at the university the previous month.[88]

In early May, PAX sent a "market survey" to over two hundred peace, labor, religious, and liberal organizations across the country about the possibility of a strike.[89] Labor groups immediately opposed the idea because it would mean that most wageworkers would suffer from a day without pay.[90] Sam Brown, a Harvard Divinity School student and former youth coordinator for the McCarthy campaign, responded favorably to PAX's idea of nationwide action. Brown believed that the "real seedbeds of anti-war sentiment were the college campuses and the white-collar suburbs," and knew from his experience with the McCarthy campaign that these constituencies would find a strike "too militant."[91] Brown suggested that PAX organize a day of discussion and debate and call it by the less forceful "Vietnam Moratorium."[92] The planners capitulated, and while they abandoned the strike idea, the organizers decided to stage the protest on a Wednesday in October to dramatize that it marked a "refrain from business as usual."[93] PAX members placed Brown in charge of coordinating the national effort. Brown soon moved to Washington, where he formed the Vietnam Moratorium Committee, recruiting David Mixner, David Hawk, and Marge Sklencar to help him mobilize college campuses.

At the same time, Grossman and PAX concentrated on plans for Massachusetts and decided to primarily target the suburbs just as they had done during the McCarthy and ABM campaigns. The campaign concentrated mainly on "engag[ing] more moderate elements of the community who have recently adopted pro-withdrawal positions," because the organizers recognized the power of these residents to gain the attention of politicians.[94] Grossman and PAX stressed a local focus and believed that involving "the person who coached the Little League" or "person who helps them burn the leaves" would help destigmatize the issue for many suburbanites who had "not yet expressed themselves through political action."[95] Grossman, who emerged as the moratorium's public face, contributed to providing the event with a moderate and pragmatic bent. He told a local Chamber of Commerce publication, "I feel that as a businessman I have a vested interest in stability, and I think that one of the most insane things about the Vietnam War is the way it has insinuated instability in our society and our economy."[96] Lexington organizers took up a similar refrain in trying to seek local support. Dubbing the war "a tax drain," organizers asked rhetorically, "Should responsible citizens be involved in the quest for peace, or shall students be left alone in this desire?"[97] These statements provided an effective way to convince white middle-class suburbanites to embrace the moratorium-related activities.

The support for the moratorium in the Massachusetts suburbs took off even beyond the organizers' "wildest imagination."[98] "This is a real grass roots affair now," longtime PAX member Helen Rees of Newton declared. "The people have taken over."[99] The response from previously politically inactive communities and residents was largely due to the fact that many people had grown frustrated by the continuing war and Nixon's handling of it. "Last year I tried to get a McCarthy write-in campaign started in this town and I coudln't [sic] even get it off the ground," Joan Stander of Weston observed. "With the moratorium it's been completely different. We've had a wonderful response. I think people are just fed up to the teeth with the war."[100] Nixon's dismissal of the moratorium at a September press conference and declaration that it would not persuade him only served to further catalyze public interest. Natick housewife Pam Kaufman described the participants in her community as largely "the people who voted for him. How long can he ignore that?"[101]

The strong interest in the moratorium also had to do with the particular contours of the event and its lack of partisan or ideological affiliation. As

Grossman later explained about the participants, "You could be against the war for whatever reason you liked," but still find a way to get involved.[102] The positive response from formal institutions and professional groups also underscored the moderate tone and breadth of opinions that the moratorium came to encompass.[103] While McGovern and McCarthy had been early champions, support among national politicians spread. A delegation of twenty-three US representatives requested "special orders" to speak on the House floor on the moratorium's eve in order to keep Congress in an all-night session. At the state level, the Massachusetts Senate and its president, Maurice Donahue, officially decreed the day a chance "to give moral witness" against the war's continuation.[104] The selectman in even the area's most Republican suburbs released proclamations of support, and the traditionally conservative Boston City Council passed a resolution asking Nixon to end the war.[105] Governor Sargent used the events to stake out his own position, asserting that "the war in Vietnam must end" as it is "costing America its soul," which also defined him as one of the nation's leading antiwar Republicans.[106]

The outpouring of support from powerful institutions provided the event an increased legitimacy and respectability, yet it also further galvanized opposition from the Left. Along with the American Legion, Students for a Democratic Society (SDS) was one of the few organizations to publicly oppose the moratorium, and its response revealed fissures within the factions of the antiwar movement.[107] The Boston chapter of SDS dismissed the event as "just old wine in new bottles" and a "Cover not a Solution" that would "draw people away from real anti-imperialist fights" and "get them engaged in meaningless symbolic actions."[108] Even members of PAX grew concerned that perhaps the pendulum had swung too far and that endorsements deeming it a day of contemplation obscured the original focus of applying pressure on the Nixon administration. Several members began to joke that the event had become so "establishment-oriented" that before long, Nixon himself would announce his support. "When we first organized this we were afraid of getting co-opted from the left," Ken Hurwitz explained. "Now it's happening from the other side. The danger is from the right."[109]

The day of activities quelled these concerns and anxieties. More than fifty thousand suburban residents in 130 communities around metropolitan Boston took part in activities ranging from small church services, rallies, and candlelight vigils on village greens to readings of the eighty-nine thousand names of the war dead. Dozens of suburban high schools scheduled special seminars or let students out early to attend local activities.[110] A mixture of over a hundred thousand college students and suburbanites converged at a rally on the Boston Common. Keynote speaker Senator McGovern applauded those present at the biggest demonstration in Boston history as practicing "the highest patriotism." Frank Rizzo, a graduate student long active in the antiwar movement, declared of these participants and the event as a whole, "To even think five years ago about this kind of a crowd—and I don't mean just numbers because most of these people are middle class types—would have been impossible."[111]

The composition of the large crowd on the Boston Common also exposed some of the constraints on the organizers' vision. The participants in moratorium events in Boston and around the nation predominantly consisted of white middle-class college students and suburbanites. PAX and the National Moratorium Committee had consciously sought to target these groups. Yet by doing so, they excluded other parts of the population from getting involved.[112] Just five years earlier, PAX and other peace organizations had established efforts like the Day campaign to demonstrate the links between military spending and racial and economic inequality. While working on the McCarthy campaign, some members of the movement had suggested that the group try to engage the black community.[113] The campaign organizers basically ignored these ideas, deciding to concentrate instead on the Route 128 suburbs like Lexington, Concord, and Newton. The decision pushed the grassroots liberal groups further away from a structural critique of the war and creating coalitions that transcended race or class lines.

The middle-class emphasis of the moratorium and movement as a whole, therefore, concealed the racial, class, and spatial inequalities at the heart of the Vietnam War itself. Members of the suburban peace movement never publicly pondered the criticisms of the wounded veteran from Dorchester who pointed out the disproportionate number of war casualties from his neighborhood as compared to "fancy suburbs" such as Lexington, Milton, and Wellesley. "You'd be lucky to find three Vietnam veterans in each of those rich neighborhoods," the Boston soldier cracked, "never mind three that got wounded."[114] Historian Christian Appy calculated that while the towns of Lexington, Milton, and Wellesley combined had the same hundred-thousand-person population as Dorchester, those suburbs lost eleven residents in the war, while the city neighborhood had forty-two casualties and many more injuries. Appy discovered the same disparity throughout the affluent Route 128 suburbs, thus deducing that "boys who grew up in Dorchester were four times more likely to die than those raised in fancy suburbs."[115] At the same time, an equally skewed ratio of citizens in these suburbs got involved in the moratorium activities as compared with residents of working-class Boston neighborhoods like Dorchester.

The tactics of PAX and its allies consistently overlooked that for the most part, the war took an immediate burden and everyday toll on low-income communities, not white upper-middle-class suburbanites. A working-class mother who lost her son in Vietnam pointedly exposed this reality, dismissing the protesters, like those who organized the moratorium, as primarily "rich women" from "the rich suburbs" whose kids were in college rather than the military. "I'm against the war too—the way a mother is. The way a mother is, whose son is in the army, who has lost a son fighting in it," the women told psychologist Robert Coles. "The world hears those demonstrators making their noise. The world doesn't hear me, and it doesn't hear a single person I know."[116]

When most of the PAX members and their allied organizations looked at the crowds on the Boston Common or at candlelight vigils on suburban greens, they did not immediately notice the absence of the soldiers and their relatives. Instead, the moratorium confirmed to them the potential and importance of stimulating support for their cause among white middle-class suburbanites in order to gain mainstream attention. The moratorium received a great deal of media attention before, on, and after October 15, appearing on the front page of most newspapers across the country and on the major television network newscasts. *Time* magazine placed it on the cover of its October 17, 1969, edition with an article claiming that by making "moratorium" a "household word," the event meant that now "Nixon cannot escape the effects of the antiwar movement."[117] The moratorium marked an important turning point in public sentiment about the Vietnam War, especially in the suburbs, shifting the conversation away from not *if* but *when* the United States would withdraw troops.

The organizers still considered the moratorium a great success even though the event did not lead Nixon to declare an immediate and full troop withdrawal, as they had initially hoped. Groups like PAX, however, recognized the singularity of the event and decided not to participate in the larger protest that the student organizers staged in Washington in November 1969, which involved over five hundred thousand people and became the biggest demonstration in US history.[118] PAX and its collaborators instead returned to working more directly within the political system and electoral politics as a means to change the course of the war.[119]

"Our Father Who Art in Congress"

In December 1969, Paul Counihan, the former chair of McCarthy's Massachusetts campaign and his local anti-ABM committee, who would also emerge as a leading advocate for affordable housing in the suburbs, hosted a meeting at his Concord home of "politically aware" residents to discuss ways to make the priorities and representatives of the Democratic Party both more socially liberal and explicitly antiwar. As Counihan later explained, "The moratorium's day was done. That's why we moved over to finding a candidate."[120] Despite the heightened liberal and antiwar activity in Massachusetts, traditional Democrats who largely supported the direction of US foreign policy continued to dominate its congressional delega-tion.[121] The activists saw Massachusetts's Third District as the ideal place to apply their new strategy and demonstrate how congressional races could both build grassroots support and shape national policy in opposition to the Vietnam War.

The district had traditionally consisted of small rural and blue-collar towns in the central part of the state, but reapportionment in 1967 had dropped two clusters of western towns from the district, and added the suburbs of Newton, Concord, Lincoln, and Weston along with Watertown and Waltham. Seventy-one-year-old Philip Philbin, a hawkish Democrat "party hack" who served as vice chair of the House Armed Services Com-mittee, had represented the district for twenty-seven years.[122]

CPP member and Newton resident Arthur S. Obermayer joined the quest to find the ideal candidate to challenge Philbin. Obermayer, a chem-istry PhD, was president of a Cambridge-based chemical research company called Moleculon. His company relied on Department of Defense contracts, and like many technical professionals, Obermayer deeply resented politi-cians like Philbin who squandered money on needless and dangerous pro-grams. Obermayer wanted to replace Philbin with a candidate who saw foreign and domestic issues in moral terms.[123] He thus conceived of an un-usual choice: Robert Drinan, a Jesuit priest and dean of Boston College Law School. Drinan had never sought public office, but had been an outspoken supporter of peace, civil rights, and other liberal issues including birth con-trol. When Obermayer approached him about running, the forty-nine-year-old priest agreed to throw his hat into the ring. Drinan believed that there was no bar to a "clergyman entering the political process," and said, "Perhaps now is the time." Drinan's candidacy immediately earned the enthusiastic support of many longtime suburban-based activists such as Grossman, who saw him as "a model of integrity, a brilliant speaker and a person of con-science" similar to H. Stuart Hughes.[124]

The group of activists enticed Drinan to participate in a caucus to bring together liberal voters in the district to select the candidate best capable of defeating Philbin in the Democratic primary. The all-day caucus took place on Saturday, February 21, 1970, in the Concord-Carlisle High School audi-torium, drawing two thousand citizens. Drinan joined a field that included three Democratic state representatives as well as John Kerry, a twenty-six-year-old Vietnam veteran making his first run for political office.[125] While the organizers invited all members of the Third Congressional District, most of the participants had ties to the suburban peace movement. After three rounds of ballot-based elimination voting, the field narrowed to Kerry and Drinan. Before the fourth round, Kerry withdrew his name, and Drinan went on to win the unanimous endorsement of the caucus as the candidate most likely to achieve success in the September primary.[126]

The organizers and participants at the caucus positioned the event and its success in context to earlier efforts. Grossman saw the caucus as the direct culmination of three previous activities: "the McCarthy organization, the Moratorium organization and the Citizens for Participation Politics organization." PAX member Ray Dougan acknowledged that the caucus also showed the movement's new commitment to working more directly within the conventions of electoral politics. He observed, "The McCarthy campaign was energy without form. Now we are together in a really rational way."[127] The caucus had also not deviated from the middle-class white liberal and suburban composition of earlier activities. Several observers raised concerns about how the more moderate voters throughout the district would respond to the unusual first-time candidate who had the manners of an academic and wardrobe of a priest.[128]

The effort to secure Drinan's nomination in the Democratic primary developed into one of the most-well organized and suburban-focused campaigns in American political history. In one of his earliest decisions, campaign manager John Marttila commissioned a private polling company to conduct a systematic survey of the district. Drawing on its data, the pollsters from the Oliver Quayle Company instructed the organizers, "If Father Drinan has to select one major focus of the campaign, it must be the suburbs."[129] The pollsters' advice provided the basic outline for Drinan's campaign strategy. Marttila began operating on the belief that "one idealistic housewife is better than all the ward heelers you can get." He set out to prove that "you can campaign on principles" and "really battle for people's minds."[130] The Drinan campaign coordinated a districtwide canvas that combined simple old politics and new technology with the earlier tactics of the antiwar movement. During the summer of 1970, thirty-five hundred Drinan volunteers each went to an average of twenty-five homes and together made direct contact with residents in forty-one thousand households, or about 70 to 80 percent of the voters in the district, to determine the sentiment of the residents toward the candidate, and then focused on the people with the most potential to support Drinan.[131] In one of the earliest examples of targeted direct mailing, the canvasers entered the information from the conversations into a computer, and then followed up by sending literature and making phone calls tailored to individual's concerns.[132] Several pamphlets presented Drinan as not merely a peace candidate but an "issue-oriented" politician distributing information with his positions on the economy, health care, housing, labor, and drugs. In the overwhelmingly white and nonurban Third District, few, if any, of these pamphlets had racial minorities as the target audience and instead played directly to white suburban anxieties. One piece of literature featured a picture of a white, long-haired teenage girl in a skirt sitting on her floral bedspread, injecting heroin. The image sat above the tagline, "If the thought of hard drugs in your town makes you feel scared and helpless, maybe it will make you read the other side."[133] The back outlined what Drinan proposed to do about local and national drug abuse. Thus, if the priest's habit was not enough, the flyer assuaged any concerns that Drinan's opposition to the war aligned with radical proclivities.

The zeal of the middle-class suburban Drinan volunteers and their college-age counterparts resembled that of a "moral crusade."[134] On primary day, despite rainy conditions, the volunteers amassed an unprecedented turnout in suburban precincts. "If there was a reasonably liberal housewife at home with her four kids almost anywhere in the district," a *Boston Phoenix* reporter half kidded, "someone who would probably vote for Drinan but who would be discouraged by the rain—on election day she was probably called two, possibly three times. The Drinan group would provide a babysitter while she voted, and a ride both ways."[135] Drinan beat Philbin by a vote of 28,612 to 22,132. The *Globe* deemed it the "political upset of the year."[136] Not surprisingly, Drinan's strongest support came from the district's affluent suburbs.[137] He received 69.4 percent of the vote in Newton as opposed to only 29 percent in the more blue-collar Fitchburg. The low turnout in certain areas was also part of the campaign strategy. Based on the advice of the private polling analysts, organizers had decided that targeting more working-class communities would have brought more votes for Philbin and therefore avoided them altogether.[138] Further contributing to the upset, the incumbent had done little more to campaign than to distribute a few mailings and bus posters. The results revealed the potential of congressional primaries as a space for challenging party regulars and incumbents.

Drinan would go on to narrowly defeat moderate Republican John Mc-Glennon in the general election on November 3, 1970. In addition to the fact that Drinan was a priest and had run on one of the more "overtly dovish" platforms in the country, the campaign received national press attention for the way it showed a reshaping of the political process.[139] Drinan himself credited his victory to the fact that he and his suburban liberal volunteer base "were organized and computerized," and "held together right up until the last minute."[140] The election also signaled a shift of the suburbs toward the Democratic Party. "The conclusion seems pretty clear," Drinan stated of the results. "The belief that the suburbs are conservative and power blocks for the Republican Party just isn't the case."[141]

The success of Drinan's race marked for many in the movement the culmination of the efforts that had begun eight years earlier with Hughes's symbolic senate campaign. The difference in outcome of the candidacies exposed larger changes in the state, national, and international landscape between 1962 and 1970 as well as the increased effectiveness of the movement to work directly within the political system.[142] "We made peace the single-most important issue here and we made the politicians take us seriously," Grossman declared in the early 1970s. "Nobody's frigging around with us anymore." J. Anthony Lukas similarly observed that the movement was not the largest in the country, but that its impact went far beyond membership numbers because it constituted the "strongest, most effective, such force of anywhere in the United States."[143]

The moratorium and Drinan campaigns also confirmed that peace and opposition to the Vietnam War constituted the arena where liberal grassroots activists would experience their widest reach and their greatest ability to influence state and national elections. As Grossman and his allies increasingly shifted their attention to the upcoming presidential race and the campaign of South Dakota senator and moratorium speaker McGovern in 1972, it would further illuminate their ability to impact state and national politics. The effort would also expose both the increasing importance of postindustrial professionals in redirecting the economic and foreign policy agenda of the Democratic Party, and the success and constraints of the suburban liberal activists, especially as they confronted larger changes in the economy.

Part II Massachusetts Liberals

6

A New Center

Just days before the Massachusetts presidential primary in April 1972, the Association of Technical Professionals (ATP) invited Democratic candidate George McGovern to speak at Bentley College in Waltham, adjacent to the Route 128 highway. During the early 1970s, the end of the Vietnam War produced significant shutdowns and layoffs in Route 128 industry and offered an early foreshadowing of the nation's economic woes. The ATP had emerged to provide emotional support and political clout to unemployed scientists and engineers. McGovern spoke directly to the professional anxieties and political concerns of his audience. "Each one of you has an extra specialty that is unrelated to your training," he asserted. "You know a great deal about the nation's failure to plan for the transition to a peace economy." He used the speech to outline his ideas for economic reconversion, describing a "major re-ordering of spending priorities" for R & D. McGovern suggested shifting the focus away from war and nuclear weapons and toward improving the nation's environment, mass transit system, schools, and infrastructure would "guarantee a bright future" for workers in the tech industry.[1]

McGovern's ideas for economic conversion combined the foreign policy, economic, and quality-of-life agenda of many of the people who lived and worked along Route 128, and contributed to his victory in the Massachusetts presidential primary the next week. After his success in Massachusetts, McGovern refined these talking points in speeches around the country, especially in defense-oriented areas like Southern California where federal cutbacks had created similar economic uncertainty.[2] The support of suburban professionals spurred McGovern to victory in the California primary in June, which secured him the Democratic nomination the following month. McGovern eventually lost the November general election by an ignominious landslide. The lopsided results cemented the view of both McGovern as the far Left candidate and the iconoclastic liberalism of Massachusetts, which obscured another important implication of the electoral returns. The 1972 election results also signaled the shift of the Democratic Party campaign toward a new center in the suburbs and among knowledge workers, not just in Massachusetts, but across the nation. McGovern, in fact, represented the first Democratic presidential candidate to do better with white-collar rather than blue-collar voters, winning 42 percent of knowledge professionals nationally and making considerable gains in affluent suburbs throughout the country.[3]

In the aftermath of the election, many observers and strategists popularized the hypothesis that McGovern had lost because he had aimed to fight a nostalgic campaign tailored for the political causes of the 1960s rather than the realities of the 1970s. McGovern himself would even take this stance, agreeing with Hunter S. Thompson's suggestion that he had "run a sixties campaign in the seventies."[4] As McGovern's speech to the ATP reveals, antiwar politics alone did not serve as the driving force for McGovern's success in Massachusetts and seeming failure everywhere else. Throughout the race, McGovern connected opposition to the Vietnam War to economic, environmental, civil rights, and other social and quality-of-life concerns. The McGovern campaign did not represent the strategy of the "last election of the 1960s" but instead offered a precursor to the Democratic Party's growing commitment to knowledge workers and economic policies that touted the government's stimulation of private sector high-tech industry.[5] Democratic candidates Michael Dukakis, Paul Tsongas, Al Gore and McGovern campaign manager Gary Hart all later refined many of the economic ideas about military reconversion proposed by McGovern. This agenda promoted the individual skills of knowledge professionals as the means to ensure both economic growth and the viability of the party following the economic turmoil of the 1970s and Democrats' landslide defeat.

The McGovern campaign in Massachusetts converged with and benefited from the suburban-centered peace movement's drive to work directly within the political system to end the Vietnam War. It built on the base of antiwar sentiment that peace activists affiliated with groups like Massachusetts Political Action for Peace (PAX), Citizens for Participation (CPP), and Voice of Women (VOW) had cultivated in earlier mobilization efforts, such as the Vietnam Moratorium as well as the Eugene McCarthy and Father Robert Drinan campaigns. The McGovern campaign also offered activists from groups like PAX and CPP a way to extend their commitment to the grassroots ideals of "new politics."[6] The activists applied new politics ideas directly to reforming the presidential nomination process, serving themselves as delegates to the Democratic National Convention in Miami, which had long-term effects in changing the power dynamics within the party.

The 1972 election marked a key moment in moving the party's center of gravity toward suburbanites on Route 128 and away from its traditional urban union base, a shift that had been occurring in Massachusetts and other postindustrial regions since the 1950s. The McGovern campaign also symbolized and exacerbated the tensions between the Democratic Party and organized labor. As knowledge professionals became an ever more crucial Democratic constituency, the shift created impediments to developing both political coalitions and policies that promoted organized labor.[7] The

1972 election results along Route 128 ultimately demonstrate that scientists and engineers, like the ones who sat in the audience at the ATP event, and the issues that concerned them, had moved to the center of the party's new electoral coalition. At the center of the constituencies' priorities were now not just civil rights, environmental protection, taxes, property values, and opposition to the Vietnam War, but also inflation and especially unemployment. This set of concerns revealed that neither the 1972 election nor the Route 128 area was an outlier but a portent of the economic problems and political tensions of the decade to come.

Down and Out on Route 128

Between the time in which McGovern had delivered the keynote speech on the Boston Common in October 1969 as part of the Vietnam Moratorium to when he launched his presidential bid in January 1971, Route 128 had transformed from a sign of the nation's economic success to one of its growing problems. The Nixon administration's attempt to wind down the Vietnam War, coupled with stricter wage and price controls, severely shrank the number of contracts awarded to Massachusetts corporations by the Department of Defense and NASA.[8] The federal cutbacks hit especially hard in the R & D arena, which constituted most of Route 128 business. Raytheon, the largest beneficiary of defense dollars in Massachusetts, sharply reduced its missile production and research, causing its workforce in the state drop from more than thirty thousand to thirty-five hundred.[9] In 1969, nearly fifty thousand engineers and scientists worked in companies on Route 128, but in the following year alone, ten thousand technical professionals lost their jobs, and many others faced sharp salary reductions.[10] In 1968, the *New York Times* ran an article with the headline "Boston's 'Golden Semicircle'" that touted Route 128 as a "symbol of technological boom." Yet just two years later, another *Times* article titled "Down and Out Along Route 128" addressed the plight of the many newly unemployed professionals.[11]

Route 128 professionals represented a small portion of the overall unemployed workers in Massachusetts. Yet the image of the people whose expertise and skills had helped to build defense weapons systems, launch space discovery, and spearhead the dawn of the computer age standing in the unemployment line served as particularly distressing symbols of the growing crisis and received a great deal of media attention.[12] Companies often first dismissed mid-career engineers with advanced degrees because they had highly specialized skills and higher salaries and could be replaced by younger workers willing to work for less money. The layoffs had a reverberating effect on families throughout the Boston suburbs. The wife of one Lexington engineer told the members of the couples club at Hancock

Congregational Church, "We just live day to day." Similar comments, the *New York Times* reported, could be heard at "dinner parties, church meetings and country clubs in Needham, Wellesley, Newton, Waltham, Weston, Lincoln, Concord, Bedford, Burlington and other suburbs that border Boston's Route 128."[13] Even for residents who maintained their jobs, the torrent of pink slips among their neighbors and colleagues spread a sense of doom.

Labor activists saw the new employment instability and sense of despair less as a crisis than as an opportunity to reach out to engineers and scientists who had long proved an especially difficult sector to organize.[14] By the early 1970s, less than 6 percent of the nation's engineers belonged to a union.[15] A small minority of engineers and scientists believed that collective action would provide the only means to create meaningful change, prevent large plant closings and layoffs, and establish standardized practices.[16] The vast majority of engineers and scientists still saw unions as antithetical to the emphasis on independence, objectivity, and the meritocratic principles of advancement through skill that defined their professions. "Unions kill creativity" and "destroy critical judgment," and "Engineers want to be and should be individualists ... and unions cater to the masses," represented typical responses to inquiries about organizing.[17] When engineers and scientists had joined unions, it was often less out of a sense of solidarity with fellow employees at the company, and instead a means to protect their distinct and specialized position.[18] Sociologist Paula Leventman found among engineers that "a veil of professionalism blunted awakening class consciousness," which prevented them from joining an organizing drive, even among those Route 128 employees who had lost their jobs.[19] *Science* reporter Deborah Shapley was herself even blunter, contending that an "inevitable snobbism" of engineers toward the "blue-collar connotations of unionization" was one of the main impediments.[20] She also believed the division between engineers who had maintained their jobs and those who were unemployed might have created a further barrier. An official from the largest professional engineering association similarly observed, "The only ones who are yelling about the unions are the ones that got laid off." The official offered another reason for the fields' low rates of unionization: "Engineers tend to be more management-oriented than labor-oriented anyway."[21]

These types of responses to the possibility of unionization showed the challenge of creating a sense of commonality and solidarity across skill and economic class lines, even among people who had lost their jobs due to a similar set of causal circumstances. Although law, medicine, and academia did not experience the heightened level of unemployment in the early 1970s, a similar set of factors had made the drives for unionization in the fields in which the majority of Route 128 residents worked equally difficult. Unlike many business owners or executives who often voiced open hostility to all organized labor, many knowledge professionals did not overtly or theoretically oppose unionization among blue-collar workers but saw it as incompatible with the skills and objectives of their own careers.[22]

While Route 128 engineers and scientists might have eschewed collective bargaining, they did not entirely dismiss collective action. Some instead turned to forming grassroots groups that fell more in line with the prerogatives and organizing strategies of postwar liberalism and suburban politics. The spark for this type of organization occurred when laid-off Needham resident Gerald Wallick told his local minister, "I was a successful engineer. Now I don't belong. I don't fit anywhere."[23] Reverend Charles Lemert of the First Unitarian Church, also one of the founders of the local fair housing committee, encouraged Wallick to create an organization in Needham to serve as a combination discussion group and placement service for others in Wallick's position. The concept quickly spread to towns along Route 128, including Topsfield, Sudbury, Wayland, Bedford, and Lexington, often founded by a group of unemployed professionals with the help of a local minister.[24] Like the fair housing movement's lists of units available to potential African American buyers, the placement component of the self-help groups relied on area contacts to generate possible job opportunities. The groups also developed seminars based on practical advice, such as applying for unemployment, one-on-one résumé writing sessions, and information on starting small businesses.[25] The focus on specific skills rather than rights as employees or laborers underscored the political leanings of the activities and how they differed from unions.

The preference of the groups to refer to themselves as "self-help" organizations further signaled their ideological and political outlook. On the one hand, the term suggested the ways in which the groups operated independently of government or corporate influence, and instead developed along lines similar to the mutual aid societies of the early twentieth century. The term "self-help", on the other hand, spoke to their therapeutic dimensions. Paul Jackman, the founder of New Meadows in Topsfield and a former program developer at a Route 128 technology company, explained that his group was "not just an employment referral service. . . . We try to do more than that," Jackman said. "We try to deal with some of the real problems— some of the real raw emotional problems, like the ego."[26] With a headline "Groups Help Jobless Help Themselves," a *Boston Globe* story on the group featured a picture of a meeting at the Topsfield Congregational Church where white males in ties gathered in a circle resembling a board meeting. As the wife of one unemployed Needham physicist put it, "Misery loves company." The meetings helped her husband see he was "not alone," and had "somewhere to go and improve his self-image."[27] Like consciousness-raising sessions formed by suburban feminists around the same time and in similar spaces, groups like New Meadows provided the male participants with a forum to speak openly about their problems.

The optimistic name "New Meadows" sounded more akin to a suburban subdivision or substance abuse treatment facility and directly contrasted with the technological expertise of its members. The leader, nevertheless, placed the group's goals in distinctly professional and gender-specific terms. Jackman explained that New Meadows aimed to show each member that "he has a lot to offer outside of the technical world he's used to, outside of the military-industrial complex, that had been paying him well, but had also been restraining his creativity and confining his talents to a specialized area." These messages and "informal rap sessions" may have helped many participants improve their self-esteem and sense of cooperation, yet the focus of the discussion on the experiences of white male professionals also impeded their ability to see shared experiences or potential coalitions across gender, class, race, or spatial lines.[28] Reverend Robert Faramelli of the more radical Boston Industrial Mission publicly dismissed the self-help groups approach as "largely personal, when what we need is a systemic analysis of what caused this unemployment situation."[29] Faramelli's criticism underscored that, similar to the fair housing movement and other grassroots causes, the therapeutic dimensions of the groups emphasized shared experiences, but in ways that raised individual consciousness rather than class consciousness.

Despite the fact that the self-help component intimated a seemingly conservative ideological thrust, the unemployment groups maintained the fair housing movement's more characteristically liberal commitment to working within the political system to get legislation passed to advance a cause. When he founded the Lexington Seven, Ephraim Weiss, a laid-off physicist and one of the leading figures in the Lexington Civil Rights Committee, envisioned it primarily as a political action group to promote legislation to channel the resources of engineers into other professions. Weiss contended that the unemployment of R & D professionals "threatens to dry up a national resource essential to the economy, standard of living, its military strength and its role as a world leader."[30] His organization proposed using federal funding to redirect R & D professionals to the issues of pollution, transportation, public health, public housing, and urban renewal as well as to sponsor Fulbright grants for tech professionals to work abroad. The Lexington Seven had even met with their congressmen Bradford Morse to explore the idea.

As the unemployment groups like the Lexington Seven sought to expand their lobbying and placement activities, the ATP emerged as an umbrella organization, but eventually largely absorbed the local groups, reaching a membership of over a thousand members spread throughout the Route 128 area by 1972. Arthur Obermayer, who served as president of the ATP, gave the organization its particular focus on political action. A trained chemist, and the founder and president of the chemical research company

Moleculon, he was an active member of Newton's chapter of CPP, and as discussed in chapter 5, was instrumental in launching Drinan's 1970 congressional campaign. Obermayer was committed to electing candidates who promoted federal investment in science and technology for the purposes of peace not war. He provided the ATP with his extensive experience and contacts within both the science and peace communities as well as his connection to politicians like Drinan. Obermayer recognized that the local groups needed to focus not only on securing placements but also on job creation, and stressed using their political power to do so.[31]

Obermayer drew on existing ties to convince Massachusetts' leading liberal politicians to press the federal government to address the problems of unemployment among tech workers. Drinan made the issue of the "128 jobless" a top priority on entering Congress in January 1971, dubbing "the complete absence of any governmental plan or program for the re-training and re-employment of these highly skilled professionals" a "travesty."[32] Obermayer worked closely with Drinan on legislative proposals related to economic reconversion and organized several trips to Washington to meet with members of Congress.[33] In June 1971, twenty members of the ATP testified before a congressional subcommittee considering legislation to re-train scientists and engineers to work in new domestic areas, such as housing, transportation, health care, environmental pollution, and crime.[34] The ATP members offered impassioned and personal anecdotes of unemployed engineers and scientists pumping gas and putting up wallpaper to pay the bills. "None of us ever expected to find ourselves in the nightmarish situation which has enveloped the Route 128 area," Robert Fraser, an unemployed engineer from Lincoln told the lawmakers. "We find ourselves faced with a desperate situation which continues to worsen, and which is becoming too much for any of us, as an individual to handle."[35] During his own testimony, Obermayer declared, "The unemployed technical professional doesn't blame his former employer for his desperate condition. . . . He blames the Administration and its spending policies and priorities."[36]

Obermayer's testimony captured both the ways in which the organization sought to demonstrate the political power of its members and the fact that many technical professionals saw unemployment in partisan terms. The precarious state of the economy had left many engineers and scientists disillusioned and their political allegiances in flux, which proved particularly important with the impending presidential election. "My wife and I raised $2,000 for McCarthy. I was against the war in Vietnam, and against ABM, and for all the stock liberal causes. Now I don't know where I am," one laid-off engineer asserted in 1971. Another Route 128 engineer supported Obermayer's testimony, declaring of Nixon, "I'll vote for anybody but him. I am not political, but I would even go out and campaign for a Democrat."[37] Few of the Route 128 employees who participated in a roundtable organized by

Science magazine in June 1971 mentioned McGovern. Yet McGovern's opposition to the war and ideas for reconversion as well as his ability to tap into their sense of alienation would eventually earn this constituency's attention and make him an increasingly attractive candidate.

Long Shot

The suburban peace movement in Boston also proved crucial to getting McGovern's campaign off the ground. McGovern's candidacy both aligned with and enlivened the goals of activists affiliated with CPP and PAX, which was essential to his eventual success in the state. Following the moratorium and Drinan's election, many CPP and PAX members had committed themselves to harnessing the increasing suburban opposition to the war, and directing it toward electoral politics as part of their larger new politics agenda. By 1971, the CPP and PAX had turned toward the presidential election, and had begun the process of identifying appropriate candidates who shared their vision and antiwar attitude.

McGovern proved to be just such a candidate. Since arriving in the Senate from South Dakota in 1963, McGovern had been an especially outspoken figure for peace. He had opposed heavy military spending and the procurement and use of nuclear weapons and was the first senator to speak against US involvement in Vietnam. These ideas connected with the vision of many of the activists who had founded PAX around the same time.[38] McGovern firmly stood against the construction of the ABM system and had served as a speaker at both the March 4, 1969, research stoppage and for the events on the Boston Common in October 1969, helping to align him with the antiwar cause in Massachusetts.

McGovern was one of the nation's main proponents of economic reconversion. Soon after arriving in Washington in 1963, he worked with Columbia University economist Bernard Mehlman to draft the Economic Conversion Act, which would have required defense contractors to provide contingency plans. McGovern's bill had earned virtually no support in the Senate.[39] Yet he continued to promote the idea, and in the official announcement of his candidacy for the presidency, McGovern had dubbed "the conversion of our economy from the excesses of war to the works of peace" as "a major test of the 1970's" and suggested that it would create "work for all" if the nation "set about the job of rebuilding our cities, renewing our rural economy, reconstructing our transportation system, and reversing the dangerous pollution of our air, lakes and streams."[40] In April 1971, he cosponsored the Emergency Transition Allowance Act designed to provide both economic assistance and educational training incentives for "workers at all levels" experiencing the impact of the "current aerospace emergency."[41]

McGovern addressed several of these ideas in his 1969 speech at the MIT research stoppage, which earned the early support and assistance of members of the Boston academic community. His existing ties to members of that community helped McGovern, a former history professor himself, place early stakes in Massachusetts and develop many of the key points of his campaign platform. Members of the faculty at Harvard and MIT worked with McGovern to develop his "alternative defense budget," which offered a line-by-line reduction of every item he would eliminate in military spending, together representing a thirty-one billion dollar cut.[42] In the spring of 1971, Harvard and MIT faculty members organized several working groups in the fields of foreign policy, economics, and science.[43] Edwin Kuh, an economist and supporter of McCarthy in 1968, took the lead in developing the economic group with many of his Harvard and MIT colleagues, including John Kenneth Galbraith and Lester Thurow. The group soon expanded to include James Tobin of Yale and William Branson at Princeton.

Academic advisers like Kuh worked with the Democratic Town Committees of Concord and Lexington to host a visit by the candidate to the Route 128 suburbs in October 1971. The schedule of events included a cocktail party at the Lincoln home of Thomas Boylston Adams and a speech by McGovern at the Lexington Armory.[44] McGovern received "thunderous applause" from the 750-person crowd for his promise to end the war within hours of taking office, cancel the ABM system altogether, and reorder national priorities away from the military.[45] "Your visit to Lexington," Kuh reported back to McGovern, "began with a lot of support and wound up with a great deal more."[46] Although he remained a long shot, this interest propelled him closer to success in the Massachusetts primary. McGovern's reform-oriented platform, honest and moral reputation, and innovative ideas for conversion of wartime industry secured him the support of a growing contingent of employed and unemployed Route 128 area residents.

The senator recognized from the start of his presidential bid that "'chic,' suburban issue oriented liberals," like those who lived in the Route 128 area and were affiliated with groups like CPP and PAX, would supply invaluable financial and volunteer support.[47] In the winter of 1971, McGovern's campaign sent out two hundred thousand letters to grassroots contacts across the country, which yielded a million dollars and many interested individuals.[48] The solicitation earned early converts like Lexington residents and CPP members Emily Frankovich, Harriet Kaufman, and Alice Piece, who launched "Massachusetts Citizens for McGovern," using Piece's home as their first makeshift headquarters. In the winter and spring of 1971, the women organized informal meetings, distributed leaflets and bumper stickers, and published a newsletter tracking McGovern's activities.[49]

A presidential caucus organized by members of PAX and CPP provided the ever-growing McGovern forces with the first major chance to prove

Figure 6.1 Democratic presidential candidate George McGovern talking with Lincoln residents at a campaign reception at the home of Thomas Boylston Adams in Lincoln, MA, on October 30, 1971. McGovern engaged in early outreach in the Route 128 area, which proved important in helping him build support in the state. Photo by Frank C. Curtain. Courtesy of the Associated Press. © 1971 The Associated Press.

their legitimacy and cast an even wider net of support. In the fall of 1971, PAX and CPP members formulated a proposal to hold an event where participants could select one candidate to endorse in the April 1972 state Democratic primary, building on the successes of the Third District caucus and Drinan campaign.[50] The organizers enticed candidates to get involved by promising both an endorsement to the winner and the mailing lists of CPP and PAX, which amounted to fifty thousand names. Eugene McCarthy, however, was the only candidate to attend the event held on January 15, 1972, at Assumption College in Worcester. McGovern and Shirley Chisholm sent proxies. Edmund Muskie and John Lindsay declined to participate in any capacity.[51] The caucus produced a similar response from state party officials, who refused to endorse the event or its selected candidate, reinforcing the long-standing cleavages between the Democratic "regulars" and the "reformers" of CPP and PAX.[52]

Many local civil rights and labor activists took a similarly resistant view, but for different reasons. Marvin Harrell, chair of the Massachusetts Minority Political Committee, publicly criticized the organizers for not including "viable minority input at the planning stages" and not providing a way to present a "slate of minority issues." In a telling rebuke, Grossman responded that the caucus intentionally included "a certain kind of people—peace and reform Democrats—the people behind the revolt of 1968" and was "not trying to represent the entire state."[53] African American activists Hubie Jones and Byron Rushing nonetheless believed that only way to political progress would have "to be in alliance with white liberals," and they saw the caucus as the first step in that process. Jones and Rushing made a late-in-the-game push to get people of color to attend the caucus.[54] Frankovich, who by that time was state fund-raising chair for the McGovern campaign, also pleaded with Gary Hart to "get as many people to the caucus as possible," stressing, "We can't afford to lose it."[55] The results of the January 15, 1972 caucus proved the foresight of Rushing, Jones, and Frankovich. The three thousand attendees gave McGovern 62 percent of the votes. Chisholm received 23 percent, McCarthy got 13 percent, and Muskie, Lindsay, and Kennedy split the remaining 2 percent between them.

The victory marked a turning point in the McGovern campaign locally and nationally.[56] Although staffers conceded that the caucus in Massachusetts did not represent a cross-section of the electorate, McGovern's success at the event enabled him to lay claim to the title of "liberal candidate."[57] McCarthy dropped out of the race soon after, and McGovern received endorsements from similar conventions of liberal Democrats in Pennsylvania, Florida, and New York. The events together provided the first indication that McGovern was a serious contender for the Democratic nomination, and helped shift power away from the party establishment and toward anti-war new politics activists who had new momentum.

A Political Test Tube

After receiving the caucus endorsement, McGovern received a phone call from Ted Kennedy telling him that the support of CPP and PAX meant "you are on your way now. That group is hardworking and effective. They will kill themselves for you."[58] Kennedy's analysis and prediction proved remarkably accurate. While most polls indicated a crushing victory for front-runner Muskie in Massachusetts's April primary, the newly fortified McGovern campaign sought to counter the statistics. Members of CPP and PAX borrowed the campaign model established during Drinan's successful run for Congress two years earlier, conducting extensive neighborhood canvasing across the state to identify McGovern supporters.[59] The process successfully excited, in the words of Hart, "those housewives and those students who spend nights and days organizing their neighborhoods. That's what wins primaries."[60]

The campaign did more than speak to students and housewives, however. It also focused on building support among knowledge professionals and blue-collar voters, who organizers had recognized would be equally essential to winning the primary. In the run-up to the April primary, the McGovern campaign intensified its outreach to the members of the science and engineering community in Massachusetts. The speech sponsored by the ATP in April 1972 was a key part of that effort. Some members of the audience had entered the Bentley College auditorium on April 17, 1972, skeptical of McGovern since his alternative defense budget had called for the types of cutbacks in spending that many saw as the main cause of the problems of the Massachusetts economy and their professions. In order to attract their support, McGovern drew on Obermayer's advice to make private sector innovation a more integral part of his reconversion agenda. The previous fall, Obermayer testified before Congress that small research corporations like the one he founded provided "a remarkable percentage of the important inventions and innovations," despite receiving far less attention and funding than behemoth corporations like Raytheon or Lockheed.[61] Obermayer believed that the way to stimulate high-tech innovation was by granting "liberal patent protection" to small businesses rather than giving contracts to large aerospace companies that were isolated from the civilian market.[62] McGovern built on these ideas in his ATP speech. He conceded many of the proposals for reconversion through improving mass transit and environmental protection were not as R & D intensive as traditional defense contracts. Instead, he suggested the need "to find effective methods of stimulating research in the private sector," especially "smaller technical enterprise," which "consistently produced far more than their fair share of important new ideas and innovations."[63]

Obermayer reported back to McGovern's legislative assistant in Washington that the "response from scientists and engineers" who were either in the crowd or read copies of the speech that the ATP later circulated was "excellent." He was "certain it produced a large number of McGovern converts."[64] McGovern's ideas appealed particularly to professionals who felt that they had little control over the type of opportunities available to them, which had forced them into work on defense weapons. Leventman found in her study of engineers and scientists that those most likely to support McGovern in the primaries, like those who had voted for McCarthy in 1968 and had opposed the Vietnam War, were most likely to feel like "innocent pawns" in the military-industrial complex.[65]

The McGovern platform's combining of opposition to the war with pocketbook worries about high property taxes, inflation, and especially unemployment tapped into the sense of alienation of blue-collar people, who campaign organizers had understood would be essential to winning the Massachusetts primary in particular as well as the party nomination. The campaign made a concerted effort to appeal to blue-collar voters by staging events at manufacturing plants and the homes of Irish Catholic families.

McGovern's campaign scheduler later explained, "We understood the importance of identifying with the historic FDR party component."[66] McGovern
used the campaign stops to highlight some of the more economically populist dimensions of his campaign platform. This strategy had already proven
successful in Wisconsin, where McGovern had captured the early April primary with strong support not just from suburbanites, youths, and African
Americans but urban workers and farmers as well.[67]

McGovern's qualified support for court-ordered busing posed a particular challenge to his campaign to win traditional Democrats in Massachusetts, especially in Boston's heavily white blue-collar wards.[68] During campaign stops McGovern placed the issue in economic terms, telling a group
of working-class voters in Boston that Nixon and George Wallace concentrated on busing to make the public "forget about unemployment and inflation and crime and make us think that Public Enemy Number One is the
old yellow school bus."[69] McGovern also staged an event at the Dorchester
home of Boston City Hall housekeeper Mary Houston. McGovern told the
assembled reporters about how Houston spent 14 percent of her paycheck
on the property taxes on the modest house, which he declared proved the
need to "break the bond between education and property taxes" through
more education funding by the federal government.[70] Even though they
might have seemed to share little common ground with one another, such
ideas appealed to blue-collar workers in South Boston as much as professionals in the suburbs, since both were frustrated by the cost of state and
local taxes.[71] In fact, leading up to the primary, campaign pollsters discovered that across all households, McGovern's popularity in Massachusetts
drew from how he "related economic issues to the war so that many people
bagan [sic] to tie the two together."[72]

The strategy led McGovern to a decisive victory in the Massachusetts
presidential primary on April 25, 1972. He won an overwhelming 48 percent of the vote, more than twice that of second-place Muskie and third-
place Wallace. McGovern captured not just college students but also "the
huge academic-research complexes" and "better-educated, independent-
minded voters," or what one reporter identified as "growth areas of American politics."[73] In many of the state's heavily white working-class wards, especially in Boston, McGovern beat Muskie by a two-to-one ratio. Some
people actually credited Wallace in part for this success. Wallace had campaigned for just one day in the Bay State, but in the words of one reporter,
he "had just warmed up the voters" to support McGovern.[74] "Wallace is saying what the people want to hear," a New Bedford bar owner explained of
his voting decision, "but McGovern is saying how to fix it."[75] Although the
most committed antibusing activists endorsed Wallace, the primary results
showed that in 1972, two years before the mandatory desegregation of the
Boston schools, the war and economy trumped busing in influencing how

the majority of residents voted. In fact, at one South Boston precinct in the heart of Louise Day Hicks's congressional district, which poll watchers characterized as filled with "poor Irish" and "Catholic conservative" factory workers, McGovern received 45 percent of the vote, while Wallace received only 18 percent.[76]

Following the 1968 election, journalist Paul Wieck had dubbed Massachusetts as "a test tube in the Northeast," since "its politics reflect the basic tensions found in the late sixties between the guardians of the old order of ward politics and the new generations of cause-oriented voters along Route 128."[77] McGovern's success with both factions in the "test tube" of the Massachusetts primary augured well for his ability to gain wide appeal in other state Democratic primaries and the general election. *Boston Globe* political columnist Robert Healy observed that the election results indicated the rise of a new Democratic coalition comprised of "the young, the suburbanite liberal and the blue collar worker."[78] McGovern himself stated of the Massachusetts primary results, "We are forming a new center (of the Democratic Party)."[79] The campaign sought to use that message to strengthen his appeal in other states.

Peace and Jobs

The McGovern campaign aimed to replicate the coalition of blue-collar residents, college students, and suburbanites created in the Massachusetts primary throughout the country, especially in the key battleground state of California. It focused on making even tighter the links between the economy, the war, and employment in the minds of voter and the platform of the candidate. The campaign also made gaining the support of defense workers an increasingly central part of its mission and strategy. Obermayer continued to be integral to that effort.[80] McGovern campaign leaders later deemed Obermayer "by far our most valuable asset" in reaching out to the science and technology community nationally but especially in the Golden State.[81] In the spring of 1972, Obermayer took a trip to Southern California, where he met with employees at several aerospace firms. He reported back to campaign staffers that most engineers he talked to "would prefer non-defense work and see the weaknesses as clearly as you do in aerospace management and the defense establishment." Yet he also found that they were "desperately afraid" that McGovern's plans to cut the defense budget by thirty-two billion dollars would lead to more job loss.[82] Obermayer critiqued the "current McGovern program" as "much too general to satisfy an engineer." He suggested making the plan more specific by stressing the use of R & D resources to solve the growing energy crisis, which was of particular concern to the people of California. The McGovern campaign took this advice to heart. At the airport news conference to officially kick off his California campaign, McGovern did not discuss the antiwar position that had earned him headlines but instead highlighted his ideas about reconversion. "Peace, not war, is the only dependable employer," he exclaimed, promising that "preparation now for a peace-time economy," coupled with reforming the tax structure and reducing arms expenditures, "will free the resources to assure . . . a life of true security and real opportunity."[83]

McGovern took Obermayer's advice for making his platform more detailed to gain more credibility with engineers and other white-collar voters.[84] He was seemingly less concerned with the specifics of his economic agenda than other parts of his platform. The issue of reconversion remained, nevertheless, close to his heart and a crucial part of the campaign's strategy for winning the California primary.[85] In late May, the McGovern campaign formed the Committee on Peacetime Jobs, which was headed by the prominent labor leader Victor Reuther and included Senator Fred Harris, Clarence Gregory of the United Aerospace Workers, Engineers and Scientist Guild executive secretary Lois Williams, and Lester Lees, director of environmental control at the California Institute of Technology. Reuther explained the committee's mandate as concentrating on "ways to bring America's technical capabilities to bear on commercial needs," specifically "the current unemployment situation in aerospace industry."[86] The committee set about to "demonstrate to the technical community that such reconversion can be a smooth and secure process," and create a program for "a prosperous and technically competitive peacetime American economy."[87]

With the help of the Committee on Peacetime Jobs, McGovern refined his ideas of reconversion to fit the California context and gain the support of aerospace and other technical professionals. McGovern traveled through the state, giving a version of the stump speech he had first tested on engineers and scientists on Route 128. Speaking to workers at TRW, Inc., in Redondo Beach and gatherings of Lockheed employees in Los Angeles and San Diego, McGovern put a stronger emphasis on the specific problems confronting the aerospace industry.[88] The campaign passed out leaflets at Lockheed plants in California that declared "Your Job and Peace: If You Vote for McGovern, You Won't Have to Choose Between Them." The flyers also proclaimed that Nixon had "deliberately forced people out of work." McGovern announced a proposal to provide an immediate investment of ten billion dollars for two million jobs in transportation, environmental protection, and communications and to establish programs to protect 80 percent of displaced workers' income as they moved from wartime to peacetime production.[89]

In the California primary, McGovern even more pointedly linked the nation's heavy dependency on the military to pocketbook and quality-of-life issues as part of an effort to target not just aerospace workers but all

Figure 6.2 Democratic presidential candidate George McGovern outlining his plans for military reconversion to the employees of the aerospace company TRW, Inc., Redondo Beach, CA, on May 25, 1972. McGovern made a concerted effort to reach out to aerospace employees, combining the issues of "peace and jobs," based on the strategy he first cultivated in Massachusetts and that helped him win the California primary. Photo by David Smith. Courtesy of Associated Press Images. © 1972 The Associated Press.

suburban voters. The campaign included in McGovern's talking points more connections between the "growing congestion and pollution and estrangement in our suburbs" and the issues of employment and peace. In his speeches and campaign literature, McGovern discussed the ways in which his ideas for the aerospace conversion would take the "highly trained and specialized" skills of scientists and engineers to promote "quiet clean and dependable transportation systems" and other forms of energy production and environmental protection. He asserted that such policies would provide not only "more good jobs for California workers" but also a solution to "the acute problems of foul water and air, clogged freeways, mounting property taxes, shrinking energy supplies, drugs and crime, inadequate housing, which plague arms and aerospace workers and everyone else."[90]

The strategy expanded support for McGovern throughout California's sprawling postindustrial office parks and subdivisions. In Orange County, the McGovern campaign became the "liveliest political shop in town." Campaign leaders Marilyn Pelkofer, a forty-one-year-old former teacher, and Bettyann Roberts, the wife of a scientist and mother of four, oversaw a dedicated cohort of hundreds of housewives and college students who went door-to-door throughout the county's streets in an attempt to contact every local Democrat.[91] In total, the California campaign set up 283 storefront offices and sent more than ten thousand volunteers to visit more than two million homes.[92] These tactics helped boost McGovern to a narrow victory over Humphrey in the June primary, especially in white-collar areas.

As McGovern moved from long shot to front-runner and secured the California primary, journalists repeatedly dubbed him "the Goldwater of the Left."[93] McGovern and Goldwater immediately eschewed the comparison, claiming "Mr. Conservative" was more iconoclastic than his purportedly liberal counterpart. The connection, however, did expose that McGovern, similar to Goldwater, relied on a base of young and enthusiastic students together with science-based and other white-collar residents of "comfortable suburbia" to build a grassroots network from Massachusetts to conservative strongholds like Orange County and Phoenix. This base of support secured McGovern's position as the likely nominee going into the Democratic National Convention held in Miami Beach in July 1972.[94]

The Democratic National Convention

The 1972 Democratic National Convention revealed the direct impact of the reforms to the delegate selection process and the shift in the party's center of focus both in Massachusetts and the nation. The reforms offered another indicator that the party had increasingly prioritized the professional and technocratic skills and strategy of activists associated with CPP and PAX to the exclusion of traditionally Democratic groups and issues, especially those involving organized labor.[95] Following the 1968 election, many members of the party had voiced outrage that despite the fact that McCarthy had won more state primaries, Humphrey had still emerged from the Chicago convention as the candidate. As a result, the Democratic National Committee appointed the Commission on Party Structure and Delegate Selection to examine reform. The body, better known as the McGovern Commission, mainly sought to help state parties change their nominating processes, particularly by putting more of an emphasis on grassroots participation.

The McGovern Commission organized hearings throughout the country to gain input into reforming the process. When the commission came to Boston in July 1969, members of the local peace movement contributed to the dialogue. Jerome Grossman testified to "the overwhelming need for the deepest kind of reform of the party structure both nationally and within Massachusetts." He argued that the new system must take note of the shift in the Democratic nucleus from the white working-class in South Boston toward suburban middle-class residents in places like his hometown of Newton. "A new electorate is on hand," Grossman warned, "which is highly-issued oriented, demanding rapid change and non-responsive to the ethnic loyalties which have created the sinecures of so many current political figures."[96]

Samuel Beer, Harvard professor and former head of both the state and national Americans for Democratic Action, took part in the proceedings, and was surprised not by Grossman's statement but instead by the lack of testimony in Boston and elsewhere by party regulars and the traditional constituencies like labor and white ethnics, and by "the fact that Negroes and the people in the cities were not the slightest bit interested in the whole thing."[97] The absences indicated to Beer that the entire effort to reform the process "was really a suburban, white, middle-class movement," which would undoubtedly have an impact on the direction that the recommendations took.[98] The McGovern Commission eventually created a set of guidelines for state delegate selection designed to promote the fair representation of minority views, and ensure that the elected officials and party regulars could not assert control. The body urged that every delegation include among its ranks racial minorities, women, and young people and that the state central committees only appoint 10 percent of the delegates. The rules transformed how the Democrats selected their presidential nominee and would have wide-reaching effects.[99]

The reform process represented the changing role of organized labor in the Democratic Party and the McGovern campaign. As Jefferson Cowie and others have suggested, the McGovern Commission signaled and contributed to both the end of labor leaders as central kingmakers and power brokers in national Democratic politics and the fragmentation of labor's political voice.[100] The reforms angered AFL-CIO president George Meany, but his hostility had predated the release of the guidelines.[101] He and other labor leaders voiced open antagonism to the entire premise of the commission, and some had flat-out boycotted the hearings. McGovern would later remark that by "remaining aloof from the reform effort," labor "kept itself isolated from what had become the dynamic mainstream of the party."[102] As much as the guidelines revealed Meany and other labor leaders' intransigence, they also illustrated the attitude of postindustrial professionals toward organized labor. The commission's structures and reforms paralleled the position of many Route 128 engineers and other knowledge professionals about unions and their potential to corrupt the ideals of equality of opportunity, fairness, and individual skill. The short- and long-term effects of the changing power relationships within the Democratic Party and the delegate selection process would become especially clear in Massachusetts.

The McGovern Commission findings had propelled the ongoing effort of new politics groups to reform the state Democratic Party. In 1966, Massachusetts had passed a law that made Bay State voters' delegate choices non-binding and gave the parties the power to determine representation at the national convention. This law had effectively allowed the Democratic establishment in Massachusetts to marginalize McCarthy and his delegates from the national convention. The combination of the McGovern Commission's findings and grassroots lobbying pressure convinced the state legislature to reevaluate the process and eventually pass a law to remove the nonbinding stipulation and abolish the winner-take-all approach.[103] The Massachusetts State Democratic Party also voted to essentially remove itself from the delegate selection process.[104] These reforms placed a stronger emphasis on arithmetic and less on the ability to make backroom deals, thereby privileging the professional and technocratic skills and strategies of activists associated with CPP and PAX, which enabled them to assume an instrumental role in delegation selection.[105]

Since CPP and PAX leaders had actively participated in the reform process, they had the foresight to recognize that "the future course of the Democratic Party is also much involved in the choice of delegates."[106] Thus, at the same time that CPP and PAX campaigned for McGovern in the primary, members worked to develop district delegate slates that not only met the new rules for race, gender, and age balance but also were "truly representative of the peace and new politics constituency."[107] In the week before the primary, CPP distributed leaflets, sample ballots, and more than twenty-five thousand brochures emphasizing how diverse slates "could result in a spectacular change of the state and national party."[108] Many members of the groups themselves ran as delegates in their respective districts. Newton resident and VOW leader Anita Greenbaum's campaign literature explained that she and her fellow delegate candidates were not "professional politicians" but "conscientious citizens from the grassroots who wish to revive and democratize the Democratic Party."[109] Dubbing her "NOT YOUR EVERYDAY HOUSEWIFE," and declaring "Just as *McGovern's* record speaks for itself so does *ANITA'S*," the homemade campaign flyer also listed Greenbaum's participation in various peace and political activities, including a rap sheet of arrests at antiwar demonstrations.[110]

When McGovern won the state primary, it meant that Greenbaum, not Representative Tip O'Neill, would represent the state at the Democratic National Convention in Miami. O'Neill and the majority of the state's Democratic Party faithful, including Mayor Kevin White, Massachusetts Senate president Kevin Harrington, and future Governor Dukakis, had run as Muskie delegates, and when he lost, they did too.[111] Instead, the 153 Massachusetts delegates included a large contingent of liberal intellectuals, women, minorities, and young people as well as Grossman and many other members of PAX, CPP, and VOW. In perhaps the clearest indicator of the changing face of the state Democratic Party, when the delegation had met in May it selected Drinan as chair, Ruth Batson as vice chair, and as secretary Ron Deiner, a Harvard history PhD student about to take his general exams.

The Massachusetts delegation served as a microcosm of all delegates to the convention. The fact that 80 percent of the delegates who traveled by plane, train, and Volkswagen bus were attending their first national convention underscored the ways in which the combination of the reforms and the McGovern campaign had together fundamentally transformed the Democratic Party's image in just four years. The eclipsing of stalwarts like Richard Daley and George Meany by political neophytes changed both the tenor of the event and future of the party. Less than 10 percent of the delegates in Miami had union affiliation; almost two-thirds had not held even the most local office; between 15 and 20 percent were African American, Chicano, Asian American, or Native American; 38 percent were women; and about 25 percent were under the age of thirty.[112] The Massachusetts participants discussed the importance of taking part in the "unique experience" of "men and women, blacks and whites, and all kinds mixed together." "The best thing about the week in Miami," one delegate from the Route 128 area later enthusiastically asserted, "was being able to do political things day and night without your family around telling you what a stupid way to spend your time."[113]

The Massachusetts delegation symbolized both the Democratic Party's new composition and its new tensions.[114] Prior to the convention, the delegates proudly described themselves to the national McGovern campaign headquarters as "exceptionally passionate" in "pursuit of liberal ideology, our delegates are often short on pragmatism and may present a problem or two on the floor of the convention."[115] This depiction proved true. Several members of the delegation recognized that certain components of McGovern's platform, particularly on busing, abortion, party reform, and Vietnam, were too conciliatory and centrist for their taste. The fact that McGovern and his advisers made many decisions behind closed doors bothered the most liberal delegates even more because it betrayed his commitment to "new politics."[116] Leading dissenter Jean Rubenstein of the Lexington CPP stated, "If you are going to fill a hall with 'new politics' people, you've got to deal with the issues that brought them there."[117] The critique revealed the clear frustration that some grassroots peace activists experienced working within the structure of traditional political parties.

An informal discussion among the Massachusetts delegates on the convention floor unexpectedly escalated into an open disagreement. Just before the balloting, several new politics activists threatened revolt. They only capitulated after John Kenneth Galbraith counseled nomination night in the front row of the convention hall was an inappropriate time and place for a fight.[118] Similar tensions erupted among the delegates from New Jersey, while the Connecticut representatives narrowly averted a fistfight on the convention floor.[119] These disagreements exposed deeper fissures between McGovern supporters and the Democratic Party that would continue to haunt both in the future. More than a few Massachusetts delegates as well as their supporters at home came away from the historic convention feeling disillusioned rather than energized.

No Engineers for Nixon

In the Bay State and nationally, McGovern's campaign flagged considerably following the Miami convention, especially after vice presidential nominee Thomas Eagleton unceremoniously relinquished the post when the press uncovered his history of psychiatric treatment. The controversy lasted for three weeks and constituted, in the words of Bruce Miroff, "the greatest campaign fiasco in modern times," severely harming McGovern's campaign and reputation.[120] McGovern himself recognized that his support among residents in the "affluent suburbs" across country, the foundation of his success in the spring primaries, had waned by the fall.[121]

The McGovern campaign was determined to woo back its suburban professional base by reemphasizing economic reconversion and linking peacetime jobs and the federal government's spending on defense to everyday taxpaying and parenting concerns. In October, McGovern told a Connecticut crowd that his plan for eliminating pollution and building better mass transit, housing, schools, and recreation and child care centers, would require the services not just of blue-collar workers but also "every engineer, aerospace worker, every college graduate."[122] McGovern took Obermayer's suggestion to heart and promised that if elected, "no aerospace or defence [sic] job will be eliminated until a comparable civilian job has been created." McGovern also proposed changes to patent laws in order to "encourage vigorous free enterprise in the field of technology," which would both reduce unemployment and restore the US edge in the international trade balance on electronic products.[123] *New Scientist* magazine praised the proposals as the type of "radical shake up" that would "encourage technological entrepreneurs of the sort responsible for the Route 128 boom."[124] The promises reignited the support of science professionals across the country, but especially in Massachusetts. "You won't find many 'Engineers for Nixon' around here," one Boston area engineer exclaimed in the fall of 1972.[125]

The campaign in Massachusetts also remained vibrant due to the strength of the state Democratic Party. Following the Miami convention, McGovern's staff sought to repair the rift created during the caucus and primary between its supporters and state Democratic regulars. The campaign staged a "unity breakfast" in August and received endorsements and pledges of help from major operators, including Kennedy, O'Neill, and Hicks. In the

Table 6.1 Party Registration and 1972 Election Results in Lexington, Newton, and Boston

Town	Lexington	Newton	Boston
Total registered voters	15,744	51,356	274,178
Registered Democrats	34.9%	42.6%	71.5%
Registered Republicans	29.5%	22.6%	8.2%
Unenrolled	35.6%	34.8%	20.3%
Votes for McGovern	52%	59%	64%
Votes for Nixon	46%	39%	32%

fall, the state party mobilized its own grassroots network of local committees and district supporters in a range of campaign activities, such as voter registration, fund-raising, and canvasing.[126] Kennedy also threw his own popularity and that of his family in Massachusetts behind the candidate, and campaigned locally to invigorate party loyalists.[127] While the national McGovern campaign focused the bulk of its attention on other parts of the country, the combined efforts of Massachusetts party politicians and suburban grassroots volunteers filled the leadership void. Polls in the weeks leading up to the election placed McGovern with a solid ten-point lead in Massachusetts over Nixon, by far his best numbers in the country.[128] Although most polls and pundits had predicted Nixon with a strong lead, few anticipated the lopsided results that followed.

Building Something

On Election Day, McGovern carried the Bay State with a decisive 54.8 percent of the vote. Just as in the primary, McGovern did particularly well among students and blue-collar urban voters (capturing all twenty-two wards in Boston) and in the Route 128 suburbs, winning Newton by a two-to-one margin.[129] Other than the District of Columbia, however, Massachusetts was the only state Nixon did not win. The fact that it was the first time in American history that such an electoral aberration had occurred did not embarrass most Massachusetts residents but solidified their sense of the state's exceptionalism. J. Anthony Lukas visited Massachusetts a few weeks after the election and observed that it was "obsessed with its singularity." Buttons and bumper stickers reading "Massachusetts—We'd Rather Be Right," "The Lone Star State," "The One and Only," and "Don't Blame Me—I'm from Massachusetts" circulated on lapels and cars across the Commonwealth, further inscribing this sense of distinctiveness into the public consciousness.[130]

The focus on the state's exceptionalism overlooked the key trends that actually made the election results in Massachusetts align with national patterns, especially the growing importance of suburbanites and knowledge workers as major forces within the Democratic Party. From Westchester County, New York, the New Jersey suburbs, the Main Line of Philadelphia, and Montgomery County, Maryland, to Winnetka and outside Chicago, Los Angeles County, San Mateo and Marin counties near San Francisco, and the Pacific Northwest, the Democrats made considerable gains among affluent suburbs and educated professionals in both the presidential and congressional races in 1972.[131] Pollster Louis Harris found this constituency to "feel strongly about the quality of life, and want tougher measures taken to curb air and water pollution," tended to favor "legalized abortions" and were "committed to change—concrete and pragmatic, not ideological."[132] "This year McGovern is the tool in helping us build something," Mike Rappeport, a statistician, father of two, and Democratic delegate from Metuchen, New Jersey, presciently explained. "People like me are going to own the party in 1976."[133] By the mid-1970s, pollsters on both sides of the partisan divide, from Patrick Caddell to Kevin Phillips, agreed and identified voters like Rappeport as the new center of the Democratic Party.[134]

Writing in the aftermath of the 1972 election, national political strategist Lanny Davis argued in *The Emerging Democratic Majority* that the results in the Bay State represented not a sign of the party's failure but actually a blueprint for subsequent action. He confidently declared, "Massachusetts is a prototype of the new coalition of blue-collars, blacks and New Politics activists of which the Democratic Party is capable across the nation."[135] While this assessment might have indicated the party's key sources of votes in presidential races, it proved difficult to hold such a coalition together on other critical political, social, and economic issues. The challenge of sustaining such a permanent coalition indicated many of the broader forces in play during the election cycle. The 1972 presidential results solidified the image of Massachusetts, especially of its suburbs as bastions of liberalism. Yet the election also previewed the economic, social, and cultural troubles and divisions that would come to plague the state and nation throughout the decade. As the subsequent chapters reveal, these issues brought to light the contours and constraints of liberalism in the suburbs and beyond.

7

Open Suburbs vs. Open Space

"I have always thought of my community to be the bastion of suburban liberalism," lamented a Newton resident in 1970. "However the recent controversy over the Newton Community Development Foundation have shown my assumptions to be mistaken."[1] The commentator, Frederick Andelman, referred to the vicious battle that engulfed his suburb after the Newton Community Development Foundation (NCDF), a local interfaith organization, attempted to build five hundred mixed-income and government-subsidized units scattered across ten sites around the suburb. During the 1960s, Newton had garnered a national reputation for its progressiveness. *Newsweek* deemed the suburb a "seedbed for liberal causes, from vigorous antiwar activity to exuberant civil rights activity." Reacting to the suburb's identity of liberal distinctiveness, the chair of the affordable housing initiative had confidently declared, "If Newton can't do it, who on earth can?" The answer to this exceptionalist question soon became clear as the efforts to build the mixed-income project developed into a protracted nine-year controversy that proved largely quixotic. It led one disillusioned local resident to conclude: "I guess it's true that liberalism stops at your own driveway."[2]

Newton and the Route 128 suburbs stood on the front lines of what experts had deemed "The Battle over the Suburbs." At the outset of the 1970s, several observers identified "opening up the suburbs" as "the major domestic social and political battle of the decade ahead." Experts, politicians, and activists across the nation argued that exclusionary zoning and metropolitan fragmentation served as the root causes of the related problems of urban poverty and school segregation, and that the suburbs represented the next frontier in the ongoing struggle to create social and racial equality. This call sparked a three-pronged assault at the federal, state, and local levels. Groups of residents in the Route 128 area responded to the demands to address the consequences of suburban exclusionary zoning with a two-pronged strategy of grassroots mobilization and legislative action.[3] An outgrowth of metropolitan Boston's fair housing movement, groups created plans for the construction of small government-subsidized affordable housing developments like the one in Newton while simultaneously spearheading lobby efforts for the passage and enforcement of Chapter 774, or the "Anti-Snob Zoning Act."

The law passed in 1969 distinguished Massachusetts as the first state to try to curb the exclusionary zoning practices of suburban municipalities.[4]

Other Route 128 residents, however, saw the projects and laws as a threat to property values, tax rates, school quality, and open space, which constituted the very reasons they had opted to move to Newton and its corollaries. By the mid-1970s, a war of attrition ensued in town meetings, the state courts, and environmental agencies, which led developers to either significantly scale back or discard altogether plans for the mixed-income projects in the Route 128 ring and made laws like the Anti-Snob Zoning Act all but nullified. This trend paralleled what took place throughout the country, bolstered by the federal government and courts turning away from the cause as well. Whereas in 1971, *Newsweek* had dubbed the opening of the suburbs as a "close-to-home domestic war whose headlines dwarf all others in local newspapers," by the end of the 1970s the issue had faded from both the national and local spotlight.[5]

Although the failure to open up fell in lockstep with what occurred in municipalities across the country, the demise of the projects took on heightened meaning in the Route 128 area, whose identity had come to rest so heavily on the ways in which the communities were "bastions of liberalism" and distinct from the "ordinary suburb." Perhaps more than any other issue, the fights to create affordable housing illuminate the interlocking constraints that limited even committed suburban residents from challenging the forces of metropolitan fragmentation and changing entrenched economic, spatial, and racial structures. The battles that ensued in Newton and Concord in particular show the external challenges that activists confronted and exposed many of the internal tensions and limits of suburban liberal politics.

The housing campaigns suggest the obstacles to suburban liberals' strategy of working at the grassroots level and through the formal channels of government to challenge inequality. This approach was successful in securing policies such as fair housing laws, getting support for voluntary integration, and stopping highway and missile construction, but proved less effective at forcing other town members to come to terms with the consequences of exclusionary zoning policies and other forms of privilege. At the same time, for most residents who might have identified or been characterized as liberal, and even initially endorsed the initiatives, it was far easier to demonstrate their values by signing a housing pledge or placing a placard for McGovern in their front yard than to sustain interest in a multiyear campaign to bring a handful of affordable housing units into their communities. The problem became ever clearer against the changing political and economic backdrop of the 1970s. The fights brought to the surface the continued presence of a "silent majority" of conservative residents in strongholds of liberalism like Newton and emboldened them to be not so silent. The sharp rise in local taxes coupled with the downturn of Route 128 industry and the growing economic turmoil at the national level posed an even greater challenge as these circumstances made local residents across the political spectrum ever more protective of the seemingly imperiled privileges of suburban residency.

The desire of affluent suburbanites to preserve their individual quality of life and property values bolstered another traditionally liberal cause: environmentalism. In Concord, the long commitment to conservation issues intensified with the changing economic climate of the 1970s, since growth control measures served as a means not just to protect open space but also the local property tax rate. The construction of affordable housing represented a perceived threat to both these forms of preservation and propelled opposition to the developments. The quests for affordable housing did not upend economic exclusivity and concerns about property values and quality of life but rather made them ever more salient features of affluent communities like those along Route 128. These controversies and their outcome ultimately show that liberalism did not stop at the proverbial driveway of local residents, and instead expose the continuities in and adaptations of the political culture of the Route 128 suburbs and liberalism more broadly in the 1970s.

The Battle Opens

In the winter of 1968, the National Advisory Commission on Civil Disorders codified into a government report what civil rights activists had been warning about for over twenty years.[6] "To continue with our present policies is to make permanent the division in our country into two societies: one largely Negro and poor, located in central cities; the other, predominately white and affluent located in the suburbs," the commission ominously declared in the Kerner Report.[7] The majority of Americans and their elected officials would eventually ignore these powerful warnings. But the release of the report did spark an initial discussion of the need to increase the housing opportunities for people of color and the poor outside central cities. While the 1968 Fair Housing Act did not explicitly address the findings, the Housing and Urban Development Act passed that same year called on the federal government to increase and diversify housing in the suburbs.[8] When George Romney became secretary of Housing and Urban Development in 1969, he built on the discussion and made reducing the barriers of suburban exclusion a top priority.[9]

The Kerner Report's warnings compounded by the King assassination in April 1968 reignited a debate in the Route 128 area about how suburban residents could help alleviate the problems of racial inequality and unrest. Concerned citizens in Brookline, Newton, Lexington, Concord, and Lincoln all sponsored townwide study groups or forums to discuss the report's findings and, in the words of the Lexington group, examine "what bearing our community has on the ability of the metropolitan area as whole to meet the needs of the impoverished and minority-group."[10] The conversation in Concord had led residents to confront the fact that although its African American population had increased 188 percent from 72 to 208 people between 1960 and 1970, the vast majority consisted of white-collar professionals and their families. "The need now is for low-income housing," a group of residents concluded. "Suburbanites should work against resistance to such housing in their own towns and help those who might like to move out of the ghetto."[11] Concord citizens recognized that they could play a particularly important role in alleviating the interrelated problems of economic and racial inequality due to the town's proximity to companies on Route 128, whose jobs had largely eluded lower-income minorities in part because of a lack of transportation and affordable housing.[12]

The heightened attention to the issue of diversifying the suburban housing stock aligned with the shifting priorities of the local fair housing movement. Since the late 1950s, the local committees had focused on increasing racial tolerance by helping African Americans, but had come to see the limits of their endeavors. Many members of the movement had realized that the tactics were only effective in helping African American professionals purchase homes, and the Massachusetts Federation for Fair Housing and Equal Rights recognized that to achieve its goals, more affordable apartments and rental units in the suburbs were necessary.[13] The Federation thus urged its local chapters to initiate "aggressive programs" to implement the Kerner Report's recommendations.[14]

Residents in Newton and Concord led the charge to put these ideas directly into practice. In the spring of 1968, a bipartisan and interfaith group of local clergy, lawyers, academics, architects, and other white-collar executives with experience in fair housing and local politics established the NCDF. Robert Casselman, a former MIT faculty member with a background in state and local government, agreed to act as board chair. In the summer of 1969, the group opened an office and hired attorney Marc Slotnick as its executive director. The Concord Home Owning Corporation (CHOC) spawned from a similar group of local professionals with ties to fair housing and peace activism and expertise in law, finance, architecture, and engineering. The board included attorney Paul Counihan, a leading figure in the peace and McCarthy campaigns, MIT electrical engineering professor Richard Thornton, assistant dean at Boston University School of Law John Wilson, and Carl Koch, the architect of Conantum who was an innovator of modernist and prefabricated design. The organization elected as its president James Craig, who like Koch and many other members was a resident of the Conantum neighborhood. Craig also had over twenty years of experience as a commercial real estate executive, which would prove important as the organization sought to navigate bureaucratic channels of building codes and government funding.[15]

The projects underscored the simultaneous optimism and pragmatism of grassroots liberal activists about their ability to create change. The leaders of the two endeavors often confidently presented their projects as a model in shaping the future of state and federal housing policy. The CHOC stated that the project would "encourage similar efforts in surrounding communities," and the NCDF was even bolder, claiming that towns around the country would watch its response to "the nation's housing crisis."[16] At the same time, the leaders recognized that their approach would not completely solve the dilemmas of racial segregation, economic inequality, and metropolitan fragmentation, which in the words of Craig could only be achieved through "massive income redistribution."[17] Still, the leaders stressed that the programs represented a significant first step in contributing to a comprehensive solution. NCDF chair Casselman asserted that the Newton plan was not intended as the sole solution to metropolitan Boston's housing or urban crisis. The proposed project "can't even solve Newton problems," he conceded, but "if Newton can pull it off, then 20 other suburbs can do it too. That's 10,000 units. And that begins to cut into the metropolitan problem, which the suburbs have to help solve."[18] The battles that would emerge would prove the drawbacks of this localist, grassroots approach to opening up the suburbs.

The planners were as attentive to the national spotlight as they were to the local political culture and aesthetics of their communities, which the blueprints and promotional literature make clear. The designs marked a conscious departure from the modernist public housing structures erected in Boston and other urban centers immediately following World War II, and instead aligned with a more suburban aesthetic. The NCDF's plans consisted of two-story wood-frame townhouses that would blend into the existing built and natural topography of Newton and would be "low rent," but *not* "low cost" construction.[19] The plans included many trees, and every site reserved over 40 percent of the land for open space in order to uphold the suburb's reputation as the "Garden City." The NCDF promised that its scatter-site approach of ten developments ranging in size from thirty-five to fifty-nine units each spread through ten different neighborhoods funded by the Federal Housing Administration through Section 236 of the National Housing Act would not just help to disperse the burden. The scattering also provided a way to avoid "the obvious sociological, financial, and governmental problems of single-site, massive housing projects."[20]

The CHOC, which received funding from the Massachusetts Housing Financing Agency (MHFA), also sought to make the project uphold Concord's physical and philosophical identity.[21] Koch drew up the plans based on many of the same ideas and principles as his design for the Conantum neighborhood in the early 1950s. He and his team created a model for a fifty- to sixty-unit development of townhouses with clapboard frames, pitched roofs, and patios, in clusters around large landscaped courtyards. Paralleling many residents' sense that Concord was special and distinct from the mass-produced, uniform architecture of typical postwar suburb, the CHOC stressed that its design would create a "feeling of identity and individuality" and "human scale and variety," in sharp contrast to the associations with public housing projects and their perceived problems.[22] CHOC board members, like their counterparts in Newton, remained dedicated to maintaining Concord's "country environment," which they recognized made their community distinctive. The plans provided "maximum open space," and the design sought to make the physical structure and inhabitants of the project integrate into the existing community in order to have minimal effect on the property values or quality of life of the abutters and the town as a whole.[23] These plans aligned well with the existing architecture of Concord, and like in Newton, had involved the input of many experts. In both cases, the organization paid less heed to the ideas or concerns of potential inhabitants or involve those people in the planning process, which undoubtedly shaped the direction of the designs.[24]

The blueprints did anticipate the potential concerns of local residents, especially fears that the additional housing and new population would place pressures on the local tax rate and public schools. The organization limited the unit sizes to between one and four bedrooms and restricted the number of children housed in each development, in compliance with federal and state housing regulations. The CHOC estimated that this design would mean that the project would house at the most forty school-age children, which it calculated would cost about $41,000, or $1,035 per child.[25] Yet it believed that the amount would be equivalent to the revenue the town would gather from the inhabitants' taxes. The NCDF released similar estimates and suggested that the scattered-site approach allowed for the flexibility to coordinate placements with open classrooms seats.[26]

In order to defuse the racial and class anxiety that accompanied the terms "low-income" and "subsidized" housing, the promotional literature made other assurances that the inhabitants would not overburden the tax rate or cause a sharp decline in property values.[27] The CHOC had explicitly stated in its application for funding of the proposal that it hoped a "substantial proportion would be occupied by people living in the center city, particularly Blacks from the Roxbury ghetto area."[28] Yet asides about wanting to recruit some METCO families and a mention of "prejudice" represented the only racially coded references in either public proposal. Throughout their literature and public presentations, the NCDF and CHOC usually described the potential inhabitants as "young marrieds," "people who grew up here but cannot afford to bring their children up here," town employees who provided mail and sanitation services, but "whose wages have not

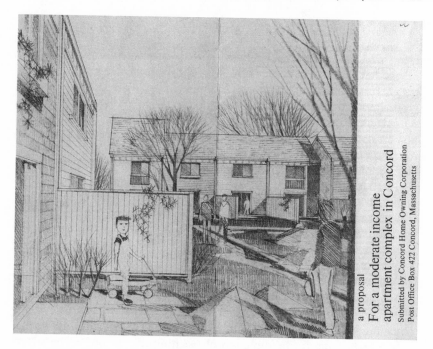

a proposal
For a moderate income
apartment complex in Concord
Submitted by Concord Home Owning Corporation
Post Office Box 422 Concord, Massachusetts

Figure 7.1 Architectural drawing on the cover of the "A Proposal for a Moderate Income Apartment Complex in Concord," ca. 1970, prepared by the Concord Home Owning Corporation as part of its effort to develop affordable housing in Concord. The design created by renowned architect and Concord resident Carl Koch countered the assumption that public housing would not blend in with Concord's "country environment." The plan called for townhouse style, low-rise housing with open space to promote "individuality." In an effort to confront potential racial fears and stigmas of Concord homeowners about public housing, the architect rendered the potential residents as white. Courtesy of the Records of Concord Home Owning Corporation, Concord Special Collections, Concord Free Public Library, Concord, MA.

caught up with the inflationary economy," and local senior citizens with fixed incomes who can "contribute to the life and vitality" of the community.[29] The NCDF also created mechanisms to give local residents oversight of the tenant application and selection process, and planned to set the rent for the units at 25 percent of a family's income, which it predicted would range from $120 to $170 per month, thus keeping the potential inhabitants well above the state poverty line. The CHOC hoped that at least 25 percent of the units would be moderate income, 25 percent low income, and 25 percent at market level.[30]

The endorsements from local residents in the local newspaper and at forums underscore how the plans complemented the aesthetic, fiscal, political, and exceptionalist sensibilities of both communities. One Newton resident asserted, "The scattered site concept is imaginative and realistic," and confidently predicted that it would avoid the "adverse social and economic effects [that] so often characterize massive single-site housing developments."[31] A Concord resident approved of the ways the plan would "preserve the charm of Concord," and not "relocate the most disadvantaged minority groups" or "convert Concord to a high rise town."[32] Many residents endorsed the ways in which the grassroots-based initiatives privileged the home rule and localist dimensions of suburban political culture. Stephen Adelson extolled the NCDF proposal as "Newton's solution to Newton's own problem." He believed that complying with the NCDF plan was a better alternative than enduring "some massive project enforced upon it by the State or Federal Government."[33] Local residents also approved of the fact that projects would not rely on an outlay of local tax dollars for the construction or subsidy of rents, which the federal and state governments would pay for, and the tenants would not be exempt from paying local property taxes. Some sympathizers, moreover, embraced the argument that projects would improve local services, especially the public schools. "There will be great benefits for our kids in going to school and playing with children from a more mixed background than that which they are presently acquainted," as one Newton couple suggested. "The Metco program has been a feeble step in the direction of teaching this lesson."[34] The strong statements of support were by no means unanimous. It proved easier for organizers to get government funding for the mixed-income housing projects than to change both local zoning codes for and residents' attitudes about such developments.

No Ordinary Suburb?

The fierce battle that erupted in Newton during the spring of 1970 over the NCDF's quest to revise existing zoning ordinances to allow for the sites demonstrated the wide range of potentially divisive issues encompassed by the mixed-income housing developments. Following the release of the plans, resident Robert Stiller formed an opposition group called the Newton Land Use and Civic Association (NLUCA) and recruited people throughout the city to join. Stiller firmly believed that "Newton owes nothing more to the city of Boston," and rejected the argument about the need for "urban ghetto blacks to get out of the ghetto and follow industry on Route 128." "Why must you live where your job is?" he asked. He denied, however, that "racism" drove his resistance, and instead stated that he was "opposed more strongly to densities, the negative impact on the schools, the higher taxes."[35] Stiller's group quickly began holding meetings, canvasing neighbors, and printing pamphlets in order to build support for their oppositional cause.

NLUCA flipped the terms of the argument about fiscal and property concerns put forward by the NCDF. The group's literature focused primarily on how the mixed-income housing would imperil all the features of Newton residents' high quality of life. One flyer asked, "Why must Newton with its limited amount of open space and one of the highest property taxes in the nation be selected for an experiment?" NLUCA contended that the scatter-site proposal would "overload" and hamper "Newton's ability to maintain its excellent school system," cause flooding and drainage problems, increase traffic flows, and remove local control from Newton residents over land use policy. Most alarming, NLUCA estimated that the new residents would require an additional annual outlay of $1 million to pay for educational and other city services, such as trash collection, snow plowing, and fire and police protection, which would add to the already "skyrocketing tax rate."[36]

These fiscal arguments took on heightened meaning in 1970, given that the local tax rate had grown rapidly over the previous few years. Newton residents had long taken pride in the suburb's superior services, particularly the local schools, and that had motivated many families to move there. The city's annual budget, however, had crept up from $36 million in 1967 to $50 million in 1970, causing the property rate to rise from $76.20 per $1,000 in 1967 to $113.00 in 1970, and reach $139.60 by 1972. Although still less than the city of Boston, the rate in Newton was two to three times higher than in neighboring towns.[37] The downturn of Route 128 industry, on which a large portion of Newton families depended for their livelihood, made this rise even more daunting, and made many citizens question the community's spending priorities.

The high tax rate and economic uncertainty had contributed to one of the reasons that Newton needed the affordable units in the first place, and the NCDF was sympathetic to some of the economic concerns of local residents. In establishing the need for the project, it stated, in noticeably passive voice, "economic forces over which the city has no control are conspiring to upset the traditional patterns, and cause changes that cannot be dealt with by traditional means."[38] Yet these same concerns and "forces" had made citizens even more resistant to any form of development, especially since Newton, like many other suburbs, had used single-residency zoning as a means to limit population, thereby lessening the demand and cost of municipal services. Reflecting the attitude of the many of those who opposed the plan, Mr. and Mrs. Bernard Gitlin firmly stated that Newton "cannot allow our tax rate to soar ad infinitum."[39] The NCDF was less understanding of people like the Gitlins who reduced the entire issue to taxes alone. "Taxes are a specious argument," NCDF director Casselman later remarked. "In reference to the potential impact it could have on schools or other municipal services," he declared, "anybody that feels housing is such a remote need that it is not worth a 2 percent tax increase is not looking at this problem rationally."[40] Casselman underestimated the extent of residents' fears about taxes and desire to maintain their high quality of life.

The plan also tapped into existing class tensions within Newton. Many residents believed that the developments would place a disproportionate burden on the more solidly middle-class portions of the city while the richer neighborhoods would be exempted. "You don't see any NCDF members upset because they put sites next to their homes," one abutter complained. "They all live in big expensive homes and are trying to ruin the neighborhoods of people like me, who have worked hard to be able to live in a moderate but comfortable home in Newton."[41] NCDF members and sympathizers tried to suggest that the sites extended to all parts of the city, and would actually help to sustain the economic heterogeneity of the community by providing more moderate-income people a foothold to stay or means to move into Newton. Rarely, however, did the potential inhabitants, either those who lived in or out of Newton, speak up in support of the project. Just as prospective inhabitants did not have much input in the planning process, seldom did they participate in the discussion about the proposal either in Newton or Concord. The debate over the developments remained dominated largely by people, for and against, who would never actually live in them, and as the fight intensified, it further marginalized the opinion of those who might.

Throughout the spring of 1970, the NCDF proposal sharply divided the citizens of Newton. Seven hundred residents signed a petition in support of the NCDF, which NLUCA countered by gathering nine thousand signatures in opposition to the proposal. Residents for and against the proposal overflowed the local newspaper with a profusion of passionately worded letters, and more than a thousand people turned out for the first public hearing. The discussion lasted until 1:45 a.m.[42] At another meeting that went until 3 a.m., the booing, hissing, and catcalls reached such a high pitch that local officials had to remind the audience it was not a baseball game.[43] The case soon reached the national stage. Secretary Romney praised the NCDF plan as the type of "rational" and "responsible" approach to the problem that he advocated.[44] Despite Romney's endorsement, the city's aldermen remained unconvinced, and officials voted against rezoning the ten sites to allow for the projects to proceed.[45] Although chastened, the NCDF did not abandon the proposal and pledged to continue the fight.

Are There Not Other More Suitable Sites?

The battle in Concord brought into even sharper focus the ways in which the land use policies and priorities of the Route 128 suburbs pitted the quest to create affordable housing directly against the agenda of the environmental movement. As chapter 4 explored, conservation had proved essential to Concord's identity and political culture. Throughout the postwar period, residents had inscribed their commitment to open space into a series of local laws and mechanisms, leaving little land available for potential development of even a single-site of mixed-income housing. Moreover, to build apartments Concord required a two-thirds vote of the town meeting as well as local Board of Appeals approval and confirmation that the project was "not injurious or detrimental to the area."[46] These factors made the CHOC's quest to realize its plans extremely difficult. The first barrier that the CHOC confronted was finding a plot of land for the project. Concord had only twenty-nine acres of land (0.025 percent of the total zoned land) available for multiunit development, and the few eligible parcels had either significant water problems or unwilling sellers.[47]

CHOC eventually found a 5.5-acre plot on Sudbury Road near the town center, for sale by the Wheeler family. Close to retail stores, local schools, and the commuter rail station, the site appeared an ideal location for a mixed-income project. But water and soil conditions on the property created a serious obstacle since the parcel was part of a ninety-acre watershed.[48] Town officials had, in fact, repeatedly denied prior plans to place apartments on the site, pointing to adverse water and soil conditions, and had tried unsuccessfully to buy the property for park and recreational purposes. CHOC members with backgrounds in engineering and ecology conducted feasibility studies of the property and concluded that the site's water and drainage problems could be solved, although they recommended that the units not have basements.[49]

The residents of the South Meadow neighborhood adjacent to the property did not agree, arguing that the five-acre plot sat directly on the watershed of Swamp Brook and exhibited the characteristics of an inland wetland, and any development would disrupt the area's already-precarious ecology.[50] The residents stressed that they already had overworked sump pumps and septic systems, and believed that the new development would further flood their basements and backyards. The South Meadow residents eventually adopted the name Swamp Brook Preservation Association (SBPA), a picture of a hand-drawn turtle as their logo, and a platform that conjoined concern about flooding and property values with an explicitly ecological appeal and a commitment to open space preservation. Edith Sisson, who lived down the road from the Wheeler land and taught courses at the Massachusetts Audubon Society, led this effort. Sisson and several other members who were engineers provided the SBPA with a level of heightened scientific expertise, especially about wetland ecology.[51]

The issue of wetlands had served as a pivotal concern of the conservation movement in Concord and the surrounding communities since the 1950s. The local conservation commissions had stressed the value of these areas as extremely rich natural habitats for wildlife, major sources of flood and mosquito control, and essential to the basic productivity of the larger ecosystem.[52] In addition to purchasing a great deal of wetlands throughout the Route 128 suburbs, the commissions had successfully lobbied for the passage of a series of state laws, which protected these areas and sparked awareness about the problem.[53] The Concord Town Planning Board had recognized that wetlands "provide essential public benefits" as a "giant sponge" that reduced "the need for costly flood control," helped "remove contaminants from water," and created a "wildlife habitat," and had taken several steps to protect them.[54] This existing recognition of the ecological value of wetlands bolstered the SBPA's arguments about the problems with the CHOC's proposal.

The members of the SBPA never denied the need for moderate-income housing in Concord, but, rather, emphasized a shift in the location of such a project. The SBPA even circulated a pamphlet throughout the community asking, "Are there not other more suitable sites in Concord for high density development?"[55] And Sisson publicly declared that she hoped the CHOC proposal would stimulate "serious and constructive consideration to problems of housing in our Town."[56] Despite these statements of sympathy, the SBPA took no affirmative steps to assist CHOC members in finding an alternative site for their project or to create a local coalition to change Concord's zoning policies so that they addressed both mixed-income housing and environmental concerns.

Throughout the postwar era, Concord town officials followed the land use principle that large-acre single-family zoning and open space acquisition offered the best means to keep the population density down, tax rate low, and quality of life high. Yet despite its aggressive agenda, Concord's tax rate continued to rise in the late 1960s. The rate jumped from $42.40 per $1,000 in 1968 to $51.40 per $1,000 in 1969. By 1970, the tax payment on a $30,000 house was $1,176—a 34 percent increase since 1965.[57] The town had taken steps to reevaluate residential property values in order to lower taxes, but the topsy-turvy rate gave the argument about limiting development renewed meaning and credence. In 1970, the Concord Finance Committee asserted that the "single most important" way to achieve "a long term stabilization of the tax rate" rested in "the withdrawal of vacant land from potential development" and promised that "a dollar spent one year for the purchase of open land will be returned many times over in saving on school and other municipal costs."[58] These ideas aligned with the agenda of the local department of natural resources, which around the same time had decided to revise and broaden its conservation and preservation efforts, since Concord was not "just another suburban town," but a "special case" as a "unique piece of national heritage."[59]

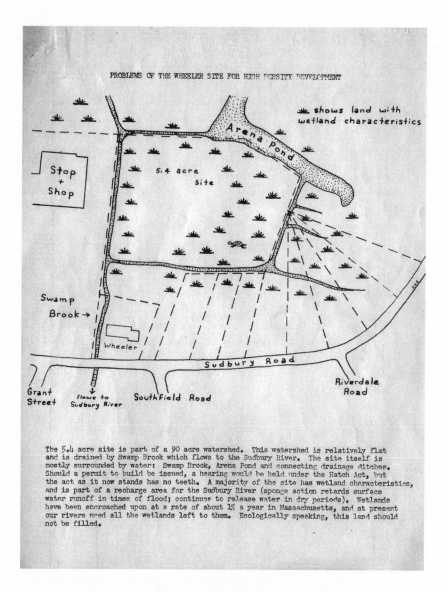

PROBLEMS OF THE WHEELER SITE FOR HIGH DENSITY DEVELOPMENT

🌿 shows land with wetland characteristics

Arena Pond

Stop + Shop

5.4 acre site

Swamp Brook →

Wheeler

Sudbury Road

Grant Street

flows to Sudbury River

Southfield Road

Riverdale Road

The 5.4 acre site is part of a 90 acre watershed. This watershed is relatively flat and is drained by Swamp Brook which flows to the Sudbury River. The site itself is mostly surrounded by water: Swamp Brook, Arena Pond and connecting drainage ditches. Should a permit to build be issued, a hearing would be held under the Hatch Act, but the act as it now stands has no teeth. A majority of the site has wetland characteristics, and is part of a recharge area for the Sudbury River (sponge action retards surface water runoff in times of flood; continues to release water in dry periods). Wetlands have been encroached upon at a rate of about 1% a year in Massachusetts, and at present our rivers need all the wetlands left to them. Ecologically speaking, this land should not be filled.

Figure 7.2 The "Problems of the Wheeler Site for Density Development" flyer created by Swamp Brook Preservation Society, whose members largely consisted of residents living adjacent to the site, to oppose the Concord Home Owning Corporation's plans to build a moderate-income development on land owned by the Wheeler Family in Concord. The flyer sought to show that the wetland characteristics of the proposed site made it unsuitable for the construction of the low-income housing project. Courtesy of the Records of Swamp Brook Preservation Association, Special Collections, Concord Free Public Library, Concord, MA.

The SBPA's pleas coupled with these larger concerns about limiting development persuaded the Concord Board of Appeals to unanimously reject the CHOC's building petition in April 1971, on the grounds that granting a permit "would not be consistent with local needs, as it could be detrimental to the health and safety of the residents of the Town."[60] The decision did not deter CHOC members. Following the ruling, the group, like its counterparts in Newton, began to shift its fight toward the structures of state government in order to use the mechanisms established by a controversial law recently passed by the Massachusetts legislature.

The Anti-Snob Zoning Act

The push for the passage of a state law challenging the exclusionary zoning powers of suburban municipalities both enhanced and constricted the efforts of groups like the NCDF and CHOC. A study sponsored by the Massachusetts legislature in 1967 found extensive evidence of the role of zoning polices in excluding minorities and lower-income families from the suburbs.[61] The study led the members of the legislature to acknowledge what many activists had already pointed out: Massachusetts had some of the most extensive fair housing laws in the nation, but the statutes had no oversight over local zoning ordinances. In 1969, Martin Linsky, a liberal Republican state senator from Brookline, began working with members of the fair housing movement to create legislation to challenge exclusionary zoning policies and increase mixed-income housing in the suburbs, which earned the indelible title as the Anti-Snob Zoning Act.[62]

The drafters were well aware of the strong resistance to subsidized housing and infringement on home rule, and took painstaking efforts to make the law able to withstand the objections of local communities. Thus, the provisions were somewhat vague and confusing, and did not fully restrict the exclusionary zoning powers of municipalities.[63] Instead, the Zoning Appeals Bill proposed a two-step administrative process. First, in communities where such dwellings comprised less than 10 percent of the total number of units, the proposed statute provided a mechanism for low-income housing developers to appeal local zoning, building, public health, and subdivision control regulations. Second, it vested the power to override local decisions in a state-appointed special committee operating under the Massachusetts Department of Community Affairs.

The fair housing movement became a central force in mobilizing support for the bill, spearheaded by longtime suburban housing activist Helene LeVine. She relied on existing contacts from earlier campaigns for the passage of state fair housing laws and the Racial Imbalance Acts. LeVine and her collaborators circulated a question-and-answer sheet directly designed to assuage the anxieties of suburbanites that echoed many of the arguments of the NCDF and CHOC.[64] Supporters stressed that the new laws would neither affect property values, tax rates, or the "character" of communities nor violate home rule. Proponents also sought to remove the racialized stigma associated with the issue of low-income housing. They promised that the bill would not create an influx of poor blacks into suburbs, and instead described the potential beneficiaries as "local municipal employees, police, fireman, teachers, young couples and returning Vietnam veterans."[65]

This strategy of depicting the issue in race neutral terms also extended to lobbying efforts. LeVine had recognized the importance of building cross-racial support for the law and initially tried to solicit participation from the area's African American community. Organizations like the NAACP and United Front rejected LeVine's outreach attempts because the bill did "not go far enough" and was "too middle class to deserve their support."[66] Many minority activists also took issue with the broader campaign to bring affordable housing to the suburbs because it would take away resources and government funding from inner-city areas.[67] After these rebuffs, LeVine abandoned her active pursuit for support of such organizations for fear of making the proposal into a "black bill."[68] While this strategy might have had short-term benefits, it contributed to preventing the formation of a broader metropolitan coalition committed to addressing issues of residential inequity.

The proponents of the Anti-Snob Zoning Bill instead discovered unlikely, but crucial allies among a group of Boston's white urban state representatives. This unusual support from traditionally racially conservative Boston legislators derived less from their newfound sympathy for the cause and more because they recognized the bill as an opportunity to "punish the do-gooder suburbanites" for their support of the Racial Imbalance Act four years earlier.[69] Suburban politicians and their constituents had served as the primary supporters of the legislation aimed at reducing segregation in public schools despite (or more likely because of) the fact that it did not affect their districts. Liberal politicians like Linsky initially balked at cooperating with legislators like William Bulger who they usually disagreed with, but eventually recognized that the Zoning Appeals Law's success depended on such endorsements and embraced these "strange bedfellows" in a "rather unholy alliance."[70] This "unusual coalition of liberals and urban conservatives" successfully overcame the strong opposition of many moderate and conservative suburban representatives, and led the Zoning Appeals Bill to passage.[71] On August 23, 1969, Governor Sargent signed into law Chapter 774 (or as it is more commonly now known, 40B).[72]

Chapter 774 earned Massachusetts the status as the first state to pass legislation directly targeted at spatial discrimination—an impressive accomplishment given the suburban slant of the Commonwealth of Massachusetts' population and legislature. As the Racial Imbalance Act had done four years earlier, Chapter 774 enhanced the Bay State's liberal image and reputation for innovative legislation. Also like the Racial Imbalance Act, the law had more symbolic than statutory power. To make the measure politically palatable, the drafters had preserved most local zoning control. Thus, in spite of the more active response implied by the term "anti-snob zoning," the act's enforcement was far more passive.[73] Unlike the policy that New Jersey would enact (under court order) a few years later that *required* the construction of affordable housing, Chapter 774 set quotas for units in terms of minimums, not maximums, and that percent only became enforceable when a developer proposed a project. Furthermore, the two-step administrative procedure injected methods of delay, which thwarted rather than eased the development of subsidized housing in the suburbs.

By the time the NCDF and CHOC began the Chapter 774 process, a wide variety of observers had started to question the law's effectiveness. Louise Day Hicks smugly noted in the winter of 1970, "Not a single spade of dirt has been dug yet to implement the new law."[74] A year later this fact was still true. *Boston Globe* reporter Anthony Yudis observed that the national press and HUD officials often praised the law as a "pacesetter" and "imaginative" model for other states.[75] Yet in an article titled "Anti-Snob Zoning Batting Big .000," Yudis contended that these favorable endorsements of Massachusetts as a "forward-thinking state" obscured the limitations of the law, especially its mechanisms for delay.[76] The statute placed the burden of launching an appeal on the developer, and few wanted to take the financial risk. The appeals period provided no return on the investment, and defeat in court would amount to a financial loss, which most nonprofit and limited-dividend developers could not afford. The NCDF and CHOC represented the few suburban nonprofits to show "the expertise" and "staying power" to sustain this process.[77] Many state legislators recognized these deficiencies, and proposed a variety of amendments to clarify and strengthen the original law. None of these provisions, however, were enacted.[78]

The bill's progenitor Linsky responded to skeptics by clarifying the Anti-Snob Zoning Act's legislative history and intent. "We never saw Chapter 774 as a miracle cure to the critical housing shortage," Linsky stated. "We wanted to make it clear to suburban communities that their land use allocations were not sacred, nor in a vacuum, and the legislature is taking a deep interest in their decision."[79] He suggested that the law acted as a "catalyst" for local initiatives, particularly since many communities misunderstood the law's provisions and, fearing a top-down intervention, decided to implement their own programs in order to reach the 10 percent mark.[80] Linsky and other proponents saw the act as successful in providing a "backdoor" means to create 10 percent affordable housing in suburban community and

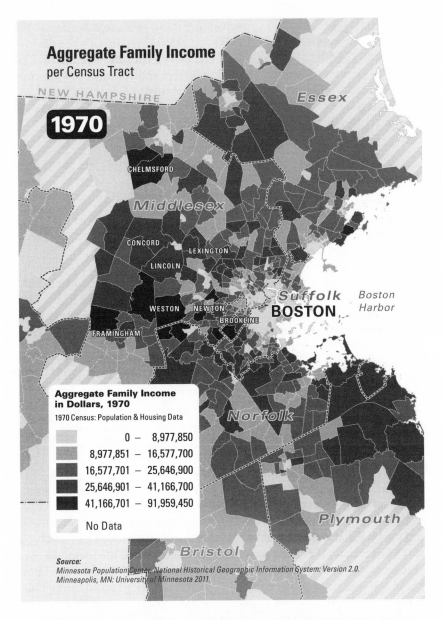

Aggregate Family Income
per Census Tract

NEW HAMPSHIRE

Essex

1970

CHELMSFORD

Middlesex

CONCORD

LEXINGTON

LINCOLN

Suffolk   Boston

WESTON   NEWTON   BOSTON   Harbor

BROOKLINE

FRAMINGHAM

**Aggregate Family Income
in Dollars, 1970**

1970 Census: Population & Housing Data

0 –	8,977,850
8,977,851 –	16,577,700
16,577,701 –	25,646,900
25,646,901 –	41,166,700
41,166,701 –	91,959,450
No Data	

Norfolk

Plymouth

Bristol

Source:
Minnesota Population Center, National Historical Geographic Information System: Version 2.0.
Minneapolis, MN: University of Minnesota 2011.

Figure 7.3 Aggregate family income in metropolitan Boston, 1970. The map highlights the economic inequities that existed between municipalities in part due to exclusionary zoning, and what the affordable housing movement and Anti-Snob Zoning Act aimed to combat. *Source*: US Census Bureau, *Census of Population and Housing, 1970* (Washington, DC: US Census Bureau, 1970).

combat the larger problems of exclusion.[81] Most of these towns' projects, however, concentrated on housing for the elderly, and actually constituted an effort to skirt the goal of economically and racially diversifying the suburbs. The opposition that ensued in Lexington, and continued in Newton and Concord, underlined the law's limited ability to force the majority of suburban residents to accept responsibility for the consequences of the exclusionary zoning policies of their own towns.

"Subsidies"

The controversy that erupted in Lexington shed light on how the combination of local resistance and a lack of federal enforcement together conspired with the limitations of Chapter 774 to further impede the effort to lessen exclusion in that town and its neighboring communities.[82] After several proposals by housing groups had failed, the town meeting finally approved a 106-unit project in 1971 intended primarily for moderate-income elderly white residents.[83] Homeowners in the neighborhood adjacent to the proposed project decried the vote and immediately formulated an aggressive opposition campaign, framing their resistance around issues of water drainage, traffic, tax increases, and the problems of high-density development in a single-family neighborhood. The developer's attorney, Frank Conroy, pierced through this seemingly mundane list of concerns. "The word subsidy is scaring people," Conroy observed. "People feel their taxes are too high. They think that subsidized housing is going to cost them money."[84] As Conroy's comment intimates, the opponents were either unaware of or did not want to acknowledge the multitude of ways that the federal policies had long "subsidized" the home purchases of white middle-class people, including the vast majority of Lexington residents. The Lexington abutters instead called for a townwide referendum asking if citizens upheld the town meeting vote.[85] Rainy conditions did not deter 15,317 people from going to the polls in May 1971, and they voted two-to-one to overrule the town meeting's approval of the proposal.[86]

The implications of the referendum extended beyond the fate of the specific project or even the town of Lexington to the future of affordable housing in the suburbs in general. News of the vote quickly spread throughout Boston's metropolitan ring as observers tried to make sense of its meaning.[87] Observers did not just focus on the outcome of the Lexington referendum because of the town's historic reputation as the "Cradle of Liberty" and a "tabernacle of current liberal dogma," but also because the vote came just a week after the US Supreme Court had delivered a serious setback to the cause of opening the suburbs. In *James v. Valtierra*, the Court upheld California's constitutional provision that local voters approve by referenda all public housing projects and adopted a very narrow interpretation of the equal protection clause that excluded zoning and other exclusionary practices from its purview.[88] The referendum and *Valtierra* ruling did not permanently shut the door on mixed-income housing in Lexington and elsewhere. Yet the two decisions showed how difficult it was to achieve without active federal and public support.

The type of resistance to affordable housing in Lexington occurred in subdivisions throughout the nation in the early 1970s, especially in the northeastern suburbs that shared a similar demographic, political, and physical profile. Several Westchester County towns thwarted the effort by Governor Nelson Rockefeller's Urban Development Corporation to bring low- and moderate-income housing into the suburbs using many of the same arguments about tax rates, school quality, and effect on the "character" of their communities.[89] A study of the area discovered that 53 percent of Westchester residents surveyed did not oppose subsidized mixed-income housing in principle, but 71 percent objected to such a development in their own community. One resident of the wealthy town of Bedford, NY, explained bluntly, "A project is a project is a project."[90]

President Nixon's stance on the issue of affordable housing construction in the suburbs further fueled this position. In June 1971, he released an eight-thousand-word "Statement of Equal Housing Opportunity," which endorsed local control over land use, advocated a limited role for the federal government, and encouraged suburbs to "provide fair, open and adequate housing" on a voluntary basis.[91] The list of towns actively resisting proposed developments clearly proved the impossibility of relying solely on voluntary action, but that did not chasten the Nixon administration. In January 1973, Nixon went even further and announced a moratorium on the production of all new federally funded housing projects. This announcement directly constrained the efforts to build mixed-income housing in the suburbs of Massachusetts and elsewhere in the nation even more. In addition to providing a new justification for suburban residents to oppose local projects, the new policy further circumscribed the plans of nonprofit developers who relied on Federal Housing Administration funding. Likewise, the moratorium coincided with the national recession, and state governments, including the Massachusetts legislature, began to cut back on funding mixed-income housing developments, leading to a sharp decline in new construction after 1973.[92]

The combination of these local, federal, and legislative circumstances led advocates in Massachusetts to see the state courts as their last and best means through which to challenge the structures of suburban exclusion. The groups aimed not only to create tangible units of housing but also to solidify permanent legal remedies to address the problem. The CHOC, with the heavy concentration of lawyers and law professors on its board, led the way in gaining the Massachusetts courts' sanction and enforcement of the Anti-Snob Zoning Act.[93] In March 1973, the Massachusetts Supreme Judicial Court upheld the constitutionality of Chapter 774 in a joint decision involving a petition by the CHOC and an appeal raised by the town of Hanover over a proposal to build eighty-eight units for the elderly. In a sixty-seven-page unanimous ruling, the state's highest court confirmed that Chapter 774 did not violate home rule and affirmed the power of the Housing Appeals Committee (HAC) to override local exclusionary practices.[94]

The verdict's impact reached far beyond Concord by potentially paving the way for thousands of units proposed and pending under the umbrella of Chapter 774.[95] By 1975, however, HAC had overruled twenty-two of the twenty-four local zoning cases that had come before it, but most of the losing parties had opted to appeal the decisions in state courts, further postponing construction.[96] Lexington residents became experts at the Chapter 774 appeals process in the 1970s. The Lexington Interfaith Housing Corporation's six-unit Interfaith Apartments broke ground in 1974 only after several rounds of court hearings and three years of delays.[97] Similarly, the Archdiocese of Boston endured appeals to the HAC and the Superior Court to get the town to issue a permit for the construction of a sixteen-unit mixed-income development on the St. Brigid's Church property.[98] Although both projects did ultimately prevail, the twenty-two units that resulted hardly seemed worth the significant time, resources, and legal fees that both of these organizations expended, and still left Lexington far short of meeting Chapter 774's 10 percent affordable housing marker.[99]

The NCDF's continued quest for its scattered-site project punctuated how the legal process did not ease but further delayed construction. Following its defeat in 1970, the NCDF recognized that an appeal under the Chapter 774 law represented the only way to keep its project alive.[100] In May 1971, the NCDF submitted a petition for a modified plan, funded by the state instead of the federal government, reducing the number of sites from six to ten, and the number of units from 508 to 367.[101] But just as the NDCF had revised its strategy, so too had its adversary. The Newton Civic Land Use Committee announced that it was "fully prepared to use all legal means available to prevent encroachment of NCDF in the city of Newton."[102] When the Board of Alderman again rejected the NCDF's proposal and the nonprofit appealed the case to the state HAC, NLUCA had the chance to fulfill this promise.

NLUCA used the hearings required by HAC to put the case into "slow-motion," thereby exhausting the NCDF's financial resources and options on the properties. Between August 1971 and October 1972, the HAC held 42 hearings in the Newton case. The NCDF presented its entire argument that the project was "consistent with local needs" within the first hearing, calling only one witness. Roger Cohen, a Newton resident and attorney affiliated with NLUCA, filibustered the appeal by calling an endless list of witnesses. Cohen himself, though, did most of the talking, leading one member of the HAC to declare, "The theater has been deprived of a considerable talent."[103] Cohen defended his tactics not as stalling but as trying to ensure that HAC interpret the law "correctly." His technique earned national media attention and served as a warning to other states trying to implement laws similar to Chapter 774. "The whole purpose," NCDF head Slotnick observed of his opponents, is "to wear us down so we'll run out of time and money."[104] The NLUCA strategy worked, but the dwindling of the large nucleus of local residents who had provided letters, made appearances at hearings, and contributed financially further weakened the NCDF.

The lack of sustained support for the development in Newton and elsewhere exposed important factors affecting the grassroots suburban campaigns for mixed-income housing in the early 1970s. The campaign lost a key anchor of institutional backing as many of the local liberally oriented churches experienced both internal tensions and declining memberships.[105] The majority of fair housing groups, which had proven instrumental in getting the issue off the ground and lobbying for Chapter 774, had also "lost their cohesion or dissolved" after 1970.[106] Many members of the groups had turned toward other issues like feminism and ecology, which scholar Michael Danielson dubbed a "severe competition for support" to "open-housing," especially among "better educated and affluent suburbanites."[107] The national recession, inflation, rise in unemployment, and increase in women entering the paid workforce, moreover, left many suburban residents with less time and money to devote to the increasingly improbable cause.

In the case of Newton, the combination of a lack of both money and local enthusiasm caused the NCDF to abandon five of its six sites. In 1974, six years after the NCDF had formed, the Board of Alderman approved plans for a fifty-townhouse project, which became the first low- and moderate-income development built in Newton.[108] The celebration of this accomplishment remained relatively muted. The NCDF succeeded in initiating a discussion about the need for mixed-income housing in Newton and easing the path for developers with more moderate plans for units for elderly residents.[109] Yet the developments remained a token solution to the problem and paled in comparison to the initial plans of the NCDF.

Open Suburbs vs. Open Space

The final chapter in the battle over the Wheeler property in Concord revealed that even for groups that weathered the anti-snob appeals process, environmental laws and politics provided further impediments to the construction of affordable housing. The CHOC had celebrated the Massachusetts Supreme Judicial Court's 1973 ruling as a "sign-post decision" for both its group and proponents of low-income housing throughout the state.[110] The ruling, however, did not automatically usher in construction on the Wheeler property. Even with its sanction from the state's highest court, CHOC still had to follow environmental regulations for building on potential wetlands, which proved an even more difficult hurdle.

In 1965, the Massachusetts legislature had passed the Hatch Act, which required a developer considering projects involving the dredging or filling of inland wetlands to apply for a state permit.[111] The process outlined in the law's procedures provided the members of the SBPA with an alternative means of preventing the CHOC project. Local advocates raised legitimate concerns that the terms of the Supreme Judicial Court's ruling not only put the Wheeler property in jeopardy but also established a precedent that could "endanger marginal wetlands throughout the state," which already had "feeble protection" and were "fast disappearing."[112] These objections moved the conversation surrounding the Wheeler property even further away from a meaningful debate about the issues of suburban responsibility and spatial inequality that had initiated the CHOC project five years earlier. Sisson publicly admitted that she would be "naïve" to say that racial and economic discrimination were not present, but it was incidental to the larger issue of wetlands.[113] Yet the technical focus on runoff, silt, and water levels throughout the various confrontations and hearings excluded from the discussion any residents who did not have engineering or ecology expertise and prevented an extended dialogue about many of the larger issues embodied in the proposal.

In the summer of 1974, the CHOC's application eventually reached the state DNR, which after four hearings denied the application on the grounds that the organization had failed to demonstrate that its development would take the proper protections against flooding.[114] The decision issued a major blow to the CHOC, and having exhausted its financial resources to pay for the legal case, the group decided to abandon its campaign.[115] At least one Concord resident could not ignore the connection between the final defeat of CHOC during the fall of 1974 and the busing crisis raging on the streets of Boston at the same time. In a letter to the *Concord Journal*, resident A. K. Lewis wrote, "Let's put all euphemisms aside" and "admit that Concord had denied an effort to allow black families to move in the community," which "leaves us free at breakfast time to shake our head over newspaper reports of South Boston and deplore all bigotry." Lewis asked that residents take "time to look in the mirror," and consider "how much of this injury and maiming, in history's long light, will belong to us?"[116]

Concord continued to prove that it privileged open space over open suburbs and socioeconomic diversity. Throughout the 1970s, even the state and

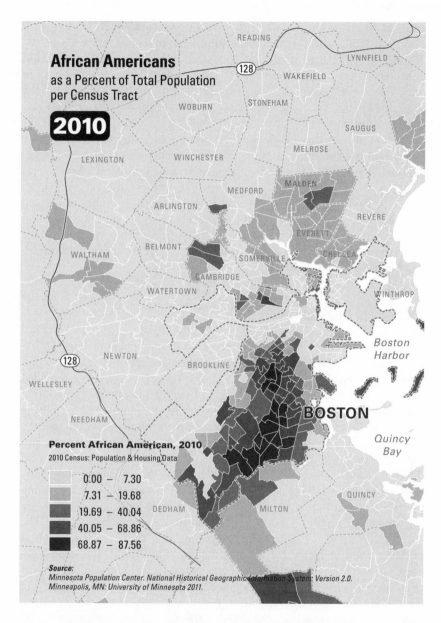

African Americans
as a Percent of Total Population
per Census Tract

2010

READING
LYNNFIELD
WAKEFIELD
STONEHAM
WOBURN
SAUGUS
MELROSE
LEXINGTON
WINCHESTER
MALDEN
MEDFORD
ARLINGTON
REVERE
EVERETT
BELMONT
WALTHAM
SOMERVILLE
CHELSEA
CAMBRIDGE
WATERTOWN
WINTHROP

*Boston
Harbor*

NEWTON
BROOKLINE
WELLESLEY

BOSTON

NEEDHAM

*Quincy
Bay*

Percent African American, 2010
2010 Census: Population & Housing Data

	0.00 – 7.30
	7.31 – 19.68
	19.69 – 40.04
	40.05 – 68.86
	68.87 – 87.56

DEDHAM
MILTON
QUINCY

Source:
Minnesota Population Center. National Historical Geographic Information System: Version 2.0.
Minneapolis, MN: University of Minnesota 2011.

Figure 7.4 Distribution of African American population in metropolitan Boston, 1970 and 2010. This map shows the lack of reduction of racial segregation in metropolitan Boston since the 1970s, due in part to the ineffectiveness of the Anti-Snob Zoning Act and failure of many of the campaigns to open up the suburbs by constructing affordable housing. *Source*: US Census Bureau, *Census of Population and Housing, 2010* (Washington, DC: US Census Bureau, 2010).

national recession did not slow the town's commitment to land acquisition.[117] In 1977, the town meeting approved an article to purchase the Wheeler property for twenty-nine thousand dollars in order "preserve and enhance Concord's rural character" and its wetlands.[118] The acquisition of the Wheeler site and other plots of open space undoubtedly enhanced the attractiveness of Concord as well as its conservation, population, and tax rate control objectives. At the same time, by making even less land available for development it further heightened the barriers to bringing mixed-income housing to the community. The outcome in Concord represented a larger national trend. From Oyster Bay, Long Island, to Boulder, Colorado, and Contra Costa County outside San Francisco, similar cases of conflict between the housing and environmental activists occurred.[119] The cases forced local housing activists and environmentalists to fight one another, and a vast majority of the contests ended with the same results as in Concord: the preservation of open space and economic exclusivity and a dearth of mixed-income housing and racial and economic diversity.

The Road to Segregation

If the Kerner Report offered one bookend to the campaign to bring affordable housing to the Boston suburbs, then the publication by the US Commission on Civil Rights of *Route 128: Boston's Road to Segregation* provided the other. Released in 1975, at the height of the mandatory desegregation of the Boston Public Schools, the commission's report interpreted the busing crisis as the direct result of the failure of suburban municipalities to take the warnings of the Kerner Commission seriously. Using statistical evidence and expert testimony, the report demonstrated that residential segregation and discrimination in metropolitan Boston had intensified during the 1960s. The authors placed the major blame for this pattern on exclusionary zoning practices and put to rest any question that resistance to mixed-income housing constituted anything less than a clear form of racial discrimination. The commission assailed Chapter 774, suggesting that through tactics such as building housing for the elderly only, the law "stimulate[d] suburban communities with new strategies for circumventing racial inclusion." Despite its criticism of the law, the report recognized that the only chance for rectifying the problems of suburban exclusion rested in increased regulation by the state. The commissioners warned, "Unless the state acts swiftly, forcefully and effectively, suburban residential patterns are likely to be firmly established in a manner which cannot be changed for generations."[120]

State officials and white suburban residents largely ignored the Civil Rights Commission's recommendations, and this dire prediction became a reality. In 1989, twenty years after Chapter 774's passage, only 28 of 351 communities had fulfilled the 10 percent benchmark, and most of these were cities like Boston, Worcester, and Springfield.[121] While Chapter 774 helped increase the number of affordable housing units throughout the state of Massachusetts, it was not able to fulfill the original intention of challenging the exclusivity of Boston's suburbs.[122] In fact, the majority of Massachusetts' wealthiest towns failed to build even a single low-income unit, continuing to assert "herculean efforts" to challenge any plan to bring mixed-income housing to their communities.[123] Newton and Concord, for their part, tried to transcend the controversy that had dominated local politics for protracted periods. The communities built a limited number of affordable housing units primarily to serve elderly white residents, but that did little to change the predominantly upper middle-class demographic of either suburb.

It is easy to dismiss the fights that occurred over affordable housing in Newton and Concord as emblematic of the "Not In My Backyard" politics and practices of supposed bastions of liberalism. This reading of the events, however, erases the sincere dedication of many residents in these communities to reducing metropolitan segregation and their willingness to take responsibility for and action against suburban exclusion. This interpretation also does not take seriously the genuine environmental concerns many of the projects raised. Yet as the Concord campaign reveals, the controversies often positioned housing and environmentalist advocates against each other and prevented local residents from grappling with the ways in which stringent zoning policies made probable wetlands the only plots available for affordable housing developments or why their towns needed the developments in the first place. The controversies also thwarted a discussion of the broader forces that pitted affordable housing and environmental activists against each other and prevented an alliance to combat together the forces that unified them.[124]

Instead, these campaigns did not challenge but actually made concerns about property values and tax rates even more central to the political worldview of affluent suburbanites across the political spectrum. A 2005 poll by the Citizens Housing and Planning Association in Massachusetts showed that this problem persisted, transcending party lines as fear of lowered property values and increased educational costs serve as the primary forces in fueling suburban homeowners' opposition to the construction of affordable housing in their communities.[125] The platforms of both political parties also reflected this stance as neither proposed any systematic effort to racially or economically integrate the suburbs.[126] Yet, if the cause of opening up the suburbs quickly faded, concerns about tax rates and the quality and cost of schools and other municipal services did just the opposite, which became even more apparent in the controversy that erupted over the METCO program in the same Route 128 communities at the height of the Boston busing crisis.

8

Tightening the Belt

In September 1974, federal judge W. Arthur Garrity received a poignant handwritten request from an African American girl sent to South Boston High under his court order for the mandatory desegregation of the Boston Public Schools. The girl explained that she and her nine siblings were so scared, they had only gone to school twice. She instead asked the judge for a specific seat reassignment for herself, her siblings, and their friends. "I know a girl who goes with Medco to suburb and she is gonna go to college cause they teach you a lot and no one is a scared to go to school," she implored. "I rely want to go to good school where there is good kid and I will be able to get a good education, so we don't have to be called poor any-more . . . cause the people in better neighborhoods like us better. They would not try to kill us or anything like that."[1]

The girl referred to the voluntary and privately run program, the Metro-politan Council for Educational Opportunity (METCO), over which Gar-rity had no discretion, so he could not help her. Her plea, however, provides a point of departure to consider both the imagined and actual role of the program and suburbs in the desegregation controversy. Explorations of the dramatic events that surrounded the Boston busing crisis have often fo-cused on the ways in which "suburban liberals" like Judge Garrity, himself a Wellesley resident, passively stood by as working-class whites and blacks in the city endured the burden of school integration.[2] The residents along Boston's Route 128 belt were not as removed from the events and issues as those depictions might suggest. The discussion about METCO during this period of turmoil illuminates how the various forces of suburban politics influenced the remedies to school desegregation and racial and economic inequality.

The busing crisis provided an important moment of opportunity for ex-panding METCO. By the time of the mandatory BPS desegregation in the fall of 1974, the eight-year-old METCO program was placing twenty-six hun-dred students in more than thirty communities, all funded by the state of Massachusetts. The program had garnered praise as the largest, most success-ful voluntary integration initiative in the nation. Amid the confusion caused by court-ordered busing, several suburbs sought to either get involved for the first time or increase the number of black students currently transported to their predominantly white school systems. Yet the busing crisis coincided with the state and national recession, and the Massachusetts government's budget problems meant it could not afford to finance this rise in participation. Instead, it requested that suburban towns "tighten their belts" and accept limited financial responsibility to keep the program going.[3] Many residents strongly refused to accept even limited responsibility and began relinquishing their commitment to the program altogether.

The controversy over METCO further wedded the busing crisis and issues of school desegregation to the national, state, and local economic crises of the 1970s. The debates over the future of METCO simultaneously offer insight into the contours of the political culture of the Route 128 suburbs as residents and how their local officials sought to navigate the new economic and political circumstances. The fights over METCO, similar to the quests to construct affordable housing, expose both a strong contingent of suburban residents committed to addressing the problems of race and class inequality and the vibrant strains of political moderation and conservatism that existed even in such supposed bastions of liberalism. The very localized issues of property taxes and public schools provided ordinary citizens a means to express anger at the larger economic problems and social changes of the 1970s, over which they had seeming less control.[4] The reaction to the program also demonstrates that although at the national level, ideas about fiscal policy and busing for integration often delineated along party and ideological lines, at the local level, especially in the suburbs, an individualistic ethos transcended political affiliation and made the differences between liberal and conservative attitudes about taxes and metropolitan responsibility less distinct.

The struggles over METCO also show that as much as any election, the issues of tax rates, quality education, and local control dominated the local and national political discussion of the 1970s. The implications of the fights extend far beyond the budgetary battles of 1975 and 1976, or even the busing crisis. The struggles crystallized notions of taxpayer rights and control over school spending, which culminated in the passage of the state property tax cap Proposition 2½ in 1980, discussed in chapter 10. The position of suburban municipalities permanently ended the conversation about adopting more comprehensive metropolitan integration in and around Boston, or even expanding the METCO program, which remained a small solution to the larger problems of educational, racial, and economic inequality. Just how limited the remedies were would come into sharp relief by the end of 1970s, when affirmative action increasingly replaced mandatory desegregation as the primary route that liberal policymakers and politicians advocated for achieving educational equality.

Send Wellesley's Children to Roxbury Schools

Garrity's ruling in *Morgan v. Hennigan* unleashed the worst resistance and violence to desegregation of the 1970s, making the words Boston and busing permanently linked. From the moment that the ink dried on the Racial Imbalance Act in 1965, the BSC willfully evaded the state's government demands for desegregation of the BPS, and its various forms of delay actually increased the rate of racial segregation. By 1971, Boston had sixty-seven racially imbalanced (meaning more than half nonwhite) schools as opposed to forty-six in 1965, and more than four thousand white students attended schools with no children of color. The following year, the local NAACP chapter filed a class action suit in US District Court on behalf of fifteen black Boston parents, claiming that schools officials had intentionally maintained a segregated school system and thereby denied black children equal protection under the Fourteenth Amendment. Garrity agreed with the claim. In *Morgan v. Hennigan*, he ruled that Boston school authorities had "knowingly carried out a systematic program of segregation affecting all the city's students, teachers, and school facilities and had intentionally brought about or maintained a dual school system." Thus, "the school system of Boston is unconstitutionally segregated."[5] The 152-page opinion, released on June 21, 1974, was at least five times the length of the rulings concerning desegregation in most other cities, which Garrity did purposefully to both prevent reversal on appeal and overwhelm the busing opposition through a preponderance of evidence.[6]

Garrity concentrated his attention more on confirming the existence of the BSC's segregationist policies than on coming up with an effective remedy. With only three months until the start of the school year, he decided to implement the Phase I plan already developed by the Massachusetts Board of Education that called for busing seventeen to eighteen thousand students. A group of state officials who had little expertise with the racial dynamics of Boston had conceived of the plan, which one later admitted was "mechanically drawn."[7] The plan matched Roxbury and South Boston high schools, which would prove to have disastrous consequences. From the first day of school in September 1974 onward, several city neighborhoods became engulfed in violence. Mobs sought to prevent implementation of the court order through a combination of bricks and slurs. The governor eventually called in the National Guard, but it did little to quell the violence. The showdown lasted for two years, and became a national flash point of attitudes about racial equality and metropolitan segregation. Some interpreted the conflict as evidence of the pervasiveness of white working-class racism, and some as the problems of elite suburban liberal social engineers like Garrity trying to impose their vision onto poor whites and blacks. For others, it called into question long-held regional distinctions about the supposed backwardness of the South and enlightenment of the North, captured by the US Civil Rights Commission's bold claim, "Boston has become for the 1970's what Mississippi represented in the 1960's—the major battleground for human rights."[8]

Boston residents themselves, especially those in opposition, also understood the order's meaning in terms of privilege, residency, and politics, but with a geography on a more localized scale. One white student transferred to Roxbury High School laid out the economic, racial, and physical geography of the order in a letter to Garrity. He pointedly asked, "Why should I be descriminated [sic] against because I live in South Boston and not in Newton or Wesley [sic] or any other rich suburban town who do not want the black people of Boston living in their town or going to their schools"? The student protested that Garrity, Governor Francis Sargent, and senators Edward Brooke and Edward Kennedy could not possibly understand the situation since they did "not live within the city of Boston."[9] The fact that the *Morgan* ruling exempted many of the state's leading officials because they lived in the suburbs or sent their children to private schools fueled a sense of victimization, which residents often framed in geographic terms. Parental choice, one enraged white Boston resident quipped, had become "reserved now for Brookline and Dover," the respective hometowns of Michael Dukakis and Sargent, the two candidates in the 1974 gubernatorial race.[10]

No figure throughout the controversy earned more ire than Garrity, and no town more mention than the affluent and exclusive Route 128 suburb of Wellesley where he and his family lived. Garrity's own four children attended Wellesley's public schools, and the town had long prided itself as one of the founding and largest participants in METCO, but the program's 130 students represented most of the nonwhite faces. He received a deluge of letters addressed simply to "Judge Garrity, Wellesley," that mentioned all these factors and documented the sense of geographic inequity driving much of the antibusers' anger.[11] Enraged missive writers suggested modifications to the order, demanding that Garrity instead send students from Roxbury to Wellesley, or even more boldly "Send Wellesley's Children to Roxbury Schools," as one resident wrote across a newspaper clipping about an African American man robbing a white woman.[12] Further drawing attention to the exemption of Wellesley children from the burdens of the desegregation plan, the leading antibusing group, Restore Our Alienated Rights (ROAR), staged several protests at Garrity's home throughout the 1974–75 school year. The largest of these trips took place one Friday night in early October, when entire families from various parts of Boston joined a motorcade to Wellesley with signs reading "Put Garrity on a Bus" attached to their cars. Almost three thousand demonstrators filled the street outside

Figure 8.1 Members of the antibusing group ROAR picket outside the colonial home of Judge Arthur Garrity, in the suburb of Wellesley, on October 5, 1974. The protesters from Boston hold signs that read "Put Garrity on a Bus" to oppose his order for the mandatory desegregation of Boston's public schools and how it denied "freedom of choice." ROAR staged several protests outside the judge's home during the 1974–75 school year, waving American flags and picket signs as a means to highlight the fact that the city of Boston bore the burden for the desegregation order, while in the suburbs, Garrity, and politicians like Senators Edward Kennedy and Edward Brooke, listed in the sign in the foreground, remained exempt. Courtesy of Associated Press Images. © 1974 The Associated Press.

the judge's white colonial house on Radcliffe Road, chanting "Here We Go Southie" and "We Want Garrity," and reciting a mock pledge of allegiance accusing the judge of providing "liberty and justice for none."[13]

The accusations shocked and dismayed Garrity. He was part of the generation of upwardly mobile, liberal-leaning knowledge professionals who had moved to Wellesley in the early 1950s. Garrity had grown up in a middle-class Irish Catholic home in Worcester, attended Holy Cross and Harvard Law School, and remained closely affiliated with the Democratic Party, serving as part of Kennedy's 1960 campaign staff before his appointment to the federal bench in 1966. Like many of his engineer and scientist neighbors, Garrity firmly believed in fairness, rationality, following the rules of procedure, and using expertise to solve social problems.[14] He scrupulously applied these principles to his judicial philosophy in general and the *Morgan* decision specifically. Garrity's surprise at the explosive responsive to the order and the personal attacks he received, as J. Anthony Lukas suggested, symbolized suburban technocrats' lack of understanding of the social complexities of the city, where they might have traveled by car or commuter rail every day, but did not live.[15] He thus emerged as a convenient synecdoche for antibusers' resentments about suburban liberals as a whole. One city resident penned a letter in the voice of Garrity, capturing this anger and sense of hypocrisy: "What was a more segregative act than my own and thousands like me who chose to reside in Wellesley and other racially isolated places?" The letter went on to decry, "Our action was a rather cheap way of showing our liberalism."[16]

Busing opponents found the METCO program another effective trope to point out the inequities of the court order and hypocrisy as well as the racial and economic exclusivity of suburban liberals. Conservative journalist Dick Sennott and BSC member John Kerrigan helped their supporters draw connections between the program and the contradictions in suburban liberal attitudes. In his widely circulated column, Sennott often denounced "suburban liberals" for telling white Bostonians "what 'racists' we are because we object to forced busing. And they go home to their Newtons, their Wellesleys ... where a select few minority kids come out and spend six hours in their schools but are forbidden to live there."[17] Kerrigan had long denounced "friggin' liberals in suburbs," and before Garrity's ruling, had frequently called for a tenfold expansion of METCO. He believed such an expansion would test the values of "cocktail party liberals who have damned us from one end of the Commonwealth," but "who sit comfortably in their lily white communities with their lily white schools."[18] During the desegregation phase, many ordinary white citizens pinned their sense of victimization and helplessness over the court order on METCO.[19] Several white parents from neighborhoods throughout the city invoked ideas of reverse discrimination to challenge the race-based admissions policy of the program. "METCO busses black children to suburban schools which are supposed to have a better educational system," one white parent complained in a letter to Garrity. "Yet if I am dissatisfied with the Boston educational system, I am being discriminated because of my white race and do not have the same right to bus the child to that suburban school."[20] The young girl who wrote Garrity on behalf of herself and her siblings was one of thousands of African Americans who tried to get into METCO before and after Phase I of the court order began. The program was only equipped to take a few hundred new students each year and turned down the majority of the applications. METCO, therefore, symbolized the limited options for many members of the city's black community as well.[21]

State and city politicians joined ordinary citizens and antibusing agitators in invoking METCO as a possible remedy to Boston's problem of school segregation, and made "metropolitanization" another key word in residents' growing lexicon of busing terminology. During the period before and after Garrity's ruling, Boston Mayor Kevin White, Governor Sargent, and future governor Dukakis separately proposed alternative plans to the compulsory integration of the BPS that suggested substantial increases in METCO.[22] A bill proposed by BSC member Kathleen Sullivan and State Representative Michael Daly in the winter of 1975 went even further, advocating a one-way busing program based on the METCO model that would require all communities within a twenty-mile radius of the city with an above-average household income to open 10 percent of their school seats to inner-city children, both black and white.[23]

"The whole idea of metropolitanization would be great," Garrity stated, publicly responding to these suggestions, "if there was a constitutional way to do it."[24] Just weeks after Garrity handed down the *Morgan* decision, the Supreme Court voted 5–4 in *Milliken v. Bradley* to overturn a federal court consolidation decree demanding that the suburbs of Detroit, not just the city proper, be held responsible for remedying segregation and therefore included in school integration plans.[25] The Court thereby ruled that suburban areas outside a city's district boundaries could not be required to join in an urban desegregation remedy. Garrity had clearly read the *Milliken* ruling closely, and saw that while the Supreme Court had not entirely shut the door to metropolitan remedies, it had made most options extremely legally tenuous. He publicly indicated that he would not require full-scale metropolitan integration in his final desegregation order, but would probably recommend the expansion of METCO and other voluntary integration programs as a means to bridge the political and social divisions between Boston and the suburbs.[26]

The leaders of METCO themselves objected to proposals to make the voluntary program a significant component of the BPS desegregation plans. As Garrity deliberated over Phase II of his remedy order, METCO representatives wrote him that they hoped the program could serve as a model for developing an integration plan and would gladly offer their services to the court, but as a private organization it was "not equipped or prepared" to be a major part of the long-term solution for the problem of systemic school segregation.[27] The organization stressed that regardless if they came from Sullivan, Kerrigan, Sargent, or Dukakis, the various proposals involving METCO sought to turn the program into an "escape hatch" and attempted to circumvent "intra city desegregation."[28] Garrity ultimately decided not to make METCO central to the second phase of his court order.[29] The continued focus on Boston as the major site for the desegregation remedy coupled with the sound defeat of the Daly-Sullivan bill did little to reduce the emphasis on METCO.[30] But increasingly, it was suburbanites leading the way to keep the program in the spotlight.

The Suburban Response

The dismissive lobs of the antibusing movement helped to transform the term "suburban liberal" into one of disrepute and hypocrisy within the local and national political discourse. The term, however, naturalized a depiction of suburbanites as uniformly liberal and unresponsive to the situation in Boston. Similar to the debates that erupted surrounding affordable housing, the busing crisis in reality highlighted a spectrum of attitudes about suburban responsibility and political affiliation. Although the suburban fair housing and civil rights infrastructure had weakened considerably since its height in the mid-1960s, a network of liberals residing in the communities along Route 128 offered the first and most vocal concern. Throughout the fall of 1974, activists met frequently to discuss ways to help alleviate the situation in the city and counter "the country's largest anti-busing movement."[31] Herbert and Helene LeVine, leaders of a variety of suburban grassroots campaigns related to fair housing and civil rights, hosted a brunch at their Newton home to develop a strategy for suburban support. Citizens for Participation in Political Action (CPPAX), the result of a merger between the two peace organizations PAX and CPP, staged several rallies and meetings and even proposed creating an event similar to the Vietnam Moratorium to demonstrate suburban concern. The participants in the events and discussions did not openly challenge the viability of Garrity's ruling but instead argued that the "image of busing" had obscured bigger problems of systemic inequality and access to quality education. Some progressive suburbanites, drawing on the language and imagery of the Kerner Commission Report, suggested that the network of activists must force their fellow citizens to recognize that they "belong to the white noose which surrounds and partly strangles our central cities." They advocated for the "metropolitanization of schools and the sharing of finance" policies to "end snob-zoning and develop fair housing" in order "to achieve full equality."[32]

Committed liberal activists found it difficult to build serious support for metropolitanization and resource sharing in the suburbs and decided to advocate for the modest expansion of METCO instead.[33] Despite the fact that by 1974 METCO boasted the involvement of over thirty suburbs the majority of the students attended school in fewer than half the participating municipalities, with by far the largest enrollments in the historically liberal suburbs around Route 128.[34] Thus, these activists believed that expanding participation where the program was already popular would offer an easy, uncontroversial way to begin to signal suburban support for educational integration and assume partial responsibility for the situation in Boston. Suburban sympathizers initiated a grassroots campaign in the fall of 1974 to increase participation in METCO in their own communities. In Lincoln, proponents asserted that "increasing the Metco enrollment in Lincoln is not enough to reduce tension in Boston, but it is a significant symbolic step in that direction."[35]

Several Newton residents made more candid pleas about the limits and benefits of the program, suggesting that adding more METCO students "poses no
threat to the largely advantaged residents of Newton," especially since the
"state reimburses Newton for each of its METCO students" and should "be
welcomed as an opportunity to take positive action in line with their social
consciences."[36]

The idea of increasing participation in METCO extended to more politically conservative and squarely middle-class communities, which before
had not been involved. Despite ROAR's acerbic assumptions, several opinion polls revealed that suburban residents throughout metropolitan Boston
supported racial integration as long they did not have to use local tax dollars to pay for it, and the busing went in one direction and involved the
placement of only a few minority students in each classroom.[37] METCO
boosters had long touted the ways in which the voluntary program did not
violate but actually enhanced local control. METCO's emphasis on voluntary action and one-way busing, therefore, became particularly appealing to
residents as a possible way to circumvent a compulsory or two-way busing
scheme in the future.[38] "I see Metco as a way to avoid forced busing," Winchester School Committee chair Stephen Parkhurst announced about why
he advocated for the town to participate, and Mrs. Horace Prindle of Norwood urged, "The suburbs should initiate positive voluntary action to aid in
the problems of segregation before we face a court order later on."[39] Advocates of affordable housing in Newton and Concord had also embraced this
argument by suggesting that their units offered a desirable alternative to
large projects mandated by the state or federal government.

State education officials themselves bolstered and encouraged this positive
reaction to METCO. During the fall of 1974, Massachusetts Education Commissioner Gregory Anrig publicly urged suburban school committees to
open up seats for METCO students and promised that the state would fully
subsidize them. He announced that Massachusetts had the funds for over a
thousand more children to join the program. "All we need is a commitment
to open the seats," he stated.[40] He even issued a veiled threat to suburban communities that failure to participate in METCO at this juncture might result in
mandatory metropolitan integration in the future. This strategy intitally
proved successful. The combination of grassroots initiatives and government
encouragement led seven new communities, including Burlington, Norwood,
and Woburn, to join the program. Lexington, Sudbury, Newton, and Wellesley
opened up dozens more seats for METCO children. Many other suburbs
made inquiries about joining in the future.[41]

Not every suburbanite took such an enthusiastic view of METCO, and
the plans for expanding the program simultaneously set off fierce resistance.
Most moderate and conservative suburbanites had offered little vocal or
organized opposition to METCO in its first decade of operation, but the

fears of full-scale metropolitan integration and the expansion of the program into new communities produced a sharp backlash. During the 1974–75 school year, more than a dozen grassroots groups emerged in the suburbs with the shared goal of preventing metropolitan integration and METCO's expansion. The groups' titles all included the words "Citizens," "Responsible," and "Education," although their acronyms had slight variations based on the names of the towns they represented, such as CRAB in Beverly, CRAM in Middleton, CREED in Randolph, and CREW in Winchester.[42]

Observers initially interpreted the opposition movement as an extension of the reactionary populism displayed by working-class whites on the streets of South Boston and Charlestown. When the group in Middleton spread rumors that METCO students in other towns had robbed and raped local residents, it only upheld such assumptions.[43] Dedham, Quincy, Beverly, and Randolph, which emerged as the strongest outposts of anti-METCO organizing, had experienced a steady increase in migration of blue-collar Irish and Italian Americans from Boston over the previous decade.[44] Most of the organizers of the groups, nevertheless, sought to distance themselves from the antibusing movement in Boston by stressing they were not "Archie Bunker-style bigots" like ROAR.[45] As Dedham State Representative Charles M. McGowan summarized his position and that of many of his constituents, "I am not opposed to the black man who can buy a house next to me and afford to take care of his property and raise his children in the same way I do."[46] He and others did oppose any kind of busing because it violated their rights as suburban parents and taxpayers to have full freedom of choice in decisions about their children's education. Carole Stacinski, a mother of five who led the opposition to voluntary integration in Dedham, explained, "If you start losing one of your freedoms, that's the beginning of the end."[47]

The leaders of the opposition rejected the pragmatic view that participation in METCO would provide a way to avoid metropolitan busing and maintain local control, and instead saw the program as the gateway toward metropolitan integration. The Daly-Sullivan bill, with its call for twenty thousand students to enroll in suburban schools, coupled with warnings by conservative politicians that the program was the "entering wedge" to bring a thousand more inner-city children into the suburbs, fanned the flames of outrage.[48] The Winchester anti-METCO group called Citizens for Responsible Education in Winchester extended messages of the loss of local control when it circulated a flyer with a drawing of "school busing" as a runaway train with steam spelling out "METCO" about to roll over a group of horrified and helpless Winchester citizens lying on the tracks.[49] Yet in Winchester and other affluent Route 128 suburbs, it demonstrated what the speeding METCO represented, and what resident feared most, was an increase in the local tax rate. Inflation and the fiscal crisis proved far more effective at stopping METCO's entrance into Winchester than CREW's organizing campaign.

The Belt Tightens

The effort to expand the METCO program provides a window into the inter-related fiscal problems at the national, state, and local levels in the 1970s. The issues of unemployment and taxes discussed during the 1972 presidential election offered a preview of the nation's severe economic problems. In-creases in stagnant growth, inflation, and unemployment converged to im-pact both the tax rate and finances of most Americans. In 1974, the national inflation rate reached 11 percent and pushed many middle-class citizens into higher marginal tax brackets, which with the rise in the payroll tax meant a sharp rise in federal tax bills.[50] The downturn of Route 128 industry and continued deindustrialization of the manufacturing sector transformed the national recession into a statewide depression. By 1974, the unemployment rate in Massachusetts had reached 11.2 percent. The state's tax rate had also grown considerably. Confirming the state's "Taxachusetts" nickname, be-tween 1963 and 1973, state and local taxes had increased from 9.6 to 14.8 percent of the average personal income, which gave Massachusetts the sixth-largest tax burden in the United States.[51] Higher taxes did not ease the bud-get problems of the state, which sat on the brink of bankruptcy.[52]

The difficulties carried over to local towns, even affluent ones like those on the Route 128 ring. Unemployment among professionals in the technol-ogy sector remained high, and many families struggled to stay afloat.[53] Other sectors were confronting similar jobs shortages. A study by the Mas-sachusetts Bar Association found that there were ten times more lawyers in the state than available jobs for them, and the teaching profession had a similar surplus.[54] Further compounding the economic worries, local tax rates continued to rise rapidly even in towns that had taken aggressive mea-sures to limit costs through density controls. The increases were particularly pronounced in places known for lavish public school expenditures. Even though student enrollments had steadily dropped through the early 1970s, inflation coupled with the growing cost of utilities and transportation kept expanding the school budgets of many communities each year.[55] By 1975, the school budget in Concord had jumped to $5 million although the school population had dropped to 2,835, or 44 fewer students than the pre-vious year. Newton's budget had grown 8.8 percent to over $31.9 million, roughly half of which went to finance public education.[56]

The state and local budget shortages had a direct impact on METCO. The program had expanded in 1975 as new towns joined and others opened more spaces to children from Boston. Yet 26 of the 36 participating commu-nities asked for a sizable increase in money for each student involved for the 1975–76 school year. In a particularly extreme example, Belmont raised its rate from $792 for each of the 70 METCO children in 1974–75 to $1,257 for 74 students in 1975–76.[57] When the Massachusetts government allocated a

Table 8.1 The Annual Tax Rate per $1,000 of Selected Route 128 Suburbs and Boston, 1965–76

	Boston	Brookline	Concord	Lexington	Lincoln	Newton
1965	99.80	56.50	38.80	44.00	77.00	70.40
1966	115.00	56.50	44.80	43.60	35.00	72.20
1967	101.00	65.00	42.40	47.00	37.00	76.20
1968	117.80	41.50	51.40	53.80	37.50	88.60
1969	129.20	49.00	36.80	59.80	47.50	98.40
1970	156.80	59.00	39.20	65.00	52.60	113.00
1971	174.70	63.50	43.30	63.80	54.40	121.60
1972	196.70	71.50	48.00	65.00	57.00	139.60
1973	196.70	73.00	51.00	68.90	63.80	134.60
1974	196.70	80.00	54.00	70.40	61.80	150.40
1975	196.70	84.00	52.00	72.00	63.50	159.00
1976	252.90	89.00	54.00	80.20	69.20	N/A

$5.3 million budget for METCO for 1975–76, it had not taken into consideration the sharp increase in participation or reimbursement requests, thus creating a major shortfall.[58]

Governor Dukakis, who had defeated Sargent in the November 1974 gubernatorial race, was the former state representative from Brookline and a longtime champion of METCO, having sponsored the initial legislation to make the state fund the program in 1966. Yet he had made fiscal austerity the center plank of his first year in office and announced that he would re-fuse to grant the full $6.2 million that the Board of Education estimated these additional reimbursement requests would cost. With the first day of school rapidly approaching, in late August 1975 the state implored subur-ban communities to be more flexible in their reimbursement requests. Ed-ucation Secretary Paul Parks and Commissioner Anrig both sent pleas to all the participating communities asking that they make at least a 10 percent reduction in their budgets. Parks wrote to local officials that he was "not insensitive to the fiscal pressure which you also face" and "the policy con-cerns being expressed in your communities about the critical national de-bate on school desegregation." He requested simply that towns "tighten their belts and absorb the 10 percent cut until we are out of our present fi-nancial crisis."[59] Charles Glenn, the long-serving director of the Bureau of Equal Educational Opportunity, also tried to spark a sense of collective re-sponsibility. He presented the situation in mathematical terms, suggesting that if every town agreed to the 10 percent cut, METCO could replace the 107 students who graduated and add four hundred more Boston participants to the program. These entreaties had little effect.

Several suburban communities offered very conditional support for METCO, announcing that without 100 percent reimbursement, they would no longer honor their commitment to enroll the Boston students.[60] The Massachusetts government eventually agreed to fund 90 percent of the re-quested budget, averting a conflict momentarily. As the fiscal crisis in Mas-sachusetts worsened by the month, however, Dukakis continued to see METCO as one place that he could impose budgetary restraint. In the win-ter of 1976, Dukakis proposed a $5.48 million budget to the legislature for METCO's operation in the upcoming school year, or $1.5 million less than the Department of Education had recommended. He also announced a stricter set of guidelines for participating suburbs to ensure that no commu-nity either made a profit on the program or allocated the state funds toward reducing local taxes. Dukakis stated that he understood "well the pressures that local supporters are under, and at the same time, I would hope that suburbanites will recognize the severe fiscal constraints under which we have been operating."[61] Most suburban communities were once again not as sympathetic as Dukakis had hoped.

The budget crisis created mounting doubts about the viability of the program's future.[62] Headlines began to appear on the front pages of area newspapers with such warnings as "Suburbs Cooling to Metco as Funds Fade," "METCO, Money, and Race," "The Crisis at METCO," and "Is METCO Effort Dying in the Suburbs?"[63] Several towns threatened that without the proper funding, they would permanently withdraw from the program. Win-chester officially rescinded its participation since the state could not promise the full $110,000 it needed to enroll forty-five Boston students. The persistent turmoil in Boston and fears of metropolitanization it had spawned undoubtedly contributed to this "cooling." The budget situation, nevertheless, played a more pivotal role in rapidly shifting the discussion away from whether METCO could provide the infrastructure for a metropolitan remedy to whether the program could survive at all.

Many supporters of metropolitan integration stressed that suburban residents used fiscal anxieties as cover for larger racial hostilities about two- and even one-way integration.[64] A school board member in one Route 128 suburb asserted, "People aren't going to say: 'Get the God damned niggers out of there.' But they feel that way." *Boston Globe* columnist Mike Barnicle pointed out some of the hypocrisy of protesting METCO because of tax rates. "How many town meetings were held about the money being spent on the B-1 bomber?" He asked. "Why is it that people get more upset at METCO than they do at the Pentagon?" Barnicle provocatively suggested the answer was a "disease called racism."[65] For most suburban residents, race and economics failed to operate in such neatly contained categories. Thus, additional answers to Barnicle's question could be that for many suburbanites, METCO represented something more tangible and immediate to constrict and challenge than military spending, or that for a large contingent of residents, their local fiscal concerns superseded national issues. Lee Berube of Beverly's reasons for why she opposed the town joining METCO centered on "the economic conditions of today" and "present financial crunch," but with clear racial undertones. "I don't mind helping people if I felt I was financially able to do it," she explained, but "if I can't help my own, how can I possibly help anyone else?"[66]

Some commentators interpreted reactions to METCO like Berube's as a signal of a larger suburban political realignment. "Increasing financial difficulties and growing suburban conservatism," the *Boston Globe* editorialized, "may be just the one two punch necessary to knock METCO out of the suburbs in the next decade."[67] Observers who construed the hostility to METCO as a sign of increased conservatism failed to acknowledge that these sentiments constituted not a break but a continuation in suburban attitudes about the program. Since METCO's inception, support for the program by residents from across the suburban political spectrum had rested on the fact that participation did not require the outlay of local tax dollars and offered local communities full control over participation. The boundaries of this commitment had not truly been tested since the state had always provided adequate funding and most suburban communities had operated in the black. Yet the recession laid bare the fact that even suburbanites who voiced concern about the problems in Boston and racial discrimination did not want to assume even the most limited local financial responsibility to remedy them. METCO boosters' arguments about the full control and lack of financial obligation that the program offered the suburbs had perhaps worked too well. In the mid-1970s, communities became even more assertive in their discretion over participation and ever less willing to make any financial sacrifice in order to do so.

These dynamics became particularly apparent in the town of Lincoln, which had a reputation for liberal politics, one of the highest per capita incomes in the state and country, and a long-standing commitment to METCO. The town's 120 METCO students in 1975 were 15 percent of the kindergarten to eighth grade school population, which represented the largest percentage of any participating municipality. Lincoln had long touted the benefits of the program, especially the ways that exposure "to children of a different race and cultural backgrounds" had "enriched the community as a whole."[68] The threat of having to kick in local tax dollars muted much of this enthusiasm. David Livingston, a local school official, aptly summarized the situation. "So far it's been a simple issue: Do you believe in integrated education?" Livingston explained. "But if the commonwealth reduces the level of funds so I have to say: Do you believe in integrated education enough to invest local funds to continue the program. That's a very different story."[69] The town showed its response to these questions by voting to accept fewer students and reduce support services for the program for the 1975–76 school year. Lincoln, however, continued to allocate money generously to its open space program, making several more land purchases in the mid-1970s that had a larger impact on the local tax rate than would have been the case if the town maintained full participation in METCO.[70]

The decisions of suburban municipalities like Lincoln to scale back involvement in METCO earned the sharp condemnation of Secretary of Education and longtime civil rights activist Paul Parks. He contended it was clearly in "no way related to fiscal or funding problems," but "a practice of social retrenchment."[71] While Parks interpreted the shift in attitudes toward METCO as a racial backlash, William Herbert of the Massachusetts Teachers Association noted that it exposed the fiscal contours of liberalism in the suburbs. "In good times it is easy to be liberal," Herbert declared. "Prejudices are overcome to a certain extent, but when money is tight, people become frightened."[72] Newton resident Marjorie Arons similarly bemoaned in an editorial in the local paper, "It was easier during the Vietnam War—you were either for it or against," but in the 1970s, "belt-tightening seems to have choked off this spirit of altruism, even of equity. . . . The community is uptight. We dig a moat."[73] These observations confirm that the response to METCO was clearly a fusion of racial and fiscal concerns. Yet Parks, Herbert, or Arons did not address the fact that support for the program outside a small circle of activists was always relatively shallow and conditional on it being free. Nor did they acknowledge that since proponents had long presented the program as good for white middle-class children, it made the fact that many suburban residents viewed METCO in self-interested, individualistic, and consumer-oriented ways less shocking and more understandable.

In Newton, the controversy that erupted over keeping METCO operational made these factors all too obvious.

Where Are Liberals Going?

Newton's exceptionalist identity had long rested on the intertwined issues of its liberal population and excellent public schools. In the 1960s, leading national education experts like James B. Conant dubbed Newton the embodiment of "lighthouse schools that point the way to excellence in education," and Jonathan Kozol praised his hometown as having "one of the few really great school systems in the world."[74] Since World War II, Newton had consistently maintained the highest per pupil expenditures in the state and had also initiated many progressive curricular innovations including METCO.[75] In early 1975, METCO executive director Jean McGuire had called Newton's METCO program "a showpiece for the country," praising it for being the biggest, the most successful in hiring minority staff members, and the most innovative in making curricular changes to incorporate more attention to African American life and history.[76] In response to the violence that accompanied desegregation in the fall of 1974, the Newton School Committee decided to take the lead once again, and agreed to accept one hundred more METCO students in January 1975 and gradually expand its involvement over the next few years until the suburb achieved a 9.4 percent minority student population.[77] By the following year, the community had begun to demonstrate a different attitude toward the program. In 1975, the school committee voted to add fifty additional METCO students. It refused, however, to answer the state's request to reduce its tuition so that more students could participate in the program and instead increased its request for reimbursement to $675,000.[78]

This decision reflected the swift sea change in Newton's political climate provoked in large part by the economic downturn. While there had been few objections during the 1960s, the recession, inflation, and the suburb's burdensome tax rate made many Newton residents question the high cost of education. In the spring of 1975, a group of citizens formed a grassroots group called VOICE with the goal of curbing the "excessive spending" of Newton's local government, especially the "spendthrift" and "out of touch with reality" school committee.[79] The group of "politically moderate people of all parties" announced as its goals the creation of "high-quality education for our children within the constraints of a reasonable tax burden," a return to a curricular focus on basic skills, and the preservation of neighborhood schools.[80]

VOICE's stance had more in common with the opposition to affordable housing that took shape in Newton than with ROAR and urban-based antibusing groups. In fact, VOICE had many literal and figurative overlaps with the movement that had emerged in opposition to the construction of scattered-site mixed-income housing in the suburb a few years earlier. Robert Stiller, the leader of the grassroots resistance movement in the earlier campaign, became a VOICE-backed candidate for alderman, and Roger Cohen, the lawyer who successfully frustrated the NCDF's plans though creative delay tactics, was one of the group's choices for the Newton School Committee in the November 1975 election. VOICE candidates sought to galvanize the same anger among Newton residents that had led to the significant scaling back of the moderate-income development. In order to arouse grassroots anxiety, Cohen made antimetropolitanization a central feature of his candidacy, stressing that the school committee must "cope with the problems of the City of Newton, not the problems of Boston."[81] On Election Day, VOICE candidates defeated four incumbents, including the chair and vice chair, creating a clear conservative majority on the school committee. Only one self-identified liberal candidate, Honora Kaplan, achieved victory. After winning by a large margin, Cohen later declared, "All of a sudden it was an advantage to be labeled a conservative."[82]

The first issue to demonstrate the new era of school governance in Newton centered on integration, but involved another voluntary metropolitan program. The fight that unfolded in early 1976 over a program called Metropairways, operated by the Metropolitan Planning Project (MPP), illuminates continuities and changes in the attitudes toward METCO within Newton and other Route 128 suburbs. MPP had begun in 1973 through a grant from the federal government's 1972 Emergency School Aid Act for the development of metropolitan programs in urban areas. The project constituted a separate entity from METCO, although they had largely overlapping boards. MPP also shared METCO's racially liberal premise that individual interaction led to tolerance and equality, but emphasized remedies that involved the two-way voluntary transportation of students. In order to encourage students of all backgrounds to "participate in a multi-cultural, multi-ethnic learning experience," MPP used its $980,000 federal grant to sponsor fifty-six programs that brought students from Boston and the surrounding suburbs together in educational endeavors on topics such as African American history, Chinese and Spanish culture and language, theater, and fine arts.[83] Newton served as one of MPP's inaugural partners and had participated in the Metropathways project, where high school students from both the suburbs and Boston explored the ecology, geography, and history of the Charles River. In the winter of 1976, MPP developed an additional program called Metropairways for younger students that matched five suburban elementary schools with five in the city. The plan included pairing 125 students at the Angier School in the Waban neighborhood of Newton with the same number of children from the David A. Ellis School in Roxbury to meet about ten times for two hours between mid-March and June, alternating between the two schools and at other sites such as the Museum of Science.[84] The program was to be entirely voluntary, giving parents the option to allow their children to participate. The planners sought to assuage potential suburban concerns by promising that the Roxbury school was in a "stable neighborhood" with no problems of physical safety for the children. They also assured parents that the program would last only for a year and there were "no strings attached" for a future commitment to metropolitan education.[85] The proposal received overwhelming support from teachers, administrators, and parents at the Angier School.

For the new members of the Newton School Committee, however, Metropairways represented a threat to the three pillars of their shared governing philosophy: traditional education, local control, and taxpayer accountability. Committee member Edward Prince immediately denounced the program as a clear diversion of Newton's educational efforts by seeking to affect social change rather than teaching children basic skills and knowledge. He and his fellow committee members also interpreted MPP's broad mission of "eliminat[ing] racial and ethnic isolation in Greater Boston" as a dangerous first step toward mandatory metropolitan integration.[86] Fusing fears about loss of local control with claims of taxpayer rights, committee chair Alvin Mandell ignored assurances that the program would be entirely federally financed and asked rhetorically, "Am I going to pay Newton taxes to have some of my children educated in some other part of the Greater Boston School District?"[87] The school committee's stance provoked residents throughout the community to voice fears about comprehensive metropolitan integration. These citizens emphasized that they had no problem with their children attending school with African American children, but did not want them to take buses into Roxbury.[88] The objections revealed many residents' highly racialized anxiety about urban crime and drugs and the overall dangers of the city. These fears partially explain why most Newton residents did not publicly object to METCO's one-way integration, but the idea of sending white suburban children into Roxbury through Metropairways evoked such a strong public response.

"I certainly wouldn't want to accuse anyone of being a racist," observed Angier principal Roland Barth, "but if we were planning the program with an elementary school in Wellesley, I don't think you would have seen the same sort of concern about not enough basic education. There's a hell of a lot of fear of the unknown."[89] Barth's comment underscores that Wellesley also held a key location in the spatial imaginary of many white suburbanites, yet with a different connotation than how the antibusers in Boston invoked Garrity's hometown. Defending his school's participation in Metropairways, Barth pointed out that since Wellesley had the same predominantly white and affluent population as Newton, it would negate the educational advantages of the program. "It is the presence of these black kids that make the program educationally important," he explained. "Many Angier children know no Black people; this isolation perpetuates stereotypes."[90]

Several Newton residents agreed with Barth's interpretation of the benefits of Metropairways and offered an alternative vision of quality education and taxpayer entitlements. Like many of the advocates for METCO and affordable housing, Metropairways supporters did not focus on the issues of systemic inequality or even the circumscribed opportunities for African American children. Advocates instead stressed that not participating in integrated educational opportunities compromised the education of white children. "I want my kids to live successfully in the year 2000, and I also want them to learn something," Angier parent Edward Lerner stated. "I think this program provides serious content as well as helping children learn together."[91] *Globe* columnist Carole Surkin, whose daughter was in the fifth grade at the Angier school, declared in one of her weekly pieces that "the rising tide of racism in the community" threatened to "deprive" her daughter of an important and innovative educational opportunity.[92] She shared the sentiment of a broader coalition of Newton residents who proclaimed that the rejection of participation in Metropairways "undermined the rights of parents to . . . choose racially integrated programs."[93] Several of the residents who rose up to defend the program mentioned that they had decided to move to Newton because the schools "were so progressive," but the stance of the school committee had led Surkin and several of her peers to threaten to move away. Some observers thus warned that rejecting Metropairways could "depress real estate values, push up the tax rate and throw heavier burdens on the budget-minded fears."[94]

When the Newton School Committee voted on March 8, 1976, not to participate in Metropairways, it ignited further outrage and concern about the transformation of the community, showing that the majority of Newton residents did not publicly adopt a conservative position, even during a recession. Many citizens stated that the vote had made them "saddened" and "ashamed," and proved the amount of "ragweed in the Garden City."[95] The response to the vote immediately transcended Newton's municipal boundaries. Longtime community activist and state representative Mel King of Roxbury denounced the decision on the floor of the Massachusetts legislature, saying it sent the message, "Put the niggers back in their place, we've done too much for the them."[96] Erik Van Loon, one of the lawyers who had represented African American parents in the *Morgan* case, damningly predicted that if an attorney in the future wanted to make an argument "that the suburbs should be involved because they had contributed to the segregation of the Boston public schools, they might be able to use the Newton decision . . . as one little piece of the puzzle."[97] This case did not arise, yet Newton became the bellwether of suburban attitudes toward METCO amid the fiscal crisis and the larger political, racial, and economic issues that the debate embodied.

The $82,000 Question

The Metropairways controversy established the context for the Newton School Committee to address the issue of Dukakis's limits on METCO's funding for the 1976–77 school year and a revised policy that the state initiated. Upon their swearing in, committee members almost immediately decided to refuse to add more students to the program for the upcoming year and increase the amount of reimbursement it requested. This staunch stance became compounded after Dukakis declared that the demands for full funding represented another way that upper-middle-class suburbs were "failing the core city."[98] He instructed the Massachusetts Department of Education to develop new guidelines to assure that no community would make or lose money through its participation in METCO. The state issued a list of itemized expenses that it would reimburse and established a new rule that if the funds did not cover the projected costs, the town could adapt by accepting fewer students or reducing its services. The new policies aimed to ensure equity among participating communities and in some ways actually gave suburban municipalities more discretion over their participation.[99] But Dukakis publicly described the intent of the new policy differently.

"Brookline, Newton, and Weston won't get full funding," Dukakis announced in the spring of 1976. "It's not costing those communities $1,400 or $1,500 to put a child in an empty seat."[100] The accusation pushed the already-volatile Newton School Committee over the edge. Committee chair Mandell issued a public letter to Dukakis pointedly disagreeing with the governor's claim that adding a few METCO pupils to a class would come at no cost to suburbs like Newton. Relying on a euphemistic view of the aptitude of inner-city youths, Mandell contended that "underachieving" students required more tutoring, extra teachers, and "more of the assets of the system than the resident students," and thus Newton actually lost money by participating in the program.[101]

Newton school officials calculated that Dukakis's budget would provide the suburb with $256,000, but still leave it $82,000 short of its requested reimbursement. The Newton School Committee thus realized that it could either scale back the budget or take the required $82,000 from the city's general tax fund. The suggestion outraged many local residents like Joyce Morrissey Beatty. She dubbed METCO "a very valid program," but felt already "overburdened," and did not want the program's future to rest on her local tax bill.[102] "As a parent, taxpayer, and lifelong resident of Newton who is faced with a tax bill of $2,000 on my modest six-room home," George Poirer declared, capturing the sentiment of many residents, "I vigorously protest the attempt to use my tax dollar to make up for the state-created deficit in the METCO program."[103] With these attitudes in mind, the committee voted 5–4 to cut the METCO budget by $82,000. METCO officials stressed that they would not send students into the community without the support services that the cut eliminated. Newton School Superintendent Leon Fink characterized the action as "tantamount to killing the program."[104]

Newton continued to contain a large contingent of residents who strongly and vocally opposed the school committee's stance. Many of these people firmly believed that the suburbs must take responsibility for the problem of school desegregation and initially advocated increasing Newton's participation as the most limited way to do so. The fight over the budget, which took place throughout the spring and summer of 1976, left such residents trying to preserve the participation of a small number of children, and restricted them from advocating for other ways to alleviate the problems of metropolitan inequality or even just expanding the program beyond the one or two students in each classroom.[105] METCO's defenders tended to de-emphasize the issues of inequality and instead relied on more self-interested arguments to preserve the program.

Local supporters of the program not only supplied well-worn assertions about METCO's dual benefits for both black and white children but also emphasized its tangible economic advantages. Advocates claimed that by removing the 350 METCO students, Newton would lose the $256,000 in state funding that supplemented both the program and other educational services in the suburb, which in turn assisted the entire school system. Some residents went as far as to suggest that Newton made a profit from the program, and "without it tax rates would go up."[106] Many residents shared the conviction of their adversaries that the local tax rate was too high, but stressed that "dropping Metco is not the way to save money" and the $82,000 cost to maintain the program, when dispersed throughout the ninety-thousand-person community, would lead to a "miniscule" increase in individual tax bills.[107] METCO's main office further supplemented this campaign to preserve participation efforts directly by couching its benefits in fiscal terms. In the spring of 1976, the organization released a statement underscoring that METCO placed no "financial drain on local real estate tax base," and in fact, took many steps to ensure that it was "one of the most cost effective programs in the public sector" and "one of the best bargains in education."[108] Executive Director McGuire continued to stress publicly that it offered "a real advantage to the white suburban child."[109] Many residents and local officials in Newton agreed about the benefits for local children, but also held the conviction that they should not have to expend local tax dollars to receive them.

As the battle in Newton extended throughout the summer of 1976, Mayor Theodore Mann called a special school committee meeting in early July, but five of the nine members, including Mandell, the chair, boycotted the session, explaining that the blame for the cuts lay with the state's failure to fully fund METCO. The session did draw 250 Newton residents, who read statements defending the program and denouncing the committee's action. METCO officials, parents, and Newton host parents also testified. McGuire adopted the commonly invoked imagery of spatial isolation, warning the suburban community, "If you build walls, remember: they keep you in, as well as keeping us out."[110] Following the meeting, Mandell stated that he and the school committee were sympathetic to METCO's defenders, but were "sincerely and honestly trying to protect the Newton taxpayer." Mandell feared that if the suburb replaced the shortfall, it would set a dangerous precedent, and "Newton will be asked to pick up more and more of what should be the state's responsibility."[111] He urged the Massachusetts government to restore the funding so that "Newton may continue its' service to the 350 youngsters in the largest Metco program in the State."[112]

The controversy inescapably placed those 350 METCO students in the middle of the cross fire. Many of these children had been students in the Newton schools since kindergarten and feared that the decision compromised their short- and long-term educational opportunities. One Boston student, Linda Silva, worried that the vote placed her plans to attend Dartmouth and then medical school in jeopardy. Eliza Paige, another METCO student, stated, "If they shut down the program, I think that would upset me more than anything." While the Newton School Committee's decision "shocked and upset" her, Paige was not completely surprised since "the whole busing situation has definitely hardened attitudes against Metco."[113] These comments added a clear human dimension to the problem, demonstrating that it was actually the future of children, not tax dollars, that sat at the center of the issue. This concern had received very little attention throughout the fight in Newton and budget controversy as a whole.

The response to the threat of METCO's end in Newton by a white student also exposed the issues at stake in the budget crisis and program in general. White high school junior Ellen Sasahara noted that despite the fact she never got to know any METCO students personally, she would "really miss seeing them around" if the program was dismantled. "There were two in my art class and they had a very happy go-lucky attitude," she observed.[114] When placed in contrast to the concerns of the Boston students about their educational future, Sasahara's comment highlights that in spite of all the discussion of racial equality surrounding the program and its continuation, METCO had fundamentally different stakes for the white and black students. The comment, therefore, also unintentionally undercut the arguments about the ways in which METCO prepared white suburban children for a multiracial world, and proved the difficulty of achieving this goal by adding one or two minority students to a classroom.

A group of state officials and politicians tried to plead with the Newton committee, alleging that their vote would not just effect their own community but also could put the entire program in jeopardy. Invoking METCO and the suburb's intertwined history, Commissioner Parks declared, "It was Newton citizens who took to the front lines in carrying METCO to a reality." Parks thus warned, "If this city turns its back, you have contributed to the destruction of the whole Metco program. Town after town will step forward and do the same thing."[115] State Senator Jack Backman agreed, stating, "My colleagues will look to Newton for leadership (and may take more drastic action). I assure you that the ramifications will go far beyond $80,000."[116] The vote's impact reverberated into the chambers of the federal government. Senator Brooke and Congressmen Drinan and Michael Harrington sent a public letter to the Newton School Committee stressing that they were "deeply concerned about the implications of these reductions," which would lead to "the darkening of the one of few bright spots in Boston's recent educational history" and serve "to enhance the isolation of and despair of those in Boston's inner city communities."[117]

The crisis in Newton eventually diffused at the eleventh hour when, after a number of closed-door meetings at the State House, Dukakis and the state legislature agreed to jointly offer METCO a budget of $5.75 million. The governor gave $150,000 from his "unforeseen emergency" fund to keep the program in Newton and elsewhere operational.[118] The decision to provide the money during a severe budget crisis underscored both the political importance of METCO and Dukakis's desire to appease suburban voters. While many Newton residents and officials let out a sigh of relief at the end of this game of brinkmanship, others continued to question the impact of the situation on both the METCO students and community's progressive standing. Evelyn Kaye worried, "You can't wash away the impression that's been given that METCO wasn't wanted in Newton" and "no one really cares about the black children unless there's money to pay for them."[119]

Conclusion

In September 1976, Ian Menzies, who covered the suburbs for the *Globe*, like many others interpreted the controversy in Newton as a sign that the future of METCO stood at a crossroads. "Times have changed," he conceded. "These are not the mid-60s, the years of the inter-racial freedom marches and the Great Society, when suburbia was gung-ho for liberal causes." Menzies believed that the program's future was uncertain, but not doomed. "What suburbia really has to decide," Menzies insisted, "is whether the rationale that first made it support the program still exists—that white students benefit from METCO integration as much as blacks. If the answer to this question is as it should be ... then suburbia has to fight for growth funding for METCO."[120]

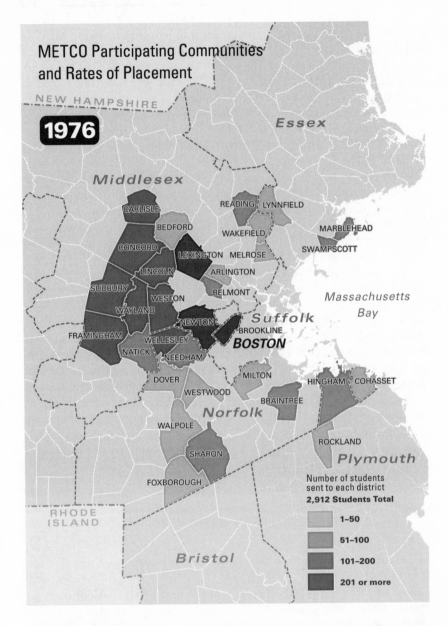

Figure 8.2 METCO participating communities and rates of placement, 1976 (left) and 2011 (right). These maps show that despite METCO's popularity, the program did not grow significantly following the busing and budget crises of the 1970s. *Sources*: Massachusetts Department of Education, Bureau of Educational Opportunities, "Schools and Programs of Choice: Voluntary Desegregation in Massachusetts," April 1977, Massachusetts Department of Education, Bureau of Educational Opportunities, Boston City Archives, Boston, MA; Massachusetts Department of Elementary and Secondary Education, "Metco Program, Metco Districts, and Grant Allocations, 2011–2012," available at http://www.doe.mass.edu/metco/.

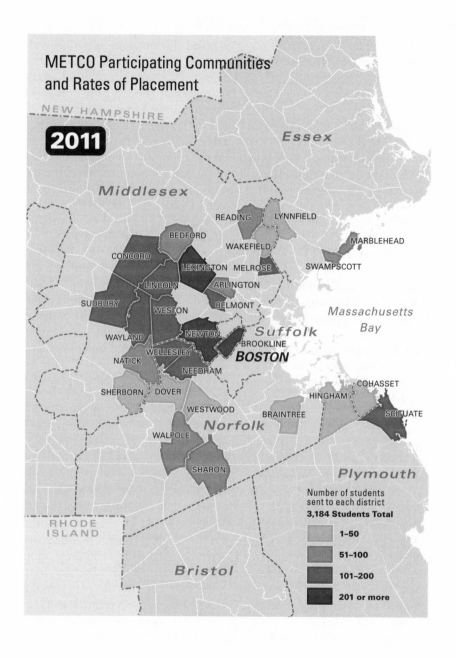

METCO Participating Communities and Rates of Placement

NEW HAMPSHIRE

2011

Essex

Middlesex

READING   LYNNFIELD

BEDFORD   WAKEFIELD

CONCORD   LEXINGTON MELROSE   MARBLEHEAD

LINCOLN   ARLINGTON   SWAMPSCOTT

SUDBURY   WESTON   BELMONT

WAYLAND   NEWTON   Massachusetts
                                                    Bay
WELLESLEY   BROOKLINE   Suffolk

NATICK   NEEDHAM   BOSTON

SHERBORN   DOVER   COHASSET

WESTWOOD   HINGHAM

WALPOLE   BRAINTREE   SCITUATE

Norfolk

SHARON   Plymouth

RHODE
ISLAND

Bristol

Number of students
sent to each district
3,184 Students Total

1–50

51–100

101–200

201 or more

In the three decades since Menzies posed this question, suburban residents have repeatedly responded both yes and no. Members of participating communities consistently reaffirmed their shared commitment to voluntary integration and frequently stressed the important benefits of the program for local children. These suburbanites also continued to voice a firm belief that they should not have to expend any local tax dollars to pay for participation in METCO or build more affordable housing, so the majority of minority students still had to be bused into their communities.[121] The funding fights of the 1970s ultimately enabled suburban communities to set the parameters of the program's limited operation, even after the national recession and state and local fiscal crises receded. Despite the fact that the waiting list of Boston students hoping to get a seat in the program exponentially multiplied, METCO did not grow significantly beyond its size in 1976.

The Newton METCO program remained the largest in metropolitan Boston. In 2013–14, the community received $2.1 million in state funds for 402 students—almost double that of any other participating community.[122] Newton and other municipalities used roughly the same language to endorse the value of the program as they did in the 1960s. "Metco helps the Newton schools look and feel more like the diverse society that our kids are going to have to function in as citizens and leaders," Newton school superintendent Jeffrey Young asserted in 2007. "It's about enriching our lives."[123] This response revealed the suburban-centered ideals that provided both a powerful and limited justification for the program in places such as Newton.

METCO's success and limitations embodied the tensions that have long animated the debate surrounding affirmative action. As public and political backlash together thwarted the quest for mandatory desegregation following the Boston busing crisis, the courts largely abandoned busing-based remedies, and the challenges to exclusionary zoning also faltered, affirmative action became the central mode through which advocates came to promote racial equality in education. Echoing METCO's champions, proponents often countered the argument that affirmative action provided preferential advantages to minorities by focusing on the tangible benefits that diversity offered to whites as well. Supreme Court Justice Lewis Powell's decision in the *California Regents v. Bakke* case officially codified this "diversity argument" into law. Powell's assessment in the 1978 case that diversity served a compelling public interest because it exposed the nation's future leaders "to the ideas and mores of students as diverse as its many peoples" directly paralleled the appeals that METCO's advocates long made about the necessity of program in the suburbs.[124]

The increased promotion of affirmative action as the route to achieve racial equality by liberals had direct links to the material and fiscal priorities of suburban professionals, and persisted far after the economic crises of the 1970s subsided. The diversity argument proved essential to maintain the support of both METCO and affirmative action by white homeowners in places like the Route 128 suburbs, who endorsed racial and social equality at an abstract level as long as it did not create any burden on their tax bills or their children's education, and could even potentially enhance it. Yet the notion that METCO and affirmative action's primary function was to enhance diversity and individual opportunity made fostering a sense of collective responsibility for, and the adoption of policies aimed to address, structural inequities in education ever more difficult to achieve.[125]

No One Home to Answer the Phone

In April 1975, as the struggle over mandatory desegregation continued to embroil the city of Boston, a coalition of women from the antibusing group ROAR and antiabortion organization Massachusetts Citizens for Life (MCFL) disrupted a rally in support of the state Equal Rights Amendment (ERA) at Boston's historic Faneuil Hall. The several area feminist groups that organized the event anticipated it would be a relatively staid affair comprised only of people who supported attaching an amendment to the state constitution articulating the broad notion of equal rights for women. The protesters upended these expectations. Carrying signs declaring "Feminists Do Not Represent the American Majority" and "ERA Will Destroy the Family" along with placards reading "Busing Stinks," the participants represented a broader coalition that saw the ERA, like mandatory integration and legalization of abortion, as a direct threat to their religious, political, and social beliefs.[1] The signs and chants of "Stop ERA" halted the rally, and even the intervention of the Boston police failed to quell the crowd. A custodian at Faneuil Hall, which had served as a space for free speech since before the American Revolution, remarked, "We never had anything like this before."[2]

The confrontation exposed how the busing crisis and national recession collided with the rise of feminism and debates over family values of the 1970s to impose new constraints on and open up new possibilities for suburban liberal politics. In response to the anti-ERA movement, the members of the Boston-area chapter of the National Organization of Women (NOW) and its allies formulated an aggressive strategy for the amendment's passage. Building directly on the suburban networks and tactics established in earlier liberal and feminist campaigns, they created an extremely well-organized grassroots-focused movement that involved over five thousand volunteers in almost a hundred cities and towns throughout the state. These efforts convinced Massachusetts voters to endorse the state ERA by an overwhelming majority in the 1976 election. The vote served as the high point of mainstream feminism in Massachusetts in the 1970s. In contrast to the difficult and ongoing battle over the federal ERA at the national level, the successful campaign solidified Massachusetts' position as a leader on the issue of equal rights for women. The fight for women's equality in Massachusetts, however, remained far from over. Just three years later, Massachusetts passed the most restrictive abortion statute in the country, which brought into focus the continued tensions within the state's Democratic coalition.

In examining liberalism during the 1970s, political historians have traditionally concentrated on the fracturing of the New Deal coalition and the economic problems and racial backlash that accompanied it both locally and nationally, and bracketed feminism's accomplishments and failures as a symbol of the Democratic Party's abandonment of class-based concerns.[3] Yet women's activism and feminism did not stand apart from the dynamics of economic restructuring, political realignment, or class politics and in fact provide a way to better understand these processes and these forces.

Feminism illuminates the continuities and changes in liberalism over the 1970s, especially in the suburbs. The movement emerged directly from the ideological and organizational infrastructure of the local fair housing and peace movements and shared many of its members and political ideals. The recession and the battles over mixed-income housing and METCO did not spell the full retreat of liberal activism in the Route 128 suburbs. In line with their position on issues of fair housing, voluntary integration, open space, and environmentalism, however, liberally minded residents in places like Lexington and Newton tended to support the elements of feminism, such as the ERA, that promoted abstract ideals of equality and opportunity, promised to enhance individual rights and quality of life, and did not burden tax rates, or demand sacrifice or redistribution. The movement's promotion of the market-oriented, class-blind idea of "choice" enhanced the individualist dimensions of suburban liberal ideology. The elevation of the language and commitment to choice and opportunity also further naturalized the forms of economic and racial inequality in the priorities of suburban liberalism. Historian Rickie Solinger has deemed choice "the most essential consumerist concept of our time."[4] Framing women's equality and reproductive rights in market-oriented, individualist notions of choice appealed directly to the ways in which fiscally minded suburban residents of both parties approached political and social issues. From voluntary integration to zoning codes, this constituency had long put a strong emphasis on policies that promoted individual and local control. Consistent with this view, residents in the Route 128 suburbs responded more favorably to arguments that pro-choice policies aimed to enhance their individual rights and freedom, while the pro-life movement tried to use the state to impose restrictions on it. The word choice thus joined the pantheon of terms that provided white suburban professionals a means to combine a commitment to abstract notions of equality and self-interest with more specific forms of class privilege.

The increasing wedding of feminism with suburban politics had key trade-offs for the larger cause of women's equality. The sensibility and organizing strategies of suburban liberal politics were both crucial to the success of several campaigns, especially the passage of the ERA. The pivot also helped the movement further earn the notice and attention of politicians eager to win suburban votes. Yet the relationship hardened the middle-class orientation of second-wave feminism and elevated class-blind and consumerist ideas of choice. In the process, white, middle-class, mainstream feminist organizations became even more unlikely to forge coalitions across lines of race, class, space, and sexual orientation or to address issues such as sexual and domestic violence, welfare rights, subsidized child care, and access to health care that concerned a wide range of women.[5]

Suburban Feminism

The story of Wellesley resident and Boston NOW president Patricia Caplan's path to feminist activism seemingly followed the basic narrative of the *Feminine Mystique*. "The trees and grass and clean air are great for the kids, but I was bored," she recalled about her days as a housewife. "I would drive around town in my station wagon and see all these other women driving around in their station wagons."[6] She contemplated the fact that she had always been a "private feminist," but then decided to channel her nascent commitment to women's rights and frustration with suburbia publicly by joining the area's NOW in the late 1960s.[7] Caplan quickly rose in the organization's ranks, serving first as the editor of its monthly newspaper and then president of the Boston-area chapter. A 1971 article in the local paper included a picture of Caplan with long hair, wearing a skirt and blouse, and smiling with her small children against a backdrop of floral wallpaper. "I really like living with my family," she commented. "I wouldn't want it any other way."[8]

An article about Caplan in the *Boston Globe* less than a year later offered a different image. The former debutante had separated from her husband, cut her hair, traded in her skirt for pants and a turtleneck, and moved to a Cambridge apartment she shared with the bearded proprietor of a nearby hammock store. By that time, Caplan had relinquished primary custody of her four children to her husband, Alan, who had gone through important changes as well. He decided to resign from his job at his family business to work as a lawyer at a community action agency, moved with his children from Wellesley to a single-family house in Cambridge, and had also traded in his suit for a turtleneck and jeans. "I credit the women's movement with the whole thing," Caplan asserted. "Without the support of the movement and my work I might have been like so many other people dragging around hating their husbands."[9] Alan too praised feminism for the changes, emphasizing that the couple was closer and more honest after their separation.

The metamorphosis of the suburban country-club members into self-realized hippies in a matter of months offers an accelerated model of the impact feminism had on the lives of many suburban families in the Route 128 ring. The individual and collective experiences simultaneously altered the political and social activity of the Route 128 suburbs in the 1970s and beyond. Caplan differed from many other suburban women she encountered through NOW, whose entrance into feminism evolved from earlier involvement in grassroots political causes. Throughout the postwar period, women had stood at the forefront of the Route 128 suburbs' vibrant network of organizations devoted to civil rights, peace, and environmentalism. Bonnie Jones, a member of the Lexington fair housing and peace movements, later observed that though the groups included a lot of men, "women did most of the work," and "the real energy and enthusiasm for a lot of this stuff came from women." She recalled that during the 1960s, she and the other "women in town were, by and large, not working," and able to put "a lot of energy into political activity.[10] The personal friendships forged in the planning meetings and envelope-licking sessions of fair housing and peace groups created both a personal network and ideological infrastructure for feminist activity. Commenting on the influence of 1960s' activism on the rise of feminism, Jones recalled, "It was no accident that the Women's movement came out of that same period."[11] By the early 1970s, Jones herself had started a consciousness-raising group, become president of the Lexington NOW chapter, and was pursuing her master's degree in social work.

The experience of participating in civil rights and antiwar groups had propelled many women like Jones to go back to school, get jobs, and renegotiate their familial responsibilities in the 1970s. "Voluntarism wasn't enough for most of us," explained Anita Greenbaum, a longtime VOW member and veteran of several other liberal political causes. Many of these suburban women saw employment as a continuation of earlier social activism, launching or reviving careers as social workers or teachers, or in politics.[12] Moreover, many of the toddlers who had come to meetings or marched alongside their mothers were in high school or college, which meant many suburban women had fewer domestic responsibilities and more time to pursue employment opportunities.[13]

The decision of many women to enter the paid workforce also signaled larger changes in the economy. The same factors that had led many suburban residents to refuse accepting financial responsibility for the METCO program, including the rise of inflation and federal and local tax rates as well as soaring utility bills and college tuitions, led many women to pursue paid labor opportunities.[14] The economic downturn of Route 128 industry that began in 1970, and had led to a rise in the unemployment of male engineers and technology professionals, had motivated many of their wives to seek full-time employment.[15] Even if they did not have to deal with unemployment, many middle-class families could no longer survive on a single salary. By 1973, as the national recession was reaching full swing, 41.1 percent of all women in Lexington had joined the labor force, up from 22.1 percent in 1960.[16] In a 1978 report, Lexington officials observed that "given the current inflation rate and other accelerating costs, it is not surprising that close to 50% of the households in Lexington find it necessary to have an income to supplement that of the primary 'breadwinner.'"[17] The other Route 128 suburbs experienced parallel developments as increasing numbers of female residents sought out part- and full-time job opportunities.

Financial pressures and job insecurity put strains on the marriages of many suburban families. The number of divorced households in Lexington grew from 354 in 1970 to 411 in 1978, which was 13.7 per 1,000 people, substantially higher than the national average of 4.6 per 1,000.[18] As the experience of the Caplan family suggests, the economy was not the sole factor propelling the divorce rate to rise, but regardless, changing family dynamics produced new economic and familial responsibilities to navigate. By 1979, Lexington school officials had organized support groups for the estimated 30 percent of students who experienced the effects of divorce. The groups mirrored the consciousness-raising activities that their mothers had joined to address the changes as well.[19]

These thousands of individual decisions and life circumstances had a powerful collective impact on the effectiveness of liberal organizations and rise of feminist activity in the Route 128 suburbs. The influx of many women into the paid workforce or taking on new familial arrangements contributed to the eventual disbanding of organizations like the MFFHER and VOW. Sue Berkeley, a longtime participant of peace and fair housing groups in Newton, noted that while the movements had long depended on "housewives in the suburbs," by the mid-1970s, "you don't find women at home to answer the phone anymore."[20] At the same time, many of these women turned their energy toward feminism, which fueled the rise of organizations like NOW in the suburbs.

Led by Betty Friedan, a group of prominent women first began NOW at the national level in 1966 with the goal of creating a civil rights organization for women, and it quickly gained a reputation as the feminist organization most committed to working through the channels of political power to create female equality.[21] Several "professional women and well-meaning liberals" established the first chapter in Massachusetts in 1969. Early member Carol Kountz summarized the group's philosophy and plan of action: "We can make a difference in women's lives by changing laws."[22] The national headquarters dubbed it both the "cyclone chapter" and "Boston Brain Trust," as it quickly became the second-largest chapter of NOW in the country and the largest and most politically visible feminist group in the Boston area.[23] From the outset, leaders understood that their success depended on presenting

Table 9.1 Changing Family Characteristics of Route 128 Suburbs and Boston, 1970 and 1980

Municipality	Concord	Lexington	Lincoln	Newton	Brookline	Boston
Population, 1970	16,148	31,886	7,567	91,066	58,886	641,071
Percent of married women in workforce, 1970	35.1%	36.6%	N/A	36.1%	39.8%	40.1%
Percent of women in workforce, 16+, 1970	41.3%	41.1%	32.7%	43.1%	51.8%	47.8%
Median income per family, 1970	$16,463	$17,558	$17,361	$15,381	$13,701	$9,133
Population, 1980	16,293	28,479	7,098	83,622	55,962	562,994
Percent of women in labor force, 16+, 1980	55.6%	55.7%	54.4%	54.7%	57.6%	52.7%
Median income per family, 1980	$34,353	$34,989	$31,543	$30,436	$25,389	$22,473

NOW as a counterpart to existing Boston-based female liberation organizations, which had younger and more leftist membership bases.[24] Several suburban women who joined NOW had attended meetings of more radical groups like Bread and Roses, but became alienated by their approach and the organizers' attitude that housewives represented "the most oppressed members of society."[25] The women preferred NOW both because of its dedication "to achieving its goals within the existing system," and because the organization provided a means to improve rather than fully reject the patterns and practices of their daily lives.[26]

By the early 1970s, NOW chapters had emerged in several towns along the Route 128 ring and gave members the tools to fight for gender equality within their own communities.[27] The Newton and Lexington chapters developed a campaign to eradicate sex discrimination in public schools. Members in Newton and other communities worked with the local school board to adopt a more gender-neutral curriculum that taught both male and female students how to sew a button or make a bench.[28] The Lexington chapter conducted an intensive study of the gendered stereotypes in assigned social study and history textbooks.[29] The project, called "Putting Women in Their Place," eventually exposed the inadequate attention to women's history in most assigned texts and offered an extensive set of materials for teachers to rectify this imbalance in the curriculum.[30] Lexington members also worked with the career counseling department at the high school to expand the options for female students beyond "typing" and marriage," and encouraged students to start a feminist column in the school newspaper. This effort relied on an argument similar to that used to advocate for voluntary integration by contending that the gendered curriculum, like the racially homogeneous one, damaged and disadvantaged white middle-class students. Diane Lund of Lexington's NOW declared, "It is hard to think of any justification for depriving half of our junior high population of organized sports opportunities."[31] "My children are individuals whose interests and creativity should not be stifled at age five," one Newton member asserted. "It really makes me mad to think my child's being told she's a cookie baker and a nose wiper and that's all and I'm paying for it."[32]

The efforts helped to reduce the overt practices of gender discrimination in many Boston area schools. By the mid-1970s, the Brookline, Newton, and Lexington NOW affiliates reported a rise in both sex equality in the curriculum and the athletic opportunities for female students. The Lexington committee even persuaded the high school to establish an ice hockey team for girls in 1976, which was particularly impressive given the tight fiscal restraints of the mid-1970s.[33] These projects undoubtedly had a positive impact on the education of individual female and male students in both the short and long term. The rise of girls' sports teams, in fact, marked one of the largest and most tangible impacts of feminist activity on suburban communities in Boston and the nation. The policies also helped to enhance the reputation of the school systems in places like Lexington and Newton as cutting edge, and served as another feature making the communities attractive to perspective homebuyers who wanted to raise their children in a progressive environment. By the early 1970s feminism joined civil rights, environmentalism, and the antiwar movement as another example of the liberal political views of residents in the Route 128 suburbs.[34]

The growth of the organization in these communities brought visibility and credibility to feminism, but it had drawbacks for the movement's larger cause of trying to improve opportunities for women of every race, class, sexual orientation, and political persuasion. Before she had fully embraced a bohemian lifestyle, Caplan stated her belief that NOW's wider contribution "may well be our so-called elitist middle-class orientation. We are educated, resourceful," and "know the people who run things."[35] NOW members frequently discussed how the organization could use its "middle-class orientation" and connections with the "establishment" on behalf of less powerful groups, such as "women on welfare," "black women," "gay women," and "women in prison."[36] The ideological and geographic realities of NOW made creating these types of alliances and coalitions difficult to achieve.

The consciousness-raising components of groups like NOW further demonstrate the difficulty of creating connections across lines of class, race, space, and sexuality. Although consciousness-raising first emerged as a tool deployed by radical activists, the groups and strategies became increasingly popular in affluent suburbs.[37] In *Rebirth of Feminism*, published in 1971, Judith Hole and Ellen Levine observed, "Suburban housewives, who might well hesitate to call themselves feminists, are among the frequent employers of the small group technique."[38] The discussions provided a way for women to address a variety of personal issues, especially the isolating and oppressive facets of suburban life. By the fall of 1972, Lexington's NOW had four consciousness-raising groups in operation and a wait-list of women wanting to join.[39] The groups paralleled and even inspired the self-help organizations of unemployed male engineers, which appeared in the Route 128 communities at the same time and may have involved many of their husbands. For women in a similar position as Caplan, consciousness-raising helped to reevaluate major changes in their lives while giving them a sense of self-worth and independence. The groups also offered a means of building connections and solidarity with other women in their communities. These explorations of the political aspects of their individual and shared personal experiences, however, often led suburban women to address a racially, economically, and spatially specific set of concerns.[40]

The politics of consciousness-raising, when removed from its radical origins, more closely resembled the arguments and tactics of the suburban fair housing movement in the early 1960s. Echoing the racial liberal philosophy of the fair housing committees, consciousness-raising rested on the belief that one-on-one conversation and changing "hearts and minds" provided the means to inspire political action and create social equality. For some women, the groups marked the first step toward a collective political consciousness. For many other participants, the discussions about transforming individual relationships helped to make their marriages and own family lives more equitable by promoting the sharing of household duties. Yet this emphasis enhanced not only the individual consciousness of the members involved but also the racially, class-, and geographic-specific focus of the movement as a whole.

The consciousness-raising groups in the Route 128 suburbs usually operated at the neighborhood level, and thereby, predominantly consisted of a dialogue among upper-middle-class white women.[41] In 1973, a group of master's students conducted a study of several groups in Lexington and found that the women involved were almost all white, uniformly upper income, highly educated, and 77 percent were married to men with either a master's, PhD, legal, or medical degree. The members also overwhelmingly shared a liberal political worldview articulating unanimous support for ecology and civil rights issues and a belief in working within the formal channels of the political system to increase individual rights.[42] The insular bent made the participants ever more inclined to use the attitudes and needs of white middle-class educated women to stand-in for the experiences and goals of all women, which would become a criticism that more radical and activist women of color would frequently deploy against second-wave feminism.[43] The lack of diversity within the groups also created barriers to forging alliances and coalitions with people of different races, socioeconomic classes, places of residence, sexual orientations, and political persuasions. The consciousness-raising groups thereby provide a microcosm of many of the strengths and limits of the movement as whole, which the battle over the ERA further illuminates.

Simple Justice

In contrast to the difficult and ultimately failed battle over the federal ERA, the campaign for the state ERA served as a high point of second-wave feminism in Massachusetts. This campaign built directly on the political gains and suburban middle-class membership of groups like NOW and showed their effectiveness at working within the political system. Despite the referendum's overwhelming victory in November 1976, the campaign also revealed certain organizational and ideological limits to the movement.

The idea of a federal ERA dated to the immediate aftermath of suffrage, but the US Congress had consistently defeated it. Upon its formation, the national NOW had made passage of the amendment a top priority. Although the federal government had by that time enacted a series of laws to promote sex equality, including Title VII, NOW and its allies believed that the ERA contained both additional protection and important symbolism. In 1972, Congress finally passed the ERA. Just a few months later, by a vote of 205 to 7, Massachusetts became the twentieth state to ratify the amendment. The quick change of attitude by local and national politicians demonstrated the growing acceptance of women's equality and the recognition that the ERA would not make radical changes to law or society. Yet the national momentum for passage halted in the remaining states needed for ratification and a lengthy, heated struggle ensued.[44]

With the future of the federal amendment in doubt, Boston NOW decided to submit a virtually identical ERA at the state level in 1973. It read, "Equality under the law shall not be denied or abridged because of sex, race, color, creed or national origin," and changed the clause "all men are born free and equal" to "all persons are born free and equal." NOW activists believed that whether or not the federal amendment passed, the state statute would at least serve as "a symbolic gesture" and at most supply women "with a legal handle" to challenge discriminatory laws and practices.[45] It was still a bureaucratically tedious task to change the state constitution. Massachusetts law stipulated that an amendment had to pass two separately elected bodies by a majority vote and then be put on the ballot for ratification. The amendment easily cleared the first hurdle as the state legislative bill passed almost unanimously and with little debate in August 1973. After this painless victory, NOW and its allies confidently placed the issue on the back burner as it waited for the chance to bring it before the electorate.

The campaign's architects drastically underestimated the growing opposition to the ERA among antibusing forces. With mandatory desegregation first a threat and then a reality, the antibusing movement became an increasingly organized force in Massachusetts politics. Groups like ROAR had initially not articulated much concern for gender issues or the ERA. Yet as several feminist organizations, especially the Governor's Commission on the Status of Women (GCSW), had repeatedly refused to acknowledge mandatory busing as a women's issue, it sparked the outrage of ROAR's largely female base. In early 1975, eighty ROAR members disrupted the GCSW proceedings at a city hall meeting in Boston by breaking into song. Chair Ann Blackham tried to restore order by chiding the ROAR members, "You are our guests here and if you don't behave, I will have to ask you to leave." The reprimand inflamed ROAR leader Pixie Palladino. Gesturing toward the commission, whose members came mostly from the Route 128 area, she quickly shot back, "You're *our* guests. This is *our* City Hall. No bunch of ladies from the suburbs is going to kick the women of Boston out of their own City Hall."[46] The dismissive treatment by the GSCW members awakened a sense for Palladino and her allies that feminists were just another example of suburban liberals using the government to encroach on their way of life.[47]

ROAR discovered a set of allies in its anti-ERA mission among the state's grassroots antiabortion movement, especially within the MCFL. Founded in 1970, the MCFL had rapidly developed a large and predominantly Catholic membership base throughout the state. MCFL leaders believed that the ERA would both increase the accessibility of abortion and destroy traditional family norms, and therefore helped to combine the issues of busing, abortion, and antifeminist and antiliberal sentiments. One observer half joked that the campaign made the ERA appear as a law to create "forced busing across school boundaries to have abortions."[48] But the combination of these issues had begun to shift the heavily Catholic state legislature against the amendment, and many of its constituents followed suit.

The Stop ERA effort in Massachusetts received a great deal of support from conservative firebrand Phyllis Schlafly, who recognized the symbolic importance of defeating the amendment in the purportedly most liberal state in the nation. Through her relentless campaign against the ERA, the Illinois activist had become a household name by the mid-1970s. In 1975 and 1976, Schlafly made several visits to Boston, where she deemed the ERA "the opening wedge to the destruction of the American family" and issued a sweeping warning that it would force the courts to validate homosexual marriages, strip churches of tax exemptions if they refused to ordain women, and stop states from regulating abortion.[49] While the Massachusetts Stop ERA forces aligned with Schlafly and the broader national effort, they continued to anchor the issue in other local concerns, particularly busing and abortion.

These state Stop ERA groups conflated the amendment and feminism with a broader set of negative assumptions about liberalism. The national campaign similarly sought to draw attention to the connections between the amendment and the problems of liberalism, but the context of the busing crisis and state's crippling economic recession gave such arguments heightened meaning in Massachusetts. ROAR's largely working-class, female base already felt victimized by high taxes, the weak economy, the poor education of their children, and the growing divorce rate. The members perceived feminism and the ERA not as an opportunity to gain new entitlements but rather as an attack on their right to a traditional nuclear family.[50] Tapping into these existing fears, Stop ERA warned that the amendment would create a "gender-free society" where women were to be "liberated" from "responsibilities of their homes and families."[51] Agnes Smith, cochair of the local Stop ERA Committee, was also a member of ROAR, the John Birch Society, and George Wallace's American Party. The combined platform of these organizations supplied the ideological underpinnings of

Smith's argument that the ERA would destroy the traditional family and take away the right of a woman to be supported by her husband. The ERA also, Smith held, constituted a clear example of "governmental intrusion" on individual rights.[52]

The largely urban white members of ROAR, however, were not the only Bay State residents to experience anxieties that liberalism, feminism, and the ERA represented an attack on the nuclear family. Several of the key leaders of the Stop ERA campaign emerged from coffee klatches on quiet tree-lined suburban streets, not from the working-class protests outside South Boston High School. The movement grew in clusters of suburbs on both the North and South Shore, drawing residents through existing affiliations to antiabortion groups and organizations like the John Birch Society and Eagle Forum.[53] It also attracted people without such tried-and-true conservative credentials. Stop ERA leader Margaret Mahoney was a lawyer from Winchester who had voted for McGovern and opposed exclusionary zoning laws. At the same time, she fiercely objected to claims of gender inequality and often pointed to her own professional success as evidence for lack of necessity for the ERA.[54] Although Mahoney came from a different class and geographic vantage point as Smith and the majority of ROAR members, she shared their Catholic faith and similarly emphasized the significance of religion in her life. Faith and religious affiliation represented common characteristics among ERA opponents nationally. But the predominance of Catholics differentiated the members of the movement in Massachusetts from their counterparts in the South and Midwest, who were primarily conservative Protestants.[55] Clearly not all the state's 40 percent Roman Catholic population shared this view of the ERA. These opponents, nevertheless, underscored the role of religion, especially Catholicism, in campaigns related to social issues like feminism and abortion, and the ways it transcended the spatial and class dividing lines that had structured controversies like the busing crisis.

Eyeshadow and the ERA

Just as Schlafly and her allies acknowledged the national implications of the defeat of ERA in the epicenter of liberalism, so too did the members of many Boston-area feminist groups. "If the Massachusetts amendment goes down we can kiss the federal ERA goodbye," one leader asserted. "They know it and we know it."[56] Members of several leading feminist and liberal groups joined forces to establish the Committee to Ratify the Massachusetts State Equal Rights Amendment, with Ann Kendall as chair, and it evolved into an extremely well-organized campaign.[57] ERA proponents worked within the rhetorical parameters established by the opposition, setting out to "combat" many of the rumors and misinformation surrounding the legislation. Supporters stressed that the state ERA would not affect abortion, the school busing issue, maternity leave policies, or bathrooms. They also clarified that the state amendment would impact neither social security benefits nor the military draft, both of which were federal issues.

During the first six months of 1976, the campaign enlisted twenty-six coordinators, who oversaw the formation of committees in about a hundred towns across the state, with the largest concentration in the Route 128 suburbs. The grassroots volunteers sponsored sales of household items and t-shirts with the amendment written on the front, wine and cheese parties, sock hops, and clambakes. One town provided the answer to the question "Can one support the ERA and still wear eyeshadow?" by holding a series of makeup parties to raise funds for the campaign.[58] A group of housewives launched a project called "Dial a Day for the ERA," where supporters pledged to call one friend every day to help sway the vote. Through these efforts, the ERA campaign raised fifty thousand dollars and recruited over five thousand volunteers and many more nonactive supporters.

Using these funds and some volunteers, the Committee to Ratify took several other steps to emulate an electoral campaign. In the place of a campaign bus or whistle-stop tour, the Committee to Ratify sent an "ERA Truthmobile" around the state to shopping plazas and parking lots, where volunteers aboard answered questions and passed out information emblazoned with the campaign slogan, "The ERA sounds simple and it is."[59] In one of their most effective moves, the organizers replaced the candidate stump speech with a bureau of speakers trained by the committee to deliver a prepared set of talking points, describing how the ERA would provide a woman with the right to "choose how she lives her life," be it as "homemaker, teacher, businesswomen, construction worker," and ensure that all women "rights and the freedom to live as they wish."[60]

The fights for the ERA in other states had showed that the viability of the cause depended on people who did not necessarily support feminism or legalized abortion but did endorse broad ideas of civil rights and individual liberties. A poll conducted by the *Boston Herald* in March 1976 confirmed that this tendency held true in Massachusetts as well. The poll showed that while more than 80 percent of women strongly rejected the feminist label, roughly the same percent supported the ERA and many of the other basic goals of the feminist movement.[61] Thus, the committee consciously worked to make the issue as moderate and nonthreatening as possible, distancing it from the negative associations of feminism, and instead focusing it on issues of rights and opportunities that echoed the fair housing movement.

The language of individual rights and choice was crucial to separating the campaign from the images of special privileges and identity politics that often made feminism, affirmative action, and busing so controversial. Nancy

Adler, the committee's Lexington coordinator, publicly stated that she would have doubted the prophecy if someone had told her she would be leading the charge for the ERA. Adler explained that she "never identified herself as a 'women's libber' or 'feminist,'" but believed the ERA "was not an issue for feminists alone."[62] The campaign stressed that the amendment would offer universal entitlements, or as one local coordinator declared, "The ERA isn't just for feminists. Citizens of all sexes and colors will benefit from it."[63] The growing appearance of the pro-ERA slogan on bumper stickers, t-shirts, and bracelets on children and adults in subdivisions throughout the state revealed the effectiveness and breadth of this message.

The campaign's language and argument also aligned with the fiscal sensibilities of many suburban residents who endorsed abstract ideals of equality as long as it did not place any burden on their own rights or property values, or require the outlay of any local tax dollars. Similar to the fair housing movement, the committee frequently framed its campaign in a market-oriented language of choice and opportunity, suggesting the ERA gave women "a choice" to "decide for themselves what they want to be and do in their own lives . . . and find fulfillment."[64] Many of the supporters also inverted this logic, articulating a fear that the absence of the ERA would put themselves and their daughters at a disadvantage. A suburban father became involved in the campaign out of the concern that without it, his daughters faced unfair handicaps to the education for which he had paid.[65]

If the campaign sought to de-emphasize special privileges, conversely it aimed to highlight its civil rights dimensions. Bill Ramsey, an African American MIT educated engineer, became the ideal poster child for this message. He spent his weekends going door-to-door through his Newton neighborhood to pass out literature and speak to his predominantly white neighbors, explaining to them that the ERA was "more than a 'women's law'"; it was "a commitment, a statement by the Commonwealth that it will protect all our rights."[66] Yet Ramsey was one of the few people of color to join in the Committee to Ratify. In perhaps a sign of the selective embrace of the civil rights cause, the committee made virtually no attempt to build an alliance with local black community activists, feminists of color, or welfare rights groups, even though the language of the proposed amendment officially included the category of race. The amendment's support did transcend partisan divisions with endorsements from Governor Dukakis, Senators Brooke and Kennedy, and presidential candidates Jimmy Carter and Gerald Ford.[67]

In the November 1976 election, the ERA secured the approval of 61 percent of the voters statewide and won by almost two to one in Route 128 suburbs like Lexington that had large chapters of the Committee to Ratify. The referendum helped Massachusetts to "buck" the national trend of low turnout in the 1976 presidential election. In fact, most liberal political activists during the fall had opted to put their energy into the amendment campaign rather than Carter's presidential bid.[68] Several observers immediately saw the strong support for the ERA as a sign of the intrinsic liberalism of the Massachusetts electorate and took the passage as a sign of the strength of feminism in the state. This celebratory interpretation overlooked how it was actually the moderate and symbolic dimensions of the amendment that fueled its passage, and how the campaign constrained rather than expanded the feminist cause.

The passage of the amendment owed much to the Committee to Ratify's well-organized grassroots campaign. By encouraging voters to support the ERA without endorsing the broader feminist movement, the campaign failed to instill permanent support for feminist issues and causes within the electorate. Moreover, the year-and-a-half effort demanded a great deal of resources and energy, and made the movement less able to address other important issues and concerns, such as welfare, access to abortion, and publicly subsidized child care. Many of these decisions were undoubtedly strategic, and a means of navigating between the constraints imposed by the anti-ERA campaign and priorities of large swaths of the electorate that supported ideas of equality and individual rights, but not redistributive measures to achieve them. Yet the campaign's discourse of equality of opportunity resulted in shifting the strategy and ideology of many feminists in the suburbs even more toward a focus on enhancing the choices and privileges of middle-class women. The choice-based rhetoric created a discursive framework that would become increasingly central to the fight to preserve legal abortion at the end of the 1970s. As the movement combated a powerful oppositional threat, it further narrowed the issue while also obscuring the multitude of structural factors preventing low-income and minority women from taking advantage of the ERA of reproductive rights.

Abortion Politics

The ERA battle offered a glimpse of the power of the Massachusetts antiabortion movement, which had gathered strength following the *Roe v. Wade* decision and gradually transformed the state into a national epicenter of pro-life sentiment. The state's leading antiabortion group, the MCFL, embraced the strategy of mobilizing supporters at the grassroots to work directly within formal channels of state government to restrict access to abortion. By 1977, the MCFL boasted around a hundred chapters, a mailing list of ninety thousand, a full-time lobbyist, and a twenty-four-hour hotline that reached over eighteen thousand callers to inform members of legislation pending on Beacon Hill.[69] During the 1977 legislative session alone, the group filed six bills and testified seventeen times at public hearings opposing abortion. Remarking on the MCFL's success, one reporter noted, "The anti-abortion lobby in this state is a vast persistent grassroots network, a one-issue constituency that will vote for or against a political candidate solely for his or her stand on abortion."[70] As part of this one-issue crusade, in the late 1970s the MCFL turned its attention to the issue of publicly funded abortion, leading a campaign throughout the metropolitan region that exacerbated racial and economic discrimination, political polarization, and the fiscal concerns of suburban taxpayers.

The case of Kenneth Edelin first set the terms for the controversy surrounding publicly financed abortion, and demonstrated the racial, economic, and political dimensions of the issue.[71] In 1974, an all-white jury convicted Edelin, the first African American chief resident in obstetrics at Boston City Hospital, of manslaughter for allegedly causing the death of a twenty-four-week-old black male fetus during a legal abortion. The case coincided directly with the mandatory desegregation of Boston's public schools and involved many of the same Irish Catholic politicians, punctuating the racial undertones of the case and its verdict. The sense of inequity and racism became even further pronounced when in response to the pressure of the case, Boston City Hospital officials decided to forbid abortions except in medical or psychiatric emergencies. Since the hospital was one of the only places in Boston where those who could not afford to pay a fee could legally end unwanted pregnancies, the policy added another burden to the lives of poor women in the city. The Supreme Judicial Court unanimously overturned the conviction the following year, but the case had much broader and long-lasting repercussions. The conviction led several cities, including Detroit, Pittsburgh, Nashville, and New York, to place strict restrictions on the availability of second-trimester abortions and other hospitals to pass policies making the procedure extremely expensive.[72]

This case propelled the shift in the national strategy of activists and politicians away from trying to fully overturn *Roe* and instead toward limiting the availability of abortion. This process gradually transformed abortion from a universal right into a privilege for those who could afford it. During the mid-1970s, members of the US Congress repeatedly introduced legislation to restrict public funding for abortion, thereby essentially cutting off the service for welfare recipients.[73] The effort finally succeeded in 1976 with the passage of the Hyde Amendment, named for its author, Illinois Republican Henry Hyde. This amendment prohibited the use of federal money to pay for or encourage abortions. The issue provided politicians like President Carter with a way to stake out a middle ground on abortion very much in line with their position on mandatory school desegregation and affordable housing: supporting the concept of equality, but not economic or class-based remedies to achieve it. When asked to comment on the restriction on Medicaid funds for abortion, Carter stated, "There are many things in life that are not fair, that wealthy people can afford and poor people can't."[74]

The Supreme Court codified this attitude into law with a set of rulings announced in June 1977 determining that states had no constitutional obligation to provide public funding for the procedure. In sharply worded dissents, Justice Harry Blackmun compared the decision to Marie Antoinette's decree "let them eat cake," and Justice Thurgood Marshall predicted it would "relegate millions of people to poverty and despair."[75]

The Supreme Court rulings opened an important door for politicians throughout the country to increase the attack on reproductive rights and implement Hyde Amendment–style policy at the state level. Massachusetts led the way. The day after the Supreme Court announced its decision, state Representative Ray Flynn, the future mayor of Boston, along with his colleague Representative Charles Doyle submitted a bill to prohibit spending any state funds for Medicaid recipients to receive both "elective" and "therapeutic" abortions.[76] The proposed statute limiting the right to an abortion raised immediate opposition from several state officials including Governor Michael Dukakis, a vocal abortion rights supporter, who promised to veto it or any other attempt to limit publicly funded procedures.[77] Several state legislators also spoke out against it. Many, such as Representative David Swartz of Haverhill, opposed abortion on philosophical and religious grounds, but disliked the fact that the Doyle-Flynn bill discriminated against the poor and contained no exceptions for drastic cases.[78] "How can we tell a wealthy woman from Wellesley that she can have an abortion because she doesn't want to defer her European trip for a year," he asked his colleagues, "while we tell the poor women who knows she and her fetus are affected by rubella that she can't have an abortion?"[79] These arguments failed to create a sense of contrition in the minds of most state's legislators, who confronted considerable pressure from the state's antiabortion movement.

Massachusetts activists recognized the Doyle-Flynn bill as a crucial foot in the door for their broader campaign to make abortions completely illegal. Outlining its strategy, MCFL chair John McNulty proclaimed, "The prolifers don't want to lose momentum. Our objective is to deny everyone, rich or poor."[80] The group relied on contacts within the state's large Catholic community in order to maintain this energy. The state's Catholic newspapers all offered editorials in favor of the Doyle-Flynn bill, and the Diocese urged parish priests to devote homilies to the "Respect Life" theme, stressing the necessity of the legislation.[81] Church leaders throughout the state distributed literature and delivered sermons aimed to encourage grassroots lobbying, and helped to craft arguments that would appeal to the predominantly Catholic legislature.

The antiabortion movement also sought to expand support for the bill among middle-class suburbanites by couching the issue in taxpayer concerns. The MCFL adopted a multifaceted argument that simultaneously raised "objections to the use of tax funds to destroy unborn children" and stressed that "human life should not have a price tag."[82] The letters that Doyle-Flynn supporters sent to the State House as part of the lobbying effort underscore this fusion of moral and fiscal opposition. In letters to Senator Jack Backman, suburban constituents like Josephine Di Gregorio stated that it was unfair to "tax people who are struggling to support their own families"; Katherine Keefe pointed out that it "was wrong to give tax dollars to the poor so they can kill their unwanted babies"; and Newton resident Jane Crimlisk asserted that she would "rather see my tax dollars being spent to help poor people get jobs and get ahead rather than having tax dollars spent on eliminating them from society."[83]

Feminist activists, who viewed the legislation as a threat to all women, not just to welfare recipients, launched a counterattack challenging the act and antiabortion movement. This effort also drew links between concerns about taxes and reproductive rights. In the summer of 1977, NOW and other female activist and civil liberties organizations formed a coalition called Mass. Citizens for Choice (Mass Choice) that built on the infrastructure developed during the fight for the state ERA to match the grassroots power of the antiabortion movement.[84] The Mass Choice leaders understood that the majority of people who received abortions were not welfare recipients but instead middle- and upper-income women, and therefore made this constituency and their concerns a centerpiece of the campaign. Echoing the tactic employed in the ERA campaign, Mass Choice used a broad language of individual rights that submerged race and class differences to arouse the suburbanites' concern. These forces emphasized the call of Newton state representative Lois Pines, who stated that the Doyle-Flynn bill was "but an opening skirmish in the battle by anti-abortionists to deny *all* women the right to freedom of choice."[85] NOW and its allies further stressed the universal components of the bill in an effort to target the self-interest of its white middle-class membership base in a flyer warning "DON'T BE COMPLACENT! WE COULD EASILY LOSE THE RIGHT TO CHOOSE."[86]

Although Mass Choice downplayed some of the class-specific components of the legislation, it embraced an economically conscious argument. The coalition circulated a series of Department of Welfare statistics to suggest that in the long run, social service costs would be significantly higher if poor women lost access to publicly funded abortions. In 1976, the state had subsidized 3,862 procedures, which amounted to about 14 percent of all the abortions performed in Massachusetts and cost about $750,000, roughly 90 percent of which the federal government paid before the Hyde Amendment. During the same year, the state had spent $4.6 million on maternity costs and $15.4 million in Aid to Families with Dependent Children payments.[87] Mass Choice calculated that the maternity expenses of the women who had Medicaid-funded abortions would increase the cost of welfare by

$2.2 million per year. The statistics appealed directly to the anxieties of suburban taxpayers such as Lexington physician Harris Funkenstein, who believed that financing abortions would "ultimately save the state an enormous amount of money," and Harris Kodis, who observed, "I think the state would have a bigger burden to pay... in terms of unhappy people it would have to support, people with a lot of problems. Economically it doesn't make sense."[88]

The protracted battle over versions of the Doyle-Flynn bill spread across several rounds of wrangling and two vetoes by Dukakis.[89] Antiabortion forces eventually prevailed in 1979, and the legislature passed an even more restrictive statute prohibiting any publicly financed abortions, including those of state employees, and made no exceptions for cases of rape or incest. One supporter enthusiastically declared, "It's a glorious day, a great, great day for the people of Massachusetts, especially the poor."[90] Reproductive and welfare rights proponents disagreed, given that the law effectively cut off the right of many poor women to obtain a legal procedure and meant that Massachusetts now had on its books the most restrictive abortion law in the nation. The legislature added to this distinction the same year when it passed an informed consent law that required all women seeking an abortion to sign a detailed form outlining the development of a fetus, procedure to be used, and risks involved. In addition, the law stipulated that a teenage girl needed her parents' approval or a superior court judge to deem her "mature," or the procedure in her "best interest."[91]

The passage of the restrictive abortion laws reveals the ways in which the Catholic and growing conservative tenor of state and national politics in the late 1970s imposed key constraints on the strategies of suburban liberal activists. While suburban liberals had long navigated successfully the structures of state politics on a variety of issues, from fair and affordable housing, voluntary integration, peace, and environmentalism, and even women's rights, abortion proved one issue where their strategies were unable to sway the largely Catholic legislature. Abortion rights activists achieved some victories circumscribing the effects of these laws through the state and federal courts, but these rulings still did not provide unfettered access to abortions for all women in Massachusetts.[92]

The legislature did not, however, represent the attitude of the vast majority of Massachusetts citizens about the legalization of abortion. A poll conducted in 1978 found that 83 percent of Massachusetts residents from across the political, religious, and economic spectrum surveyed believed that the "choice" to have abortion was a "private matter" that should be made by an individual without state intervention, and 53 percent supported government funding of the procedure for those who could not afford to pay.[93] A large percentage of Bay State residents, therefore, endorsed abortion rights in the abstract and remained appalled at the idea of laws that denied such rights to low-income women.[94] Yet most of these residents—especially white, affluent, liberal-leaning professionals—interpreted abortion politics in terms of their individual rights and options. The majority of these white suburbanites recognized that *Roe v. Wade* and their ability to pay for the procedure preserved their own abortion rights. This fact meant that as the battle over the Doyle-Flynn bill dragged out, most people in the Route 128 suburbs became complacent about fighting hard against restrictions on the availability of abortion for low-income women. This class-blind understanding of abortion politics increasingly came to shape the struggle to preserve the legality of the procedure at both the state and national level.

As American as Apple Pie

In the aftermath of the passage of the new abortion laws, the Massachusetts Organization for Repeal of Abortion Laws (MORAL) decided to shift its strategies to fall even more closely in line with the individualistic attitude of white suburban professionals. Newly appointed executive director Jean Weinberg, a community organizer who had worked with NOW, acknowledged that despite the fact that most Massachusetts citizens supported the right to abortion, the group had a far weaker grassroots network than its antiabortion counterparts. "There are a lot of smart people in the community who care what's happening," Weinberg explained of her strategy, "but they don't know what to do about an issue."[95] Polling results convinced Weinberg that in order to preserve and expand reproductive rights, MORAL had to *"mobilize this majority"* not by changing views but by channeling existing sentiment into "effective political action."[96] MORAL decided to organize the members of the public already sympathetic to its cause to create an abortion rights constituency that matched the singularly focused pro-life vote.[97]

Like many previous liberal initiatives, MORAL hoped to tap into the effectiveness of suburban middle-class voters to work within the political channels and persuade politicians to uphold and expand abortion rights. MORAL implemented a plan to develop local committees in each of the state's forty senate districts to stage house parties "identical to Tupperware parties'" to sell not plastic but reproductive politics.[98] Using a strategy similar to a pyramid scheme, MORAL encouraged the fifty to a hundred people in attendance at every house party to invite friends and neighbors over for coffee to tell them about specific ways to get involved. By expanding the network, more local residents learned about the political process, became involved in lobbying efforts, and set up registration drives to increase the pro-choice vote.[99] By 1979, MORAL had established committees in twenty-one districts, and by 1981 had staged four hundred meetings and reached four thousand Massachusetts residents. The effort to "politically activate pro-choice people" proved most effective in traditionally liberal communities like Newton that had an existing base of support from the ERA campaign.[100]

MORAL's recognition of the importance of self-interest as a force in motivating political action also contributed to its success in challenging many suburbanites' sense of complacency on the abortion issue. In order to do so, the campaign framed the issue of abortion in the nonthreatening language and imagery of white middle-class norms. The campaign's adoption of the slogan "As American as Apple Pie: A Women's Right to Choose" most clearly symbolizes this strategy and message.[101] This language followed in close step with ERA supporters' efforts to present the amendment not as a demand for particular rights for women but rather as a quest for class- and race-neutral ideals of choice and opportunity.[102] The concept of the "right to choose" aligned with and enhanced the ideology of white middle-class residents in places like the Route 128 suburbs dating back to the fair housing movement in the early 1960s when they sought to provide stable middle-class black families the "right to choose" to live in affluent suburbs.

The goal of enhancing choice, nevertheless, further obscured the fact that the laws like the Doyle-Flynn bill, Hyde Amendment, and informed consent requirements prevented a large portion of women from electing the option of abortion.[103] The focus on choice might have sparked middle-class suburbanites to channel their support of abortion politically, but it made groups like MORAL even more unlikely to address the variety of economic and social conditions that led most women to claim reproductive rights in the first place. Embracing tactics like Tupperware parties and bake sales also made it difficult for MORAL to create a coalition with poor and minority women in order to preserve abortion rights. In spite of the issues exposed by the fight over the Doyle-Flynn bill, MORAL, NOW, and many of their allies also opted not to make welfare rights and poverty central components of their campaign. Thus, these efforts did not numerically or ideologically include the constituency most affected by the new limits on abortion.

This single-issue strategy also limited MORAL from addressing other feminist issues inextricably linked to abortion such as health care, rape, domestic violence, and employment equality, which created tensions with other women's and abortion rights activists. More progressive-leaning organizations such as the Abortion Action Coalition, a group that had worked closely with MORAL on the Doyle-Flynn bill, experienced a sense of alienation from the focus "on abortion as a single-issue struggle." The coalition members grew increasingly frustrated with MORAL and NOW, especially their "formulation of this struggle as essentially a question of choice" and "their strategic commitment to purely legislative and judicial work." In a

1980 letter to members of the abortion rights community, the Abortion Action Coalition leaders also contended, "By pushing the choice position the liberals ignore the fact that the availability (and for that matter the non-availability) of abortion services changes the meaning of *all* the options."[104] These critiques aptly conveyed the forms of class and racial inequality that became further inscribed into abortion, feminist, and liberal politics through the single-issue strategy.

The class-dimensions of MORAL's approach became reproduced and magnified at the national level. The rapid success of MORAL's recruiting campaign and single-issue strategy inspired the national abortion rights movement to take similar action.[105] In 1979, the National Abortion Rights Action League (NARAL), the nation's leading abortion organization, tapped Weinberg to launch "Impact '80: Protecting the Right to Choose" in order to mobilize a "politically astute pro-choice constituency" that would lay the foundation "for a major pro-choice victory in 1980."[106] The initiative, which NARAL announced on the steps of the State House in Boston, aimed to expand the "Massachusetts model" to a national scale.[107] Weinberg and other MORAL representatives began traveling around the country, providing training and materials to activists in other states to spread the campaign's slogan, "I'm Pro-Choice and I Vote."[108] Weinberg described NARAL's process as "bringing inactive pro-choice supporters into one end of a funnel and sending campaign workers out the other end."[109]

Impact '80 underscored the ways in which the strategies that liberal activists had long successfully implemented at the grassroots along Route 128 shaped and inspired national action. The shift toward grassroots organization and a single-issue, pro-choice agenda had clear trade-offs. In the short run, Impact '80 failed to mobilize enough opposition to stop the victories of Reagan and other antiabortion politicians. In the long term, this effort encouraged the abortion rights movement to narrow its lens and work through institutionalized channels of power to create change. This emphasis, in large part a defensive response to the growing power of the pro-life movement, increasingly directed the movement's demands toward keeping abortion legal, and away from such issues as regaining Medicaid funding or demanding other services from public hospitals.[110] The strategy assisted the pro-choice movement in successfully developing an electoral constituency, but one that was overwhelmingly middle-class, white, and ascribed to a narrow view of the issue.[111]

By the mid-1980s, MORAL's tactics had ensured that a pro-choice stance joined civil rights, environmentalism, and peace as litmus tests of liberal values, and served as a basic prerequisite for Democratic politicians seeking to gain the support of knowledge professionals, particularly those in the suburbs. The notion of choice also helped politicians earn the votes of many independent and moderate Republicans who supported preserving the legality of abortion from government intrusion, but were strongly opposed to using state funds to pay for it.[112] The position enabled politicians since the late 1970s to embrace the symbolic ideals of the movement without having to commit to economic or social policies that would ensure actual equality in reproductive rights.[113] Pro-choice politics thereby aligned with other facets of the Democratic agenda in the 1980s and beyond, especially as the party continued to adapt to the processes of economic restructuring, growing power of the conservative movement, and continued influence of suburban knowledge workers, which the following chapter explores.

10

From Taxachusetts to the
Massachusetts Miracle

In late November 1982, newly reelected governor Michael Dukakis addressed the Massachusetts High Technology Council (MHTC) at its annual meeting at a Newton hotel abutting the Route 128 highway. The presidents of the major high-tech firms in the Route 128 area had formed the MHTC in 1977 to fight the policies that had earned the state the reputation of "Taxachusetts." In 1980, the organization had served as one of the driving forces in passing the ballot initiative Proposition 2½, which had placed Massachusetts beside California as a front-runner in the nation's tax revolt. Howard Foley, president of the MHTC, introduced Dukakis by declaring, "He wants our industry to prosper in Massachusetts" and is determined to "make Proposition 2½ work." Dukakis used the opportunity to thank the executives. "Your help has been invaluable," he exclaimed, and "just the beginning of a strong and productive relationship" to position Massachusetts as "the leading edge of a world economy based on knowledge."[1] The event solidified a partnership that would contribute to the rebounding of the state's economy in the 1980s, later dubbed the "Massachusetts Miracle," and to the rejuvenation of Dukakis's political career.

Dukakis's decisive defeat in the 1988 presidential race further cemented an inextricable association between the liberal iconoclasm of Massachusetts and decline of the Democratic Party established after the 1972 presidential election. Since that moment, the label "Massachusetts liberal" has proven to be one of the most perennial of political pejoratives. The time line embedded in the label, nevertheless, creates a direct link between the 1972 and 1988 elections that overemphasizes the decline of the Democratic Party and the Republican Party's political rise.[2] Tracing the change in the state's reputation from Taxachusetts into the Massachusetts Miracle and Dukakis's political career over the period from 1974 to 1988 counters those assumptions, and instead illuminates the growing centrality of high-tech growth and engineers and other knowledge-based professionals in the priorities of the Democratic Party in Massachusetts and nationally. The debates in boardrooms and town meetings along the Route 128 corridor surrounding the pocketbook concerns of low tax rates and high quality of life over the 1970s, moreover, underscore the inextricable relationship between public policy and the political agenda of suburban knowledge professionals. This set of issues brings into sharp focus how the combined legacy of New Deal consumer-oriented policies and Cold War defense spending priorities shaped the political culture of the Route 128 suburbs and the ideology of many of its residents even as both the New Deal order and Cold War came to an end.

While Silicon Valley has received a great deal of attention as the locus of the new tech economy in the 1970s and the dawn of the "wired workers" constituency, Route 128, which served as the epicenter of the minicomputer revolution, also played a central role in fusing the rise of the Information Age to the changing fortunes of the Democratic Party. The relationships forged between the MHTC and Dukakis show that the political mobilization of business interests to stimulate economic growth and shape tax policy did not just occur on the Right and the Republicans but influenced and reinvigorated the Democratic Party as well in the 1970s and 1980s.[3]

Dukakis's efforts to harness and fuel high-tech development illustrate how the Democratic Party responded and adapted to the economic recession of the 1970s and Reagan revolution of the 1980s. His agenda of private sector business growth, low taxes, and market-oriented solutions explicitly recast the Democratic Party's long-standing approach to economic development, welfare, and organized labor. Dukakis's approach accentuated and reinvigorated the technocratic dimensions of liberalism, and extended and refined many of the ideas and goals first articulated by George McGovern in his 1972 bid, though with an even more pronounced probusiness and private sector bent. Dukakis stood at the forefront of a group of politicians known as the Watergate babies and later Atari Democrats, such as Gary Hart, Jerry Brown and Paul Tsongas, who all represented suburban districts, and focused on government reform and stimulating private sector economic growth especially high-tech industry. This reform- and issue-oriented cohort offered an alternative middle ground between the urban ethnic old guard of the Democratic Party and progressive constituencies, like the Rainbow Coalition, advocating for social equality and economic justice. In Massachusetts, Dukakis in particular pioneered many policies including public-private partnerships, a balanced budget, a welfare-to-work program, environmental protection, and transportation initiatives as well as support for reproductive rights and other liberal causes that combined a technocratic ethos, business-oriented reform, and quality-of-life issues.

Although this platform might not have propelled Dukakis to the White House in 1988, it did directly influence the New Democrats, the Democratic Leadership Council (DLC), and the agenda that Bill Clinton ran on and later implemented as president in the 1990s. The emphasis stimulating Route 128 style growth was crucial to the Democratic Party's competitive-

Figure 10.1 The cartoon "At Least I Know Who My Running Mate Would Be" appeared in the Massachusetts High Technology Council's newsletter in early 1987 as Michael Dukakis was contemplating a run for the presidency. It suggested that his running mate would be a computer, and that Dukakis would run on the slogan "Duke and Tech in '88." The cartoon highlighted the centrality of the tech industry to Dukakis and the Democratic Party's agenda in the 1980s, and depicted the close relationship that Dukakis had developed with the consortium of tech firms over the course of his political career. Cartoon by Glenn Foden, courtesy of Glenn Foden. *Source*: *Mass High Tech*, January 19–February 1, 1987.

ness, particularly in presidential elections as it appealed directly to suburban professionals throughout the country. This private sector and tech-oriented agenda, however, did not resolve the fundamental tensions between blue- and white-collar workers within the Democratic electoral coalition at the state and national levels. The party's concentration on high-tech growth, knowledge-based professionals, low taxes, and welfare reform also resulted in a set of policies that continued, and exacerbated, forms of economic and racial inequality throughout metropolitan Boston and the nation.

"Mike Dukakis Should Be Governor"

Dukakis's biography encapsulated many of the facets of suburban liberal politics. A forty-year-old, first-generation Greek American son of an obstetrician, Dukakis had grown up in a gracious colonial house in Brookline and graduated from Brookline High School, where his classmates voted him "most brilliant."[4] He returned to Brookline after attending Swarthmore and Harvard Law School, and joined his local fair housing committee. Dukakis launched his political career as one of Brookline's state representatives, serving as a key ally to suburban liberal activists in the quest for passage of laws related to METCO, environmental protection, improved mass transit, and women's equality.[5] But he experienced his greatest legislative accomplishments through less sensational issues such as insurance reform and changing the structure of state government. During his tenure at the State House, Dukakis cultivated an image as a socially liberal technocrat and frugal reformer who refused to toe the party line and consciously set himself apart from the powerful ethnic Democratic machine that dominated the legislature. He, like many young suburban Democrats, expressed frustration with the tenor of the state party, and in the early 1960s orchestrated the creation of the short-lived reform organization the Commonwealth Organization of Democrats to challenge the urban ethnic old guard.[6]

The goal of changing the direction of the state Democratic Party coupled with problems of unemployment, inflation, and high taxes set the tone for the political battles of the subsequent decade, but especially established the backdrop for Dukakis's gubernatorial campaign in 1974. Dukakis made revitalizing the state's economy the centerpiece of his platform. Many of his ideas paralleled those of McGovern, who during his 1972 bid for the presidency had emphasized the importance of private sector growth in converting the talent and resources of state's technology sectors away from their dependency on the Pentagon. In announcing his own candidacy for governor two years later, Dukakis discussed his plans to "aggressively" recruit new businesses into the high-tech sector, and develop new forms of mass transit and environmental protection. He stressed that the state's pool of professionals "with unique and technological skill" would offer the best "magnet" for new industries.[7] Dukakis's agenda intrigued many professionals along Route 128, where the levels of unemployment had reached an all-time high.

The *Boston Globe* interpreted Dukakis's success in the gubernatorial primary as the official passing of "mantle of the Democratic Party" from the "working class three decker neighborhoods" to "the more affluent and single family homes of suburban Massachusetts."[8] Even his campaign slogan "Mike Dukakis Should Be Governor" reflected the confidence and competitive, meritocratic ethos of postindustrial professionals. Dukakis's success in the general election still depended heavily on the support of the party's traditional constituencies. On most issues, Dukakis staked out a position further to the right than his opponent, Republican governor Francis Sargent, losing him the votes of many minority and progressive constituencies that maintained their support for the incumbent.[9] Instead, he gained the votes of those blue-collar workers hardest hit by the economic downturn with bold promises to close the deficit, balance the state budget, reduce the unemployment rate to the national average, and deliver better social services at lower costs.[10] Dukakis's running mate, Thomas P. O'Neill III, further buffeted his support among dyed-in-the-wool Democrats. O'Neill's father, Tip, curried significant influence among party regulars and contributed that to the campaign. Dukakis did not reject this assistance, despite his long critique of patronage and party politics. Dukakis won the November election with his best showing in the cities most affected by inflation and unemployment.[11]

Dukakis's victory brought him in concert with a group of politicians including California governor Brown, Colorado senator Hart, and Massachusetts congressman Tsongas that in 1974 gave the Democratic Party its greatest midterm triumph in decades.[12] Known as the Watergate babies, the members of this cohort had all earned reputations as issue-oriented, reform-minded politicians from suburban and heavily white districts. These politicians shared a desire to distance themselves from the "old politics" of the New Deal regulars and offer a new era of leadership for the Democratic Party and country.[13] Dukakis and the other Watergate babies quickly discovered that it was far easier to pledge reform than to implement recovery.

On the campaign trail, Dukakis had promised to "introduce the idea of productivity and efficiency goals and standards into state government," and pledged to cut the budget by $150 million and implement no new taxes once in office.[14] But confronted with a deficit of $500 million, in the fall of 1975 he instituted a 7.5 percent across-the-board increase to the income and sales taxes, amounting to the single-largest hike in state history. He did uphold his promise to make cuts to a wide range of social programs. The METCO program represented just one by-product of this action. The state's welfare program faced the most dramatic and symbolically significant cuts. In his boldest move, which anticipated Clinton's welfare reform by almost two decades, Dukakis eliminated employable persons under forty years old from General Relief, the part of the welfare system entirely financed by state funds. In order to be eligible for the program, a recipient had to have a family income that fell 20 to 30 percent below the national poverty line. It was difficult to imagine the surplus of employment opportunities for the over fifteen thousand welfare clients who fell into this category given the state's endemic unemployment problems.[15] Critics declared that these cutbacks placed undue hardship on those least able to handle them.[16] In a further testament to the direction of his welfare policy, after his first secretary of human services resigned in protest, Dukakis appointed a replacement with a background in finance not social policy.

Dukakis saw welfare reform as a site to demonstrate his technocratic and market-oriented approach to social issues. He introduced an initiative called the Work Experience Program (WEP) as a way to simultaneously reduce the state's soaring unemployment rate and welfare rolls.[17] The idea of workfare had become synonymous with the harsh initiative that Reagan instituted while governor of California, but Dukakis sought to make the idea more palatable and turn himself into a national spokesperson for it.[18] Targeted at men, WEP made as a condition of welfare payment performing basic maintenance duties such as painting guardrails, "roadside and brush clearing," and "litter pick up." The recipients also had to undergo employment and personal counseling and conduct job hunts under state supervision.[19] The idea met with controversy in many interlocking circles in Massachusetts, but piqued the interest of Jimmy Carter, who acknowledged Dukakis's leading position in "helping solve the welfare problem," and credited the Massachusetts governor with having a major role in shaping Carter's own Program for Better Jobs and Income.[20] The Massachusetts legislature eventually passed a much more limited version of the WEP proposal, and the law made little impact on the state's rates of welfare or unemployment. Yet WEP and Dukakis's advocacy helped implant a new attitude into the national discussion about the best way to help the poor, which would later return in the welfare agenda of Massachusetts and the Democratic Party in the 1980s and beyond. Rather than an issue created by southern New Democrats of the DLC, welfare reform emerged from the same political culture of New England liberalism that produced pioneering civil rights, environmental politics, and antiwar activism.[21]

Dukakis more explicitly aimed to dispel the stereotype of New England's political culture as "anti-industry" by stimulating the growth of the high-tech sector. In the late 1970s, Massachusetts companies Digital Equipment, Data General, and Wang Computers led the remaking of Route 128 into the epicenter of minicomputer innovation, which ushered in the end of the area's downturn and start of the Information Age. In order to prove that "Massachusetts means business," the Dukakis administration established a combination of tax incentives as well as the Massachusetts Technology Development Corporation and Massachusetts Industrial Financing Agency to launch new companies and help older ones make the transition to commercial markets.[22] This stimulus contributed to the rise of the minicomputers industry from the ashes of closed R & D labs along Route 128.[23] In just two years, the Bay State added four hundred companies and over two hundred thousand jobs, with the majority of new growth occurring in the high-tech sector.[24] Employment in engineering and scientific instrument firms expanded by more than 70 percent, computer programming increased by 65 percent, and the construction of office machines and computers rose by 43 percent between the end of 1976 and 1978.[25] These new job opportunities greatly reduced the white-collar unemployment epidemic in the Route 128 area and enhanced approval for Dukakis's policies. A poll in March 1978 found that 56 percent of those Massachusetts residents surveyed rated Dukakis's performance as good or excellent, and he had high hopes of winning a second term.[26]

Taxachusetts

The passage of property-tax limitation measure Proposition 13 in California significantly altered the parameters of the impending Massachusetts gubernatorial race. The initiative, which passed by a two-to-one margin in June 1978, required California municipalities to limit property tax rates to 1 percent of the assessed value, restricted future assessment to 2 percent a year, and mandated a two-thirds majority by the legislature to increase state taxes and a similar fraction of voters to approve any new local levies. The law led to an immediate reduction in revenues by more than seven billion dollars. California went from being far above to far below the national average in property taxes. Proposition 13, however, quickly became important less for its direct effect on the tax revenue in the Golden State than for signifying public resentment against the burden of taxes throughout the nation.[27]

Immediately following the passage of Proposition 13, Massachusetts residents and politicians anticipated that the state would become one of the key sites for the national debate around taxes. When Howard Jarvis, "the father of proposition 13," came to visit Massachusetts in the fall of 1978, he told a crowd of seven hundred at Newton North High School, "I never thought I'd find a state where property taxes are worse than California, but I have and you are here."[28] Observers suggested that if a measure identical to Proposition 13 passed in Massachusetts, it would look as though Californians got cheated, since a 1 percent limit would slash Massachusetts' property taxes statewide by 77 percent.[29] State fiscal experts warned that such cuts would either create a loss in basic services or new burdens on the state government. Experts pointed to the fact that California in the late 1970s had a large state budget surplus that could cover the loss in local revenue, while Massachusetts still hovered near bankruptcy.[30] A tax-cutting measure would have the greatest impact on deindustrialized cities where the per capita property values were lower and thereby the tax rates were particularly high.[31] Further indicating the potential divisiveness of the issue, polls revealed that while three out of four Massachusetts voters supported a 45 percent reduction in property taxes, the respondents differed about which basic municipal services to cut.[32]

The passage of Proposition 13 put the issue of taxes and Edward King's candidacy in the spotlight of the 1978 Democratic gubernatorial primary. King, an Irish American Catholic, former professional football player, and executive director of the Massachusetts Port Authority, had never before held elected office.[33] To overcome this lack of experience, he adopted a strategy that one aide later explained as putting "all the hate groups in one pot and let it boil."[34] King consciously fed on the wounds and divisions of the busing crisis, and used his staunchly pro-life position to gain the support of the well-organized antiabortion movement. Yet it was King's fiscally conservative stance that truly put the proverbial fire under his campaign.

King seized the opportunity of Proposition 13 to stake out a place in the election, declaring his support for the implementation of a similar type of reform in Massachusetts. Dukakis had said of Proposition 13, "Massachusetts voters are too smart to fall for such a simplistic proposal," to which King retorted that this was the classic response of a "limousine liberal." King pledged to reduce property taxes by five hundred million dollars if elected.[35] In the September Democratic primary, King received 51 percent of the vote to Dukakis's 42 percent. Cambridge mayor Barbara Ackermann, who had earned the support of the progressive wing of the party frustrated by Dukakis's cuts to social services, finished third.

The electoral upset exposed the long-standing divide within the state's Democratic Party. King did the best in blue-collar, traditionally Catholic communities, while Dukakis had decisively won college-educated professionals and strongly carried Route 128 suburbs like Concord, Lexington, Newton, and Wellesley.[36] One observer characterized the divide as between "the older pork-chop, brass-collar" constituency and liberals who were "suburban and privileged, anti-growth, pro-abortion, anti-highway and environmentalist."[37] Dukakis himself cautioned against reading the results as a sign that traditional "backlash" voters had gained control of the Democratic Party, or state or national politics.[38] More important, the primary served as a bellwether of the national sense of despair about the economic and political climate. King was most successful in the cities and towns with the highest property tax rates and those that would be most devastated by the passage of a law like Proposition 13.[39] Extrapolating the meaning of these statistics, pollster Patrick Caddell concluded that support for antitax, antigovernment candidates constituted "a safety valve" that allowed voters to express frustration about a range of issues.[40] Exit interviews supported this interpretation. Theresa Flynn, a nurse from the North End neighborhood of Boston, spoke for many Massachusetts residents when she said Dukakis "didn't do enough for the little man. I can see why the state is called Taxa-chusetts."[41] King's promise to ease the economic burden of people like Flynn led him to victory in the general election, although not in the Route 128 suburbs where voters mainly supported his liberal Republican oppo-nent.[42] It soon became clear that the issue of tax relief and King's overall agenda had a group of supporters with much deeper pockets than Flynn.

The MHTC and Its "People-Oriented" Tax Politics

The struggle over tax policy in Massachusetts revealed the increasing politi-cal clout of high-tech industry executives led by the MHTC in shaping the directives of state politics and would have a direct impact on the battle. The council had grown from conversations between Data General head Edson de Castro and Analog Devices founder Ray Stata, who had served together on a state task force about capital formation appointed by Dukakis while he was still governor. After experiencing a rift with Dukakis over the task force's recommendations, de Castro and Stata invited fellow leaders from thirty-eight electronics and R & D firms to form the MHTC. De Castro and Stata saw the group as means to address their belief that the problem impeding economic growth in the state was not the supply of capital "but the cost of doing business in Massachusetts."[43] The organization had quickly grown by 1980 to include eight-nine firms that collectively employed around 140,000 people.

The MHTC deviated from the traditional view that the "high cost of busi-ness" in the Northeast derived from its high union wages and corporate taxes. None of the founding companies of the MHTC were unionized, and Massachusetts actually had lower production wages than other major com-puter manufacturing states in the 1970s.[44] The MHTC instead argued that the high cost of living, especially taxes, put Massachusetts' "home-grown companies" at a "distinct disadvantage for recruiting" the "well trained highly skilled engineers and managers who are short supply everywhere."[45] Tech-nology workers, especially electrical engineers, had a particularly high rate of turnover, and MHTC members believed the difficulty of securing this ele-ment of the workforce created an even higher impediment to business than corporate taxes or union wages. Characterizing its vision and agenda as "people-oriented" ones, the MHTC's concerns overlapped in some respects with groups like the Association of Technical Professionals (ATP), but rather than focusing on unemployment, the MHTC sought to address the sudden problem of an abundance of new job opportunities.[46]

The MHTC's core principles and agenda rested on the personal experi-ences of its founders supplemented by notions of supply-side economic the-ory, which had become increasingly popular the late 1970s, especially in business circles. Supply-side advocates suggested that heavy taxation impeded productivity, entrepreneurship, investment, and overall private sector economic growth.[47] Massachusetts had the nation's third-highest per capita income, but the MHTC concluded that since state and local taxes took an average of 17.8 percent of personal income, the state was much less attractive than states with which it competed, especially those concentrated in the Sunbelt, which boasted far lower percentages.[48] "We offer a guy a job and the first thing you hear is taxes," bemoaned Herbert Roth, the president of a Waltham-based electronics company.[49] Some companies, including Data General, had already moved part or all of their operations out of the state, particularly to North Carolina, which held out to workers a 20 percent cost-of-living difference through a combination of taxes, insurance, food, and lower home-heating prices.[50] De Castro described his "reluctance" about building a new facility in the Research Triangle, stating that a company of course "always likes to stay close to home." "This is not our choice," de Castro maintained, "but that of the potential employees we are trying to recruit."[51] One industry expert empathized, noting, "The electrical engineer is the linchpin of these industries and they have to go where the engineers want to live."[52]

The MHTC's purported people-oriented tax agenda demonstrated the increasing clout of corporate leaders to dictate a policy agenda in state politics on behalf of their employees. The antitax pro-Sunbelt archetypal engineer that the MHTC frequently invoked, nevertheless, did not uniformly describe the worldview of the people who worked at its companies. As Tracy Kidder portrayed in *The Soul of a New Machine*, when Data General decided to move one of its big minicomputer projects to North Carolina, many of its employees refused to relocate and felt in competition with those who had left. "I thought North Carolina sucked," one engineer candidly exclaimed. It was "not a place where I want to bring up my wife and family." He instead decided to stay put in his gray colonial house in Framingham.[53] In other Route 128 suburbs like Framingham where many engineers lived, Dukakis had outpolled King by 22 percentage points in the 1978 Democratic primary, and these communities had likewise supported King's moderate Republican opponent in the general election. In a deviation from the MHTC's campaign, Paula Leventman, who conducted interviews with professionals at the Route 128 firms in the late 1970s, found that the majority were skeptical of solutions similar to Proposition 13 because they recognized that the maintenance of many municipal services, such as quality public schools, parks, and other amenities that made their suburbs desirable places to live, depended on taxes. Such attitudes failed to slow the momentum of the MHTC and its antitax agenda.[54]

In just a matter of months, the MHTC developed a dominant presence in state politics.[55] Although the MHTC had not offered an official endorsement in the 1978 election, King received strong support from several of its members, especially after he promised to lower taxes to a level comparable to competing states.[56] Almost immediately upon King taking office, the MHTC convinced him to sign an agreement called the "Social Contract," establishing that the member firms would help create 150,000 new jobs in Massachusetts in exchange for King's promise to reduce property and income taxes.[57] The MHTC sought to fortify this agreement by urging member employees that their state representatives must "hear from the payers of taxes," providing them with form letters to support the increasingly symbiotic policies of the MHTC and King administration.[58]

The MHTC wanted aggregate reductions in the tax burden, and told state legislators that it "made little difference whether taxes are reduced through lower property or income taxes."[59] With momentum already galvanized in the aftermath of Proposition 13, the MHTC decided that focusing on property taxes offered a more politically expedient route. Between 1978 and 1980, the state legislature received more than twenty-five major proposals for tax relief from groups across the political spectrum.[60] The proposal of the grassroots group Citizens for Limited Taxation (CLT) to place a tax limit on the state ballot in 1980 emerged as the plan with the most staying power.[61] The measure shared many of Proposition 13's features, but in addition to a 2.5 percent limit on the assessed value of property, it allowed tenants to deduct 50 percent of their rent from their state income and called for a reduction in the automobile excise tax.[62] Local officials immediately spoke out against the measure with warnings about the devastating effects of such a proposal on the ability to adequately manage municipal governments, especially in populous, low-income areas.[63] Robert Coard, executive director of a Boston antipoverty agency, succinctly predicted, "Wealthy suburban communities will be minimally affected. Urban areas will be devastated."[64] Officials from many affluent suburbs offered an alternative prediction, issuing sober assessments about employee layoffs and the decline of municipal services.[65] State officials and politicians chimed in, calling Proposition 2½ "irresponsible" and potentially "disastrous."[66]

The mounting opposition helped proponents of the measure fashion a populist-laden campaign as the underdogs, which would prove pivotal to their eventual success. The CLT led this effort. Edward F. King (no relation to Governor King), a seasoned lobbyist for business organizations, had started the CLT with several close friends, and the group had grown in strength over the 1970s. Still, it remained a self-described "low-budget," "grassroots" organization that operated out of a small office run by volunteers.[67] Executive director Barbara Anderson, a Marblehead housewife turned outspoken antitax crusader, served as the public face of the organization and its Proposition 2½ campaign. While many suburban women became politically active after reading Betty Friedan, Ayn Rand was the catalyst for Anderson's awakening.[68] In 1978, Anderson decided to switch her hobby from teaching swimming at a local pool to volunteering at the CLT. She had ascended to the post of executive director in 1980 just in time to lead the fight for the ballot initiative and earn the reputation as the "Mother of Proposition 2½." Anderson's image as a suburban mom enhanced the homeowner-driven portrait of the campaign she led. "The way I see it, she's a housewife who raised a family and woke up one morning just fed up with what's going on," one erstwhile supporter later declared.[69]

Throughout this campaign, Anderson and the CLT adopted arguments about homeowner and taxpayer rights similar to those that Jarvis and his allies had used in California, never turning down an opportunity to draw a reference to the Boston Tea Party or the Lexington Minutemen. In its literature, the CLT frequently discussed how "homeowners need protection," particularly against the "special interest groups."[70] At the same time, these rallying cries downplayed the role of "special interests" in the CLT's own campaign. The group would often tout the fact its donations came "from individual taxpayers, who sometimes sen[t] in $2 in crumpled envelopes."[71] In truth, only 54 percent of the contributions came from individuals; the rest was from the coffers of several business interests, especially in the high-tech field.

The CLT forged a partnership with MHTC members, which proved essential to the success of Proposition 2½. The consortium gave over $240,000 to finance the CLT campaign, but this contribution did not end the extent of the high-tech community's involvement. In the fall of 1980, Foley, MHTC president, established Concerned Citizens for Lower Taxes in order to circumvent campaign tax law and raise additional funds. In the span of two months, Concerned Citizens for Lower Taxes raised $269,085, with the vast majority coming from the firms that comprised the MHTC, including a $16,000 check from Data General, and $12,000 each from GenRad, Teradyne, Prime Computer, and Computervision.[72] Foley also hired the political consulting firm Dresner, Morris, and Tortorello, led by Dick Morris, who later became one of Clinton's most trusted advisers. The consultants urged the campaign architects to downplay the links to business and "conservative limited government concept" because "it just won't wash that way in liberal Mass. Sell it instead as a liberal compassionate measure."[73]

Political scientist Daniel Smith would later characterize the Proposition 2½ campaign as "faux populist" because of the influential, but invisible role of the high-tech executives.[74] While Anderson later admitted that Proposition 2½ would not have passed without the money raised by the MHTC and the advertisements it sponsored, she also countered accusations that she merely operated as a "populist front" for the political agenda of the high-tech industry, calling her relationship with the MHTC "symbiotic."[75] The MHTC's advertisements and the CLT's grassroots energy worked in tandem to capitalize on voter confusion about Proposition 2½. Polls showed that Bay State residents supported the measure primarily because they believed that taxes were "too high," and not because they necessarily wanted fewer services or a smaller state government.[76] Likewise, while the majority of Bay State voters endorsed the proposition, they remained confused as to exactly its purpose and consequences.[77] The CLT thus began to emphasize the somewhat-deceptive idea that Proposition 2½ was the last chance voters had to alter the tax system. Many citizens recognized flaws in the measure, but believed it offered what Newton resident Arthur Adelman saw as "the lifetime chance for us taxpayers to assert ourselves."[78] This typical sentiment played a central role in raising widespread support for Proposition 2½ in a matter of months.

Proposition 2½ and the Suburbs

The suburbs surrounding Route 128 served as a major battleground over Proposition 2½, and the debate it engendered in 1980 exposed not only the divide between the personal and professional priorities of many scientists and engineers but also the individualist and consumerist ethos of suburban residents. Similar to the Vietnam era, when many Route 128 engineers opposed the war despite the fact that their livelihood depended on defense spending, so too did their personal opinions of Proposition 2½ put them at odds with their employers' agenda. Several professionals shared the criticism of one academic from Wellesley that the measure represented a "poorly worded" and "haphazard approach to much needed tax reform."[79] In line with their commitment to rationality, these professionals believed both that Proposition 2½ appeared deceptively simple and there was no quick fix to resolving the issues of tax reform.[80]

Issues of school financing became a central part of this debate, exposing many of features and fault lines of Proposition 2½ and suburban fiscal politics more broadly. Public education had been one of the primary reasons that many engineers and other professionals commonly cited for moving to places like Newton or Lexington. Education also constituted the most substantial part of the local budgets, and many proponents saw Proposition 2½ as a way to rein in growing educational costs. Arthur Masucco, a resident of the Route 128 suburb of Natick who worked as a consultant for a Boston-based engineering firm and paid $1,828 per year in property taxes, found it frustrating that $14 million of the $20 million of his town's revenue went to the public schools.[81] Even though his own children benefited from this education, Masucco contended that individual parents, not all taxpayers, should finance such "special" services as violin, extra reading instruction, tennis, cross-country skiing, or football. Others proponents suggested that

the measure could help do away with METCO and instead focus on "traditional education."[82] These suggestions, rooted in notions of freedom of
choice, touched off fierce disagreements at PTA and school board meetings
about what programs were essential or extraneous.

Many parents adopted a language and attitude to oppose Proposition 2½
similar to that which their neighbors had used to support it. The president
of the Newton PTA, Bonnie Armor, stressed that defeat of the proposition
would "preserve the educational system which has made Newton a desirable place to live."[83] Echoing the arguments that proponents adopted to
support participation in METCO, the building of affordable housing, and a
more gender-neutral curriculum, Lexington superintendent John Lawson
warned that Proposition 2½ "would create a lower than average school system for an above average student population." Lawson dubbed such an outcome "a tragedy."[84] Despite such invocations of disadvantage, rarely did
those suburbanites, either those for or against the measure, discuss the ways
in which Proposition 2½ might affect children in Boston's public schools,
who just a few years early had stood at the center of the violent battle over
mandatory desegregation and continued to struggle with its fallout.[85]

In the November election, Proposition 2½ won by a 59 to 41 percent
margin, achieving its greatest success in the state's middle-class suburban
communities and urban districts where homeowners felt most squeezed by
property taxes.[86] The debate over Proposition 2½ had overshadowed the
1980 presidential race, but in the end Reagan won by a narrow victory in
Massachusetts. Reagan's assurance of reducing federal taxes and the size of
the government enticed many of the same voters who welcomed the cuts
promised by Proposition 2½. Reagan received his largest gains in the
middle-class suburbs of the North and South Shores, consistent with national voting patterns.[87] The vote was far closer in the Route 128 suburbs in
part due to the third party candidacy of John Anderson, who was quite
popular with independent voters in these communities.[88] Anderson ended
up winning 15 percent of the Massachusetts electorate, which was a significantly greater share than his national showing. The MHTC would later intimate to Reagan "either we have you to thank or perhaps you have us" for
the "coincidence" of Proposition 2½ passing the same year that he carried
the state.[89] Yet this claim was not entirely true. Several of the urban precincts in Boston that favored Proposition 2½ did not extend their support
to Reagan, while his opponent, President Carter, received almost the same
number of votes in Boston among white working-class voters as had Proposition 2½.[90]

The more affluent Route 128 communities remained squarely divided
over Proposition 2½. In Lexington the measure won by fewer than four hundred votes, while it failed to pass by a similarly narrow margin in Brookline,
Lincoln, and Newton.[91] The results often highlighted an occupational divide

Table 10.1 Percentages Voting for Proposition 2½
and the Presidential Race, 1980

| | Proposition 2½ | | Presidential race | |
	Yes	No	Reagan	Carter
Concord	57%	39%	41%	35%
Lincoln	45%	52%	37%	31%
Lexington	49%	47%	40%	37%
Newton	47%	48%	35%	45%
Brookline	37%	56%	30%	50%
Boston	50%	38%	32%	52%
State total	56%	40%	41.20%	41.05%

as people in upper-managerial positions such as company executives, CEOs, and business owners voted for the measure, while knowledge professionals did not.[92] In fact, college-educated professionals joined low-income minorities and public service employees as the constituencies that were least likely to support the measure. These results illustrate that the "people-oriented" agenda of the MHTC leaders in the case of Proposition 2½ trumped the political desires and choices of many of their employees. It also showed the limits of suburban professionals' ability to influence large-scale policy.

Education, however, proved one sphere where engineers and other suburban residents with means did have the ability to exercise their individual choice. Many professionals in the Route 128 area responded to Proposition 2½ by choosing to take their children out of local public school systems. In the weeks immediately following the 1980 election, Boston-area private and parochial schools received a flood of inquiries and a record number of new applications primarily from upper-middle-class parents from Boston,

Cambridge, and the Route 128 suburbs.[93] Reflecting the attitude of many middle-class residents, Laurence Auros explained that such a change would create a "financial burden" for him, but he could not deprive his daughter of "a good sound education."[94] The Cambridge school superintendent empathized with people like Auros, insisting, "You can't blame parents for considering the private sector especially when I'm forced to make massive cuts in aesthetic subject areas."[95] The thousands of individual decisions had powerful consequences on racial and class composition and quality of schools throughout metropolitan Boston. The *Boston Globe* called this pattern of departure the "single most chilling result" of Proposition 2½.[96] Many officials warned that this trend would not simply remove many of the brightest and most dedicated students. It would also remove their parents, who often played a crucial role in lobbying for quality public education, and cause great harm to students without the resources to enroll in private schools. Few, if any, parents publicly voiced concern about the impact of their decision on other people's children.

The direct warnings by officials about drastic looming cuts in municipal services, especially education, produced panic in cities and suburbs across the state.[97] Many residents began to regret their vote and implored the state legislature to compensate for the revenue loss.[98] Even King's secretary of economic affairs and MHTC member George Kariotis dubbed it "a disaster," and declared that "the biggest irony is that it's not going to provide tax relief" in the towns where "these high tech engineers all live, like Weston, Lincoln, Wellesley."[99] The MHTC called on the state to "carry the load" by "squeez[ing] 4% out of its budget without starving the poor, emasculating public higher education or laying off state troopers."[100] The Massachusetts legislature approved such a measure, which offered some relief to municipalities, but it did not permanently assuage the anxiety of residents and budget choices of local officials.

The implementation of Proposition 2½ magnified the socioeconomic inequality embedded in the geography of Massachusetts. During its first year of implementation, Proposition 2½ led to a $311 million reduction in property taxes statewide, but the Revenue Department noted it had an "extremely diverse" effect on communities commensurate with existing patterns of wealth and privilege. The greatest impact fell on lower-middle-class, working-class, and low-income urban areas.[101] In the years immediately after the law passed, affluent suburbs such as Lexington, Weston, and Wellesley endured some minor hardships, like fewer library hours, book purchases, streetlights, and trash collection days, while urban locales such as Boston and Somerville made major cuts to police and fire service, and the city of Quincy laid off 294 teachers.[102]

The override provision contained in Proposition 2½ further contributed to the pattern of spatial inequality. In the weeks after the 1980 election, Dukakis's hometown of Brookline led the fight to allow municipalities to avoid full compliance with the measure. "Many people moved to Brookline for its high level of services and want to maintain that standard," stated Juan Cofield, the leader of this campaign.[103] The reaction led the legislature to modify the law to enable the voters of a city or town to approve an override to Proposition 2½ through an election.[104] Indeed, since 1980, many municipalities used overrides to finance the construction of new schools, fire stations, and recreation facilities, purchase conservation land, or increase education funding. The proposals created discord in many towns, often pitting residents against one another in fights over fiscal priorities. But more significantly, the override mechanism proved an easier device to invoke in smaller communities, while virtually impossible in larger municipalities with no budget surplus and few residents willing to spend money on items such as a new school building or conservation land. The provision thus had the unintended consequence of enhancing the disparities in municipal services and privileges between smaller suburbs and larger cities. In spite of these divisions, most scholars have concluded of Proposition 2½ that "neither its costs nor its benefits have been as great as predicted."[105] Bay State residents and officials for the most part learned how to adjust to the law and forms of metropolitan inequity it has engendered.[106] Yet the same was not true for King. By the early 1980s, the public had grown increasingly dissatisfied with his tenure, which paved the way for Dukakis to resume his political career and platform of economic growth.

Rematch

Amid the uncertainty created by the implementation of Proposition 2½, Dukakis decided to run to reclaim his old job as governor, but updated his message to fit the new political climate of the state and nation at the dawn of the Reagan era.[107] During his four years in office, King implemented the socially conservative, probusiness policy on which he campaigned.[108] His positions on abortion, welfare, and the economy had earned him the reputation as Reagan's "favorite governor" and "favorite Democrat."[109] King proudly embraced those labels, disillusioning the state's Democratic loyalists. A series of scandals and charges of corruption involving the members of his administration also led many to question his leadership. With these negative factors mounting against King, Dukakis launched a campaign to retake the governorship.

The 1982 gubernatorial primary, like the one four years earlier, highlighted the divisions between the two sides of the Democratic Party, with lower- and middle-income white ethnics concentrated in the older cities on one side and suburban liberal professionals on the other.[110] The King campaign strategy focused on intensifying this cleavage in order to appeal to blue-collar white voters.[111] Relying on antiliberal stereotypes, a King aide called the contest the difference between the "Chablis-and-brie-crowd and Joe Six Pack."[112] Dukakis made competence and integrity the overriding themes of his campaign in order to contrast the King administration's scandals and corruption charges. But he focused on projecting this image without the self-righteousness that had plagued him throughout his first term.[113]

Dukakis had spent the time out of office teaching at Harvard's Kennedy School of Government, where he was exposed to a clique of academics touting government's role in stimulating growth in the private sector, especially in the high-tech industry. During his campaign, he made overtures to the leaders of the high-tech sector, promising to "spearhead a new era of investment" of state money in smaller- and medium-size growth companies, and make Massachusetts an "attractive place to do business."[114] Dukakis also pledged to crack down on crime and drunk driving and enhance environmental protection, energy conservation, and support for women's "right to choose."[115] This platform mobilized a huge turnout for Dukakis among what observers deemed the "high-tech," "free-choice" Democrats who lived in the suburbs.[116] King spent two million dollars on a series of television, radio, and print advertisements that criticized Dukakis as the prototypical ineffectual liberal, yet such depictions failed to rattle Dukakis or deter his supporters.[117] Dukakis's retooled image and strategy led him to a win by a decisive margin of more than eighty thousand votes in the September Democratic primary, followed by an easy victory in the November general election.[118] Dukakis stated that the win gave "him something one rarely gets in American politics—a second chance."[119] During his "second chance "as governor, Dukakis refashioned a brand of liberal politics and Democratic leadership that culminated in his presidential bid in 1988.

The Massachusetts Miracle

During his second round in the State House, Dukakis made economic development his primary area of focus, riding on and increasing the wave of the Commonwealth's rebounding high-tech industry. He became "a born-again business booster," working aggressively to improve Massachusetts' reputation, and transform it into the "vanguard" and "very model of the high-tech state."[120] By the time Dukakis secured his reelection, the state's high-tech industry was at the height of its boom. The turnaround confirmed that within the new rules of the postindustrial economy, knowledge, expertise, and the heavy concentration of research institutions once again represented Massachusetts' most valuable resources.[121] The rapid rebounding also made

Route 128 a model for other parts of the country trying to stage similar transitions from industrial to service-oriented economies.[122]

The MHTC continued to play a key role in this transformation and the political support it earned. As MHTC member and president of the Millipore Corporation Dee D'Arbeloff framed it, politicians from both sides of the aisle had gone from asking "what's high tech?" to "what does high tech want?"[123] Fulfilling that observation, in January 1983 Reagan toured Millipore's Bedford facility and delivered an address to MHTC members. The president praised the organization for its "vision" and "taking action," and promised to be "something of an apostle for your success story here."[124] In his address to the MHTC after winning the 1982 race, Dukakis took an equally complimentary and cooperative view of the organization. Repairing the rift with the leaders of the high-tech community that had led to the MHTC's formation, Dukakis told the audience, "No one has done more to create jobs than you have—as individuals, as companies, as a vital industry." He maintained that it would be essential to a "good business climate" for "the business community and the state government to talk to each other, listen to each other's problems, and work together to solve important problems."[125] He fulfilled that model during his second term.

Dukakis adopted a set of policies that bolstered the growth of the high-tech industry to the state's and his own advantage. He also relied heavily on the ideas of trusted advisers like Harvard and MIT economists Robert Reich, Lester Thurow, and Lawrence Summers, and Harvard management guru Rosabeth Moss Kanter, who convinced him that "the key to successful economic revitalization [lay] in specific investment strategies that link public investment with private opportunities."[126] With this maxim of "public-private partnerships" in mind, the Dukakis administration worked to broker deals between high-tech companies and Boston-based venture capital firms. The creation of these partnerships led to the surge of new software, data processing, and computer manufacturing corporations in the state.[127] The Dukakis administration also drew heavily on the work of MIT economist David Birch, whose influential article "The Job Generation Process" had demonstrated that independent businesses with fifty or fewer employees created 52 percent of all new jobs, and 80 percent of all new job growth occurred in companies that were four years old or younger.[128] These ideas echoed the argument of tech executive and activist Arthur Obermayer, who since the early 1970s had stressed to McGovern and other politicians that small firms should be the priority of the party's economic development platform.

Despite the new attention directed at small businesses, many of the state's larger companies like Digital, Wang Computer, and Raytheon also became part of the new focus on public-private relationships. Massachusetts companies also managed to jockey Reagan's prodefense position to gain myriad contracts from the Pentagon to make software and hardware for military weapons. Raytheon received $2.3 billion in government contracts in 1985 alone. Overall, the economic growth generated 50,000 new businesses and 160,000 jobs in two years. By 1985, Massachusetts had the highest percentage of workers in the service sector of any state in the country, lowest unemployment rate of any industrial state, and greatest average per capita income in the nation.[129]

Dukakis joined a group of Democratic politicians involved in shifting the party's economic priorities over the 1980s toward high-tech growth. Called by many either neoliberal or Atari Democrats, this group represented the maturation of the so-called Watergate babies, and included Senators Bill Bradley, Christopher Dodd, Al Gore, Hart, and Tsongas.[130] Although often liberal on foreign policy, rights issues, and especially the environment, the group eschewed the party's traditional focus on full employment and adequate housing as the favored means to create social equality, and instead concentrated on stimulating entrepreneurship and private sector growth.[131] Tsongas, perhaps the most quintessential Atari Democrat, had launched his career from a congressional district that included both his hometown of Lowell and Route 128 suburbs like Lexington. He had long derived his success from his combination of working-class ethnic roots, socially liberal defense of abortion rights, affirmative action, and the environment, and an emphasis on using market incentives and high-tech growth to solve economic and social problems.[132]

The focus on expanding the high-tech sector had clear advantages for changing the fortunes of the economy as well as the agenda of Dukakis and the Democratic Party. This form of development, however, produced an economically and geographically uneven distribution that privileged middle-class professionals and enhanced structural inequities. High-tech industry primarily created jobs for scientists, engineers, computer programmers, and data analysts that paid well, but these opportunities demanded a high level of expertise, experience, and training and were nonunionized.[133] Throughout the 1980s, the MHTC continued to include not one unionized firm in its over one-hundred-member consortium.[134] The manufacturing jobs that did exist at both large and small computer companies were not just nonunion but low-wage with little long-term security. Moreover, the focus on creating jobs in high-tech companies and related service sector businesses made employment overly dependent on the boom-bust cycles of the postindustrial economy, and therefore provided even greater job insecurity and uncertainty for workers at all levels. The high overall numbers in Massachusetts actually masked the fact that in the state's predominantly minority and low-income neighborhoods, the unemployment rate continued to hover at 31 percent in the mid-1980s, while the Massachusetts manufacturing sector continued its rapid decline, losing fifty-five thousand jobs between 1980 and 1987.[135] In the 1980s, furthermore, many high-tech firms shifted construction of their headquarters and plants to I-495, a semicircular highway thirty miles from downtown Boston where land was cheaper and more abundant than the famed Route 128 highway.[136] Population migration quickly followed suit as large shopping centers and subdivisions joined the industrial parks, rapidly transforming the former farming communities along this corridor and making I-495 a national symbol of exurban sprawl.[137] The area between I-495 and Route 128 gained 124,700 residents, accounting for nearly 40 percent of the state's growth in the 1990s.[138] Few residents of color joined in the I-495 migration, and thus the area remained about 93 percent white.

The Dukakis administration tried to offset the consequences of such uneven growth through its economic development and job-training programs. Updating his older planning agenda, Dukakis actively encouraged industrial growth beyond Route 128 and throughout the state, helping start-ups to establish corporate headquarters and factories in older deindustrialized mill communities like Lowell, Springfield, and Taunton.[139] The Dukakis administration contended that rerouting development away from Route 128 and toward economically distressed cities would also reduce the problems of rapid growth, traffic, and soaring home prices, which threatened the environment and quality of life of the suburban residents who lived along the highway.[140] Like, many Atari Democrats, Dukakis argued that with proper planning, environmentalism and growth could be complementary.[141]

Dukakis used his technocratic approach to make the relationship between unions and companies more compatible. In order to secure the endorsements of the state's labor leaders in the 1982 election, he had promised to promote a measure requiring advance notification of any plant closings—a idea to which the business community had been hostile. Dukakis created a commission of leaders from the business, labor, government, and academic sectors to help broker a compromise. The process led to the creation of the Mature Industries Act, passed in 1984, which abandoned the demands for mandatory notification of plant closings, and instead created a "voluntary" "social contract" that "encouraged," but did not require, companies to give employees at least a ninety-day notice of any plant closing. Under the law, displaced workers also received ninety days of continued health coverage, reemployment assistance and training, and state benefits if the company went bankrupt. Although it was "voluntary," companies that refused to comply could not gain access to certain forms of state financing.[142] The compromise both provided companies access to state funding incentives and gave state protections to workers. The "social contract" ultimately worked better in theory than practice, but it showed how Dukakis sought to help industry and labor adapt to economic change and served as the model for a similar policy eventually implemented at the federal level at the decade's end.[143]

Dukakis's revised welfare program further demonstrated his effort to adapt the traditional Democratic approach to bedrock social issues to fit the times. Dukakis recast the unpopular workfare program from his earlier time in the governor's seat into a new program called Employment and Training Choices (ET) launched 1983. The word "choices" in the title, Dukakis and Rosabeth Moss Kanter later explained, indicated its emphasis on "self-motivated client participation."[144] Participants voluntarily enrolled in the program and received a wide "menu" of options intended to fit the "the needs of each person," including education, training, and work opportunities in the private sector at companies such as Wang, Raytheon, and AVCO.[145] The program also provided subsidies and vouchers for child care and transportation, and supplemental health insurance along with a "sales pitch" about the benefits of work.[146] In its first four years of operation, the program placed thirty-eight thousand former welfare recipients in entry-level private sector jobs, with high enough wages that 86 percent remained off welfare for more than a year and saved the state hundreds of millions of dollars. By 1985, ET had a waiting list of sixteen thousand welfare recipients trying to get a spot and the Dukakis administration claimed it as the major factor in the 50 percent reduction of the state's welfare rolls.[147]

ET proved popular for some of the reasons that had long contributed to the success of programs like METCO. Participants appreciated the flexibility and voluntary dimensions of the program and the tangible opportunities and education it provided. Many middle-class taxpayers concurrently touted the initiative as a "wise investment," and supported the ways in which it not just saved money but also promoted individual advancement and lessened welfare dependency.[148] Private industries also favored the program because it helped industry with its personnel needs. Like METCO, ET endured criticism for the fact that took the "cream of the crop," privileging those people most excited and ready to work. The program also represented the pitfalls of an economic recovery agenda based on high technology and a welfare program connected to service sector jobs. The volatility of the high-tech industry could not provide a stable source of jobs for ET graduates, and thus the program operated most successfully in times of economic boom when there was a surplus of employment opportunities.

ET earned a great deal of national attention, nevertheless, as an innovative and effective approach to welfare reform. Some observers noted that elements of the approach were not entirely new, but praised the administration for understanding how to package and promote them in a market-oriented, meritocratic language of success that appealed to a wide range of interests. Liberal writer Robert Kuttner declared that ET combined the "conservative premise" that "most people ought to be working rather than living on the dole" with "the good-government premise that an efficient, well-managed program is good for both recipients and taxpayers."[149] David Osborne observed that in doing so, the Dukakis administration successfully "altered the national debate around welfare reform."[150] Dukakis declared in August 1987 that of all his accomplishments as governor, he was proudest of ET.[151] He boasted how the program helped "mothers and their children" become "self-sufficient, get an opportunity to move up, to lift themselves out of poverty," and gain "the dignity and confidence that comes" with "working and earning at a good job."[152] The Personal Responsibility and Work Opportunity Reconciliation Act signed by Clinton in 1996 embodied a similar notion that work and individual self-sufficiency offered the best solution to the problem of welfare dependency and the premise of combining liberal and conservative ideas in order to successfully diffuse Republican opposition.

Dukakis's fiscal policy similarly served as a model of the Democratic Party's new approach to economic concerns as it adapted to the political realities of the 1980s, especially the tax cut ethos of the Reagan administration. On returning to office, Dukakis reneged on his earlier opposition to tax limitation laws like Proposition 2½, publicly stating that "there was no doubt that taxes were too high" in Massachusetts during the 1970s.[153] Dukakis sought not to revise but work within the boundaries established by Proposition 2½ and the broader resistance to taxes among both Bay State voters and the high-tech companies. His fiscal policy managed to keep property tax rates low by replacing the revenue lost with increased state aid to cities and towns. The Dukakis administration generated the money to carry out this program through a crackdown on tax evasion called the REAP program, which yielded $900 million in three years.[154] By 1985, the state tax rate had fallen below the national average and Massachusetts had a budget surplus. Dukakis agreed to the MHTC's request to repeal the 7.5 percent surcharge on income taxes that he had imposed a decade earlier. The next year, Dukakis oversaw a $64 million tax cut, the largest such reduction in state history, bolstering both his approval ratings and image as an effective reformer.[155] Dukakis's spate of public-private partnerships and focus on investment earned notice as a model for how Democratic governors could successfully create economic success and maintain social programs in the face of the Reagan administration's "new federalism," which brought significant cutbacks in funding from Washington.[156]

The state of Massachusetts did benefit from key forms of federal funds, not just for defense, but for public works as well, due in part to the power of the state congressional delegation, especially Speaker of the House O'Neill. Dukakis and O'Neill had never had a particularly close bond, but during the 1980s, they worked together on the effort to secure federal funds for the state, especially for the megaproject the Central Artery/Tunnel Project, otherwise known as the "Big Dig." Dukakis and O'Neill had both played parts in the drama surrounding the Inner Belt dating back to the 1960s. During his first term, Dukakis had appointed Fred Salvucci as secretary of transportation. Salvucci had extracted from the Boston Transportation Planning Review a plan for moving the Central Artery highway and adding a new tunnel as a means to relieve congestion and get rid of the large highway structure that cut off downtown from the waterfront. The plan had originally created skepticism. Although perhaps initially counterintuitive, Salvucci believed that the plan supplied the means to fix earlier problems of urban renewal and to limit sprawl by reducing traffic problems and increasing ingrowth within the city.[157] During the King administration, the plans laid dormant, but when Salvucci returned to the State House, he convinced Dukakis that it would be integral to his larger economic development goals to make Boston "the hub of an expanding New England economy."[158] O'Neill also recognized the project's potential. Shortly before retiring from Congress in 1986, the speaker had worked with other members of the state's congressional delegation to secure the initial $3.1 billion in funding for project. Eventually costing more than $12 billion, the "Big Dig" became the most expensive public works project in American history. The controversial project's promise to economically and aesthetically change Boston and improve the quality of life of residents by funneling new money into the state economy and creating new construction jobs combined the various facets of the Democratic agenda.[159]

Members of the Dukakis administration frequently labeled this wide range of programs as the Massachusetts Miracle, overemphasizing the governor's singular role in the turnaround. The efforts both glossed over other significant factors that had contributed to the state's economic recovery and obscured persistent forms of inequality. Yet it was difficult to ignore Dukakis's impressive record. In 1986, the National Governors' Association anointed Dukakis "most effective governor in America," beating out Clinton and Mario Cuomo. Many people recognized him as the Democratic Party's "economic development policy expert," and he and the state had settled squarely into the national spotlight as, according to *Time*, "the pacesetter for the nation's transition to a high tech service oriented economy."[160] The praise he garnered inspired Dukakis to launch a bid for the presidency in 1988.

Competence, Not Ideology

Massachusetts liberal is the more memorable label to emerge from the 1988 presidential race, but it was the Massachusetts Miracle that led Dukakis to the front of a crowded field of Democratic candidates seeking the party's nomination. Dukakis made his successful revival of the state's economy and political structure the centerpiece of his presidential campaign.[161] During the first year of the campaign, he primarily promoted his record as governor. He suggested that he would run the nation in much the same way as he had the state of Massachusetts, stressing the growth of the high-tech sector through public-private partnerships. *Time* noted that he often appeared to be running for "Governor of the United States," and another observer dubbed him the Honda Civic of leaders: "Compact, efficient, reliable, short on style, but long on utility."[162] His remark during his convention address that "this election isn't about ideology. It's about competence" encapsulated his emphasis on rationality, meritocratic ability, and his forward-thinking ethos.[163] The very same values had long pervaded the political culture of the Route 128 suburbs.

Dukakis's style did not energize the more progressive wings of the party or many minority voters who supported Jesse Jackson as their candidate, but it did help earn him the support of other critical constituencies. Dukakis's political ideology, which one observer described as "at once a social liberal and fiscal moderate, proenvironment and pro-growth, an advocate of the poor and a friend of business," combined many of the facets that Democratic Party strategists recognized as crucial to capturing the two major groups of swing voters.[164] In order to connect with and win back "Reagan Democrats," Dukakis began highlighting his Greek ethnicity and first-generation immigrant narrative of upward mobility.[165] Yet many party regulars remained dubious of Dukakis's claims of ethnic authenticity and even circulated buttons declaring "I knew Dukakis before he was Greek."[166] His former lieutenant governor, Thomas O'Neill III, remarked, "Ethnics come from working-class city neighborhoods; Michael is from a suburb. Ethnics deal with constituents who need a job or a favor; Michael has always been an issues-oriented politician."[167]

Dukakis's suburban origins and issue-oriented style actually served as a major asset with the other constituency that many strategists recognized as key to his and the Democratic Party's success in the general election. Political consultant and Dukakis adviser Hank Morris saw Dukakis's upbringing and ethos as important in galvanizing postindustrial suburban professionals in battleground states such as California, Illinois, and New York.[168] Suburban professionals responded favorably to Dukakis's record about quality-of-life issues like traffic and air pollution, unregulated commercial growth and sprawl, declining schools, and rising drug and crime problems. Morris urged the campaign to further underscore that "he is the first presidential nominee to grow up in the suburbs and to stay there, commuting to work and mowing the lawn and knowing the concerns of suburbanites."[169] Taking the advice to heart, Dukakis made frequent references to his 1963 Sears snowblower as an emblem of his suburban sensibility and frugality.[170]

Dukakis's emphasis on stimulating high-tech growth based on the Route 128 model proved most important in enlisting him a following among both white-collar professionals in the metropolitan areas of the Sunbelt, West, and Northeast and blue-collar voters in the Midwest and elsewhere.[171] Dukakis's record on labor issues, especially his plant closing initiative, even-

Figure 10.2 Michael Dukakis trimming hedges outside his Brookline home on Sunday, July 31, 1988, at the height of the presidential race. The Dukakis campaign used such images both to accentuate Dukakis's suburban roots in order to appeal to suburban voters and emphasize his lack of pretension and frugality, so that even at the height of campaign season, he opted to do his own yard work. Photo by Susan Walsh. Courtesy of Associated Press Images. © 1988 The Associated Press.

tually earned him the official endorsement of the AFL-CIO, which had experienced a sharp decline in membership and political power during the 1980s.[172] Like McGovern, Dukakis's ability to unify suburban professionals and blue-collar workers under the same electoral umbrella did not mean that these two groups necessarily saw eye to eye on economic matters, or shared or even understood the economic interests of the other. In his influential 1991 memoir, *Which Side Are You On?*, suburban-bred and Harvard-educated labor lawyer Thomas Geoghegan observed how "shocking it would have been" if Dukakis "had stood up in Brookline and said to his supporters 'workers have a right to organize.'" Geoghegan imagined most people in the room would have "looked absolutely blank" and asked, "'Michael, what the hell are you talking about?'" Geoghegan contended that the democratizing demands and goals of organized labor were "incomprehensible" to Dukakis's liberal friends and former classmates, since they were "middle-class Emersonian individualists" who had "more in common with the Reagan right" than the average union member, even though both might have supported a Democratic candidate.[173] This tension would continue to plague the relationship between labor and the Democratic Party, but in the short run, Dukakis confronted a greater challenge.

Massachusetts Liberal

By the conclusion of the July 1988 Democratic National Convention, Dukakis enjoyed a seventeen-point lead in the polls over his Republican opponent George H. W. Bush.[174] In response to this gap, Bush and his campaign manager, Lee Atwater, borrowed and adapted the template established by previous conservative politicians to discredit Dukakis. Bush's forces transformed Dukakis's reputation as a technocrat into a sign of his elitism and depicted him as the quintessential Massachusetts liberal "out of step with the mainstream America on most social issues." The Bush campaign adopted a set of keywords including "Massachusetts," "Harvard," "George McGovern," "Ted Kennedy," "Taxachusetts," and eventually simply the infamous abbreviation the "L-word" to associate with Dukakis negative ideas about both the Bay State and left-leaning politics.[175] It mattered little that Bush's accusations did not mesh with Dukakis's fiscally moderate record or that he had actually supported the more centrist Edmund Muskie over McGovern in the 1972 democratic primary. The effectiveness of these messages showed the continuing vibrancy of "Massachusetts" and "liberal" as pejoratives.[176] Bush increasingly turned to social issues such as school prayer, gun control, and the death penalty to lure voters. He declared that there was a "wide chasm" on the "questions of values between me and the liberal governor whom I'm running against."[177]

The attack culminated with the infamous campaign advertisement "The Revolving Door," which aired in the fall of 1988. It told the story of Willie Horton, an African American convicted murderer from Massachusetts who raped a white woman during a prison furlough. Written by Roger Ailes and Larry McCarthy, the script concluded by stating "Weekend Prison Passes: Dukakis on Crime" as the screen focused on Horton's mug shot. McCarthy later proudly dubbed the advertisement "every suburban mother's greatest fear."[178] "The Revolving Door" portrayed an incomplete version of Dukakis's crime record, which he had long touted as a means to gain the support of the very same constituency that the intimidating image of Horton aimed to scare. Since his first campaign, Dukakis had consciously presented himself as tough on crime. Throughout his time in office, he had been a strong proponent for mandatory minimum sentencing, especially in drug cases, and significantly cut back on the number of sentencing commutations over the course of his three terms.[179] The furlough program had begun under Sargent, and Dukakis had restricted it to make first-degree murderers ineligible.[180]

The Dukakis campaign proved unable to muster a meaningful response, and the "Willie Horton" moment served as the turning point in the 1988 presidential race. During the fall, Bush came from behind to lead in nearly every poll.[181] In the November election, Dukakis managed to win the professionals nationally and, for the first time, in San Mateo and Santa Clara counties, which sat at the forefront of the high-tech industry. Yet Bush won a decisive 54 percent of the popular vote overall, swept the southern states and most of the West with the exception of Oregon and Washington, and handily won white, working-class voters.[182] For many, the election results proved that the Bay State still stood so far out of the mainstream that the labels Massachusetts and liberalism held enough power to sink the fortunes of state candidates at the national level.[183]

Dukakis's sound defeat sent a particular disheartening message to Massachusetts residents, especially self-identified liberals, since Bush's success largely lay in mobilizing the nation's resentments specifically against them. William Schneider, a political analyst, asserted that the election "proved most of the country does not want to be Massachusetts."[184] The identity of Massachusetts, particularly the residents of the Route 128 suburbs, had long rested on the ways in which the state's liberal credentials made it distinctive and different from the rest of the country. The commitment to this ideal relied on a consistent denial of the structures and political trends that actually made the state and its suburban residents representative and in line with the rest of the nation. Thus, when Dukakis aimed to show that he and the state represented larger economic, political, and social processes and forces, it proved difficult to transcend the boundaries and power of the exceptionalist ideology of the Massachusetts liberal label promoted by liberal residents and their critics.

Seeking to move the Democratic Party more toward the ideological center and the South following the 1988 election, the New Democrats who founded the DLC also adopted the label and narrative of Dukakis as a Massachusetts liberal.[185] This revisionist account was key to DLC members' effort to remake the image of the party. Yet it overlooked Dukakis's success with the suburban voters and postindustrial professionals who DLC strategists saw as central to the viability of the party. It also overlooked the linkages between Dukakis's record and philosophy and the DLC's own vision.[186] The DLC's proposal of "a new governing agenda that expands opportunity, rewards responsibility and fosters community" largely through "economic growth in the free markets," expanding international trade and investment, entrepreneurship, civilian-oriented R & D, and nonunionized, service-oriented employment virtually recapitulated the components of Dukakis's gubernatorial record and campaign platform.[187]

When the DLC's leader and favored son Clinton ran alongside fellow southerner and notable Atari Democrat Gore, the campaign created an advertisement deeming them "a new generation of Democrats" who "don't think the way the old Democratic Party did. They've called for an end to welfare as we know it," and "they've rejected the old tax-and-spend politics."[188] The advertisement marked a clear effort to distance Clinton from Dukakis.

It was, in fact, Clinton who delivered the nominating speech for Dukakis at the 1988 Democratic National Convention, and he used similar language as the later campaign advertisement. Clinton praised his longtime friend and fellow governor as "the kind of man who plays it straight," and had "made the hard decisions: to balance budgets, create jobs, fight crime and drug abuse, move people from welfare to work."[189] When Clinton took office just over four years later, he brought many of Dukakis's advisers, including Summers and Reich, to serve in his cabinet. Although he did so with a southern drawl and populist charisma, Clinton implemented many of the core components of Dukakis's vision such as balancing the budget, welfare to work, and public-private partnerships aimed to help Americans make the transition to a high-tech, service-based economy.[190]

Dukakis's legacy was not exclusive to the Democratic Party but had a bipartisan reach. The series of four consecutive Republican governors who succeeded him in Massachusetts after he retired in 1990 also adopted key facets of his platform and governing style. In the early 1990s, William Weld promoted a governing philosophy labeled "Volvo Republicanism," or "libertarian liberalism," that combined fiscal restraint and social moderation. While serving as Massachusetts governor, Mitt Romney similarly extended Dukakis's ideas of public-private partnerships, business development, and market-oriented approaches to economic and social policy, making him popular with the crucial constituency of "suburban commuter voters" and leading him to contemplate his own presidential bid.[191] Two pieces of policy, passed during Romney's tenure, came to set the terms of political and social debate across the nation, as Massachusetts became the first state to legalize gay marriage in 2003 and two years later adopted the first state-mandated health care system. Both of these state policies aligned with the priorities of Dukakis and the suburban knowledge professionals in the Route 128 suburbs.

The policy platform of Dukakis and the Route 128 suburbs that he represented clearly had a more lasting influence on national political developments than the term Massachusetts liberal might indicate. Although Democrat John Kerry and Republican Romney did not win, their respective presidential bids underscored that Massachusetts continued to play a central role in national politics. Each of these campaigns embodied not the divergence of Massachusetts and the nation and liberal and conservative politics since the 1970s but their increasing convergence.[192] The narrative of the Massachusetts liberal has widely obscured that the real transformation of the Democratic Party and national politics has not been a geographic shift away from the Northeast toward the Sunbelt but rather a power shift away from urban ethnics and labor unions to suburban knowledge professionals and high-tech corporations.

Epilogue

The 2004 Democratic National Convention in Boston confirmed the inextricable ties between the state of Massachusetts, Boston, and the Democratic Party. The event marked Massachusetts' effort to confront its image as out of touch with the rest of the country, the city's attempt to overcome its reputation for racism, and the national Democratic Party's endeavor to surmount the rumors of its decline. The array of events, tours, and speeches combined the area's fusion of history and modernity by showcasing Boston's booming high-tech economy, role in cutting-edge medical research, American Revolution landmarks, and multiculturalism fostered by the immigration of new generations seeking the opportunities of the state's tech industry.

The highlight of the program came with the keynote address delivered by Illinois senate candidate Barack Obama, who captured many of the convention's larger themes and goals. While his speech did not serve its immediate purpose of helping Massachusetts senator John Kerry win the presidency in 2004, it did boost Obama's own political career, and offered a preview the main message of his own campaigns in 2008 and 2012 as well as his presidency. In the widely acclaimed address, Obama drew on his biography and diverse heritage to encourage Americans to recognize that they were "connected as one people" and that there was not a "liberal America and a conservative America," and "not a black America and white America and Latino America and Asian America." At the same time he pointed out that the struggles of individual citizens affected the entire country, Obama emphasized the themes of "opportunity" and individual advancement through "hard work."[1] By advocating for transcending difference and the burdens of the past without addressing many of the structural forces that fueled these divisions, Obama's speech encapsulated the core values that since the 1950s had come define to liberalism.

The themes of equality of opportunity and meritocratic individualism proved especially crucial to Obama's popularity among high-tech-oriented professionals. Richard Florida, who initially coined the term the "creative class" to describe this cohort, defined them as "generally liberal-minded" and above all "staunchly meritocratic," offended by "inequality of opportunity" and the waste of natural resources and human capital. Yet Florida observed that the creative class had been decidedly less invested in finding collective remedies to these problems such as promoting a pro-labor agenda, which proved consistent with the outlook of suburban knowledge professionals in places like the Route 128 suburbs throughout the second half of the twentieth century.[2] In his 2012 reelection bid, Obama directly appealed to this constituency and their values and priorities. In battleground areas like the suburbs of northern Virginia, Denver, and North Carolina's Research Triangle, Obama made promises of stimulating high-tech employment and entrepreneurship, offering tax cuts for the middle class, and providing improvements to public education.[3] The strategy paid off, especially as Republican candidate Romney also heavily courted these same voters using many of the same talking points that led him to become governor of Massachusetts. In the end, high-tech workers helped Obama to victory. He earned the votes and campaign contributions of workers at companies like Google and Microsoft at remarkably high rates, building on the relationships forged between tech companies and the Democratic Party by Dukakis and the other Atari Democrats.[4] The candidates remained competitive in the suburbs overall, but Obama handily won areas where a large concentration of residents had advanced degrees and secured the support of high-tech workers nationally by an overwhelming margin. The results solidified the position of people like the residents in the Route 128 suburbs at the center of the Democratic Party's base.

The growth of racial and ethnic diversity in the Route 128 area over the last thirty years similarly embodies many of the themes and images of Obama's 2004 convention speech and biography. The new job opportunities at technology companies kindled by the Massachusetts Miracle coupled with the changes in federal immigration policy led to a surge in foreign-born residents in the Route 128 suburbs, especially from Asia. In Newton, the Asian population grew from 2 to 11.5 percent, in Brookline from 4.8 to 15.6 percent, and in Lexington from 3 to 20 percent between 1990 and 2010.[5] By 2010, one-fourth of the students in the Lexington Public Schools were Asian, and 55 percent of the Asian population of the town held an advanced degree.[6] These newcomers in Lexington, Newton, and Concord consist primarily of either the upwardly mobile children of earlier generations of immigrant families or middle-class immigrants who came to the Boston area to achieve a "high-tech version of the American dream."[7] "Most are like me," Lexington resident Sophia Ho observed. "Immigrants who, I don't want to use the word 'made it' but who've been successful. They want to raise their children in a town where education is very important."[8] These reasons echo the motivating factors that led many young white families to move to Lexington and its surrounding areas in the 1950s and 1960s. Residents in Brookline, Lexington, and Newton have touted scenes of people bringing specialties from India, China, and Korea to block parties, and how the library has sections of Chinese and Bengali books. Many white residents have celebrated how the new population helps to prepare their children for the realities of a global society.[9]

These demographic changes have helped lessen the pronounced whiteness in the Route 128 suburbs, but not the patterns of economic exclusivity.

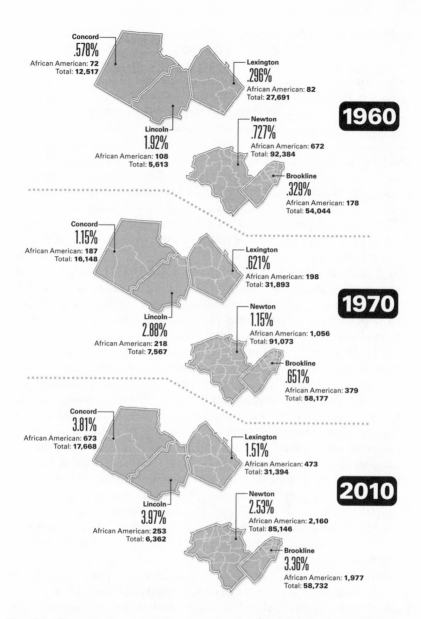

Concord
.578%
African American: **72**
Total: **12,517**

Lexington
.296%
African American: **82**
Total: **27,691**

Lincoln
1.92%
African American: **108**
Total: **5,613**

Newton
.727%
African American: **672**
Total: **92,384**

Brookline
.329%
African American: **178**
Total: **54,044**

1960

Concord
1.15%
African American: **187**
Total: **16,148**

Lexington
.621%
African American: **198**
Total: **31,893**

Lincoln
2.88%
African American: **218**
Total: **7,567**

Newton
1.15%
African American: **1,056**
Total: **91,073**

Brookline
.651%
African American: **379**
Total: **58,177**

1970

Concord
3.81%
African American: **673**
Total: **17,668**

Lexington
1.51%
African American: **473**
Total: **31,394**

Lincoln
3.97%
African American: **253**
Total: **6,362**

Newton
2.53%
African American: **2,160**
Total: **85,146**

Brookline
3.36%
African American: **1,977**
Total: **58,732**

2010

Figure E-1 African American population as percent of total population in five Route 128 sub-urbs, 1960, 1970, and 2010. This map shows how despite the increased diversity of the Route 128 area since the 1970s, the African American population had not grown substantially since 1960. *Sources*: US Census Bureau, *Census of Population and Housing, 1960* (Washington, DC: US Census Bureau, 1960); US Census Bureau, *Census of Population and Housing, 1970* (Washington, DC: US Census Bureau, 1970); US Census Bureau, *Census of Population and Housing, 2010* (Washington, DC: US Census Bureau, 2010).

By 2010, Lexington had a median family income of $150,389 and a median home value of $677,600, Newton a median family income of $109,724 and a median home value of $689,600, and Brookline had a median household income of $97,250 and a median home value of $681,200.[10] In line with national demographic patterns, while the overall suburban minority population increased during the 1990s and early 2000s, in metropolitan Boston, so did the segregation of blacks and Latinos from whites and Asians.[11] The Latino and black populations in Massachusetts have increasingly become concentrated within struggling neighborhoods and inner-ring suburbs in Boston, Chelsea, Lawrence, Lynn, and Lowell. The 2010 census revealed that Lawrence is 74 percent Latino, with roughly the same percentage speaking a language other than English at home, had a median family income of $31,478, and 28.6 percent of the residents lived below the poverty line. In the Lawrence Public Schools, 79 percent of the students qualified for free lunches during the 2012–13 school as compared to 4.3 percent in Concord.[12] In the lower-income inner suburbs of Chelsea, which had a slightly higher median household income of $43,155, 62.2 percent of the population was Latino, 8.5 percent was African American, 89.9 percent of the student population was low-income, 81.8 percent of the students received a free lunch and 91.6 percent had a high-needs designation. At the beginning of twenty-first century, Boston's African American and Latino populations remained largely concentrated in the low-income neighborhoods of Roxbury and Dorchester, and the student population of the BPS was roughly 87 percent minority and 76 percent low income.[13] The ineffectiveness at challenging the exclusionary zoning practices of suburban municipalities contributed to these patterns of inequality. Surveying the census data, the executive director of the Fair Housing Center of Greater Boston noted the high correlation between a community's resistance to compliance with the requirements of the Anti-Snob Zoning Act and municipalities' lack of racial and economic diversity.[14] The Route 128 suburbs continued to reflect this trend, falling drastically short of the 10 percent guideline outlined in the 1969 Anti-Snob Zoning Act.[15] In fact, in most suburban municipalities METCO students continued to compromise the few black or brown faces in the public schools.

While METCO remained far more popular in the Route 128 suburbs than potential affordable housing developments, the program also highlights these trends of racial and economic inequality in metropolitan Boston. White suburban residents often continued to tout the ways that METCO offers diversity and the means to transcend the kinds of racial and spatial differences that Obama outlined in his convention speech.[16] In 2014, the program remained roughly the size it was at the time of the busing crisis, and support in suburban towns for the program remained predicated on the fact that its $20 million yearly budget was still entirely state funded.[17]

Yet the wait-list of Boston students seeking acceptance into the program grew to around ten to twelve thousand, comprising one-fourth of all eligible Boston residents, and many parents signed their children up before their first birthday.[18] The list illustrates how the program still represented a means for parents of color in Boston to provide superior educational opportunities for their children.[19]

During the 1980s and early 1990s, METCO began to face criticism that it favored African Americans and did not reflect the changing racial diversity and growing immigrant population of Boston, particularly the city's growing Asian and Latino populations.[20] In 1994, the state heeded the criticisms and issued specific guidelines for METCO recruitment. The stipulations required the program to more accurately reflect the changing demographics of Boston. By the 2010–11 school year, the 3,341–pupil program included 2,513 African Americans (75.2 percent), 562 Latinos (16.8 percent), 112 Asians (3.4 percent), and 111 multiracial students (3.3 percent).[21] Although they discuss the hardship that participation entailed, the vast majority of METCO students and alumni have stated that they would participate again, or put their children in the program if they had the chance. The respondents have also consistently said that the most important thing they gained from METCO was how to operate in a white world.[22] These responses and the names on the long wait-list reveal the continued desire of many parents to offer this opportunity for quality education to their children, but how, like many liberal initiatives, METCO represents a limited solution to a much larger set of problems of educational, socioeconomic, and metropolitan inequality.

The strong desire of Boston parents of color to enroll their children in districts outside the city indicated the persistent problems in Boston's schools, where despite the use of busing since the 1970s, low-income students of color remained concentrated in underperforming schools throughout the district.[23] In 2013, the BSC took steps to eliminate its long-standing program of busing for racial diversity as a response to these patterns. The decision was also in part a way to address the governor's order of across-the-board spending cuts so as to balance the state's budget, which echoed the budget and busing crisis of the mid-1970s and its disproportionate impact on low-income people of color.[24] The elimination of comprehensive busing clearly marked an end of an era. School officials have suggested that the new program "increases equitable access to quality schools overall."[25] Yet many residents and experts have worried that the fall 2014 implementation of the plan, which includes a return to neighborhood schools, could exacerbate city's class-segregated school system and allow children students from more affluent neighborhoods to go to better-funded schools, leaving low-income children even more concentrated in underfunded and increasingly overcrowded schools.[26] The new busing plan, therefore, has not lessened the high rate of parents trying to seek one of the coveted spaces in the METCO program.[27]

At the same time that many parents and students of color continue to look outward to the suburbs for quality education, increasing numbers of creative-class professionals are opting to move into Boston neighborhoods like Jamaica Plain, the South End, Charlestown, and South Boston, or Cambridge, and Somerville rather than the purportedly bland suburbs of the exurban fringe.[28] Like their corollaries in Park Slope, Lincoln Park, Silver Lake, and Hayes Valley in other cities, residents of Jamaica Plain and the South End have updated many of the same arguments about aesthetic and cultural distinctiveness, high quality of life, and the desire to live around "like-minded people" who share a commitment to open-mindedness, liberal values, and politics that many of their predecessors used to explain their decisions to move to the Route 128 suburbs in the 1950s and 1960s.[29] Community members and the scholars and journalists who study them frequently frame qualities like diversity, cosmopolitanism, creativity, authenticity, community, walkability, and bikeability in the market-based terms of the real estate market and knowledge-oriented workplace.[30]

This trend is changing certain political, social, economic, and social dynamics, especially as many tech companies have followed suit and shifted their headquarters from the suburban fringe into urban centers, such as the Seaport area of South Boston, Williamsburg in Brooklyn, and the South of Market district in San Francisco. Yet this trend has not provided the solution to metropolitan, class, and racial inequities. The growing concentration of tech companies and creative-class people in urban enclaves has, in fact, compounded rather than reduced patterns of economic exclusivity. These shifting trends have inscribed socioeconomic and structural inequality ever deeper into the metropolitan landscape of Boston and its postindustrial counterparts, driving up property values while pushing poverty into lower-income suburbs like Chelsea outside Boston, Long Island in New York, and Contra Costa County in the Bay Area.[31]

The commitment of urban-dwelling knowledge workers to preserving their property values, providing the best education for their own children, and attaining a high quality of life reflect a similar set of individualist political priorities and class sensibility as the typical individualist, conformist suburbanite who they frequently eschew. The choice of liberal professionals to move into creative-class enclaves of major urban areas clearly has not proven a way to avoid the individualist attitudes and difficult decisions of their predecessors who migrated to the Route 128 suburbs in the 1950s, 1960s, and 1970s. While buying a house in a hip urban neighborhood and putting up a yard sign for Obama might offer a means to outwardly demonstrate a liberal political identity and commitment to socioeconomic equality, it is not the main route to confront or solve structural inequity. Indeed, the language and ideals of individual rights, meritocracy, equality of opportunity, and diversity embedded in these political and purchasing decisions seems to have even further obscured structural problems from the consciousness of many highly educated, liberal-leaning professionals.

The voting and residential patterns of knowledge-oriented professionals confirm that neither the Democratic Party nor liberalism has declined since the 1960s, but instead both have transformed. It is thus ever more important to focus not on the ways this constituency, whether they live in Lexington or Boston, the suburbs of Chicago or the Bay Area, are distinctive or exceptional. Rather, it is crucial to understand how their individualist and meritocratic outlook reflects the continuities and changes in liberalism, and has contributed to the problems of metropolitan segregation and inequality and the absence of public policies that address these issues. The emphasis on high-tech growth and knowledge workers by the Democratic Party and cities like Boston as the solution to the nation's economic and social problems shows much more of a commitment to the future than addressing many of the persistent problems of the past. Yet coming to terms with the roots of the high-tech and upper-middle-class transformation of liberalism and understanding its possibilities and limits offers an important first step in advocating for more collective, metropolitan-based solutions that transcend these class, race, and spatial divisions and benefit everyone.

Notes

Abbreviations for Frequently Cited Sources and Organizations

Archival Collections

AACR	Abortion Action Coalition Records, Archives and Special Collections Department, Northeastern University, Boston
ADA	Massachusetts Chapter of Americans for Democratic Action Records, Massachusetts Historical Society, Boston
AES	Adlai E. Stevenson Papers, Seeley G. Mudd Manuscript Library, Princeton University, Princeton, NJ
AHM	Allen H. Morgan Papers, Massachusetts Historical Society, Boston
ASN	Andrew S. Natsios Papers, Special Collections, State Library of Massachusetts, Boston
CDNR	Concord Department of Natural Resources, Division of Natural Resources, and the Natural Resources Commission of Concord, Special Collections, Concord Free Public Library, Concord, MA
CHOC-CPL	Concord Home Owning Corporation Records, Concord Special Collections, Concord Free Public Library, Concord, MA
CHWF	Charles H. W. Foster Papers, Massachusetts Historical Society, Boston
CLCT	Concord Land Conservation Trust, Special Collections, Concord Free Public Library, Concord, MA
COREP	Papers of the Congress of Racial Equality, 1941–67, Microform Collections, Microfilming Corporation of America, Sanford, NC
CPC	Concord Pamphlet Collection, Concord Special Collections, Concord Free Public Library, Concord, MA
CSC	Concord Special Collections, Concord Free Public Library, Concord, MA
CPPAX-UMB	Citizens for Participation in Political Action Records, Special Collections, Healey Library, University of Massachusetts at Boston
CRMERA	Committee to Ratify the Massachusetts State Equal Rights Amendment Records, Arthur and Elizabeth Schlesinger

	Library on the History of Women in America, Radcliffe Institute for Advanced Study, Harvard University, Cambridge, MA
FFM	Frank F. Mankiewicz Personal Papers, John F. Kennedy Presidential Library, Boston
FH	Freedom House Inc. Records, Archives and Special Collections Department, Northeastern University, Boston
FLL	Francis Loeb Library, Harvard University Graduate School of Design, Cambridge, MA
FWS	Francis W. Sargent Administration Records, Massachusetts Archives, Boston
GSM	George S. McGovern Papers, Seeley G. Mudd Manuscript Library, Princeton University, Princeton, NJ
JHB	Jack H. Backman Papers, Special Collections, State Library of Massachusetts, Boston
JWO	John W. Olver Papers, Special Collections, State Library of Massachusetts, Boston
KWC	Kalmia Woods Corporation Records, Concord Special Collections, Concord Free Public Library, Concord, MA
LER	Town of Lincoln Environmental Records, Lincoln Archives, Lincoln Public Library, Lincoln, MA
LGP	Lois G. Pines Papers, Special Collections, State Library of Massachusetts, Boston
LCRC-LPL	Lexington Civil Rights Committee Collection, Cary Memorial Public Library, Lexington, MA
LPL	Lexington Collection, Cary Memorial Public Library, Lexington, MA
LRA	Lawrence R. Alexander Papers, Special Collections, State Library of Massachusetts, Boston
LWVL	League of Women Voters of Lincoln Massachusetts Collection, Lincoln Archives, Lincoln Public Library, Lincoln, MA
METCO-NUSC	Metropolitan Council for Educational Opportunity, Records, Archives, and Special Collections Department, Northeastern University, Boston
MIT-SC	Massachusetts Institute of Technology Planning Office, MIT Institute Archives and Special Collections, Cambridge, MA
MGL	Monroe C. Gutman Library, Center for Field Studies, Graduate School of Education, Harvard University, Cambridge, MA
MHM	Mildred H. Mahoney Papers, Arthur and Elizabeth Schlesinger Library on the History of Women in America, Radcliffe Institute for Advanced Study, Harvard University, Cambridge, MA

MORAL-SL	Mass Choice Records, Arthur and Elizabeth Schlesinger Library on the History of Women in America, Radcliffe Institute for Advanced Study, Harvard University, Cambridge, MA
MSD	Michael S. Dukakis Presidential Campaign Records, Archives and Special Collections Department, Northeastern University, Boston
NARAL-Newsletters	National Abortion Rights Action League, State Affiliates Newsletter Collection, Arthur and Elizabeth Schlesinger Library on the History of Women in America, Radcliffe Institute for Advanced Study, Harvard University, Cambridge, MA
NNCC	Newton-Needham Chamber of Commerce Records, Newton Historical Society, Newton, MA
NOW-Boston	National of Organization for Women Records, Boston Chapter, Arthur and Elizabeth Schlesinger Library on the History of Women in America, Radcliffe Institute for Advanced Study, Harvard University, Cambridge, MA
NOW-Newsletters	National Organization for Women Chapter Newsletter Collection, Arthur and Elizabeth Schlesinger Library on the History of Women in America, Radcliffe Institute for Advanced Study, Harvard University, Cambridge, MA
NPL	Newton Collection, Newton Public Library, Newton, MA
PMR	Phyllis M. Ryan Papers, Archives and Special Collections Department, Northeastern University, Boston
RC	Concord Route 2 Committee, Special Collections, Concord Free Library, Concord, MA
RFD	Robert F. Drinan Papers, Special Collections, Burns Library, Boston College, Chestnut Hill, MA
RMB	Ruth M. Batson Papers, Arthur and Elizabeth Schlesinger Library on the History of Women in America, Radcliffe Institute for Advanced Study, Harvard University, Cambridge, MA
RRC	Environmental Impact of the Redesigning and Reengineering of Route 2 on Several Mass. Towns Records, Special Collections, Concord Free Public Library, Concord, MA
SBPA-CPL	Swamp Brook Preservation Association Records, Concord Special Collections, Concord Free Public Library, Concord, MA
SLM	State Library Massachusetts, Boston
VOW-SL	Voice of Women–New England Records, Arthur and Elizabeth Schlesinger Library on the History of Women in America, Radcliffe Institute for Advanced Study, Harvard University, Cambridge, MA

WAG   W. Arthur, Garrity Jr. Papers on the Boston Schools
             Desegregation Case, Archives and Special Collections
             Department, Healey Library, University of Massachusetts at
             Boston
WILPF   Women's International League for Peace and Freedom
             Records, Boston Chapter, Arthur and Elizabeth Schlesinger
             Library on the History of Women in America, Radcliffe
             Institute for Advanced Study, Harvard University,
             Cambridge, MA

Oral History Collections

COHP   Concord Oral History Program Collection, Concord Free
             Public Library, Concord, MA
LOHP   Lexington Oral History Projects, Archives and Special
             Collections Department, Healey Library, University of
             Massachusetts at Boston

Introduction

1   Ronald P. Formisano, *Boston against Busing: Race and Ethnicity in the 1960s and 1970s*
    (Chapel Hill: University of North Carolina Press, 1991), 1; J. Anthony Lukas, *Common
    Ground: A Turbulent Decade in the Lives of Three American Families* (New York: Knopf, 1986);
    Pam Belluck, "Boston Rises above Unflattering Stereotypes," *New York Times*, July 25, 2004.
2   For works that recently made this claim, see Judith Stein, *Pivotal Decade: How the United
    States Traded Factories for Finance in the Seventies* (New Haven, CT: Yale University Press,
    2010), xi–xii; Jefferson Cowie, *Stayin' Alive: The 1970s and the Last Days of the Working
    Class* (New York: New Press, 2010), 235–41.
3   For more on the conservative and Sunbelt-centered dimensions of many studies of sub-
    urban politics, see Lisa McGirr, *Suburban Warriors: The Origins of the New American Right*
    (Princeton, NJ: Princeton University Press, 2001); Darren Dochuk, *From Bible Belt to
    Sunbelt: Plain Folk Religion, Grassroots Politics, and the Rise of Evangelical Conservatism*
    (New York: W. W. Norton, 2010); Kevin Kruse, *White Flight: Atlanta and the Making of
    Modern of Conservatism* (Princeton, NJ: Princeton University Press, 2005); Michelle M.
    Nickerson, *Mothers of Conservatism: Women and the Postwar Right* (Princeton, NJ: Prince-
    ton University Press, 2012).
4   John B. Judis and Ruy Teixeira, *The Emerging Democratic Majority* (New York: Scribner,
    2002), 39–49; Nate Silver, "In Silicon Valley, Technology Talent Gap Threatens G.O.P
    Campaigns," *New York Times*, November 29, 2012; Nate Cohn, "Bankers—Abandoned
    Obama, But the Rest of the Rich Hold Surprisingly Strong," *New Republic Online*, No-
    vember 14, 2012.
5   Daniel Bell, *The Coming of Post-Industrial Society: A Venture in Social Forecasting* (New
    York: Basic Books, 1973).
6   Richard Todd, "The 'Ins' and 'Outs' at M.I.T.," *New York Times*, May 18, 1969; Kevin Phil-
    lips, *Mediacracy: American Parties and Politics in the Communications Age* (Garden City, NY:
    Doubleday and Company, 1975), 15.

7   Historian Margaret Pugh O'Mara has called Route 128 "a metropolitan-wide network of high-tech growth that was more extensive than was seen anywhere else in the country." See Margaret Pugh O'Mara, *Cities of Knowledge: Cold War Science and the Search for the Next Silicon Valley* (Princeton, NJ: Princeton University Press, 2004), 73.

8   Christopher Rand, *Cambridge, U.S.A.: Hub of a New World* (New York: Oxford University Press, 1964), 17–18.

9   Julian Soshnick, interview by Nancy Earsy, August 15, 1991, LOHP; Bonnie Jones, interview by Norma McGavern-Norland, December 3, 1991, LOHP.

10   For the long historical roots of the debate over the class position and politics of professionals, see Talcott Parsons, "The Professions and Social Structure," in *Essays in Sociological Theory, Pure and Applied* (Glencoe, IL: Free Press, 1949), 34–49; C. Wright Mills, *White Collar* (New York: Oxford University Press, 1951).

11   For an excellent discussion of the notion of the development of the term New Class, see Barbara Ehrenreich, *Fear of Falling: The Inner Life of the Middle Class* (New York: Pantheon Books, 1989), 144–95. For the various uses of these terms, see Bell, *The Coming of Post-Industrial Society*; B. Bruce-Briggs, *The New Class?* (New Brunswick, NJ: Transaction Books, 1979); Barbara Ehrenreich and John Ehrenreich, "The Professional-Managerial Class," in *Between Labor and Capital*, ed. Pat Walker (Hassocks, UK: Harvester Press, 1979), 5–45; Richard Florida, *The Rise of the Creative Class: And How It's Transforming Work and Leisure in America* (New York: Basic Books, 2002); Randall Rothenberg, *The Neo-Liberals: Creating the New American Politics* (New York: Simon and Schuster, 1984); David Brooks, *Bobos in Paradise: The New Upper Class and How They Got There* (New York: Touchstone Book 2000). For more on the formation of the postindustrial middle class and the difficulties of terminology, see Suleiman Osman, *The Invention of Brownstone Brooklyn: Gentrification and the Search for Authenticity in Postwar New York* (New York: Oxford University Press, 2011), 12–14.

12   For more on the difficulties of defining suburbs, see Robert Fishman, *Bourgeois Utopias: The Rise and Fall of Suburbia* (New York: Basic Books, 1987); Delores Hayden, *Building Suburbia: Green Fields and Urban Growth* (New York: Pantheon Books, 2003); Kenneth T. Jackson, *Crabgrass Frontier: The Suburbanization of the United States* (New York: Oxford University Press, 1985), 4–5; Becky M. Nicolaides and Andrew Wiese, eds., *The Suburb Reader* (New York: Routledge, 2006), 1–9.

13   On the challenges of defining liberalism, see Alan Brinkley, *Liberalism and Its Discontents* (Cambridge, MA: Harvard University Press, 1998), ix–xii; Robert O. Self, *American Babylon: Race and the Struggle for Postwar Oakland* (Princeton, NJ: Princeton University Press, 2003), 13–14; Gary Gerstle, "The Protean Character of American Liberalism," *American Historical Review* (October 1994): 1043–73.

14   For more on the literature surrounding liberalism and the variations on its usage, see Eric Alterman and Kevin Mattson, *The Cause: The Fight for American Liberalism from Franklin Roosevelt to Barack Obama* (New York: Penguin, 2012); Eric Alterman, *Why We're Liberals: A Political Handbook for Post-Bush America* (New York: Viking, 2008); Peter Beinart, *The Good Fight: Why Liberals—and Only Liberals—Can Win the War on Terror and Make America Great Again* (New York: HarperCollins, 2006); Douglas S. Massey, *Return of the "L" Word: A Liberal Vision for the New Century* (Princeton, NJ: Princeton University Press, 2005); Tom Waldman, *Not Much Left: The Fate of Liberalism in America* (Berkeley: University of California Press, 2008); Neil Jumonville and Kevin Mattson, eds., *Liberalism for a New Century* (Berkeley: University of California Press, 2007), 6–7; Kevin Mattson, *When America Was Great: The Fighting Faith of Postwar Liberalism* (New York: Routledge, 2004).

15   The suburban liberal label reinforces the assumption that suburban residents in the postwar era were exclusively white and middle class. A series of works have challenged that

image, and exposed the racial and economic diversity of the suburbs throughout the twentieth century. See Becky M. Nicolaides, *My Blue Heaven: Life and Politics in the Working-Class Suburbs of Los Angeles, 1920–1965* (Chicago: University of Chicago Press, 2002); Andrew Wiese, *Places of Their Own: African-American Suburbanization in the Twentieth Century* (Chicago: University of Chicago Press, 2004); Charlotte Brooks, *Alien Neighbors, Foreign Friends: Asian Americans, Housing, and the Transformation of Urban California* (Chicago: University of Chicago Press, 2009); Aaron I. Cavin, "The Borders of Citizenship: Latinos, Asian Americans, and Metropolitan Politics in Silicon Valley, 1945–2000" (PhD diss., University of Michigan, 2012); Wendy Cheng, "The Changs Next Door to the Diazes: Suburban Racial Formation in Los Angeles's San Gabriel Valley," *Journal of Urban History* (January 2013): 15–31; Timothy Fong, *The First Suburban Chinatown: The Remaking of Monterey Park, California* (Philadelphia: Temple University Press, 1994); Leland T. Saito, *Race and Politics: Asian Americans, Latinos, and Whites in a Los Angeles Suburb* (Urbana: University of Illinois Press, 1998); Matt Garcia, *A World of Its Own: Race, Labor, and Citrus in the Making of Greater Los Angeles, 1900–1970* (Chapel Hill: University of North Carolina Press, 2001); Jerry Gonzalez, "'A Place in the Sun: Mexican American Identity, Race, and the Suburbanization of Los Angeles, 1940–1980" (PhD diss., University of Southern California, 2009).

16   Ehrenreich and Ehrenreich, "The Professional-Managerial Class," 35. For more about professionals in the progressive era, see Alice O'Connor, *Poverty Knowledge: Social Science, Social Policy, and the Poor in Twentieth-Century U.S. History* (Princeton, NJ: Princeton University Press, 2002), 25–54; Daniel Rodgers, *Atlantic Crossings: Social Politics in a Progressive Age* (Cambridge, MA: Harvard University Press, 1998); Robert Wiebe, *The Search for Order, 1877–1920* (New York: Hill and Wang, 1966); Michael Willrich, *City of Courts: Socializing Justice in Progressive Era Chicago* (New York: Cambridge University Press, 2003); Doug Rossinow, *Visions of Progress: The Left-Liberal Tradition in America* (Philadelphia: University of Pennsylvania Press, 2008), 13–15; Edwin Layton, *The Revolt of the Engineers: Social Responsibility and the American Engineering Profession* (Cleveland: Press of Case Western Reserve University, 1971).

17   See Alan Brinkley, *The End of Reform: New Deal Liberalism in Recession and War* (New York: Alfred A. Knopf, 1995); Steven Brint, *In an Age of Experts: The Changing Role of Professionals in Politics and Public Life* (Princeton, NJ: Princeton University Press, 1994).

18   Peter Drucker first coined the term "knowledge worker" in 1959; see Peter Drucker, *The Age of Discontinuity* (New York: Harper and Row, 1968). For more on the growth of knowledge workers, see Stephen Schryer, *Fantasies of the New Class: Ideologies of Professionalism in Post–World War II American Fiction* (New York: Columbia University Press, 2011). See also Bell, *The Coming of Post-Industrial Society*; Ehrenreich and Ehrenreich, "The Professional-Managerial Class," 5–45.

19   Bell, *The Coming of Post-Industrial Society*, 127, 344–45.

20   See Ehrenreich and Ehrenreich, "The Professional-Managerial Class," 5–45; Ehrenreich, *Fear of Falling*, 12.

21   For more on the various government programs that fueled suburbanization, see Jackson, *Crabgrass Frontier*; Lizabeth Cohen, *A Consumers' Republic: The Politics of Mass Consumption in Postwar America* (New York: Alfred A. Knopf, 2003); Louis Hyman, *Debtor Nation: The History of America in Red Ink* (Princeton, NJ: Princeton University Press, 2011). For more specifically on how the mortgage market shaped postwar whites affluence and privilege, see David M. P. Freund, "Marketing the Free Market," in *The New Suburban History*, ed. Kevin Kruse and Thomas J. Sugrue (Chicago: University of Chicago Press, 2006), 11–32.

22   Jackson, *Crabgrass Frontier*; Andrew Highsmith, *Demolition Means Progress: Flint, Michigan, and the Fate of the American Metropolis* (Chicago: University of Chicago Press, forthcoming); Arnold R. Hirsch, "Containment on the Home Front: Race and Federal Hous-

ing Policy from the New Deal to the Cold War," *Journal of Urban History* (January 2000): 158–89; Thomas J. Sugrue, *The Origins of the Urban Crisis: Race and Inequality in Postwar Detroit* (Princeton, NJ: Princeton University Press, 1996).

23   David M. P. Freund, *Colored Property: State Policy and White Racial Politics in Suburban America* (Chicago: University of Chicago Press, 2007); Kruse, *White Flight*; Matthew D. Lassiter, *The Silent Majority: Suburban Politics in the Sunbelt South* (Princeton, NJ: Princeton University Press, 2006); George Lipsitz, *The Possessive Investment in Whiteness: How White People Profit from Identity Politics* (Philadelphia: Temple University Press, 1998). See also Mike Davis, *City of Quartz: Excavating the Future in Los Angeles* (New York: Vintage Books, 1992).

24   For more on this consumer-oriented attitude to government services, see Cohen, *A Consumers' Republic*. See also Thomas J. Sugrue, "All Politics Is Local: The Persistence of Localism in Twentieth-Century America," in *The Democratic Experiment: New Directions in American Political History*, ed. Meg Jacobs, William J. Novak, and Julian Zelizer (Princeton, NJ: Princeton University Press, 2003), 301–26.

25   For more on the impact of postwar liberalism in the producing a social compact that promoted individualism and its consequences, see Molly C. Michelmore, *Tax and Spend: The Welfare State, Tax Politics, and the Limits of American Liberalism* (Philadelphia: University of Pennsylvania Press, 2012).

26   Ellen Herman, *The Romance of American Psychology: Political Culture in an Age of Experts* (Berkeley: University of California Press, 1994); Andrew Polsky, *The Rise of the Therapeutic State* (Princeton, NJ: Princeton University Press, 1991).

27   See Gunnar Myrdal, *An American Dilemma: The Negro Problem and Modern Democracy* (New York: Harper & Bros, 1944). See also Walter Jackson, *Gunnar Myrdal and America's Conscience: Social Engineering and Racial Liberalism, 1938–1987* (Chapel Hill: University of North Carolina Press, 1987); Daryl Michael Scott, *Contempt and Pity: Social Policy and the Image of the Damaged Black Psyche, 1880–1996* (Chapel Hill: University of North Carolina Press, 1997), 93–160.

28   Sugrue, *Origins of the Urban Crisis*, 10.

29   See Lizabeth Cohen, *Making a New Deal: Industrial Workers in Chicago, 1919–1939* (New York: Cambridge University Press, 1990).

30   There has been an extended scholarly discussion spanning disciplines since the early twentieth century that has debated the question of the lack of class consciousness among knowledge workers, especially engineers. See Thorstein Veblen, *Engineers and the Price System* (1921; repr., New York: Viking, 1965); Andre Gorz, *Strategy for Labor* (Boston: Beacon Press, 1968); Robert Zussman, *Mechanics of the Middle Class Work and Politics Among American Engineers* (Berkeley: University of California Press, 1985); Richard Florida, *The Rise of the Creative Class, Revisited* (New York: Basic Books, 2012), xxiv–xxv, 35–62.

31   Matthew Lassiter has deemed this shift the "spatial turn." See Lassiter, *Silent Majority*, 7–10.

32   Alan Brinkley, "The Problem of American Conservatism," *American Historical Review* (April 1994): 409.

33   Steve Fraser and Gary Gerstle define the "New Deal Order" broadly to encompass economic and social institutions, ideologies, and electoral coalitions. See Steve Fraser and Gary Gerstle, eds., *The Rise and Fall of the New Deal Order, 1930–1980* (Princeton, NJ: Princeton University Press, 1989), x–xi. See also Thomas Byrne Edsall and Mary D. Edsall, *Chain Reaction: The Impact of Race, Rights, and Taxes on American Politics* (New York: W. W. Norton, 1992); Formisano, *Boston against Busing*; Jonathan Rieder, *Canarsie: The Jews and Italians of Brooklyn against Liberalism* (Cambridge, MA: Harvard University Press, 1985); Jonathan Rieder, "The Rise of the 'Silent Majority,'" in *The Rise and Fall of the New Deal Order, 1930–1980*, ed. Steve Fraser and Gary Gerstle (Princeton, NJ: Princeton University Press, 1989). For an excellent discussion of the problems of associating the term working class with

white men in industrial unions in the urban North, see Nancy MacLean, "Getting New Deal History Wrong," *International Labor and Working-Class History* (Fall 2008): 49–55.

34 For one of the first and clearest articulations of this investigation, see McGirr, *Suburban Warriors*. See also Joseph Crespino, *In Search of Another Country: Mississippi and the Conservative Counterrevolution* (Princeton, NJ: Princeton University Press, 2007); Dochuk, *From Bible Belt to Sunbelt*; Kruse, *White Flight*; Nickerson, *Mothers of Conservatism*; Elizabeth Tandy Shermer, *Sunbelt Capitalism: Phoenix and the Transformation of American Capitalism* (Philadelphia: University of Pennsylvania Press, 2013).

35 Brinkley, "The Problem of American Conservatism," 409. Several more recent works have helped to greatly enhance understandings of modern conservatism by shifting attention from the grassroots focus, and demonstrated the importance of corporations, think tanks, and economists in the modern Republican ascendance. See, for example, Jennifer Burns, *Goddess of the Market: Ayn Rand and the American Right* (New York: Oxford University Press, 2009); Angus Burgin, *The Great Persuasion: Reinventing the Free Market since the Depression* (Cambridge, MA: Harvard University Press, 2012); Shane Hamilton, *Trucking Country: The Road to America's Wal-Mart Economy* (Princeton, NJ: Princeton University Press, 2008); Bethany Moreton, *To Serve God and Wal-Mart: The Making of Christian Free Enterprise* (Cambridge, MA: Harvard University Press, 2009); Kim Phillips-Fein, *Invisible Hands: The Making of the Conservative Movement from the New Deal to Reagan* (New York: W. W. Norton, 2009); Benjamin C. Waterhouse, *Lobbying America: The Politics of Business from Nixon to NAFTA* (Princeton, NJ: Princeton University Press, 2013).

36 For a discussion of the diversity of political activism in the suburbs, see Michelle Nickerson and Darren Dochuk, *Sunbelt Rising: The Politics of Place, Space, and Region* (Philadelphia: University of Pennsylvania Press, 2011), 3–4.

37 This point builds on the argument about suburban ideology and mainstream politics in Lassiter, *Silent Majority*; Matthew D. Lassiter, "Big Government and Family Values: Political Culture in the Metropolitan Sunbelt," in *Sunbelt Rising: The Politics of Space, Place, and Region*, ed. Michelle Nickerson and Darren Dochuk (Philadelphia: University of Pennsylvania Press, 2011), 85–86. For more on a form of suburban politics that transcends partisan division, see Davis, *City of Quartz*, 151–221.

38 Dochuk, *From Bible Belt to Sunbelt*; Eileen Luhr, *Witnessing Suburbia: Conservatives and Christian Youth Culture* (Berkeley: University of California Press, 2009); Moreton, *To Serve God and Wal-Mart*; Daniel K. Williams, *God's Own Party: The Making of the Christian Right* (New York: Oxford University Press, 2010).

39 For a range of examples of how a small organized group of suburban residents can have a great impact on shaping public policy, see Jonathan Bell, *California Crucible: The Forging of Modern American Liberalism* (Philadelphia: University of Pennsylvania Press, 2013); McGirr, *Suburban Warriors*; Nickerson, *Mothers of Conservatism*; Lassiter, *Silent Majority*; Clayton C. Howard, "The Closet and the Cul de Sac: Sexuality and Culture War in Postwar California" (PhD diss., University of Michigan, 2010).

40 For more on the problems of trying to address controversial and progressive issues, particularly around race, through incremental rather than sweeping change, see Jennifer L. Hochschild, *The New American Dilemma: Liberal Democracy and School Desegregation* (New Haven, CT: Yale University Press, 1984).

41 Duane Lockard, *New England State Politics* (Princeton, NJ: Princeton University Press, 1959), 120–23.

42 Lockard, *New England State Politics*, 126–31. Unlike Chicago or New York, Boston and other Massachusetts cities never developed a single machine. Curley, however, represented the closest thing to a boss.

43 Lukas, *Common Ground*, 22–23; V. O. Key Jr., *American State Politics: An Introduction* (New York: Alfred A. Knopf, 1956), 157–61.

44   Edgar Litt, *The Political Cultures of Massachusetts* (Cambridge, MA: MIT Press, 1965), 34–38; Murray Levin, *Kennedy Campaigning: The System and Style as Practiced by Edward Kennedy* (Boston: Beacon Press, 1966), 104.

45   Litt, *The Political Cultures of Massachusetts*, 201, 3.

46   Lockard, *New England State Politics*, 136.

47   For a trenchant critique of the problems of using the red/blue binary to understand political history, see Matthew D. Lassiter, "Political History beyond the Red–Blue Divide," *Journal of American History* (December 2011): 760–64.

48   Litt, *The Political Cultures of Massachusetts*, 2.

49   Henry B. Cabot to Grace Gleason, April 6, 1956, box 313, folder 4, AES.

50   Joseph F. Dineen, "Brahmin from Boston," *New Republic* (February 24, 1947): 12–14; Litt, *The Political Cultures of Massachusetts*, 50–51.

51   For more on some of the problems of investment in exceptionalist narratives, see Matthew D. Lassiter and Joseph Crespino, "Introduction: The End of Southern History," in *The Myth of Southern Exceptionalism*, ed. Matthew D. Lassiter and Joseph Crespino (New York: Oxford University Press, 2009), 3–22.

1   No Ordinary Suburbs

1   Robert C. Wood, *Suburbia: Its People and Places* (Boston: Houghton Mifflin, 1959), vii–vii. Wood ended up moving into Boston in the 1970s.

2   Paul Brooks, *The View from Lincoln Hill: Man and the Land in a New England Town* (Boston: Houghton Mifflin, 1976), 3, 4; Paul Brooks and Susan Brooks, "Town with Room for Living," *New York Times*, June 13, 1971.

3   Newton Chamber of Commerce, "Newton Massachusetts," 1969, NNCC.

4   Sam Bass Warner Jr., *Streetcar Suburbs: The Process of Growth in Boston (1870–1900)*, 2nd ed. (Cambridge, MA: Harvard University Press, 1978), 1.

5   Warner, *Streetcar Suburbs*, 80.

6   *The WPA Guide to Massachusetts: The Federal Writers' Project to 1930s' Massachusetts* (New York: Pantheon Books, 1983), 71–75.

7   Charles H. Trout, *Boston, the Depression, and the New Deal* (New York: Oxford University Press, 1977), 4.

8   David Koistinen, "Public Policies for Countering Deindustrialization in Postwar Massachusetts," *Journal of Policy History* 18, no. 3 (2006): 326–27.

9   Susan Rosegrant and David R. Lampe, *Route 128: Lessons from Boston's High-Tech Community* (New York: Basic Books, 1992), 80. See also Stuart W. Leslie, *The Cold War and American Science: The Military-Industrial-Academic Complex at MIT and Stanford* (New York: Columbia University Press, 1994), 14–43.

10   John H. Fenton, "M.I.T. Offers Spur the Area Economy," *New York Times*, January 15, 1961.

11   Roger Geiger, *Research and Relevant Knowledge: American Research Universities since World War II* (New York: Oxford University Press, 1993), 63; Fenton, "M.I.T. Offers Spur the Area Economy."

12   Leslie, *The Cold War and American Science*, 35–43.

13   AnnaLee Saxenian, *Regional Advantage: Culture and Competition in Silicon Valley and Route 128* (Cambridge, MA: Harvard University Press, 1996), 13.

14   Henry R. Lieberman, "Technology: Alchemist of Route 128," *New York Times*, January 8, 1968.

15   Rosegrant and Lampe, *Route 128*, 15. See also Fenton, "M.I.T. Offers Spur the Area Economy."

16   Rosegrant and Lampe, *Route 128*, 107.

17   Massachusetts Advisory Committee to the US Commission on Civil Rights and Massachusetts Commission Against Discrimination, *Route 128: Boston's Road to Segregation* (Washington, DC: US Commission on Civil Rights, 1975), 3.

18   For more on Cabot, Cabot & Forbes, see "Mills Now Built on 'Package Plan,' " *New York Times*, January 3, 1956; Russell B. Adams Jr., *The Boston Money Tree: How the Proper Men of Boston Made, Invested, and Preserved Their Wealth from Colonial Days to the Space Age* (New York: Thomas Y. Crowell, 1977), 288–89; Barry Bluestone and Mary Huff Stevenson, *The Boston Renaissance: Race, Space, and Economic Change in an American Metropolis* (New York: Russell Sage, 2002), 93–94.

19   "Electronics, The Ideas Road," *Time*, July 13, 1959.

20   Margaret Pugh O'Mara, *Cities of Knowledge: Cold War Science and the Search for the Next Silicon Valley* (Princeton, NJ: Princeton University Press, 2004), 10–11, 74–75.

21   Greater Boston Chamber of Commerce, "The Boston Area: America's Top Spot for Industrial Research" (Boston: Greater Boston Chamber of Commerce, 1960); Massachusetts Advisory Committee to the US Commission on Civil Rights, *Route 128*, 37–38; Greater Boston Chamber of Commerce, "The New Boston, Its People, Its Places, Its Potentials" (Boston: Greater Boston Chamber of Commerce, 1961).

22   Lester Smith, "Operation 128: Boston's History-Laden Industry Blooms Anew in Suburban Towns," *Wall Street Journal*, October 21, 1954.

23   Lieberman, "Technology: Alchemist of Route 128."

24   John Fenton, "Yankee Ingenuity Helps Stem New England Industrial Blight," *New York Times*, May 24, 1959.

25   Rosegrant and Lampe, *Route 128*, 93.

26   Saxenian, *Regional Advantage*, 17.

27   Fenton, "M.I.T. Offers Spur the Area Economy."

28   Fenton, "Yankee Ingenuity"; "New England's Big Comeback: Latest Success Story," *U.S. News and World Report*, February 14, 1966; Smith, "Operation 128."

29   Leslie, *The Cold War and American Science*, 29.

30   Everett J. Burtt Jr., "Labor Supply Characteristics of Route 128 Firms," research report no. 1–1958 (Boston: Federal Reserve Bank of Boston, 1958).

31   Massachusetts Advisory Committee to the US Commission on Civil Rights, *Route 128*, 3.

32   Warner, *Streetcar Suburbs*, 116–17.

33   Kenneth T. Jackson, *Crabgrass Frontier: The Suburbanization of the United States* (New York: Oxford University Press, 1985), 146–47. For more about the complex debate surrounding metropolitan integration and development in Boston during the nineteenth century, see Noam Maggor, " 'Zone of Emergence': Boston's Lower Middle Class and the Politics of Property, 1865–1917" (PhD diss., Harvard University, 2010).

34   Matthew Edel, Elliott D. Sclar, and Daniel Luria, *Shaky Palaces: Homeownership and Social Mobility in Boston's Suburbanization* (New York: Columbia University Press, 1984), 64–67, 232; Michael N. Danielson, *The Politics of Exclusion* (New York: Columbia University Press, 1976), 17; Jackson, *Crabgrass Frontier*, 138–44.

35   Michael Rawson, *Eden on the Charles: The Making of Boston* (Cambridge, MA: Harvard University Press, 2010), 131; Charles Knowles Bolton, *Brookline: The History of a Favored Town* (Brookline, MA: CAW Spencer, 1897); Jackson, *Crabgrass Frontier*, 147; Warner, *Streetcar Suburbs*, 163–64; Ronald Dale Kerr, "Brookline and the Making of an Elite Suburb," *Chicago History* (Summer 1984): 36–47.

36   Edel, Sclar, and Luria, *Shaky Palaces*, 59–60.

37   Bluestone and Stevenson, *Boston Renaissance*, 79; Jackson, *Crabgrass Frontier*, 208; Danielson, *The Politics of Exclusion*, 13.

38   Jackson, *Crabgrass Frontier*, 101.

39   Alexander von Hoffman, "To Preserve and Protect: Land Use Regulations in Weston, Massachusetts" (Cambridge, MA: Joint Center for Housing Studies, Harvard University, November 2010).

40   Philip Simon v. Town of Needham, 311 Mass. 560 (1942), 563; David M. P. Freund, *Colored Property: State Policy and White Racial Politics in Suburban America* (Chicago: University of Chicago Press, 2007), 231.

41   James C. O'Connell, *The Hub's Metropolis: Greater Boston's Development from Railroad Suburbs to Smart Growth* (Cambridge, MA: MIT Press, 2013), 137, 152.

42   John H. Fenton, "Boston Suburbs Beset by Zoning," *New York Times*, January 17, 1954.

43   Robert Gladstone, "Downtown Boston: Market Studies for Urban Renewal" (paper prepared for the Boston Redevelopment Authority, Washington, DC, May 1963); Massachusetts Advisory Committee to the US Commission on Civil Rights, *Route 128*, 4.

44   Gladstone, "Downtown Boston"; Edel, Sclar, and Luria, *Shaky Palaces*, 69.

45   Thomas O'Connor, *Building a New Boston: Politics and Urban Renewal, 1950–1970* (Boston: Northeastern University Press, 1993), 67.

46   Herbert Gans, *Urban Villagers: Group and Class in the Life of Italian Americans* (New York: Free Press, 1962); J. Anthony Lukas, *Common Ground: A Turbulent Decade in the Lives of Three American Families* (New York: Knopf, 1986), 139–59.

47   Massachusetts Advisory Committee to the US Commission on Civil Rights, *Route 128*, 20–21.

48   Massachusetts State Advisory Committee to the US Commission on Civil Rights, "The Voice of the Ghetto" (Washington, DC: US Commission on Civil Rights, 1967); Lawrence Vale, *From the Puritans to the Projects: Public Housing and Public Neighbors* (Cambridge, MA: Harvard University Press, 2000); Lawrence Vale, *Reclaiming Public Housing: A Half Century of Struggle in Three Public Neighborhoods* (Cambridge, MA: Harvard University Press 2002); John Stainton, "Urban Renewal and Planning in Boston: A Review of the Past and a Look at the Future" (Boston: Citizens Housing and Planning Association, November 1972).

49   Massachusetts State Advisory Committee to the US Commission on Civil Rights, "The Voice of the Ghetto."

50   Bluestone and Stevenson, *The Boston Renaissance*, 33; Massachusetts Advisory Committee to the US Commission on Civil Rights, *Route 128*, iv.

51   Christopher Rand, *Cambridge, U.S.A.: Hub of a New World* (New York: Oxford University Press, 1964), 18.

52   League of Women Voters of Lincoln, "A Study of the Impact of Light Industry on the Character and Economy of Nine Boston Area Towns," April 1963, box 2, folder 24, LWVL.

53   League of Women Voters of Lincoln, "Lincoln: Guide to Government, 1963," box 3, folder 31, LWVL.

54   Massachusetts Department of Commerce and the Urban and Regional Studies Section of MIT, "The Effects of Large Lot Zoning on Residential Development," *Urban Land Institute Technical Bulletin*, no. 32 (July 1958).

55   "Report of the Historical District Study Committee to the Lincoln Historical Society," ca. 1964, box 4, folder 50, LER; Keith N. Morgan, ed., *Buildings of Massachusetts: Metropolitan Boston* (Charlottesville: University of Virginia Press, 2009), 449, 452–53.

56   Brooks and Brooks, "Town with Room for Living."

57   City of Newton, "Profile of Population," 1970, NPL.

58   Brookline Town Planning Board, "The Preliminary Comprehensive Town Plan for Brookline: A Progress Report," December 1958, FLL.

59   Rand, *Cambridge, U.S.A.*, 15.

60   League of Women Voters of Lincoln, "A Study of the Impact of Light Industry"; Peter T. Siskind, "Growth and Its Discontents: Localism, Protest, and the Politics of Development

on the Postwar Northeast Corridor" (PhD diss., University of Pennsylvania, 2002); James J. Nagle, "Shopping Center Planning Others," *New York Times*, October 14, 1951; John Fenton, "Court Ruling in Massachusetts May Spur Municipal Tax Crisis," *New York Times*, January 22, 1965.

61 League of Women Voters of Lincoln, "A Study of the Impact of Light Industry."

62 Massachusetts Taxpayers Foundation, "Who Assesses Property in Massachusetts?" ca. March 1974, ASN; Robert W. Eisenmenger et al., "Options for Fiscal Structure Reform in Massachusetts," Federal Reserve Bank of Boston Research Report 57, March 1975, unprocessed material, ASN.

63 Lizabeth Cohen, *A Consumers' Republic: The Politics of Mass Consumption in Postwar America* (New York: Alfred A. Knopf, 2003), 231.

64 Brooks, *The View from Lincoln Hill*, 4, 231.

65 Newton Chamber of Commerce, "Newton Massachusetts."

66 Massachusetts Advisory Committee to the US Commission on Civil Rights, *Route 128*, 81.

67 Brooks and Brooks, "Town with Room for Living." The Brooks did acknowledge that Lincoln's approach had contributed to the rise in real estate prices, and "discouraged all, both the established and well-to-do."

68 Massachusetts Department of Commerce and the Urban and Regional Studies Section of MIT, "The Effects of Large Lot Zoning on Residential Development."

69 Wood, *Suburbia*, viii.

70 Brooks, *The View from Lincoln Hill*, 5, 231, 240.

71 Concord Natural Resources Commission, "Natural Resources Report," July 1972, CPC.

72 Sara Lawrence Lightfoot, *The Good High School: Portraits of Character and Culture* (New York: Basic Books, 1983), 150–55.

73 Renee Garrelick, "Conantum Neighborhood Oral History," fall 1986, box 4, folder 18, KWC.

74 For instance, the Lexington Historical Commission included in its mission that "structures of the recent past—Moon Hill, Five Fields and the Peacock Farm enclaves throughout Town, among others—enhance Lexington's diverse architectural heritage" (http://ci.lexington.ma.us/committees/historical.cfm).

75 Walter Gropius, *The Scope of Total Architecture* (New York: Harper and Bros., 1955), xxi–xxii; Kevin D. Murphy, "The Vernacular Moment," *Journal of the Society of Architectural Historians* (September 2011): 308–29; "Colony of Contemporary Homes Will Be Repeated Near Boston," *New York Times*, September 13, 1959.

76 Walter Gropius et al., eds., *The Architects Collaborative, 1945–1965* (New York: Architectural Book Publishing, 1966), 37–53.

77 "Colony of Contemporary Homes Will Be Repeated near Boston," *New York Times*, September 13, 1959; David Fixler, "Hipsters in the Woods," *Architecture Boston* (Spring 2009): 26.

78 "Five Fields Advertisement," *Sunday Boston Herald*, ca. 1958, Lexington Historic Survey.

79 Linda Matchan, "An Era Ends at Five Fields," *Boston Globe*, August 20, 2013.

80 Robert Butman, "The Conantum Saga," 1995, box 4, folder 6, KWC.

81 Carl Koch with Andy Lewis, *At Home with Tomorrow* (New York: Rinehart and Company, 1958).

82 "Conantum in Concord," advertisement, ca. 1950s, box 5, folder 4, KWC.

83 Koch with Lewis, *At Home with Tomorrow*; Carl Koch, interview by Renee Garrelick, August 10, 1992, COHP.

84 "Conantum in Concord," advertisement; Butman, "The Conantum Saga." The community half jokingly awarded a gold star to men living there with no connection to Harvard, MIT, or Lincoln Laboratory. Only fifteen out of a hundred men were eligible.

85 For more on the history of universities in Massachusetts, see Richard M. Freeland, *Academia's Golden Age: Universities in Massachusetts, 1945–1970* (New York: Oxford University Press, 1992).

86   Lieberman, "Technology: Alchemist of Route 128"; "New England's Big Comeback"; O'Mara, *Cities of Knowledge*, 88.

87   Bluestone and Stevenson, *Boston Renaissance*, 93.

88   Saxenian, *Regional Advantage*, 60.

89   Greater Boston Chamber of Commerce, "The Boston Area."

90   Massachusetts Chamber of Commerce, "Massachusetts Factbook, 1963," Papers of Edward Lampiere, Office of Intergovernmental Affairs, box 3, Massachusetts State Archives, Boston. For more on these campaigns in other parts of the country, see O'Mara, *Cities of Knowledge*, 81–92.

91   William Ward, "Conversion in a Military Society," in *Conversion from War to Peace: Social, Economic, and Political Problems*, ed. William Meyers (New York: Gordon and Breach, 1972), 55.

92   Paula Leventman, *Professionals Out of Work* (New York: Free Press, 1981), 85–86.

93   Edel, Sclar, and Luria, *Shaky Palaces*, 159.

94   Peter Schrag, *Voices in the Classroom: Public Schools and Public Attitudes* (Boston: Beacon Press, 1965), 100.

95   Jackie Davison, interview by Norma McGavern-Norland, October 6, 1992, LOHP.

96   Noam Chomsky, interview by Norma McGavern-Norland, October 7, 1992, LOHP.

97   School and University Program for Research and Development, "SUPRAD and Lexington," 1963, MGL; "Lexington: A Study of the Public Schools," July 1960, MGL.

98   "Memoranda on Initial Studies of Selected Aspects of the Concord Public Schools: A Report," July 1958, MGL.

99   Town of Lexington, Massachusetts, Annual Report 1950, LPL; Town of Lexington, Massachusetts, Annual Report 1960, LPL.

100 Schrag, *Voices in the Classroom*, 99.

101 League of Women Voters of Newton, "Newton: Garden City," pamphlet, 1973, NPL.

102 Schrag, *Voices in the Classroom*, 113–14.

103 Schrag, *Voices in the Classroom*, 100–101.

104 William A. Davis, "Conantum's Search for Utopia," *Boston Globe*, April 6, 1995.

105 School and University Program for Research and Development, "Concord and SUPRAD," July 1963, MGL.

106 "Education: Experts on Call," *Time*, September 21, 1959.

107 School and University Program for Research and Development, "SUPRAD and Lexington."

108 Richard Alpert, "Professionalism, Policy Innovation, and Conflict: School Politics in Newton, Massachusetts" (master's thesis, Harvard University, March 1971).

109 Alpert, "Professionalism, Policy Innovation, and Conflict."

110 School Department, "Report of the School Committee, for the Year 1960," Lexington 1960 Annual Report, LPL; Alpert, "Professionalism, Policy Innovation, and Conflict."

111 Jerome Grossman, *Relentless Liberal* (New York: Vantage Press, 1996), 16–38; Marjorie Arons, "Jerry Grossman Reflects on Local Political Scene and Beyond through Two Decades," *Newton Times*, November 24, 1976.

112 Evening Alliance of the First Parish Church, "Directory of Organizations in Lexington and Bus Schedules," 1950, FLL.

113 Davison interview. For a similar point about another group of suburbanites, see Lisa McGirr, *Suburban Warriors: The Origins of the New American Right* (Princeton, NJ: Princeton University Press, 2001), 48. Likewise, as Jonathan Bell suggests, many suburbanites in California joined the Democratic Club movement for a related set of reasons. See Jonathan Bell, *California Crucible: The Forging of Modern American Liberalism* (Philadelphia: University of Pennsylvania Press, 2013), 96.

114 David Riesman, "The Suburban Dislocation," *Annals of the American Academy of Political and Social Science* (November 1957): 132.

115   "Churches: The Apostolic Few," *Time*, May 24, 1963. Hancock Church had eleven different clubs, including three youth groups and two different dinner and entertainment clubs for married couples (Evening Alliance of the First Parish Church, "Directory of Organizations in Lexington").

116   "Churches: The Apostolic Few."

117   For more on the new forms of religion that took shape in California after World War II, see McGirr, *Suburban Warriors*, especially 45–51; Darren Dochuk, *From Bible Belt to Sunbelt: Plain Folk Religion, Grassroots Politics, and the Rise of Evangelical Conservatism* (New York: W. W. Norton, 2010), 141–256.

118   Dana Greeley, "Liberal Religion: What It Is, What It Is Not" (Boston: Unitarian Universalist Association, 1965); "Inspiring Church Offered as Ideal," *New York Times*, June 27, 1960.

119   Andrea Greenwood and Mark W. Harris, *An Introduction to the Unitarian and Universalist Traditions* (New York: Cambridge University Press, 2011), 186–98.

120   "Unitarian Praises Benefits of Science," *New York Times*, July 27, 1959; "Inspiring Church Offered as Ideal"; Dana McLean Greeley, "Religion and Science," in *Forward through the Ages: Writings of Reverend Dana McLean Greeley, 1970–1986* (Concord, MA: First Parish in Concord, 1986), 44–46.

121   First Parish Church in Lexington Unitarian Universalist, "History of the First Parish Church," http://fpc.lexington.ma.us/index.php/history.

122   John Beuhrens, interview by Nancy Earsy, May 25, 1994, LOHP; Albert I. Gordon, *Jews in Suburbia* (Boston: Beacon Press, 1959), 24; Newton Chamber of Commerce, "Newton Massachusetts."

123   Gordon, *Jews in Suburbia*, 27; Joshua A. Fishman, "Moving to the Suburbs: Its Possible Impact on the Role of the Jewish Minority in American Community Life," *Phylon* (Summer 1963): 150; Harry Gersh, "The New Suburbanites of the 50's," *Commentary* (March 1954): 209–21. See also Gerald Gamm, *Urban Exodus: Why the Jews Left Boston and the Catholics Stayed* (Cambridge, MA: Harvard University Press, 1999).

124   Gordon, *Jews in Suburbia*, 26–27.

125   Gamm, *Urban Exodus*, 194–95; Gordon, *Jews in Suburbia*; Sherry Israel, "Moving Apart and Growing Together, 1967–1994," in *The Jews of Boston: Essays on the Occasion of the Centenary (1895–1995)*, ed. Jonathan D. Sarna and Ellen Smith (Boston: Northeastern University Press, 1995), 107–20.

126   John T. McGreevy, *Parish Boundaries: The Catholic Encounter with Race in the Twentieth-Century Urban North* (Chicago: University of Chicago Press, 1998), 84.

127   Marion Coletta, interview by Nancy Earsy, November 1, 1993, LOHP. See also Michael J. O'Sullivan, "Sacred Heart 75th Anniversary, Celebrating the Past, Present, and Future: A Historical Thesis," December 16, 2007, http://sacredheartlex.org/documents/SacredHeart LexHistory.pdf.

128   Norma McGavern-Norland, interview by Eugenia Kaledin, August 22, 1991, LOHP.

129   McGavern-Norland interview.

130   League of Women Voters of Newton, "A Historical Review of the League of Women Voters of Newton," May 1953, NPL.

131   "League of Women Voters: Eightieth Anniversary of Women's Suffrage," Barbara Anthony, Debbie Barr, Nancy Beecher, Louise Haldeman, and Annabelle Sheperd, interviews by Renee Garrelick, May 12, 2000, COHP.

132   Davison interview.

133   For more on the history and goals of the League of Women Voters, see Marisa Chappell, "Rethinking Women's Politics in the 1970s: The League of Women Voters and the National Organization for Women Confront Poverty," *Journal of Women's History* (Winter 2002): 55–79; Jane Eveyln Davis, *The Socialization of Women into Politics: A Case Study of the League of Women Voters* (Ann Arbor: University of Michigan Press, 1984); Louise Mer-

win Young, *In the Public Interest: The League of Women Voters, 1920–1970* (New York: Greenwood Press, 1989); Susan Ware, "American Women in the 1950s: Nonpartisan Politics and Women's Politicization," in *Women, Politics, and Change*, ed. Louise A. Tilly and Patricia Gurin (New York: Russell Sage, 1990), 281–99.

134 Davison interview.

135 Davison interview.

136 Adlai Stevenson Campaign, "Massachusetts Report," 1956, box 313, folder 2, AES.

137 "Brookline Volunteers for Stevenson to Herman Dunlap Smith, National Volunteers for Stevenson," October 20, 1952, box 237, folder 6, AES.

138 Coletta interview.

2 Good Neighbors

An earlier version of chapter 2 was published in Lily Geismer, "Good Neighbors for Fair Housing: Suburban Liberalism and Racial Inequality in Metropolitan Boston," *Journal of Urban History* (May 2013): 454–77.

1 Jeremiah V. Murphey, "In Lexington, Pickets Claim Bias on Rental," *Boston Globe*, September 1, 1963.

2 J. Anthony Lukas, *Common Ground: A Turbulent Decade in the Lives of Three American Families* (New York: Knopf, 1986), 95–99.

3 As civil rights scholars have successfully expanded the temporal and geographic parameters of the movement, the efforts to combat housing discrimination serve as an example of the types of interracial activism that existed in the North in the late 1940s and 1950s. See Martha Biondi, *To Stand and to Fight: The Struggle for Civil Rights in Postwar New York City* (Cambridge, MA: Harvard University Press, 2006); Thomas J. Sugrue, *Sweet Land of Liberty: The Forgotten Struggle for Civil Rights in the North* (New York: Random House, 2008). See also Tracy E. K'Meyer, "'Well, I'm Not Moving': Open Housing and White Activism in the Long Civil Rights Movement," *The Sixties: A Journal of History* (June 2009): 1–24.

4 On Proposition 14 in California, see, for example, Becky M. Nicolaides, *My Blue Heaven: Life and Politics in the Working-Class Suburbs of Los Angeles, 1920–1965* (Chicago: University of Chicago Press, 2002), 308–22; Robert O. Self, *American Babylon: Race and the Struggle for Postwar Oakland* (Princeton, NJ: Princeton University Press, 2003), 167–68. For a nuanced examination of the role of racial liberalism in shaping support for Proposition 14, see Daniel Martinez HoSang, *Racial Propositions: Ballot Initiatives and the Making of Postwar California* (Berkeley: University of California Press, 2010). On King in Chicago, see Brian J. L. Berry, *The Open Housing Question: Race and Housing in Chicago, 1966–1976* (Cambridge, MA: Ballinger Publishing, 1979); James R. Ralph Jr., *Northern Protest: Martin Luther King, Jr., Chicago, and the Civil Rights Movement* (Cambridge, MA: Harvard University Press, 1993).

5 William J. Collins, "The Political Economy of State Fair Housing Laws before 1968," *Social Science History* (Spring 2006): 15–49; Laurence D. Pearl and Benjamin B. Terner, "Survey: Fair Housing Laws, Design for Equal Opportunity," *Stanford Law Review* (July 1964): 849–99. While other scholars acknowledge the Massachusetts' fair housing laws as evidence of the state's progressive position on civil rights in the postwar period, none have examined the role of suburban groups securing the passage of this legislation. See, for example, Stephen Grant Meyer, *As Long As They Don't Move Next Door: Segregation and Racial Conflict in America's Neighborhoods* (New York: Rowan and Littlefield, 2000), 161; Andrew Wiese, *Places of Their Own: African-American Suburbanization in the Twentieth Century* (Chicago: University of Chicago Press, 2004), 222.

6 In Massachusetts in the 1950s and 1960s, participants in the movement primarily saw the issues of fair housing and civil rights in terms of a black-white binary largely due to the state's racial demographics, which included small Latino and Asian populations. Yet in California and along other parts of the West Coast, fair housing activists took a more multiracial approach—documented by a variety of scholars. See, for example, Shana Bernstein, *Bridges of Reform: Interracial Civil Rights Activism in Twentieth-Century Los Angeles* (New York: Oxford University Press, 2011); Mark Brilliant, *The Color of America Has Changed: How Racial Diversity Shaped Civil Rights Reform in California, 1941–1978* (New York: Oxford University Press, 2010); Charlotte Brooks, *Alien Neighbors, Foreign Friends: Asian Americans, Housing, and the Transformation of Urban California* (Chicago: University of Chicago Press, 2009).

7 Richard O'Donnell, "How Negroes Fare in the Bay State: Growing Population Needs Homes," *Boston Globe*, May 23, 1961.

8 Juliet Saltman, *Open Housing as a Social Movement: Challenge Conflict and Change* (Lexington, MA: D. C. Heath and Company, 1971), 29–39; Sugrue, *Sweet Land of Liberty*, 213–20; Meyer, *As Long As They Don't Move Next Door*, 133–49.

9 For a discussion of *An American Dilemma* and its influence on liberalism, see Walter Jackson, *Gunnar Myrdal and America's Conscience: Social Engineering and Racial Liberalism, 1938–1987* (Chapel Hill: University of North Carolina Press, 1987); Daryl Michael Scott, *Contempt and Pity: Social Policy and the Image of the Damaged Black Psyche, 1880–1996* (Chapel Hill: University of North Carolina Press, 1997), 93–160.

10 Saltman, *Open Housing*, 37–39. See also National Committee Against Discrimination in Housing, *Trends in Housing* 2, no. 2 (March–April 1958); National Committee Against Discrimination in Housing, *Trends in Housing* 2, no. 4 (August–September 1958); Frances Levenson, "An Overview of Grassroots Activities in Housing," ca. 1963, excerpted in *Fair Housing Key* 1, no. 1 (July 1963), LCRC-LPL.

11 American Friends Service Committee, New England Regional Office, "Proposal for Long-Range Work on Education Issues in Boston, June, 1975," box 34, folder 1188, FH.

12 Massachusetts Advisory Committee to the US Commission on Civil Rights, *Report on Massachusetts: Housing in Boston* (Washington, DC: US Commission on Civil Rights, December 1963), 31; Levenson, "An Overview of Grassroots Activities in Housing"; "200 Join Move for Fair Housing in State," *Boston Sunday Herald*, June 4, 1961.

13 The Natick Committee on Homes for Minority Groups, flyer, 1957, box 58, folder 2519, FH; Richard O'Donnell, "Committees on Housing Work for Racial Harmony," *Boston Globe*, May 24, 1961.

14 See, for example, Robert A. Storer, Malcolm R. Sutherland Jr., and Dana McLean Greeley, "Personal Faith: The Minns Lectures for 1955" (Boston: Minns Lectureship Committee, 1955). See also Stephanie Muravchik, *American Protestantism in the Age of Psychology* (New York: Cambridge University Press, 2011), 28–81; Phillip Rieff, *The Triumph of the Therapeutic: Uses of Faith after Freud* (New York: Harper and Row, 1966); Jon Butler, "Jack-in-the-Box Faith: The Religion Problem in Modern American History," *Journal of American History* (March 2004): 1376.

15 Newton Chamber of Commerce, "Newton Massachusetts," 1969, NNCC.

16 George Forsythe, "Housing Laws: Do They Work?" Negro in Boston series reprinted from *Boston Traveler*, 1962, box 55, folder 2231, FH.

17 Forsythe, "Housing Laws: Do They Work?"; Helen Kistin, "Housing Discrimination in Massachusetts," prepared by the Housing Advisory Research Committee of the Massachusetts Committee Against Discrimination in Housing as a statement to the public meeting of the Housing Subcommittee, Massachusetts Advisory Committee of the US Commission on Civil Rights, March 5, 1963, box 4, folder 13, PMR; Massachusetts State Advisory Committee to the US Commission on Civil Rights, "The Voice of the Ghetto"

(Washington, DC: US Commission on Civil Rights, 1967); National Committee Against Discrimination in Housing, *Trends in Housing* 3, no. 3 (May–June 1959).

18 Many scholars have addressed this shift in federal and state governments' civil rights agenda in the aftermath of World War II. See, for example, Biondi, *To Stand and to Fight*; Thomas Borstelmann, *The Cold War and the Color Line: American Race Relations in the Global Arena* (Cambridge, MA: Harvard University Press, 2001); Mary L. Dudziak, *Cold War Civil Rights: Race and the Image of American Democracy* (Princeton, NJ: Princeton University Press, 2000).

19 Anthony S. Chen, "'The Hitlerian Rule of Quotas': Racial Conservatism and the Politics of Fair Employment Legislation in New York State, 1941–1945," *Journal of American History* (March 2006): 1238–64.

20 For an excellent discussion of the efforts of black housing activism in the 1940s and 1950s, see Max A. Felker-Kantor, "'Freedom Means a House to Live In': The Black Struggle for Equal Housing Opportunities in Greater Boston, 1948–1968" (honors thesis, Tufts University, 2006).

21 Massachusetts Commission Against Discrimination, "Thirteenth Annual Report of Massachusetts Commission Against Discrimination, December 1, 1957 to November 30, 1958," SLM. New York, New Jersey, Oregon, and the state of Washington also had laws banning discrimination in the sale, lease, or rental of publicly assisted private housing accommodations.

22 Morton Rubin, "The Function of Social Research for a Fair Housing Practice Committee," *Journal of Intergroup Relations* (Fall 1961): 326.

23 Eph Weiss, "Informal Report to the Members of the L.C.R.C.," February 3, 1961, LCRC-LPL; Fair Housing Federation of Greater Boston, "Excerpts from Statements of Viewpoint Prepared for the Osgood Hill Conference, October 20–21, 1961," box 3, folder 9, PMR.

24 John Updike, *Couples* (New York: Fawcett Books, 1996), 229.

25 Rhoda Lois Blumberg, "White Mothers as Civil Rights Activists: The Interweave of Family and Movement Roles," in *Women and Social Protest*, ed. Guida West and Rhoda Lois Blumberg (New York: Oxford University Press, 1990).

26 "200 Join Move for Fair Housing in the State."

27 "200 Join Move for Fair Housing in the State."

28 For more on panic selling and racial steering, and the movements that emerged to stop them, see Matthew J. Countryman, *Up South: Civil Rights and Black Power in Philadelphia* (Philadelphia: University of Pennsylvania Press, 2006), 71–75; Beryl Satter, *Family Properties: Race, Real Estate, and the Exploitation of Black Urban America* (New York: Metropolitan Books, 2009).

29 "Group Works to Dispel Prejudice Fantasy and Fear," *Brookline Chronicle-Citizen*, March 17, 1960; "Property Values Don't Fall When Negroes Move In," *Brookline Chronicle-Citizen*, April 7, 1960; "200 Join Move for Fair Housing in the State."

30 Rubin, "The Function of Social Research for a Fair Housing Practice Committee," 330–31.

31 Fair Housing Federation, *Fair Housing News*, January 1962, LCRC-LPL.

32 "200 Join Move for Fair Housing in the State."

33 Lexington Civil Rights Committee, "Summary and Final Report of the First Fair Housing Workshop," March 17, 1962, LCRC-LPL.

34 Forsythe, "Housing Laws: Do They Work?"

35 Forsythe, "Housing Laws: Do They Work?"; "200 Join Move for Fair Housing in the State."

36 O'Donnell, "How Negroes Fare in the Bay State."

37 Fair Housing, Inc., "Annual Housing Report, April 1962–March 1963," LCRC. For more on the motivations of these "pioneers" for moving to the suburbs, see L. K. Northwood and Ernest A. T. Barth, *Urban Desegregation: Negro Pioneers and Their White Neighbors* (Seattle:

University of Washington Press, 1965); Harold M. Rose, *Black Suburbanization: Access to Improved Quality of Life or Maintenance of the Status Quo?* (Cambridge, MA: Ballinger Publishing, 1976); Wiese, *Places of Their Own.*

38 Robert W. Morgan Jr., "Some Thoughts about the usefulness of a Federation office in Boston, based on my first two weeks of work at the Temporary Federation, June 19, 1961," box 2, folder 2, PMR.

39 For more on the racial segregation embedded in the mortgage market and the ways in which African Americans negotiated with it, see David M. P. Freund, *Colored Property: State Policy and White Racial Politics in Suburban America* (Chicago: University of Chicago Press, 2007), 99–139, 190–93; Wiese, *Places of Our Own.*

40 Sadelle Sacks, "An Open Door to Integrated Housing in Metropolitan Boston," 1966, box 55, folder 2230, FH.

41 Fair Housing, Inc., "Annual Housing Report, April 1962–March 1963."

42 Fair Housing Federation of Greater Boston, "Report on Housing Activity, April 1961 to October 1962," October 1962, LCRC-LPL.

43 Fair Housing, Inc., "Semi-Annual Report on Housing," October 1963, box 3, folder 6, PMR.

44 Belmont Fair Practices Committee, "An Invitation to Act for Democracy!" 1961, LCRC-LPL; Lexington Civil Rights Committee, flyer, n.d., LCRC-LPL.

45 For more on how many fair housing advocates adopted and reified many of the discourses they sought to challenge, see HoSang, *Racial Propositions,* 80–90.

46 Bryant Rollins, "Fair Housing Federation Builds Mounting Enthusiasm in the Area," *Boston Globe,* February 11, 1962.

47 Rollins, "Fair Housing Federation Builds Mounting Enthusiasm in the Area"; Belmont Fair Practices Committee, "A Invitation to Act for Democracy!"

48 "Citizens Groups Look for Fair Housing Practices," *Newton Villager,* June 26, 1958; Rollins, "Fair Housing Federation Builds Mounting Enthusiasm in the Area."

49 Belmont Fair Practices Committee, "A Invitation to Act for Democracy!"

50 Jeanne Theoharis, "Hidden in Plain Sight: The Civil Rights Movement Outside the South," in *The Myth of Southern Exceptionalism,* ed. Matthew D. Lassiter and Joseph Crespino (New York: Oxford University Press, 2009), 54.

51 Brookline Fair Housing Practices Committee, press release, n.d., box 1, folder 52, PMR.

52 "Good Neighbor for Fair Housing," flyer, box 4, folder 3, PMR.

53 Lexington Civil Rights Committee, flyer, n.d., LCRC-LPL.

54 See Elaine Tyler May, *Homeward Bound: American Families in the Cold War,* rev. ed. (New York: Basic Books, 1999).

55 This point is indebted to the discussion of "respectable domesticity" in Nayan Shah, *Contagious Divides: Epidemics and Race in San Francisco's Chinatown* (Berkeley: University of California Press, 2001).

56 The civil rights committee placed advertisements in the *Lexington Minute-Man* with the names of all the residents who signed the pledge. See "The Good Neighbor Pledge," *Lexington Minute-Man,* May 10, 1962.

57 Irene Blum and Dee Zobel, "Pledge Sidelights," n.d., LCRC-LPL. Blum and Zobel accessed this information using the town directory.

58 Blum and Zobel counted 520 housewives, 120 engineers, 80 teachers, 35 physicians, 30 physicists, 25 chemists, 25 business executives, and 12 labor workers (Blum and Dee Zobel, "Pledge Sidelights").

59 "Civil Rights Pledge Here Signed by 1,500 Persons," *Lexington Minute-Man,* May 10, 1962. One resident believed that the pledge actually surpassed the American Revolution battle on the Lexington Green, dubbing the campaign as "the best thing that ever happened to the town" (Blum and Zobel, "Pledge Sidelights").

60 Fair Housing Federation of Greater Boston, *Fair Housing News*, January 1962, box 2, folder 1, PMR.

61 "Fair Housing in Greater Boston," *Boston Globe*, February 19, 1962; "Mortar for Bricks," *Boston Herald*, March 9, 1962.

62 Letter from Phyllis Ryan to Mr. Manion, n.d., box 1, folder 52, PMR.

63 Mrs. Paul F. Duggan to the L.C.R.C., June 15, 1962, LCRC-LPL.

64 Sugrue, *Sweet Land of Liberty*, 247.

65 Fair Housing Federation of Greater Boston, "Excerpts from Statements of Viewpoint, Prepared for Osgood Hill Conference," October 20–21, 1961, box 3, folder 8, PMR.

66 "200 Join Move for Fair Housing in the State."

67 Fair Housing Federation of Greater Boston, "Excerpts from Statements of Viewpoint."

68 National Committee Against Discrimination in Housing, *Trends in Housing* 3, no. 2 (March–April 1959). In 1962, these groups forged a formal coalition called Committee of the Massachusetts Committee Against Discrimination in Housing. See Letter from the Organizing Committee of the Massachusetts Committee Against Discrimination in Housing, June 1, 1962, box 1, folder "Committee on Discrimination in Housing," Records of Massachusetts Chapter of Americans for Democratic Action, Massachusetts Historical Society, Boston, MA.

69 "Minutes of Meeting," May 13, 1960, box 3, folder 28, MHM; Fair Housing Federation, "Knock on Any Door," n.d., LCRC-LPL.

70 Greater Boston Federation of Fair Housing Practices Committees, press release, March 19, 1961, box 1, folder 53, PMR; Brookline Fair Housing Practices Committee, press release, March 13, 1961, box 1, folder 53, PMR; Greater Boston Federation of Fair Housing Practices Committees, press release, June 15, 1961, box 1, folder 53, PMR.

71 Letter from Bill and Phyllis Ryan to Mr. Davis, February 7, 1962, box 2, folder 4, PMR.

72 National Committee Against Discrimination in Housing, *Trends in Housing* 3, no. 2 (March–April 1959).

73 Arthur Schlesinger Jr. to James R. Robinson, October 7, 1958, reel 21, folder 55, COREP.

74 During their early planning, the founding members considered that Boston CORE might be effective "assisting suburban committees which are working against discrimination in housing" and sought to create contact with the grassroots fair housing committees ("Report on Housing-Greater Boston CORE," June 1959, reel 21, folder 55, COREP).

75 "CORE Techniques in Housing, Greater Boston CORE," n.d., reel 21, folder 55, COREP.

76 Jean Mann to Marvin Rich, July 17, 1960, reel 21, folder 55, COREP.

77 Greater Boston CORE to National Council Meeting, Lexington, Kentucky, February 1961, reel 21, folder 55, COREP.

78 Massachusetts Commission Against Discrimination, "Sixteenth Annual Report of Massachusetts Commission Against Discrimination, December 1, 1959 to November 30, 1960," SLM.

79 James R. Robinson to Richard D. Mann, August 5, 1960, reel 21, folder 50, COREP.

80 "Housing Workshop Minutes," April 23, 1961, reel 46, folder 499, COREP.

81 Massachusetts Commission Against Discrimination v. Colangelo, 344 Mass. 387 (1962).

82 Greater Boston CORE to National Council Meeting, Lexington, Kentucky.

83 Massachusetts Commission Against Discrimination v. Colangelo, 344 Mass. 387 (1962).

84 Fair Housing Federation, *Fair Housing News*, January 1962, box 2, folder 1, PMR.

85 The Jewish Community Council later made both briefs available to the various fair housing committees. See Robert E. Segal to Chairman, Fair Housing Practices Committees, January 24, 1962, LCRC.

86 Commission Against Discrimination v. A. J. Colangelo et al., the Brief Amici Curiae, box 4, folder 60, PMR.

87   Commission Against Discrimination v. A. J. Colangelo et al., Petitioners Brief, box 4, folder 60, PMR.

88   Massachusetts Commission Against Discrimination v. Colangelo, 182 N.E. 2d 595.

89   "Precedent-Setting Decision," *CORE-lator* 62 (June 1962); Margaret Fisher, *Fair Housing Handbook* (Philadelphia: American Friends Service Committee and National Committee Against Discrimination in Housing, 1964).

90   Pearl and Terner, "Survey: Fair Housing Laws," 851; John Fenton, "Boston Awaiting New Housing Law," *New York Times*, June 29, 1963.

91   For more on Proposition 14, the ballot initiative that repealed California's fair housing law, see, for example, HoSang, *Racial Propositions*, 53–90; Nicolaides, *My Blue Heaven*, 308–22; Self, *American Babylon*, 167–68.

92   Massachusetts Advisory Committee to the US Commission on Civil Rights, *Report on Massachusetts*.

93   HoSang points out that the Rumsford Act, passed in California, had virtually identical provisions. See HoSang, *Racial Propositions*, 63.

94   Mark Moore Jr., advertisement, *Lexington Minute-Man*, December 3, 1959.

95   "LCRC Affidavit," *Lexington Minute-Man*, September 12, 1963.

96   Robert Sherman, "Moore Denies Racial Bias; Pickets Again Charge Bias in Lexington," *Boston Globe*, September 4, 1963; Greater Boston Fair Housing Federation, *Fair Housing Key*, September 1963, LCRC-LPL.

97   "C.O.R.E. Picketing Rules," n.d., reel 47, folder 516, COREP.

98   Annelise Orleck, introduction to *The Politics of Motherhood: Activist Voices from Left to Right*, ed. Alexis Jetter, Annelise Orleck, and Diana Taylor (Hanover, NH: University Press of New England, 1997), 6.

99   Liz Collins to the editor, *Lexington Minute-Man*, September 12, 1963.

100   Murphey, "In Lexington."

101   Murphey, "In Lexington."

102   For the open housing movement's effort to find "ideal pioneers," especially in the famous attempt to integrate Levittown, see Sugrue, *Sweet Land of Liberty*, 223–28.

103   Murphey, "In Lexington."

104   Murphey, "In Lexington."

105   Murphey, "In Lexington."

106   Lukas, *Common Ground*, 98–99.

107   "Probable Bias Found in Lexington Case," *Boston Globe*, September 9, 1963.

108   Arline Morrison and Michael Morrison to the editor, *Lexington Minute-Man*, September 12, 1963.

109   Fair Housing, Inc., "Annual Housing Report, September 1963–August 1964," box 3, folder 12, PMR.

110   "CORE, NAACP Join Forces to Combat Housing Blight," *CORE-spondent* 1, no. 5 (December 3, 1963).

111   Congress of Racial Equality, "One Year of Promise," n.d., box 2, folder 27, PMR.

112   "CORE, NAACP Join Forces to Combat Housing Blight," *CORE-spondent*.

113   Greater Boston Fair Housing Federation, *Fair Housing Key*, November 1963, LCRC-LPL.

114   "Fair Housing Committee Changes Name to Committee for Civil Rights," *Brookline Chronicle-Citizen*, October 12, 1963.

115   "Civil Rights Committee Now 1,000," *Lexington Minute-Man*, February 11, 1965.

116   Roy Brown, "What We Are and Where We Are," May 14, 1964, LCRC-LPL.

117   In 1960, slightly less than 13 percent of Massachusetts' white population lived in the city of Boston, and slightly more than 35 percent lived in the suburbs of Boston, whereas approximately 56 percent of the Commonwealth of Massachusetts' black population

lived in the city, yet only 12 percent lived in the suburbs (Massachusetts Advisory Committee to the US Commission on Civil Rights, *Report on Massachusetts*).

118   US Bureau of the Census, *Census of the United States, 1970* (Washington, DC: US Bureau of the Census, 1970).

119   Richard A. Powers, "Negro Move into Suburbia Still Only a Trickle," *Boston Globe*, June 5, 1964.

3   A Multiracial World

1   Lisa Hammel, "Buses That Bring Together Two Separate and Unequal Worlds," *New York Times*, April 4, 1969.

2   Hammel, "Buses That Bring Together Two Separate and Unequal Worlds."

3   See Nancy MacLean, *Freedom Is Not Enough: The Opening of the American Workplace* (Cambridge, MA: Harvard University Press, 2008); Thomas J. Sugrue, "Affirmative Action from Below: Civil Rights, the Building Trades, and the Politics of Racial Equality in the Urban North, 1945–1969," *Journal of American History* (June 2004): 145–73.

4   Massachusetts Advisory Committee to the US Commission on Civil Rights, *Report on Massachusetts: Housing in Boston* (Washington, DC: US Commission on Civil Rights, December, 1963), 7; Ruth Batson, "Statement to the School Committee," June 11, 1963, box 3, folder 15, PMR; "Teacher Overlooks One Fact," *Boston Globe*, February 27, 1964.

5   Jeanne Theoharis, "I'd Rather Go to School in the South: How Boston's School Desegregation Complicates the Civil Rights Paradigm," in *Freedom North: Black Freedom Struggles Outside the South, 1940–1980*, ed. Jeanne Theoharis and Komozi Woodard (New York: Palgrave Macmillan, 2003), 129.

6   Boston Branch, NAACP, "Statement to the Press of the Boston Branch, NAACP," June 18, 1963, box 3, folder 18, PMR.

7   J. Anthony Lukas, *Common Ground: A Turbulent Decade in the Lives of Three American Families* (New York: Knopf, 1986), 127.

8   Robert L. Hassett, "Hub Negroes Say 14,000 Will Stay Out of School," *Boston Herald*, June 13, 1963; Boston Branch, NAACP, "Statement to the Press of the Boston Branch, NAACP."

9   Harvard Center for Law and Education, "A Study of the Massachusetts Racial Imbalance Act," publication no. 6019 (Cambridge, MA: Harvard Center for Law and Education for the Massachusetts State Department of Education, February 1972). The daily average absentee rate among secondary school students was about 10 percent. The absentee list included 5,200 whites. While Louise Day Hicks claimed that many white parents kept their children at home to avoid violence, more likely, given the day's "magnificent weather," many used the boycott as an excuse to "play hooky." Ian Forman, "And Whites Play Hooky," *Boston Globe*, June 18, 1963; Boston Branch, NAACP, "Statement to the Press of the Boston Branch, NAACP"; "What about the Freedom Stay Out?" n.d., box 3, folder 15, PMR; "Statement of James Breeden," June 17, 1963, box 1, folder 33, PMR.

10   "Background Material: Freedom Schools Goals and Purposes of Freedom Schools as Developed for June 18, 1963," ca. June 1963, box 2, folder 19, PMR.

11   "Public Schools: The Spreading Boycott," *Time*, February 14, 1964; Leonard Buder, "Boycott Cripples City Schools," *New York Times*, February 4, 1964.

12   "Statement of James Breeden," ca. 1964, box 1, folder 33, PMR.

13   "Wayland Schools in Recess, Weston in Session for New Freedom Stayout Day," *Wayland and Weston Town Crier*, February 6, 1964.

14   Lucia Mouat, "Suburbs Prepare Boycott Support," *Christian Science Monitor*, February 26, 1964.

15   "Youngsters Explain Why They 'Stayed Out' for Freedom," n.d., box 8, folder 10, PMR.

16   NAACP, "Press Release: Boston Boycott 100 Per Cent Successful," February 28, 1964, box 2, folder 19, PMR. The NAACP reported that 22 percent of the city's ninety-three thousand public schools students did not attend classes, or about twice the normal absentee rate.

17   "Freedom School Curriculum," n.d., box 2, folder 19, PMR.

18   William Ryan, *Blaming the Victim* (New York: Pantheon Books, 1971), 40.

19   Ian Forman, "Who Staged the Boycott?" *Boston Globe*, February 27, 1964; Timothy Leland, "From Suburbs They Came to Back the Fight," *Boston Globe*, February 27, 1964.

20   Uncle Dudley, "The Boycott Aftermath," *Boston Globe*, February 27, 1964.

21   NAACP, "Press Release: Boston Boycott 100 Per Cent Successful"; Forman, "Who Staged the Boycott?"; John H. Fenton, "20,571 Pupils Out in Boston Boycott," *New York Times*, February 27, 1964.

22   Harvard Center for Law and Education, "A Study of the Massachusetts Racial Imbalance Act."

23   Advisory Committee on Racial Imbalance, "Massachusetts State Board of Education Interim Report," July 1, 1964, box 1, folder 16, PMR.

24   Massachusetts State Board of Education, "Because It Is Right—Educationally: Report of the Advisory Committee on Racial Imbalance and Education" (Boston: Massachusetts State Board of Education, April 1965).

25   Harvard Center for Law and Education, "A Study of the Massachusetts Racial Imbalance Act."

26   Ronald P. Formisano, *Boston against Busing: Race and Ethnicity in the 1960s and 1970s* (Chapel Hill: University of North Carolina Press, 1991), 34.

27   Lukas, *Common Ground*, 18.

28   "Excerpts Taken from Governor's Message," *Boston Globe*, June 1, 1965.

29   Harvard Center for Law and Education, "A Study of the Massachusetts Racial Imbalance Act."

30   In addition to Paul Parks and Ruth Batson, the group included Edward Barshak, who had been one of the driving forces in the fair housing movement, and Rev. Robert Drinan, who was then the dean of the Boston College Law School (Harvard Center for Law and Education, "A Study of the Massachusetts Racial Imbalance Act").

31   For a good discussion of the maneuverings within the State House, see Harvard Center for Law and Education, "A Study of the Massachusetts Racial Imbalance Act."

32   Massachusetts Federation for Fair Housing and Equal Rights, *FHER Key*, September 1965, LCRC-LPL.

33   "Another First for Massachusetts," *Time*, August 27, 1965. By early 1966, California, Illinois, and Indiana had passed similar laws. See Fred Powledge, "North Offers Tokens," *New York Times*, January 12, 1966. The law also became a model for a failed bill in the US Congress that sought to apply a similar set of standards on a national scale.

34   The BSC would later officially classify 671 Asian students at two schools in Chinatown as "white" to alleviate charges that the schools were racially imbalanced; see "Chinese 'Whites' Boston Declares," *New York Times*, October 20, 1966.

35   "Summer of Discovery," Massachusetts Federation for Fair Housing and Equal Rights, *FHER Key*, September, 1965, LCRC-LPL.

36   "Planning to Aid Negro Children from Virginia," *Newton Villager*, August 22, 1961.

37   The Metropolitan Council for Educational Opportunity, "A Program of Greater Boston Action to Improve Education and Racial Balance in Our Schools," January 1966, box 2, folder 61, METCO-NUSC.

38   Clarence G. Williams, *Technology and the Dream: Reflections on the Black Experience at MIT, 1941–1999* (Cambridge, MA: MIT Press, 2003), 231–32.

39   Ruth Batson, interview by Mel King, n.d., carton 4, RMB.

40 "Planning to Aid Negro Children from Virginia," *Newton Villager*.

41 Williams, *Technology and the Dream*, 231–32.

42 Edward J. Logue, "Proposal for Achieving Racial Balance in the Boston Area Public Schools," speech at a Massachusetts Association of Women Lawyers meeting, Boston, n.d., box 1, folder 45, PMR.

43 Lizabeth Cohen, "Renewal in American Buying into Downtown Revival: The Centrality of Retail to Postwar Urban Renewal in American Cities," *ANNALS of the American Academy of Political and Social Science* (May 2007): 84.

44 Logue, "Proposal for Achieving Racial Balance in the Boston Area Public Schools."

45 "Kiernan, "Doubts Workability of Logue Busing Plan," *Boston Traveler*, April 29, 1965; Irene Michelek and Bill Duncliffe, "Suburban School Heads Cool to Busing Proposal," *Record American*, April 28, 1965.

46 "As We See It: Logue's Scatteration," *Boston Globe*, April 28, 1965.

47 Grace Sullivan to the editor, *Lexington Minute-Man*, May 6, 1965.

48 Massachusetts Federation for Fair Housing and Equal Rights, "Minutes of Executive Board Meeting," October 25, 1965, LCRC-LPL.

49 Ruth Batson, interview by Katherine M. Shannon, Boston, MA, December 27, 1967, Civil Rights Documentation Project, box 1, RMB.

50 METCO, "Suburban Education for Urban Children [Internal Report]," ca. 1967, box 2, folder 62, METCO-NUSC.

51 Spencer F. Martin Jr. and John Barnaby, "Metropolitan Education for Boston: A Proposal for a Demonstration (Preliminary)," February 24, 1966, box 2, folder 27, METCO-NUSC.

52 "Increasing Educational Opportunities," December 14, 1965, box 6, folder 50, METCO-NUSC; "Suburbs Push Plans for Busing," *Brookline Chronicle-Citizen*, December 16, 1965; Leon Trilling letter, January 5, 1966, box 28, folder 1, METCO-NUSC.

53 "Bylaws of the Metropolitan Council for Educational Opportunity," March 24, 1966, box 1, folder 29, METCO-NUSC; METCO, "Proposed Plan for Cooperative Program of Education between Urban and Suburban Schools, Draft," February 2, 1966, box 47, folder 16, METCO-NUSC.

54 Department of Health, Education, and Welfare, "Title III Data Form," January 13, 1967, box 8, folder 30, METCO-NUSC; Leon Trilling, "For Meeting at Boston College," March 10, 1966, box 2, folder 34, METCO-NUSC.

55 The signatories on METCO's official articles of organization included many individuals who had long been active in the suburban fair housing movement such as Astrid Haussler, Helene LeVine, Edward Barshak, and Elizabeth Keil. See Commonwealth of Massachusetts, "Articles of Organization," March 24, 1966, box 1, folder 59, METCO-NUSC.

56 The founders also sought the sanction of the BSC as a means to establish the program's legitimacy. On March 28, 1966, the BSC voted three to two in favor of the program, but its approval included the contingent clause "that this program shall not require the expenditure of funds of the City of Boston" (Boston School Committee, "In School Committee," March 28, 1966, box 8, folder 4, METCO-NUSC).

57 Massachusetts Federation for Fair Housing and Equal Rights, "Report on Executive Board Meetings of 2/6/66 and 2/15/66," February 1966, LCRC-LPL.

58 Kenneth J. Cooper, "Dukakis Is Soldier, Not Leader, in Civil Rights Fight," *Philadelphia Inquirer*, August 28, 1988.

59 Ruth Batson, *The Black Educational Movement in Boston: A Sequence of Historical Events* (Boston: Northwestern University Press, 2001), 229.

60 Trilling, "For Meeting at Boston College."

61 Marianne Brinker to the editor, *Wellesley Townsman*, March 3, 1966; Hammel, "Buses That Bring Together Two Separate and Unequal Worlds."

62　Mrs. Thomas Schelling to the editor, *Lexington Minute-Man*, January 13, 1966.

63　Metropolitan Council for Educational Opportunity, "What You'll Want to Know about the METCO Program," November 1966, box 2, folder 5, METCO-NUSC.

64　"Discuss Plans for Hub Students Here," *Newton Graphic*, January 27, 1966.

65　Metropolitan Council for Educational Opportunity, "What You'll Want to Know about the METCO Program."

66　Betty Psaltis and Alice Miel, "Are Children in the Suburbs Different?" *Educational Leadership* (April 1964): 436–40; Alice Miel, *The Shortchanged Children of Suburbia: What Schools Don't Teach about Human Differences and What Can Be Done about It* (New York: American Jewish Committee, 1967).

67　Phyllis Myers, "Boston's METCO: What To Do Until the Solution Arrives," *City*, National Urban Coalition, January–February 1971, box 13, folder 33, METCO-NUSC.

68　Metropolitan Council for Educational Opportunity, "What You'll Want to Know About the METCO Program."

69　METCO, "Questions & Answers About METCO," ca. 1970, box 2, folder 35, METCO-NUSC.

70　Arthur E. Bryson Jr., "An Open Letter to the Lexington School Committee," *Lexington Minute-Man*, January 13, 1966.

71　Metropolitan Council for Educational Opportunity, "What You'll Want to Know about the METCO Program"; "Chairman Sargent Tells School Committee Plans to Bus Boston Pupils to Wellesley," *Townsmen*, February 24, 1966; David Reiner to the editor, *Lexington Minute-Man*, January 13, 1966.

72　Elizabeth C. Weaver to the editor, *Lexington Minute-Man*, January 20, 1966.

73　Hammel, "Buses That Bring Together Two Separate and Unequal Worlds."

74　In Wellesley, a small group of residents did form an oppositional group, but plans for the program went ahead. See "Operation Challenge METCO," n.d., box 8, folder 99, METCO-NUSC.

75　Batson, King interview.

76　Theoharis, "I'd Rather Go to School in the South," 129.

77　Batson's position at the forefront of the movement shows how female activism at the grassroots level was a constitutive feature of the leadership of Boston's freedom struggle. See Theoharis, "I'd Rather Go to School in the South," 131.

78　Claude Lewis, "Boston Takes Step toward School Integration by Busing," *Sunday Bulletin*, Philadelphia, June 11, 1967. Operation Exodus, a program initiated by a group of Roxbury parents in 1965, had arranged to bus 250 children from the city's predominantly black and low-income areas to open seats in schools throughout the city (James Teele, Ellen Jackson, and Clara Mayo, "Family Experiences in Operation Exodus," 1966, box 28, folder 3, METCO-NUSC).

79　Mel King, *Chain of Change: Struggles for Black Community Development* (Boston: South End Press, 1981), 86–87.

80　Ruth Batson and Robert C. Hayden, "A History of METCO: A Suburban Education for Boston's Urban Students," 1987, box 2, folder 6, METCO-NUSC.

81　Ruth Batson, "The METCO Story," Association for the Study of Afro-American Life and History, October 11, 1985, box 1, RMB.

82　Leon Trilling to Benjamin Benderson, September 21, 1967, box 8, folder 58, METCO-NUSC.

83　Ruth M. Batson, "A View from the Top, 1968–1969," ca. 1969, box 13, folder 32, METCO-NUSC.

84　Lewis, "Boston Takes Step toward School Integration by Busing."

85　Batson and Hayden, "A History of METCO."

86　Batson and Hayden, "A History of METCO."

87   For more on the ways that race and class came to assume spatial meanings in the postwar period, see Thomas J. Sugrue, *The Origins of the Urban Crisis: Race and Inequality in Postwar Detroit* (Princeton, NJ: Princeton University Press, 1996), 120–21; Matthew D. Lassiter, *The Silent Majority: Suburban Politics in the Sunbelt South* (Princeton, NJ: Princeton University Press, 2006), 9–10.

88   Batson and Hayden, "A History of METCO."

89   As far as I know, she was the only white student who has participated in the program.

90   This rule would later change when the state passed new legislation to fund special education.

91   The organization's 1967 report to the Carnegie Corporation includes many samples of this positive feedback (METCO, "Suburban Education for Urban Children [Internal Report]").

92   Thomas W. Mahan, "The Busing of Students for Equal Opportunities," *Journal of Negro Education* (Summer 1968): 291–300; Lewis, "Boston Takes Step toward School Integration by Busing."

93   METCO, "Suburban Education for Urban Children [Internal Report]"; METCO, "A Report to the Carnegie Corporation," December 18, 1968, box 2, folder 2, METCO-NUSC.

94   David R. Sargent to Francis W. Sargent, March 26, 1969, box 2, folder 73, METCO-NUSC.

95   METCO, "Suburban Education for Urban Children [Internal Report]."

96   METCO, "1969 Annual Report," box 1, folder 7, METCO-NUSC; Leon Trilling and Ruth M. Batson to Thomas J. Curtin, December 11, 1968, box 8, folder 19, METCO-NUSC.

97   METCO, "Memorandum No. II: Report of School Systems Waiving Tuition and/or Reducing Tuition," ca. May 1968, box 8, folder 69, METCO-NUSC.

98   METCO, "METCO Executive Board Minutes," March 12, 1969, box 5, folder 23, METCO-NUSC.

99   Myers, "Boston's METCO: What To Do Until the Solution Arrives."

100   Tonnie Katz, "Three Years Later—METCO Is Working," *Patriot Ledger*, May 28, 1969.

101   Batson, "A View from the Top, 1968–1969."

102   METCO, "1970 Annual Report," box 1, folder 7, METCO-NUSC.

103   Hammel, "Buses That Bring Together Two Separate and Unequal Worlds."

104   METCO, "Proposed Plan for Cooperative Program of Education between Urban and Suburban Schools."

105   "METCO in Lincoln, 1966–1976," in "Schools and Programs of Choice: Voluntary Desegregation in Massachusetts."

106   Hammel, "Buses That Bring Together Two Separate and Unequal Worlds."

107   Hammel, "Buses That Bring Together Two Separate and Unequal Worlds."

108   Hammel, "Buses That Bring Together Two Separate and Unequal Worlds."

109   "Black-White Student Dialogue Probes Value of METCO Busing," *Boston Globe*, May 25, 1969.

110   For a lengthy discussion of this sentiment, see Susan E. Eaton, *The Other Boston Busing Story.*

111   "Graduates Assess Program," *Boston Globe*, March 26, 1972.

112   Batson, "A View from the Top, 1968–1969."

113   Evelyn Keene, "Director Rates Metco," *Boston Globe*, March 26, 1972.

114   "Black-White Student Dialogue Probes Value of METCO Busing."

115   Myers, "Boston's METCO: What To Do Until the Solution Arrives."

116   METCO, "Questions & Answers About METCO."

117   METCO, "Questions & Answers About METCO."

118   David J. Armor, "The Evidence on Busing," *Public Interest* (Summer 1972): 102; David J. Armor, "METCO Student Attitudes and Aspirations: A Three-Year Evaluation," October 1970, box 32, folder 12, METCO-NUSC.

119   John B. Wood, "Avowed Integrationist Probes Busing, Finds It Has Backfired," *Boston Globe*, May 22, 1972; Robert Reinhold, "Study Critical of Busing Scored," *New York Times*, June 8, 1972.

120   Thomas F. Pettigrew et al., "Busing: A Review of the Evidence," *Public Interest* (Fall 1972): 88–118.

121   METCO, "What You'll Want to Know About the METCO Program."

122   Efrem Sigel and Gary F. Jonas, "Metropolitan Cooperation in Education: The Greater Boston Case," *Journal of Negro Education* (Spring 1970): 155–57.

4   Grappling with Growth

1   Claire Ellis to the editor, *Concord Journal*, October 19, 1972.

2   For more on the national open space movement, see Adam Rome, *The Bulldozer in the Countryside: Suburban Sprawl and the Rise of American Environmentalism* (New York: Cambridge University Press, 2001); Christopher C. Sellers, *Crabgrass Crucible: Suburban Nature and the Rise of Environmentalism in Twentieth Century* (Chapel Hill: University of North Carolina Press, 2012); Peter Siskind, "Suburban Growth and Its Discontents: The Logic and Limits of Reform on the Postwar Northeast Corridor," in *The New Suburban History*, ed. Kevin Kruse and Thomas J. Sugrue (Chicago: University of Chicago Press, 2006); Peter T. Siskind, "Growth and Its Discontents: Localism, Protest, and the Politics of Development on the Postwar Northeast Corridor" (PhD diss., University of Pennsylvania, 2002).

3   See, for instance, Ronald P. Formisano, *Boston against Busing: Race and Ethnicity in the 1960s and 1970s* (Chapel Hill: University of North Carolina Press, 1991), 165, 234.

4   For a similar movement in Marin County, see Louise Nelson Dyble, "Revolt Against Sprawl: Transportation and the Origins of the Marin County Growth-Control Regime," *Journal of Urban History* (November 2007): 39.

5   For more about the links between the growth of environmental concern in the 1960s and the ideology of postwar liberalism, see Adam Rome "'Give Earth a Chance': The Environmental Movement and the Sixties," *Journal of American History* (September 2003): 527–34.

6   Ellis to the editor.

7   Scholars have traditionally dismissed the antisprawl philosophy as a convenient medium through which to practice the exclusionary politics of suburban privilege. See Mike Davis, *City of Quartz: Excavating the Future in Los Angeles* (New York: Vintage Books, 1992), 159; Andrew Hurley, *Environmental Inequalities: Class, Race, and Industrial Pollution in Gary, Indiana, 1945–1980* (Chapel Hill: University of North Carolina Press, 1995); Matthew Klingle, *Emerald City: An Environmental History of Seattle* (New Haven, CT: Yale University Press, 2007), especially 201–80. On the other side, Adam Rome has demonstrated the central role of suburbanites in shaping the modern environmental movement while downplaying the exclusionary dimensions of their political worldview. See Rome, *Bulldozer in the Countryside*. There has been an increasing effort to take a more balanced view of this movement. See Siskind, "Suburban Growth and Its Discontents"; Sellers, *Crabgrass Crucible*.

8   Massachusetts Department of Natural Resources, "Annual Report of the Commissioner of Natural Resources, Fiscal Year 1955," SLM.

9   Charles W. Eliot and Planning and Renewal Associates, "Planning for Lincoln," December 1, 1958, box 3, folder 46, LER.

10   Roland B. Greeley, "A Proposal for Town Action to Preserve Local Space," n.d., box 1, folder "Natural Areas Council," CHWF.

11 Michael N. Danielson, *The Politics of Exclusion* (New York: Columbia University Press, 1976), 36.

12 Allen H. Morgan, "A History of the Massachusetts Audubon Society (Draft)," 1980, box 3, folder 14, AHM.

13 Barbara P. Paine, "Preservation of Open Spaces Offers a Challenge to Suburbia," *Nature Magazine* 51 (October 1958).

14 Allen H. Morgan to C. Russell Mason, January 7, 1955, box 1, folder 15, AHM.

15 Paine, "Preservation of Open Spaces Offers a Challenge to Suburbia."

16 For a look at how Boulder activists adopted a similar argument to promote open space protection, see Amy L. Scott, "Remaking Urban in the American West: Urban Environmentalism, Lifestyle Politics, and Hip Capitalism in Boulder, Colorado," in *Political Culture of the New West*, ed. Jeff Roche (Lawrence: University of Kansas Press, 2008), 251–80.

17 Rome, *Bulldozer in the Countryside*, 128–39.

18 James G. Coke and Charles S. Liebman, "Political Values and Population Density Control," *Land Economics* 37 (November 1961): 347–62.

19 Tom Connor, "Preserving Open Spaces through Land Trusts," *New York Times*, June 3, 1979.

20 League of Women Voters of Lincoln, "Lincoln: Guide to Government, 1963," box 3, folder 31, LWVL; Open Space Institute, "Landsaving, Lincoln Style," *Open Space Action* (1968), reprinted by the Lincoln Land Conservation Trust, box 3, folder 39, LER; Paul Brooks, "Suburban Land Use," *Conservation Leader* 4, no. 1 (September 1968), box 7, folder 90, LER; "Agreement and Declaration of Trust," n.d., CLCT.

21 Rome, *Bulldozer in the Countryside*, 120.

22 Andrew J. W. Scheffey, *Conservation Commissions in Massachusetts* (Washington, DC: Conservation Foundation, 1969), 30.

23 Mary Ann Guttar, "When Communities Care," *New York Times*, December 14, 1969.

24 Massachusetts Department of Natural Resources, "Annual Report of the Commissioner of Natural Resources," 1958, 1959, 1960, SLM; Monica A. Amiel, "A Comparative Analysis of Conservation Commission Enabling Legislation in Seven Northeastern States within the Context of National Environmental Policy" (master's thesis, University of Massachusetts, 1972); Scheffey, *Conservation Commissions in Massachusetts*, 59.

25 Charles H. W. Foster, "Commissions . . . a Progress Report," *Massachusetts Wildlife* (September–October 1961), box 1, folder "Conservation Commission," CHWF.

26 John H. Fenton, "Town Enacts Law to Save Streams," *New York Times*, May 14, 1967.

27 Foster, "Commissions . . . a Progress Report."

28 Massachusetts Department of Natural Resources, "Annual Report of the Commissioner of Natural Resources," 1960, SLM.

29 Linda Davidoff, Paul Davidoff, and Neil N. Gold, "The Suburbs Have to Open Their Gates," *New York Times*, November 7, 1971.

30 Siskind, "Growth and Its Discontents."

31 League of Women Voters of Lincoln, "A Study of the Impact of Light Industry on the Character and Economy of Nine Boston Area Towns," April 1963, box 2, folder 24, LWVL; Scheffey, *Conservation Commissions in Massachusetts*, 76.

32 Division of Conservation Services, "Annual Report for Fiscal Year 1966," SLM.

33 A report by the Massachusetts Department of Natural Resources from the early 1970s found that the affluent suburbs ringing Boston where "the pressures of development are the greatest, but the financial and human resources to cope with the pressures are plentiful," had consistently served as the most active participants in the program. See Massachusetts Department of Natural Resources, *Environmental Resource* 10 (Fall 1973), CDNR.

34 Scheffey, *Conservation Commissions in Massachusetts*, 81; Siskind, "Growth and Its Discontents."

35 For more on the state and national efforts to preserve natural spaces through the state and national park systems, see Samuel Hays, *Beauty, Health, Permanence: Environmental Politics in the United States, 1955–1985* (New York: Cambridge University Press, 1987), 99–136.

36 Concord Department of Natural Resources, "Natural Resources Report," July 1972, CDNR.

37 Concord Department of Natural Resources, "Natural Resources Report."

38 Concord Department of Natural Resources, "Natural Resources Report."

39 Lincoln Planning Board, "Comprehensive Development Plan for the Town of Lincoln," August 1965, box 3, folder 46, LER.

40 Ruth Rusch, "Look How Open Space Can Hold Down Your Taxes," *Planning and Civic Comment* 28, no. 1 (March 1962).

41 Concord Natural Resources Commission, "Article 46: Punkatasset," flyer, 1971, CDNR.

42 Concord Department of Natural Resources, "Natural Resources Report."

43 Paul Brooks, *The View from Lincoln Hill: Man and the Land in a New England Town* (Boston: Houghton Mifflin, 1976), 263.

44 "Conservation: A Do It Yourself Miracle," *New Englander* (January 1965).

45 Siskind, "Growth and Its Discontents."

46 Paul Brooks and Susan Brooks, "A Town with Room for Living," *New York Times*, June 13, 1971.

47 Brooks, *The View from Lincoln Hill*, 263.

48 Massachusetts Department of Natural Resources, "Conservation Commissions at a Crossroads," *Environmental Resource* 10 (Fall 1973), folder 890, JHB; Scheffey, *Conservation Commissions in Massachusetts*, 150.

49 Greater Boston Chamber of Commerce, "A Background Paper: Subject: Interstate 695, the Inner Belt, September 1964," box 15, folder 6, MITPO; Alan Lupo, Frank Colcord, and Edward P. Fowler, *Rites of Way: The Politics of Transportation in Boston and the U.S. City* (Boston: Little, Brown, 1971), 13.

50 "O'Neill, Council Join Citizens in Campaign to Stop Belt Highway," *Cambridge Chronicle*, May 19, 1960; "Belt Route Delay Seen by O'Neill," *Cambridge Chronicle*, June 9, 1960.

51 For more on the national freeway revolt, see Raymond A. Mohl, "Stop the Road: Freeway Revolts in American Cities," *Journal of Urban History* (July 2004): 674–706; Jim Hampton, "Now the Real Highway Fight Begins," *National Observer*, April 14, 1969.

52 "Highway Opposition Groups Join Forces for State House Demonstration," Boston, January 19, 1969, box 116, folder "People's March," FWS.

53 Tom Sewell, "2000 in State House Protest," *Sunday Herald Traveler*, January 24, 1969; Alan Lupo, "Road Protestors Mass," *Boston Globe*, January 26, 1969; Alan Lupo, "Roads the Case for a Moratorium," *Boston Globe*, February 1, 1970; Lupo, Colcord, and Fowler, *Rites of Way*, 45.

54 Lupo, "Road Protestors Mass"; Sewell, "2000 in State House Protest."

55 Lupo, Colcord, and Fowler, *Rites of Way*, 41.

56 Emergency Coalition Bill against 5270 to Francis W. Sargent, ca. 1969, box 47, folder "Transportation Task Force," FWS.

57 Robbins v. Department of Public Works, 355 Mass. 328, 244 N.E.2d 577 (1969); Helen E. Sullivan, "Court Ruling Nullifies Rte. I-95 Agreement," *Patriot Ledger*, February 6, 1969.

58 Lupo, Colcord, and Fowler, *Rites of Way*, 78.

59 Allen H. Morgan, "Fundraising 'Art, Science and Effort;'" *California Waterfront Age* 3, no. 4 (Fall 1987), box 3, folder 7, AHM.

60 *CPP Coordinator Bulletin*, January 2, 1970, box 6, folder 6.13, CPPAX-UMB.

61 Greater Boston Committee on the Transportation Crisis, "Letter from Susan Straight," n.d., ca. fall 1969, box 6, folder 6.12, CPPAX-UMB.

62 Greater Boston Committee on the Transportation Crisis, "Letter from Susan Straight."

63   Stephen P. Crosby to Francis W. Sargent, November 26, 1969, box 116, folder "General," FWS.

64   Francis W. Sargent to Stephen P. Crosby, December 30, 1969, box 116, folder "General," FWS.

65   Governor's Press Office, press release, February 11, 1970, box 109, folder "Gov. Speeches," FWS.

66   "Gov Francis Sargent (Republican)," July 1970, box 6, folder 42, CPPAX-UMB.

67   Sargent told the GBC that it deserved "a great deal of credit for bringing the people to understand the need for balanced transportation." See Francis W. Sargent to Father Thomas D. Corrigan, February 18, 1970, box 116, folder "General," FWS.

68   Lupo, Colcord, and Fowler, *Rites of Way*, 61.

69   Francis W. Sargent to Father Thomas D. Corrigan; Lupo, Colcord, and Fowler, *Rites of Way*, 110.

70   Francis W. Sargent, "Policy Statement on Transportation Crisis in the Boston Region," November 30, 1972, box 32, folder "Transportation Readings," FWS.

71   Lawrence Susskind, ed., *The Land Use Controversy in Massachusetts Case Studies and Policy Options* (Cambridge, MA: MIT Press, 1975), 44; Ralph Gakenheimer, *Transportation Planning as Response to Controversy: The Boston Case* (Cambridge, MA: MIT Press, 1975), 1–5.

72   See, for instance, Brookline Conservation Commission, press release, November 21, 1972, box 20, folder "Restudy Comments II," FWS; Francis X. Meaney, Eugenie Beal, et al. to Francis W. Sargent, November 21, 1972, box 20, folder "Restudy Comments II," FWS.

73   Richard A. Liroff, *A National Policy for the Environment: NEPA and Its Aftermath* (Bloomington: Indiana University Press, 1976), 3.

74   National Environmental Policy Act of 1969, Pub. L. 91–190, 42 U.S.C. 4321–47, January 1, 1970.

75   Alan A. Altshuler and David E. Luberoff, *Mega-Projects: The Changing Politics of Urban Public Investment* (Washington, DC: Brookings Institute Press, 2003), 86.

76   Department of Public Works, "Design Hearing Route 2 Acton-Concord-Lincoln and Lexington," 1970, RC.

77   Joan Mahoney, "Lincoln Families Charge DPW Harasses, Threatens," *Boston Evening Globe*, May 15, 1972.

78   Department of Public Works, "Design Hearing Route 2."

79   Sareen R. Gerson, "New Breed of Local Officials Developing During Rte. 2 Battle," *Lexington Minute-Man Supplement*, January 7, 1971.

80   "165 Lincoln Residents to the Editor," *Lincoln Fence Viewer*, April 6, 1972.

81   Citizens for Balanced Transportation, "The Proposed Route 2: A Challenge to Concord," April 15, 1971, box 20, folder "Route 2," FWS.

82   Gerson, "New Breed of Local Officials Developing During Rte. 2 Battle."

83   Howard Whitman, "Thoreau's Concord Is Willing to Leave Nature's Work Alone," *New York Times*, September 17, 1972.

84   Whitman, "Thoreau's Concord Is Willing to Leave Nature's Work Alone."

85   Cyrus F. Gibson to Al Kramer and Guy Rosmarin, October 30, 1972, box 20, folder "Route 2," FWS.

86   ROUTE, "The Environment at Walden: A Concrete Example," October 9, 1972, RRC.

87   Citizens for Balanced Transportation, "The Proposed Route 2"; Citizens for Balanced Transportation, "Facts on the Proposed Route 2 Construction," April 15, 1971, box 20, folder "Route 2," FWS.

88   George Barker to Bruce Campbell, December 15, 1971, box 20, folder "Route 2," FWS.

89   Joan Mahoney, "Citizens Groups Up in Arms over Route 2," *Boston Globe*, May 23, 1972.

90   George Barker to Bruce Campbell; Allen H. Morgan to Charles H. W. Foster, re: Route 2 Reconstruction (Lincoln-Acton), May 24, 1972, box 20, folder "Route 2," FWS; Charles H. W.

Foster to Mrs. Alan Barrett, July 28, 1972, box 20, folder "Route 2," FWS; "CBT Told Route 2 to Become State's Major East-West Highway," *Concord Journal*, February 17, 1972; "Altshuler Meets with Route 2 Coalition," *Concord Journal*, May 11, 1972; Cyrus F. Gibson to Al Kramer and Guy Rosmarin, October 30, 1972, box 20, folder "Route 2," FWS. See also Peter Koff to Steve Teichner, September 23, 1972, box 20, folder "Route 2," FWS.

91   Massachusetts Department of Public Works, "Draft Environmental/Section 4 (f) Statement for Route 2 in Acton, Concord, Lincoln & Lexington," April 1972, RRC; Priscilla Korell, "Towns to See Route 2 Designs in January," *Lexington Minute-Man Supplement*, December 12, 1974; "Minutes of Working Committee on Environmental Impact Statement for Route 2 in Acton, Concord, Lincoln, Lexington," June 19, 1975, box 1, folder "Loose Material," RRC.

92   Brad Kane, "Uncorking the Bottlenecks: State to Ease Tie-ups on Route 2 with $124m Makeover," *Boston Globe*, October 23, 2008.

93   The proposal did not completely stop all construction. As exceptions to his no-build policy, Sargent called for the creation of a special two-lane road and tunnel from downtown Boston to Logan Airport open solely to buses, taxis, and trucks. See Francis W. Sargent, "Policy Statement on Transportation in the Boston Region," November 30, 1972, box 32, folder "Transportation Readings," FWS.

94   Peter Baerstrup, "Gov. Sargent Lays Future on Freeway Line," *Los Angeles Times*, June 3, 1973.

95   Peter Baerstrup, "The Boston Freeway Halt," *Washington Post*, December 25, 1972.

96   Baerstrup, "Gov. Sargent Lays Future on Freeway Line."

97   John Lear, "The Road-Tax Rebellion," *Saturday Review*, July 4, 1970.

98   Francis W. Sargent to Republican legislators, May 13, 1970, box 116, folder "General," FWS; John A. Volpe to Francis W. Sargent, May 21, 1970, box 116, folder "Transportation Task Force," FWS; Francis W. Sargent to John A. Volpe, June 2, 1970, box 116, folder "Transportation Task Force," FWS.

99   Francis W. Sargent, "Testimony of Governor Sargent before Sub Committee of Public Roads of the Senate Public Works Committee," May 14, 1970, box 20, folder "Press Statements," FWS.

100   Altshuler and Luberoff, *Mega-Projects*, 187.

101   "Suburban Vote Becomes Powerful Influence with 131 House Seats," *Los Angeles Times*, May 1, 1974.

102   Phillip Albohn, "BTPR Transit Plans Include $45M Line to Lexington Landfill," *Lexington Minute-Man Supplement*, April 5, 1973.

103   Anne R. Sciligano, "Will Red Line End Here?" *Lexington Minute-Man*, July 19, 1973.

104   Nancy Earsy to the editor, *Lexington Minute-Man*, June 28, 1973.

105   "Residents Want More, Better Public Transit, Split between Rail, Bus," *Lexington Minute-Man*, August 8, 1974; "Commuters Demand Dependable Transit," *Lexington Minute-Man*, August 15, 1974.

106   "Commuters Demand Dependable Transit."

107   John O'Keefe, "Towns Want Slow, Planned Growth, but Fear Transportation 'Improvements,'" *Lexington Minute-Man Supplement*, November 25, 1976.

108   Stephen Pollit, "Red Line Terminal at Rte, 128 'Not Feasible,'" *Lexington Minute-Man*, June 12, 1975; "What Will the Impact of the Red Line Extension Be on Town?" *Lexington Minute-Man*, September 13, 1973.

109   John Lahiff to the editor, *Lexington Minute-Man*, January 24, 1974.

110   Phillip Albohn, "Red Line Expansion Plan Could Create Ruckus—Lexington vs. Neighbors," *Lexington Minute-Man Supplement*, May 3, 1973.

111   Tom Forstmann to the editor, *Lexington Minute-Man*, June 26, 1975.

112   Jason H. Korell, "Red Line to Rte 128? What Path, Which Terminal," *Lexington Minute-Man Supplement*, March 3, 1977. For similar arguments in the fight over rapid transit in Atlanta, see Kevin Kruse, *White Flight: Atlanta and the Making of Modern of Conservatism* (Princeton, NJ: Princeton University Press, 2005), 249.

113   Jason H. Korell, "Red Line Extension Moving Closer to 128, Most Say 'Inevitable,'" *Lexington Minute-Man Supplement*, May 10, 1977.

114   "What Will the Impact of the Red Line Extension Be on Town?"

115   "What Will the Impact of the Red Line Extension Be on Town?"

116   "Arlington Says No to MBTA Red Line," *Lexington Minute-Man Supplement*, March 10, 1977.

117   "Transportation Chief Urges Transit Growth," *Lexington Minute-Man*, June 2, 1977.

118   H. H. Seward to the editor, *Arlington Advocate*, December 9, 1976.

119   Cheryl Waixel, "Red Line Extension Receives Mixed Reaction at BTPR Hearing," *Lexington Minute-Man*, April 19, 1973.

120   "Arlington Says No to MBTA Red Line."

121   Lou Conrad, "MBTA Rail Plan Interred," *Lexington Minute-Man*, June 6, 1978.

122   John Laidler, "His Dream Was a Road More Traveled," *Boston Globe*, July 6, 2003.

123   Vollmer Associates, "MBTA Lexington Branch R.R. Right-of-Way Study," n.d., Historical Collection, Rollins Library, Arlington, MA.

124   Shira Springer, "On the Popular Minuteman Bikeway, Crowds and Towns Are Part of Its Charm," *Boston Globe*, September 19, 2010; Ethan Gilsdorf, "Popular Bike Trail Gets Even Better," *Boston Globe*, June 29, 2008. For an example of its popularity among city dwellers, see Ryan Stewart, "A Trek through the Minuteman Trail," *Boston Phoenix*, May 9, 2011.

125   Paul K. Asabere and Forrest E. Huffman, "The Relative Impacts of Trails and Greenbelts on Home Price," *Journal of Real Estate Finance and Economics* (May 2009): 408–19. Asabere and Huffman analyzed statistics on the listing and selling prices of homes in the towns through which the Minuteman Bikeway Trail runs. They found that homes near this and other rail trails in Massachusetts sold at 99.3 percent of the listing price as compared to 98.1 percent of the listing price for other homes sold in these towns, and that these homes sold in an average of 29.3 days as compared to 50.4 days for other homes.

126   "Massachusetts: No Partisanship on Environment," *New York Times*, June 19, 1996; Fred Siegel and Will Marshall, "The Quality of Life Agenda," *DLC Blueprint Magazine*, September 1, 2000.

5 Political Action for Peace

1   Crocker Snow Jr., "McGovern, Kennedy Ask Ground Troop Pullout within a Year," *Boston Globe*, October 16, 1969; Andrew F. Blake and David B. Wilson, "A Political Woodstock on Boston Common," *Boston Globe*, October 16, 1969.

2   "Strike against the War," *Time*, October 17, 1969.

3   Diane White, "'This Is Real Grass Roots,'" *Boston Globe*, October 15, 1969; Diane White, "War Rallies: All Over Towns," *Boston Globe*, October 10, 1969.

4   "On Moratorium Day," *Boston* (November 1969), box 5, folder 6.29, CPPAX-UMB.

5   Marjorie Arons, "Jerry Grossman Reflects on Local Political Scene and beyond through Two Decades," *Newton Times*, November 24, 1976.

6   The standard narratives of the antiwar movement pay virtually no attention to suburban groups. For a look at the dominant model and most easily challenged of this extensive literature, see Todd Gitlin, *The Sixties: Years of Hope, Days of Rage* (New York: Bantam Books, 1987). For a notable exception, see Amy Swerdlow, *Women Strike for Peace: Traditional Motherhood and Radical Politics in the 1960s* (Chicago: University of Chicago Press, 1993).

7   For more on the class-based issues surrounding the Vietnam War, see Christian G. Appy, *Working-Class War: American Combat Soldiers and Vietnam* (Chapel Hill: University of North Carolina, 1993). For a discussion of these issues in the Boston area specifically, see Appy, *Working-Class War*, 12–13, 54.

8   Paula Leventman, *Professionals Out of Work* (New York: Free Press, 1981), 185.

9   Lisa McGirr, *Suburban Warriors: The Origins of the New American Right* (Princeton, NJ: Princeton University Press, 2001), 173–76; Matthew D. Lassiter, "Big Government and Family Values: Political Culture in the Metropolitan Sunbelt," in *Sunbelt Rising: The Politics of Space, Place, and Region*, ed. Michelle Nickerson and Darren Dochuk (Philadelphia: University of Pennsylvania Press, 2011), 82–99.

10 E. J. Dionne Jr., *Why Americans Hate Politics* (New York: Simon and Schuster, 1991), 48.

11 Jerome Grossman, *Relentless Liberal* (New York: Vantage Press, 1996), 16–38.

12 Jerome Grossman, interview by Nancy Earsy, December 3, 1996, LOHP.

13 Grossman interview.

14 Sumner Rosen, "The Transformation of Politics in Massachusetts," in "The Hughes Campaign: 25 Years Later, 1962–1987," CPPAX Education Fund, 1987, box 29, CPPAX-UMB.

15 Jerome Grossman, "From Stuart Hughes to Robert Drinan," in "The Hughes Campaign: 25 Years Later, 1962–1987," CPPAX Education Fund, 1987, box 29, CPPAX-UMB.

16 John H. Fenton, "Candidates Push Bay State Drives," *New York Times*, June 23, 1962.

17 H. Stuart Hughes, *Gentleman Rebel: The Memoirs of H. Stuart Hughes* (New York: Ticknor and Fields, 1990), 252.

18 Grossman, "From Stuart Hughes to Robert Drinan."

19 Hughes, *Gentleman Rebel*, 252.

20 "Hughes Has Support from All Walks of Life," *Brookline Chronicle*, November 1, 1962.

21 Voice of Women–New England, newsletter, August–September 1962, box 1, folder 19, VOW-SL.

22 John H. Fenton, "Campuses Voice Some Opposition," *New York Times*, October 24, 1962.

23 Selections from "Joel Cohen's Hughes for Senate: A Campaign History," 1964, in "The Hughes Campaign: 25 Years Later, 1962–1987," CPPAX Education Fund, 1987, box 29, CPPAX-UMB.

24 Shrag, "Two Visits to the Executive Office Building," in "The Hughes Campaign: 25 Years Later, 1962–1987," CPPAX Education Fund, 1987, box 29, CPPAX-UMB.

25 "Report of Dec. 1 Meeting at the Home of Mr. and Mrs. Donham in Wayland," 1962, box 5, folder 5.5, CPPAXR; Mass PAX, leaflet, ca. 1971, box 6, folder 5.42, CPPAX-UMB; Mass PAX, press release, February 7, 1963, box 5, folder 5, CPPAX-UMB.

26 Paul Anders, introduction to "The Hughes Campaign: 25 Years Later, 1962–1987," CPPAX Education Fund, 1987, box 29, CPPAX-UMB.

27 Mass PAX, *Peace Politics*, no. 1 (October 1963), box 5, folder 5.1, CPPAX-UMB; Jerome Grossman, "The Peace 'Crowd,'" *The Nation*, January 20, 1964.

28 Grossman, "The Peace 'Crowd.'"

29 Chester Hartman, "The Noel Day Campaign and the Future of Radical Politics," *Correspondent* (Winter 1965), box 2, folder 28, PMR.

30 Hartman, "The Noel Day Campaign."

31 Cambridge PAX, "Noel Day to Announce for Congress," *Bulletin*, June 3, 1964, box 5, CPPAX-UMB.

32 Roy H. Brown to Robert D. Hall Jr., October 1964, box 2, folder 31, PMR.

33 A poll conducted by a Boston University political scientist found that only 27 percent of African Americans in Boston interviewed had heard of Day (Hartman, "The Noel Day Campaign").

34 Chester W. Hartman, "Comments on the Brumm Memorandum," 1964, box 5, folder 5.11, CPPAX-UMB.

35 To commemorate VOW's thirtieth reunion, a group of members sent out questionnaires titled "30 Years Later: Voice of Women Reunion" to members of the organization asking a variety of questions, including why the respondent originally got involved. Several of the members cited a desire to protect their children and family from the harm of nuclear war. See Voice of Women–New England, "30 Years Later: Voice of Women Questionnaires," box 1, folder 51, VOW-SL.

36 Suzanne Kelley McKormack, "Good Politics Is Doing Something: Independent Diplomats and Anti-War Activists in the Vietnam Era Peace Movement—A Collective Biography" (PhD diss., Boston College, 2002).

37 Voice of Women–New England, newsletter, May 1962, no. 5, box 1, folder 19, VOW-SL; Voice of Women–New England, newsletter, October 1964, box 1, folder 20, VOW-SL.

38 Voice of Women–New England, newsletter, March 1966, box 1, folder 20, VOW-SL; Voice of Women–New England, newsletter, November 1966, box 1, folder 20, VOW-SL; Voice of Women–New England, newsletter, December 1967, box 1, folder 21, VOW-SL; Voice of Women–New England, flyer, n.d., box 1, folder 28, VOW-SL.

39 McKormack, "Good Politics Is Doing Something."

40 Voice of Women–New England, newsletter, November 1967, box 1, folder 21, VOW-SL; Amy Swerdlow, "'Not My Son, Not Your Son, Not Their Son': Mothers Against the Vietnam Draft," in *Give Peace a Chance: Exploring the Vietnam Antiwar Movement*, ed. Melvin Small and William D. Hoover (New Brunswick, NJ: Rutgers University Press, 1992), 159–70. For more on the draft resistance movement in Boston, see Michael S. Foley, *Confronting the War Machine: Draft Resistance in the Vietnam War* (Chapel Hill: University of North Carolina Press, 2001).

41 Voice of Women–New England, newsletter, December 1967.

42 Voice of Women–New England, "30 Years Later."

43 Women's International League of Peace and Freedom, "He's Shopping with Our Money," box 1, folder 19, WILPF; Voice of Women–New England, "Phone Tax Card," box 1, folder 29, VOW-SL; Voice of Women–New England, newsletter, March 1970, box 1, folder 22, VOW-SL.

44 Jerome Grossman to Mrs. Gardner Cox, August 27, 1965, box 5, folder 3, CPPAX-UMB.

45 Grossman interview.

46 For more on the Lowenstein effort, see William Chafe, *Never Stop Running: Allard Lowenstein and the Struggle to Save American Liberalism* (New York: Basic Books, 1993), especially 262–75.

47 Grossman, *Relentless Liberal*, 41–42.

48 Mass PAX, "Executive Committee Meeting," January 8, 1968, box 5, folder 21, CPPAX-UMB.

49 Grossman, *Relentless Liberal*, 43.

50 See, for example, "McCarthy Rides on 'Student Power,'" *New York Times*, March 10, 1968; Allen J. Matusow, *The Unraveling of America: A History of Liberalism in the 1960s* (New York: Harper and Row, 1984), 407.

51 "LBJ, McCarthy Invited to Speak in Lexington," *Lexington Minute-Man*, January 28, 1968; Voice of Women–New England, newsletter, March 1968, box 1, folder 22, VOW-SL.

52 Bonnie Jones, interview by Norma McGavern-Norland, December 3, 1991, LOHP.

53 Emily Frankovich, interview by Bonnie Jones, February 28, 1992, LOHP.

54 Richard Todd, "The 'Ins' and 'Outs' at M.I.T.," *New York Times*, May 18, 1969.

55 Leventman, *Professionals Out of Work*, 177–84.

56 Sheldon Rampton and John Stauber, *Trust Us We're Experts: How Industry Manipulates Science and Gambles with Your Future* (New York: Tarcher, 2000), 210.

57 Leventman, *Professionals Out of Work*, 182–83.

58 Leventman, *Professionals Out of Work*, 184.

59   "Rocky Upsets Volpe, Nixon, McCarthy Tops JFK Record," *Boston Globe*, May 1, 1968.

60   Paul Wieck, "The Case of Massachusetts," *New Republic*, February 1, 1969, 25.

61   Theodore White, *Making of the President 1968* (New York: Athenaeum House, 1969), 466.

62   Citizens for Participation Politics, "Proposed Goals for the Citizens for Participation Politics" ca. September 1968, box 6, folder 6.19, CPPAX-UMB.

63   For more on "new politics," see Lanny J. Davis, *The Emerging Democratic Majority: Lessons and Legacies from the New Politics* (New York: Stein and Day, 1974).

64   Citizens for Participation Politics, "Proposed Goals for the Citizens for Participation Politics."

65   Matusow, *Unraveling of America*, 407.

66   Massachusetts Department of Natural Resources, "The Sentinel-Perimeter Acquisition Radar Site, Boxford State Forest, North Andover, Massachusetts," August 1970, box 54, folder "ABM Site in North Andover," FWS.

67   Victor K. McElheny, "Reading Scene for Verbal War," *Boston Globe*, January 29, 1969.

68   Mass PAX, "December 10 Meeting, First Congregational Church, Reading," December 10, 1968, box 5, folder 5.23, CPPAX-UMB; Letter from Raymond Dougan, December 16, 1968, box 5, folder 5.23, CPPAX-UMB.

69   Rachelle Patterson, "TV Blur from Radar; Crowded Schools Cited," *Boston Globe*, January 29, 1969.

70   Citizens for Participation Politics, "The Reading ABM Meeting: Citizen Action to Stop Nuclear Missiles in Massachusetts," February 1969, box 6, folder 5.1, CPPAX-UMB.

71   Noam Chomsky, interview by Norma McGavern-Norland, October 7, 1992, LOHP.

72   Todd, "The 'Ins' and 'Outs' at M.I.T."

73   Stuart W. Leslie, *The Cold War and American Science: The Military-Industrial-Academic Complex at MIT and Stanford* (New York: Columbia University Press, 1994), 100.

74   Union of Concerned Scientists, "Founding Document: 1968 Faculty Statement," http://www.ucsusa.org/about/founding-document-1968.html; Todd, "The 'Ins' and 'Outs' at M.I.T."

75   Jonathan Allen, ed., *March 4: Scientists, Students, and Society* (Cambridge, MA: MIT Press, 1970), xxii–xxiii.

76   Leventman, *Professionals Out of Work*, 184.

77   Concord Citizens Committee on ABM, "Missile Sites Near Concord, Write Now!!" ca. February 1969, box 5, folder 5.25, CPPAX-UMB; Winchester Citizens Committee on A.B.M., "Hydrogen Bombs in Winchester's Backyard? The Pentagon Wants to Put Them There," March 1969, box 5, folder 5.25, CPPAX-UMB.

78   PAX, "Steering Committee Minutes," February 23, 1969, box 5, folder 5.25, CPPAX-UMB.

79   Theresa McMasters, "Ted Urges Halt on All ABM Work," *Boston Herald Traveler*, February 5, 1969; "Remarks of Senator Edward Brooke regarding Proposed ABM System," February 4, 1969, box 5, folder 5.25, CPPAX-UMB.

80   "State Senate Asks Halt on ABM Site," *Boston Record American*, February 4, 1969; "Coordinating Committee Meeting on ABM," February 2, 1969, box 5, folder 5.25, CPPAX-UMB.

81   "Coordinating Committee Meeting on ABM."

82   The treaty did allow for one "token installation" for each country.

83   Arthur W. Brownell to Charles W. Colson, August 14, 1970, box 54, folder "ABM Site North Andover," FWS.

84   Francis W. Sargent, press release, October 30, 1970, box 54, folder "ABM Site North Andover," FWS.

85   Mass PAX, "Steering Committee Meeting," April 15, 1969, box 5, folder 5.26, CPPAX-UMB; Mass PAX, "Steering Committee Meeting," February 11, 1969, box 5, folder 5.25, CPPAX-UMB; Nancy Zaroulis and Gerald Sullivan, *Who Spoke Up? American Protest against the War in Vietnam, 1963–1975* (New York: Horizon Books, 1989), 245–56.

86   William J. Lewis, "Oct. 15 Was Born Here," *Boston Globe*, October 10, 1969.

87   Mass PAX, "Executive Assembly Meeting," April 20, 1969, box 5, folder 26, CPPAX-UMB.

88   Grossman interview. The fact that Grossman, a factory manager, would advocate for a work stoppage surprised many members of the group, but he believed that withdrawing labor power was actually a way to treat the issue of the war as a business problem.

89   Mass PAX, "Executive Assembly Meeting," June 1, 1969, box 5, folder 5.26, CPPAX-UMB; Zaroulis and Sullivan, *Who Spoke Up?* 246.

90   Grossman interview.

91   Paul Hoffman, *Moratorium: An American Protest* (New York: Tower PublicAffairs, 1970), 32–33.

92   The less forceful term displeased PAX members, and while they reluctantly agreed, they interchangeably referred to the event as the moratorium and "Vietnam Peace Action Day." Mass PAX, "Executive Assembly Meeting," July 1, 1969, box 5, folder 5.27, CPPAX-UMB; Betram G. Waters, "Peace Action Day—October 15," *Boston Sunday Globe*, October 12, 1969.

93   Robert L. Levey, "Grossman Is Pleased by Response to Idea," *Boston Globe*, October 7, 1969.

94   Levey, "Grossman Is Pleased"; Vietnam Peace Action, press release, September 4, 1969, box 5, folder 27, CPPAX-UMB.

95   Grossman interview; "Raymond Dougan to High School Students," September 20, 1969, box 5, folder 27, CPPAX-UMB.

96   "On Moratorium Day."

97   "Citizens Groups Plan War Protest Meeting, "*Lexington Minute-Man*, September 23, 1969.

98   Lewis, "Oct. 15 Was Born Here."

99   White, "This Is Real Grass Roots"; White, "War Rallies: All Over Towns."

100 Diane White, "More Adults Joining Vietnam War Protest," *Boston Globe*, October 12, 1969.

101 White, "More Adults Joining Vietnam War Protest."

102 Zaroulis and Sullivan, *Who Spoke Up?* 271.

103 Richard A. Knox, "Doctor Protest Grows," *Boston Globe*, October 7, 1969; Alan Lupo, "Hub Lawyer Group Plans to Participate," *Boston Globe*, October 7, 1969.

104 Crocker Snow Jr., "Sargent Endorses Rally," *Boston Globe*, October 7, 1969.

105 Snow, "Sargent Endorses Rally."

106 George Washington to Al Kramer, Memorandum re: The Governor's October 15 Speech on the Vietnam War, October 9, 1969, box 36, folder "Memos from Pool to Al Kramer," FWS; Stephen Kurkjian, "Moratorium Foes Heckle Sargent on Lexington Green," *Boston Globe*, October 16, 1969.

107 Jeremiah V. Murphy, "Protests Make Strange Bedfellows," *Boston Globe*, October 14, 1969.

108 Boston Chapter of Students for a Democratic Society, "The Moratorium Is a Cover Not a Solution" (Boston, 1969).

109 Crocker Snow Jr., "Everybody's Getting into the Act, " *Boston Globe*, October 10, 1969.

110 John C. Burke, "Students Form the Vanguard in Suburbs," *Boston Globe*, October 16, 1969; Robert J. Anglin, "Peace Day to Him Just That," *Boston Globe*, October 14, 1969.

111 Crocker Snow Jr., "McGovern, Kennedy Ask Groundtroop Pullout within a Year," *Boston Globe*, October 16, 1969; Andrew F. Blake and David B. Wilson, "A Political Woodstock on Boston Common," *Boston Globe*, October 16, 1969.

112 PAX had made a halfhearted attempt to arrange for moratorium events in Roxbury, but a spokesperson for Boston's black community stated that they would rather focus on domestic injustice than the war. See Snow, "McGovern, Kennedy Ask Groundtroop Pullout within a Year."

113 Mass PAX, "Executive Committee Meeting Minutes," December 4, 1967, box 5, folder 5.20, CPPAX-UMB.

114 Appy, *Working-Class War*, 12.

115 Appy, *Working-Class War*, 12.

116 Robert Coles, *The Middle Americans: Proud and Uncertain* (Boston: Little Brown, 1971), 131–34.

117 "Strike against the War."

118 Andrew F. Blake and Stephen J. Kurkjian, "2nd Rally: 500,000 to March on Washington," *Boston Globe*, October 17, 1969; Parker Donham, "Leaders of Moratorium Shy from March on D.C.," *Boston Globe*, October 18, 1969.

119 Mass Pax, "Moratorium Executive Assembly," December 28, 1969, box 5, folder 29, CPPAX-UMB.

120 Deckle McClean, "Causes and Caucuses," *Boston Sunday Globe Magazine*, April 12, 1970.

121 "Harrington Says Polls Not Used to Form Policies," *Boston Globe*, October 10, 1969.

122 Norman C. Miller, "'Good Old Phil': How One Congressman Holds on to His Seat by Wooing Home Folks," *Wall Street Journal*, September 8, 1970.

123 McClean, "Causes and Caucuses."

124 Jerome Grossman, "From Stuart Hughes to Robert Drinan," in "The Hughes Campaign: 25 Years Later, 1962–1987," CPPAX Education Fund, 1987, box 29, CPPAX-UMB.

125 Robert Healy, "Now's the Time to Participate," *Boston Globe*, March 2, 1970.

126 Carol Liston, "3d District Caucus Nominates Fr. Drinan to Oppose Philbin," *Boston Globe*, February 22, 1970.

127 John S. Saloma, "Citizens Caucus . . . a Political Innovation," *Boston Globe*, February 28, 1970.

128 "30% Don't Like Priests in Politics; Drinan Campaign Faces Big Hurdle," *Boston Globe*, March 3, 1970; R. W. Apple Jr., "Priest in Massachusetts Is Opposed as Politician," *New York Times*, June 17, 1970.

129 Oliver Quayle and Company, "A Survey of the Political Climate in Massachusetts' Third Congressional District," May 1970, RFD.

130 Eliot Friedman, "How to Win the Primary by Really Trying," *Boston Sunday Globe*, October 18, 1970.

131 Robert Healy, "Drinan Victory Upset of the Year," *Boston Evening Globe*, September 17, 1970.

132 Drinan for Congress, "You're Fighting the Vietnam War at the Checkout Counter," flyer, 1970, RFD.

133 Drinan for Congress, "If the Thought of Hard Drugs in Your Town Makes You Feel Scared and Helpless, Maybe It Will Make You Read the Other Side," flyer, 1970, RFD.

134 Friedman, "How to Win the Primary by Really Trying."

135 Vin McLellan, "Father Drinan: A Victory in the Rain," *Boston Phoenix*, September 26, 1970.

136 Healy, "Drinan Victory Upset of the Year."

137 Robert Healey, "The Message of Drinan Win," *Boston Globe*, September 27, 1970.

138 Friedman, "How to Win the Primary by Really Trying."

139 "New Politics and Old," *Time*, September 28, 1970; R. W. Apple Jr., "Some Post-Primary Observations," *New York Times*, September 17, 1970.

140 "Computer, Enthusiastic Workers," *Boston Globe*, September 17, 1970.

141 Bill Kovach, "Liberal Shift Detected in Massachusetts Vote," *New York Times*, September 17, 1970.

142 Grossman, "From Stuart Hughes to Robert Drinan."

143 J. Anthony Lukas, "As Massachusetts Went—I'm from Massachusetts, Don't Blame Me, " *New York Times*, January 14, 1973.

6 A New Center

1   George McGovern, "Address before the Association of Technical Professionals, Inc., at Bentley College," April 17, 1972; box 98, folder "Jobs," GSM.

2   Richard Bergholz, "McGovern Urges Year of Aid for Jobless Defense Workers," *Los Angeles Times*, May 21, 1972.

3   Lanny J. Davis, *The Emerging Democratic Majority: Lessons and Legacies from the New Politics* (New York: Stein and Day, 1974), 213; John B. Judis and Ruy Teixeira, *The Emerging Democratic Majority* (New York: Scribner, 2002), 38.

4   Hunter S. Thompson, *Fear and Loathing: On the Campaign Trail '72* (New York: Popular Library, 1973), 478.

5   Bruce Miroff similarly contends that the McGovern campaign produced a new generation of political operatives who came to reshape the party. See Bruce Miroff, *The Liberals' Moment: The McGovern Insurgency and the Identity Crisis of the Democratic Party* (Lawrence: Kansas University Press, 2007), 3–4, 260–78.

6   Davis, *Emerging Democratic Majority*.

7   For more about the relationship between the McGovern campaign and organized labor, see Jefferson Cowie, *Stayin Alive: The 1970s and the Last Days of the Working Class* (New York: New Press, 2010), 75–124.

8   Berkeley Rice, "Down and Out Along Route 128," *New York Times*, November 1, 1970; Gene Smith, "Slowdown on Route 128," *New York Times*, October 11, 1970.

9   Smith, "Slowdown on Route 128."

10   Rice, "Down and Out Along Route 128."

11   Henry R. Leberman, "Technology: Alchemist of Route 128; Boston's 'Golden Semicircle,'" *New York Times*, January 8, 1968; Rice, "Down and Out Along Route 128."

12   Richard D. Lyons, "Science Jobs That Were," *New York Times*, November 8, 1970.

13   Rice, "Down and Out Along Route 128."

14   For more on this debate, see Robert Zussman, *Mechanics of the Middle Class: Work and Politics Among American Engineers* (Berkeley: University of California Press, 1985), 160–73; Geoffrey W. Latta, "Union Organization among Engineers: A Current Assessment," *Industrial and Labor Relations Review* (October 1981): 29–42; George Strauss, "Professional or Employee-Oriented: Dilemma for Engineering Unions," *Industrial and Labor Relations Review* (July 1964): 519–33.

15   Deborah Shapley, "Unionization: Scientists, Engineers Mull over One Alternative," *Science* (May 12, 1972): 618–21.

16   Shapley, "Unionization Scientists, Engineers Mull over One Alternative"; Paula Leventman, *Professionals Out of Work* (New York: Free Press, 1981), 175–176.

17   Leventman, *Professionals Out of Work*, 175–76; John W. Riegel, *Collective Bargaining as Viewed by Unorganized Engineers and Scientists* (Ann Arbor: Bureau of Industrial Relations, University of Michigan, 1959), 6–7.

18   Shapley, "Unionization: Scientists, Engineers Mull over One Alternative."

19   Leventman, *Professionals Out of Work*, 175.

20   Shapley, "Unionization: Scientists, Engineers Mull over One Alternative."

21   Berkeley, "Down and Out Along Route 128."

22   "The Unionization of Attorneys," *Columbia Law Review* (January 1971): 100–117; Lionel S. Lewis and Michael N. Ryan, "The American Professoriate and the Movement toward Unionization," *Higher Education* (May 1977): 139–64. For a more contemporary discussion of the difficulties of creating alliances between labor and white-collar professionals, see Thomas Geoghegan, *Which Side Are You On? Trying to Be for Labor When It's Flat on Its Back* (New York: New Press, 1991), 3–8, 276–87.

23 Evelyn Keene, "From Pulpit, Jobless Engineer Tells What It's Like," *Boston Globe*, December 28, 1970.

24 Evelyn Keene, "Groups Spring Up to Console the Jobless," *Boston Globe*, January 17, 1971.

25 Joan Millman, "Self-Help for the Jobless," *Boston Herald*, September 5, 1971.

26 Lucinda Smith, "Groups Help Jobless Help Themselves," *Boston Globe*, June 13, 1971.

27 Keene, "Groups Spring Up to Console the Jobless."

28 Smith, "Groups Help Jobless Help Themselves."

29 Keene, "Groups Spring Up to Console the Jobless."

30 Keene, "Groups Spring Up to Console the Jobless."

31 Deckle McClean, "Causes and Caucuses," *Boston Sunday Globe Magazine*, April 12, 1970.

32 Martin F. Nolan, "Drinan Plans to Meet with '128' Jobless," *Boston Globe*, January 7, 1971; Robert F. Drinan "The Unprecedented Challenge Confronting the Economy of Massachusetts," excerpts from address at Fitchburg Rotary Club, January 4, 1972, RFD.

33 Keene, "Groups Spring Up to Console the Jobless."

34 Keene, "Groups Spring Up to Console the Jobless"; Association of Technical Professionals, newsletter, February 1, 1972, box 103, folder "Science and Technology," GSM.

35 John Thomas, "Unemployed Scientists Plead for Help," *Boston Globe*, June 24, 1971; Edward Witten, "Unemployment of Scientists and Engineers," ca. 1972, box 86, folder "Employment 1972," GSM.

36 "Testimony of Dr. Arthur S. Obermayer, Hearings on Research Development House Select Committee on Small Business Subcommittee on Government Procurement," Washington, DC, November 17, 1971, box 96, folder "Employment 1972," GSM.

37 Deborah Shapley, "Route 128: Jobless in a Dilemma about Politics, Their Professions," *Science* (June 11, 1971).

38 Miroff, *The Liberals' Moment*, 132.

39 George S. McGovern, *Grassroots: The Autobiography of George McGovern* (New York: Random House, 1977), 96–98.

40 George S. McGovern, "Remarks Announcing Candidacy for the 1972 Democratic Presidential Nomination," January 18, 1971, available online by Gerhard Peters and John T. Woolley, *The American Presidency Project*, http://www.presidency.ucsb.edu/ws/?pid=77815.

41 Citizens for McGovern, newsletter, April 30, 1971, box 33, CPPAX-UMB.

42 Davis, *Emerging Democratic Majority*, 106.

43 Robert Healy, "McGovern and the Professors," *Boston Globe*, May 14, 1971; Edwin Kuh to Ed O'Donnell, May 6, 1971, GSM; McGovern for President, "McGovern Names Economic Advisory Panel," November 7, 1971, box 95, folder "Economists-General," GSM; Robert Reinhold, "Scholars Starting to Advise McGovern," *New York Times*, June 18, 1972.

44 Charles I. Clough Jr., Daniel E. Power, and Emily Frankovich to George McGovern, July 2, 1971, box 112, folder "Massachusetts," GSM.

45 Charles I. Clough Jr., Daniel E. Power, and Emily Frankovich to George McGovern, July 7, 1971, box 112, folder "Massachusetts," GSM; "Senator McGovern Claims Jump on Candidates Helping Him Get Funds," *Lexington Minute-Man*, October 14, 1971.

46 Edwin Kuh to George McGovern, October 12, 1971, box 95, folder 95, GSM.

47 Patrick H. Caddell to Senator George McGovern, December 29, 1971, box 29, folder "Cambridge Survey Research, Patrick Caddell, General, 12/71–2/72," FFM.

48 "Sen. McGovern Claims Jump on Candidates Helping Him Get Funds," *Lexington Minute-Man*, October 14, 1971.

49 Emily Frankovich to District Contacts for the McGovern Campaign, June 7, 1971, box 33, CPPAX-UMB; Emily Frankovich to Richard Cauchi, ca. June 1971, box 33, CPPAX-UMB; "McGovern for President Organizes in Newton," *Newton Free Press*, January 12, 1972.

50 "Grossman Outlines Liberal Plan to Capture '72 Delegate Seats," *Newton Times*, October 6, 1971.

51 Bill Kovach, "McCarthy, Casually, Enters the '72 Race," *New York Times*, December 18, 1971.

52 Robert Jordan, "Mass Caucus Upsets Critics," *Boston Globe*, December 23, 1971.

53 Jordan, "Mass Caucus Upsets Critics."

54 Richard M. Weintraub, "Contest Developing for Mass Caucus," *Boston Globe*, January 9, 1972.

55 Emily Frankovich, interview by Bonnie Jones, February 28, 1992, LOHP.

56 Gordon Lee Weil, *The Long Shot: George McGovern Runs for President* (New York: W. W. Norton, 1973), 56–57.

57 Martin F. Nolan, "McGovern Staff Sees Victory in Caucus Vote," *Boston Globe*, January 19, 1972; Christopher Lydon, "Liberals in Florida and Pennsylvania Favor McGovern," *New York Times*, January 24, 1972; Thomas P. Ronan, "McGovern Gains Coalition's Vote," *New York Times*, January 30, 1972.

58 Jerome Grossman, *Relentless Liberal* (New York: Vantage Press, 1996), 68.

59 Mass PAX, *Coordinators' Bulletin*, March 9, 1972, box 5, folder 5.3, CPPAX-UMB.

60 Christopher Lydon, "McGovern's Route to the Top," *New York Times*, June 11, 1972.

61 Testimony of Dr. Arthur S. Obermayer.

62 Harvey Brooks to Arthur S. Obermayer, April 10, 1972, box 96, folder "Employment 1972," GSM. Obermayer's company, Moleculon, was itself later at the center of a high-profile patent dispute over the Rubik's cube. See David E. Sanger, "Rubik's Rival," *New York Times*, June 6, 1982.

63 McGovern, "Address before the Association of Technical Professionals, Inc."

64 Arthur Obermayer to John Holum, April 1972, box 94, folder "Economic Conversion, 1972," GSM.

65 Leventman, *Professionals Out of Work*, 191.

66 Miroff, *The Liberals' Moment*, 190.

67 Miroff, *The Liberals' Moment*, 58–59.

68 Cowie, *Stayin' Alive*, 3–7, 95–105.

69 Christopher Lydon, "McGovern Backers Decry One-Issue Image, but Vietnam Remains as the Key Factor in His Campaign," *New York Times*, February 22, 1972.

70 McGovern for President, "McGovern Education and Property Tax Relief Plan," Monday January 31, 1972, box 24, folder "Press Releases, 1/72," FFM.

71 Cambridge Survey Research, "McGovern in Massachusetts: A Short Report on the Last Poll," April 23, 1972, box 30, folder "Cambridge Survey Research: Short Report on Massachusetts," FFM.

72 Cambridge Survey Research, "McGovern in Massachusetts: A Short Report on the Last Poll."

73 William V. Shannon, "The Legends of George McGovern," *New York Times*, July 2, 1972.

74 Robert Healy, "Blue Collars, Suburbs, and Youth Give George a Big Win," *Boston Globe*, April 26, 1972.

75 John J. Goldman and David Lamb, "Boston Precinct: From Hicks to McGovern," *Los Angeles Times*, April 27, 1972.

76 "McGovern Campaign, South Boston District 9, Ward 6, Precinct 6," ca. April 1972, box 21, folder "Massachusetts," FFM.

77 Paul Wieck, "The Case of Massachusetts," *New Republic*, February 1, 1969, 25.

78 Healy, "Blue Collars, Suburbs, and Youth."

79 Jonathan Fuerbringer, "McGovern Links Victory to His 'New Democrats,'" *Boston Evening Globe*, April 26, 1972.

80 William V. Shannon, "The Legends of George McGovern," *New York Times*, July 2, 1972.

81 Larry Goldstein to John Holum, Subject: McGovern Committee on Peacetime Jobs, 1972, box 94, folder "Economic Conversion," GSM.

82   Arthur Obermayer to John Holem [*sic*], Sandy Berger, and Irena Neal, ca. 1972, box 94, folder "Economic Conversion," GSM.

83   McGovern for President, press release, May 17, 1972, box 158, folder "Primaries California," GSM.

84   H. Erich Heinemann, "McGovern Aide Calls Jobs Chief Goal," *New York Times*, July 9, 1972.

85   Weil, *The Long Shot*, 74–87.

86   McGovern for President, "California Campaign," press release, May 30, 1972, box 158, folder "Primaries California," GSM.

87   Larry Goldstein to John Holum, Subject: McGovern Committee on Peacetime Jobs; McGovern for President, "California Campaign."

88   John H[olum] to George McGovern, in re: Events Thursday, ca. 1972, Box 158, folder "California Primaries," GSM; Scientists for George McGovern, "NEW Priorities with NEW Technologies," ca. 1972, box 179, folder "Campaign Literature Target Special Groups," GSM.

89   McGovern for President, "Your Job and Peace: If You Vote for McGovern, You Won't Have to Choose Between Them," leaflet passed out at California Lockheed Plant, June 2, 1972, box 158, folder "Primaries California," GSM. There was some debate about the effectiveness of this drive, and whether Humphrey or McGovern won aerospace workers in California. See Deborah Shapely, "McGovern: Conversion Plans Spell Upheavals for Scientists," *Science* (August 11, 1972): 505.

90   George McGovern, "Peace and Jobs: An Alternative Economic Policy for California," ca. 1972, box 158, folder "California Primaries," GSM.

91   Howard Seelye, "2 Housewives Shift McGovern Drive into High Gear," *Los Angeles Times*, May 14, 1972.

92   David S. Broder, "McGovern Canvassing Tactic Tested, *Washington Post*, May 29, 1972.

93   See, for instance, Christopher Lydon, "On McGovern and Goldwater …," *New York Times*, May 6, 1972; Rowland Evens and Robert Novak, "Anybody But McGovern," *Washington Post*, April 6, 1972; "McGovern Not Goldwater," *Life*, June 16, 1972; "How Voters Assess George McGovern v. Richard Nixon," *Time*, July 17, 1972.

94   D.J.R. Bruckner, "Humphrey Has Not Shifted; the Voters Have—to McGovern," *Los Angeles Times*, June 5, 1972; Steven Roberts, "Volunteers in Storefronts Pressing McGovern's Campaign," *New York Times*, September 17, 1972; Davis, *Emerging Democratic Majority*, 164.

95   Byron Schafer, *Quiet Revolution: The Struggle for the Democratic Party and the Shaping of Post-Reform Politics* (New York: Russell Sage Foundation, 1983), 8.

96   Statement of Jerome Grossman before the National Democratic Committee's Commission on Party Structure and Delegate Selection, Boston, Massachusetts, July 10, 1969, box 5, folder 5.27, CPPAX-UMB.

97   For more on the absence of labor in the reform process, see Cowie, *Stayin' Alive*, 87–88.

98   Schafer, *Quiet Revolution*, 129.

99   For more on the McGovern Commission and its significance, see Schafer, *Quiet Revolution*; Miroff, *Liberals' Moment*, 19–23; Judith Stein, *Pivotal Decade: How the United States Traded Factories for Finance in the Seventies* (New Haven, CT: Yale University Press, 2010), 51–57.

100   Cowie, *Stayin' Alive*, 88.

101   Weil, *The Long Shot*, 128–29.

102   McGovern, *Grassroots*, 141–42.

103   "CPP Pushes for Reform Presidential Primary This Week," *Lexington Minute-Man*, July 1, 1971; Emily Weston Frankovich, "Delegate-Choosing Reform Looms for '72," *Boston Globe*, May 10, 1971; "Coming Reforms on Elections," *Boston Globe*, June 5, 1971.

104   Richard Weintraub, "Bay State Democrats Change Process of Selecting Candidate," *Boston Globe*, December 19, 1971.

105   Schafer, *The Quiet Revolution*, 8.

106   Citizens for Participation Politics, newsletter, vol. 4, no. 2 (April 20, 1972), box 6, folder 6.11, CPPAX-UMB.

107   Mass PAX, *Coordinators' Bulletin*, January 29, 1972, box 5, folder 5.3, CPPAX-UMB.

108   Citizens for Participation Politics, newsletter, vol. 4, no. 2 (April 20, 1972).

109   "Massachusetts Delegate Profile," *Boston Sunday Globe*, July 9, 1972.

110   "!!!KNOW ANITA . . . MCGOVERN SUPPORTER!!!" ca. 1972, RFD.

111   Michael Kenney, "White Sees Two-to-One Defeat for Party's Big Names," *Boston Globe*, April 26, 1972.

112   R. W. Apple Jr., "Delegate Reforms Bring New Types to the Convention," *New York Times*, July 9, 1972; "Party Delegates Are New Breed," *New York Times*, June 25, 1972.

113   Betty Levin, "Area Demo Delegates React to 'New Politics,'" *Lexington Minute-Man Supplement*, July 20, 1972.

114   Committee to Elect the McGovern Slate Letter, April 29, 1972, RFD.

115   Massachusetts Delegation, "Massachusetts, 102 Delegates," n.d., box 165, folder "Massachusetts Delegates," GSM.

116   Richard M. Weintraub, "Floor Rift Threatened Bay State Unity," *Boston Evening Globe*, July 20, 1972.

117   Levin, "Area Demo Delegates React to 'New Politics.'"

118   Weintraub, "Floor Rift Threatened Bay State Unity."

119   Warren Weaver Jr., "New York's Bloc Is a Model of Unity," *New York Times*, July 13, 1972.

120   Miroff, *The Liberals' Moment*, 1, 84–97.

121   Max Frankel, "The McGovern 'Gap' Is Closing," *New York Times*, September 27, 1972.

122   "McGovern Claims He Has Peacetime Job Plan; Nixon Doesn't," *Daytona Beach Morning Journal*, October 30, 1972.

123   Arthur Obermayer to John Holum, re: Possible McGovern Commitment to Assure Technical Community of an Orderly Transition, ca. 1972, box 94, folder "Economic Conversion," GSM; Weil, *The Long Shot*, 112–13; "McGovern Reassures Technocrats," *New Scientist*, November 2, 1972; "Response of Senator George McGovern to Questions from The Electrics Engineer," ca. 1972, box 98, folder "Jobs," GSM.

124   "McGovern Reassures Technocrats."

125   J. Anthony Lukas, "As Massachusetts Went—I'm from Massachusetts, Don't Blame Me," *New York Times*, January 14, 1973.

126   David Nyhan, "It Was a Ho-hum Presidential Campaign in Massachusetts," *Boston Globe*, November 5, 1972.

127   "McGovern Fund Day Wednesday," *Boston Globe*, October 5, 1972.

128   "McGovern 49%, Nixon 39% in Bay State," *Boston Globe*, November 5, 1972.

129   Theodore White, *Making of the President 1968* (New York: Athenaeum House, 1969), 109.

130   Lukas, "As Massachusetts Went"; Bob Sales, "To Bay Staters; The Other 49 Are Out of Step," *Boston Globe*, November 9, 1972; David Nyhan, "Bay State a Lonely Outpost of Camelot in Nixon Sweep," *Boston Globe*, November 9, 1972; Fred Pillsbury, "Bay State Now Political Island," *Boston Globe*, November 9, 1972.

131   Davis, *Emerging Democratic Majority*, 213; R. W. Apple Jr., "As Goes Skokie . . . ," *New York Times*, November 3, 1974.

132   Davis, *Emerging Democratic Majority*, 213–14.

133   Steven V. Roberts, "Democratic Delegate, '72 Version: Michael Arnold Rappeport," *New York Times*, July 11, 1972.

134   Judis and Teixeira, *Emerging Democratic Majority*, 120; Kevin Phillips, *Mediacracy: American Parties and Politics in the Communications Age* (Garden City, NY: Doubleday and Company, 1975), 191–228.

135   Davis, *Emerging Democratic Majority*, 224.

7   Open Suburbs vs. Open Space

1   Frederick Andelman to the editor, *Newton Graphic*, May 14, 1970.

2   "Liberalism in the Suburbs," *Newsweek*, July 6, 1970.

3   Charles M. Haar and Demetrius S. Iatridis, *Housing the Poor in Suburbia: Public Policy at the Grass Roots* (Cambridge, MA: Ballinger Publishing, 1974), 16–17. For more on the national efforts to "open" the suburbs, see "The Battle Over the Suburbs," *Newsweek*, November 15, 1971. See also Anthony Downs, *Opening Up the Suburbs: An Urban Strategy for America* (New Haven, CT: Yale University Press, 1973); Nancy Morgan, "N.A.A.C.P to Fight Suburban Zoning," *New York Times*, December 7, 1969.

4   Most accounts of the battles to challenge the structures of suburban exclusion have focused on the federal government and the ways in which Nixon effectively squandered this moment of opportunity by promoting a fierce opposition to government-imposed integration. See Christopher Bonastia, *Knocking on the Door: The Federal Government's Attempt to Desegregate the Suburbs* (Princeton, NJ: Princeton University Press, 2006); Charles M. Lamb, *Housing Segregation in Suburban America since 1960* (New York: Cambridge University Press, 2005). For two books that have gone beyond the purview of the federal government, see Michael N. Danielson, *The Politics of Exclusion* (New York: Columbia University Press, 1976); David L. Kirp, John P. Sawyer, and Larry Rosenthal, *Our Town: Race, Housing, and the Soul of Suburbia* (New Brunswick, NJ: Rutgers University Press, 1997).

5   "The Battle Over the Suburbs."

6   Robert O. Self, *American Babylon: Race and the Struggle for Postwar Oakland* (Princeton, NJ: Princeton University Press, 2003), 270–72.

7   US National Advisory Commission on Civil Disorders, *Report of the National Advisory Commission on Civil Disorders* (New York: New York Times, 1968), 2.

8   Daniels, *The Politics of Exclusion*, 80.

9   For more on Romney's commitment to ending residential segregation in the suburbs and building more mixed-income developments, see Bonastia, *Knocking on the Door*, 91–121.

10   "Group Proposes Formation of Responsibility Comm," *Lexington Minute-Man*, June 13, 1968; "Responsibility Committee to Begin Work by July 1," *Lexington Minute-Man*, June 20, 1968; "Lincoln Nonprofit Group to Move Houses, Plan Moderate Income Project," *Fence Viewer*, June 6, 1968; "Heat from the Audience but None from the Furnace," *Concord Journal*, February 4, 1971.

11   "WILPF Actively Works for Understanding of the 'Ghettos,'" *Concord Journal*, March 28, 1968.

12   League of Women Voters of Concord-Carlisle, "A Survey of Housing in Concord," October 1970, CPC.

13   Sadelle Sacks, "An Open Door to Integrated Housing in Metropolitan Boston," 1966, box 55, folder 2230, FH.

14   Citizens Housing and Planning Association, "Federation Instructs Suburban Chapters," *CHPA Letter* 2, no. 3, box 16, folder 9, MIT-SC.

15   Craig et al. to Conantum Residents, June 25, 1968, CHOCR; Moderate Income Housing for Concord Committee, "Minutes of Meeting," September 11, 1968, CHOC-CPL; Con-

cord Home Owning Corporation, "A Proposal for a Moderate Income Apartment Complex in Concord," ca. 1970, CHOC-CPL.

16 Newton Community Development Foundation, "Housing for Families of Moderate and Low Income in Newton," 1969, box 4, folder 3, PMR; Newton Community Development Foundation, "Facts About the Newton Community Development Foundation (NCDF)," May 1970, box 4, folder 3, PMR; Concord Home Owning Corporation, "Application to Massachusetts Housing Financing Agency, Draft," ca. 1970, CHOC-CPL.

17 Haar and Iatridis, *Housing the Poor in Suburbia*, 156.

18 Winthrop P. Baker and Jim Lightfoot, "Action on the Suburban Housing Front," WBZ-TV and radio, April 17, 1970, box 4, folder 3, PMR.

19 Newton Community Development Foundation, "Housing for Families of Moderate and Low Income in Newton."

20 Newton Community Development Foundation, "Housing for Families of Moderate and Low Income in Newton."

21 Massachusetts Housing Finance Agency, "Third Annual Report," September 1971, SLM; Concord Home Owning Corporation and Moderate Income Housing Committee, "Meeting Minutes," January 14, 1970, CHOC-CPL; Concord Home Owning Corporation, "Memo, re: Moderate Income Housing," n.d., CHOC-CPL.

22 Concord Home Owning Corporation, "A Proposal for a Moderate Income Apartment Complex in Concord."

23 Concord Home Owning Corporation, "A Proposal for a Moderate Income Apartment Complex in Concord."

24 The Concord group, however, spoke to municipal employees and senior citizens in addition to contacting METCO and several town agencies. See Haar and Iatridis, *Housing the Poor in Suburbia*, 147.

25 Concord Home Owning Corporation, "A Proposal for a Moderate Income Apartment Complex in Concord."

26 Concord Home Owning Corporation, "A Proposal for a Moderate Income Apartment Complex in Concord."

27 Newton Community Development Foundation, "Newton ... No Ordinary Suburb," December 1969, NPL.

28 Concord Home Owning Corporation, "Application to Massachusetts Housing Financing Agency, Draft."

29 Concord Home Owning Corporation, "Application to Massachusetts Housing Financing Agency, Draft"; Newton Community Development Foundation, "Newton ... No Ordinary Suburb"; Concord Home Owning Corporation, "A Proposal for a Moderate Income Apartment Complex in Concord."

30 Newton Community Development Foundation, "Housing for Families of Moderate and Low Income in Newton."

31 Martin S. Kaplan and Honora A. Kaplan to the editor, *Newton Graphic*, May 21, 1970.

32 D. Elliot Wilbur Jr. to the editor, *Concord Journal*, December 2, 1971.

33 Stephen M. Adelson to the editor, *Newton Graphic*, May 7, 1970.

34 Michael and Mary Feld, *Newton Graphic*, May 21, 1970; Mr. and Mrs. Arnold Lezberg to the editor, *Newton Graphic*, May 28, 1970.

35 Haar and Iatridis, *Housing the Poor in Suburbia*, 78

36 Newton Land Use and Civic Association, "Have You Heard What's Happening in Newton???" ca. 1970, box 4, folder 11, PMR.

37 City of Newton, "Annual Report of the City of Newton," 1967, 1970, 1972, NPL.

38 Newton Community Development Foundation, "Newton ... No Ordinary Suburb."

39 Mr. and Mrs. Bernard Gitlin to the editor, *Newton Graphic*, May 28, 1970.

40 Haar and Iatridis, *Housing the Poor in Suburbia*, 120.

41   Haar and Iatridis, *Housing the Poor in Suburbia*, 82. See also Anonymous to the editor, *Newton Graphic*, July 16, 1970.

42   "1000 Jam Hearing for Planned Housing Here," *Newton Graphic*, May 28, 1970.

43   Haar and Iatridis, *Housing the Poor in Suburbia*, 83.

44   "Secretary Romney Backs NCDF Plans," *Newton Graphic*, June 4, 1970.

45   Haar and Iatridis, *Housing the Poor in Suburbia*, 108–9.

46   League of Women Voters of Concord-Carlisle, "A Survey of Housing in Concord," October 1970, CPC.

47   Haar and Iatridis, *Housing the Poor in Suburbia*, 142.

48   Haar and Iatridis, *Housing the Poor in Suburbia*, 145.

49   James Craig to the Board of Appeals, Concord, February 10, 1971, CHOC-CPL.

50   Swamp Brook Preservation Association, "Apartments Proposed for the Wheeler Land—Again!" ca. 1970, box 1, folder 1, SBPA-CPL; Commonwealth of Massachusetts, Department of Natural Resources, file no. 137–4 Concord, Boston, May 29, 1974, box 2, SBPA-CPL; Edith A. Sisson to the editor, *Concord Journal*, January 16, 1969.

51   Edith A. Sisson, "Problems of the Wheeler Site for High Density Development," January 20, 1971, box 1, folder 1, SBPA-CPL.

52   Charles H. W. Foster, "Wetland Values: Are They Fact or Fiction?" *Massachusetts Audubon* (November–December 1958): 56–61.

53   Fred P. Bosselman and David L. Callies, *The Quiet Revolution in Land Use Control* (Washington, DC: US Council on Environmental Quality, 1971), 205–34; "Inland Wetlands Victory," *Conservation Leader*, September 1968, box 7, folder 90, LER.

54   Town of Concord Planning Board and Natural Resources Commission, "Wetlands Protection Act in Concord," n.d., CPC.

55   Swamp Brook Preservation Association, "Apartments Proposed for the Wheeler Land—Again!"

56   Edith A. Sisson to Board of Appeals, Concord, January 27, 1971, box 1, folder 1, SBPA-CPL.

57   Concord Home Owning Corporation, "A Proposal for a Moderate Income Apartment Complex in Concord."

58   Concord Finance Committee, "Annual Report of the Finance Committee and Warrant with Recommendations to the Town Meeting of March 2, 1970, Concord, MA," CSC. See also League of Women Voters of Concord-Carlisle, "A Survey of Housing in Concord," October 1970, CPC.

59   Concord Department of Natural Resources, "Natural Resources Report," July 1972, CDNR.

60   "Appeals Board Turns Down Request of Concord Homeowning Corporation," *Concord Journal*, April 15, 1971.

61   Karen Jean Schneider, "Innovation in State Legislation: The Massachusetts Suburban Zoning Act" (honor's thesis, Radcliffe College, 1970).

62   "Time to Unlock Suburbia," *Boston Herald Traveler*, August 12, 1969; "Snob Zoning Reform," *Boston Globe*, August 8, 1969.

63   Martin A. Linsky and Maurice E. Frye, "What Suburban Zoning Will Do," *Boston Globe*, August 22, 1969; Department of Community Affairs, "Rules and Regulations for the Conduct of Hearings by the Housing Appeals Committee Affairs, Draft," February 12, 1970, box 108, folder "Housing Legislation," FWS.

64   Sumner Z. Kaplan to Members of the General Court, July 1, 1969, box 112, folder "Low-Moderate-Income Housing Legislation," FWS.

65   Committee for Better Communities, "The Zoning Bill: How It Works," box 112, folder "Low-Moderate-Income Housing Legislation," FWS.

66   Schneider, "Innovation in State Legislation."

67   Evelyn Keene, "Suburbs of Boston Resist Housing Projects for Persons with Low-Income," *Boston Globe*, May 9, 1971.

68   Schneider, "Innovation in State Legislation."

69   Thomas C. Gallagher, "Reform for Reformers," *Boston Herald Traveler*, August 6, 1969.

70   James Breagy, *Overriding the Suburbs: State Intervention through the Massachusetts Appeals Process* (Boston: Citizens Housing and Planning Association of Metropolitan Boston, 1976).

71   Gallagher, "Reform for the Reformers."

72   See Chapter 774 of the Acts and Resolves of 1969 (New Chapter 40B of the General Laws).

73   Breagy, *Overriding the Suburbs*.

74   Evelyn Keene, "State's 'Snob Zoning' Law: A Challenge to Suburban Beliefs," *Boston Globe*, January 4, 1970.

75   Anthony J. Yudis, "Anti-Snob Zoning Batting Big .000," *Boston Globe*, July 7, 1971.

76   Yudis, "Anti-Snob Zoning Batting Big .000"; "MAPC Report Reveals Anti-Snob Zoning Law Ineffective since '69," *Minute-Man Supplement*, April 16, 1972.

77   Yudis, "Anti-Snob Zoning Batting Big .000." See also Samuel Mintz Testimony to Commonwealth of Massachusetts Joint Legislative Committee on Urban Affairs, Housing Conference, June 10, 1970, SLM.

78   For more on these amendments, see Bosselman and Callies, *The Quiet Revolution*, 168–69.

79   Keene, "State's 'Snob Zoning' Law"; Evelyn Keene, "Antisnob Zoning Law Fails, but Succeeds," *Boston Globe*, January 3, 1971.

80   Keene, "Antisnob Zoning Law Fails, but Succeeds."

81   Breagy, *Overriding the Suburbs*.

82   "Suburban Responsibility Comm. Discusses Program," *Lexington Minute-Man*, September 12, 1968; Roberta Leviton, "Affordable Housing in a Suburban Town: Lexington Massachusetts," November 1987, Lexington Planning Department, LPL.

83   "Final TM Session Approves RH Zone," *Lexington Minute-Man*, April 8, 1971.

84   Joan Mahoney, "Lexington Joins Housing Foes," *Boston Evening Globe*, May 4, 1971.

85   "Sufficient Signatures Secured for Referendum," *Lexington Minute-Man*, April 15, 1971; "Lexington to Vote on Housing," *Boston Globe*, May 3, 1971.

86   "Subsidized Housing Defeated 2–1," *Lexington Minute-Man*, May 6, 1971.

87   It even appeared as a streamer across the evening edition of the *Boston Globe* on the day of the vote, May 1, 1971. See Martin F. Nolan, "Hottest Issue, '70s: Low-Income Homes," *Boston Globe*, May 11, 1971; "Lexington Shuts the Door," *Boston Globe*, May 9, 1971; Tom Paine, "Lexington Says It All," *Concord Journal*, May 4, 1971.

88   James v. Valtierra, 402 U.S. 137 (1971); Matthew D. Lassiter, *The Silent Majority: Suburban Politics in the Sunbelt South* (Princeton, NJ: Princeton University Press, 2006), 137–38. For more on *James v. Valtierra*, see Aaron I. Cavin, "The Borders of Citizenship: Latinos, Asian Americans, and Metropolitan Politics in Silicon Valley, 1945–2000" (PhD diss., University of Michigan, 2012).

89   Paul Davidoff, "Pro," *New York Times*, November 4, 1973; Linda Greenhouse, "Battle Lines in the Suburbs," *New York Times*, January 28, 1973.

90   Danielson, *The Politics of Exclusion*, 85; Martin F. Nolan, "The City Politic: Showdown Vote in Northern Westchester," *New York*, June 4, 1973; "Land Use: The Rage for Reform," *Time*, October 1, 1973.

91   Lamb, *Housing Segregation in Suburban America*, 142–43.

92   William J. White, "Statement by the Executive Director," in "Annual Report 1974," by the Massachusetts Housing Finance Agency, September 1974, SLM.

93   John H. Clymer to Paul Counihan Memorandum, re: Concord Homeowning Corpora-
     tion—Common Approach to Chapter 774 Cases, August 20, 1971, CHOC-CPL; Haar
     and Iatridis, *Housing the Poor in Suburbia*, 156.

94   Board of Appeals of Hanover v. Housing Appeals Committee in Dept. of Community
     Affairs, 363 Mass. 339, 294 N.E.2d 393 (Mass. 1973); Leonard S. Rubinowitz, *Low-Income
     Housing: Suburban Strategies* (Cambridge, MA: Ballinger Publishing, 1974), 88–89.

95   John O'Keefe, "Touro Ruling Clears Way for Development of 5,548 Units of Low-Income
     Housing," *Boston Globe*, March 26, 1973; Evelyn Keene, "Snob Zoning Rule Only Opens
     Door for Developers," *Boston Evening Globe*, March 23, 1973. For more on the benefits
     and drawbacks of using state courts to challenge suburban exclusion, see Danielson, *The
     Politics of Exclusion*, 159–98. For a discussion of New Jersey's Mount Laurel case, see Kirp,
     Sawyer, and Rosenthal, *Our Town*.

96   Lawrence Susskind, ed., *The Land Use Controversy in Massachusetts: Case Studies and Policy
     Options* (Cambridge, MA: MIT Press, 1975), 11; "A Share of the Suburbs," *Boston Globe*,
     May 25, 1975; Anne Kircheimer, "Progress Report on Snob Zoning," *Boston Globe*, No-
     vember 1, 1975.

97   Anne R. Scigliano, "Appeals Decision Overruled, Interfaith Wins HAC Case," *Lexington
     Minute-Man*, August 30, 1973; Ann R. Scigliano, "Judge Rules in Favor of Interfaith
     Housing," *Lexington Minute-Man*, October 3, 1974.

98   Planning Office for Urban Affairs, "Archdiocese of Boston, Summary of the Archdioce-
     san Housing Program," ca. 1974, box 32, folder "Interfaith Housing," FWS; Susskind, *Land
     Use Controversy*, 116.

99   Leviton, "Affordable Housing in a Suburban Town."

100 James S. Craig to Robert C. Casselman, February 16, 1971, CHOC-CPL.

101 "NCDF Seeks Permit for Local Housing," *Newton Graphic*, April 29, 1971.

102 Haar and Iatridis, *Housing the Poor in Suburbia*, 116–17.

103 Liz Roman Gallese, "Suburban Stall: Housing for the Poor Blocked Despite Curb on
     'Snob Zoning' Laws," *Wall Street Journal*, October 17, 1972.

104 Gallese, "Suburban Stall."

105 For instance, the Trinity Episcopal Church in Concord roughly went from a member-
     ship of two thousand to five hundred over the course of the 1970s. Reverend David Bar-
     ney later stated that "most large New England mainline parishes or congregations . . . of
     large size in New England lost from 2/3 to 3/4 of their membership in those decades."
     David Barney, interview by Renee Garrelick, February 22, 2001, COHP.

106 Massachusetts Advisory Committee to the US Commission on Civil Rights and Massa-
     chusetts Commission against Discrimination, *Route 128: Boston's Road to Segregation*
     (Washington, DC: US Commission on Civil Rights, 1975), 57.

107 Danielson, *The Politics of Exclusion*, 126–27.

108 "NCDF, Towers Pass Board," *Newton Graphic*, February 7, 1974; Haar and Iatridis, *Housing
     the Poor in Suburbia*, 128–31.

109 "120 NHA Units of Low-Income Housing Here," *Newton Graphic*, February 25, 1971.

110 "Town Won't Appeal Supreme Court Ruling," *Concord Journal*, April 5, 1973.

111 Bosselman and Callies, *The Quiet Revolution*.

112 Edith A. Sisson to the editor, *Concord Journal*, November 25, 1971.

113 Sisson to the editor, *Concord Journal*, November 25, 1971.

114 Linda Baker, "CHOC Hearing Opens before State DNR," *Concord Free Press*, May 23, 1974;
     Commonwealth of Massachusetts, Department of Natural Resources, file no. 137–4, Con-
     cord, Boston, June 10, 1974, box 2, SBPA-CPL; Arthur W Brownell, Commissioner, Mem-
     orandum of Findings and Department of Natural Resource on File No. 137–4, Concord
     Home Owning Corporation, September 30, 1974, box 1, folder 1, SBPA-CPL.

115 "James S. Craig to Dick Neil, President Non-Profit Housing Development Corporation," October 12, 1974, CHOC-CPL; James S. Craig to Concord Homeowning Corp. Members, Memorandum, Subj: Proposed Final Meeting C.H.O.C., May 19, 1980, CHOC-CPL.

116 A. K. Lewis to the editor, *Concord Journal*, October 17, 1974.

117 Concord Natural Resources Commission, "Proposed Conservation Land Acquisitions, 1977," CPL.

118 Concord Natural Resources Commission, "Proposed Conservation Land Acquisitions, 1977." The SBPA, which had both financially and organizationally assisted in the transaction, interpreted the acquisition as a major accomplishment. Tom B. Arnold to Edith Sisson, April 22, 1977, box 1, folder 1, SBPA-CPL.

119 Richard F. Babcock and David L. Callies, "Ecology and Housing: Virtues in Conflict," in *Modernizing Urban Land Policy*, ed. Marion Clawson (Baltimore: Johns Hopkins University Press, 1972), 205–22; Danielson, *The Politics of Exclusion*, 127–28.

120 Massachusetts Advisory Committee to the US Commission on Civil Rights, *Route 128*, xii.

121 Peter S. Canellos, "After 20 Years, Anti-Snob Zoning Found Ineffective," *Boston Globe*, January 21, 1989.

122 Bonnie Heudorfer, *The Record on 40B: The Effectiveness of the Massachusetts Affordable Housing Zoning Law* (Boston: Citizens Housing and Planning Association, 2003).

123 Canellos, "After 20 Years, Anti-Snob Zoning Found Ineffective." See also Alexander von Hoffman, "To Preserve and Protect: Land Use Regulations in Weston, Massachusetts" (Cambridge, MA: Joint Center for Housing Studies, Harvard University, November 2010).

124 As a notable exception to this trend, Lincoln environmental and housing groups worked together to form the nonprofit Lincoln Foundation, which after a six-year endeavor, built a 125-unit project called Lincoln Woods. This project helped Lincoln become one of the few towns in Massachusetts that reached the 10 percent benchmark, although that was easier to reach in a community of roughly seven thousand residents.

125 Josh Harkinson, "NIMBY Notebook: Habitat for Hypocrisy," *Mother Jones*, July 2007; UMass Donahue Institute, "Housing Poll" (prepared for the Citizens Housing and Planning Association, March 23, 2005).

126 Lamb, *Housing Segregation in Suburban America*, 165–203.

8 Tightening the Belt

1 Anonymous to Judge Garrity, September 1974, box 49, folder 5, WAG.

2 See especially Ronald P. Formisano, *Boston against Busing: Race and Ethnicity in the 1960s and 1970s* (Chapel Hill: University of North Carolina Press, 1991); Emmett Buell, *School Desegregation and Defended Neighborhoods* (Lexington, MA: Lexington Books, 1982); J. Anthony Lukas, *Common Ground: A Turbulent Decade in the Lives of Three American Families* (New York: Knopf, 1986); Alan Lupo, *Liberty's Chosen Home: The Politics of Violence in Boston* (Boston: Beacon Press, 1977); George Metcalf, *From Little Rock to Boston* (Westport, CT: Greenwood Press, 1983); J. Michael Ross and William M. Berg, *"I Respectfully Disagree with the Judge's Order": The Boston School Desegregation Controversy* (Washington, DC: University Press of America, 1981); J. Brian Sheehan, *The Boston School Integration Dispute: Social Change and Legal Maneuvers* (New York: Columbia University Press, 1984); Steven Taylor, *Desegregation in Boston and Buffalo: The Influence of Local Leaders* (Albany: State University of New York Press, 1998).

3 Paul Parks to METCO Communities, August 25, 1975, box 11, folder 33, METCO-NUSC; "Memorandum from Gregory R. Anrig to METCO Superintendents," September 2, 1975, box 22, folder 11, METCO-NUSC.

4   For more about how the issue of busing became a means for many people to address broader economic concerns, see Matthew D. Lassiter, *The Silent Majority: Suburban Politics in the Sunbelt South* (Princeton, NJ: Princeton University Press, 2006); Formisano, *Boston against Busing*; Kevin Kruse, *White Flight: Atlanta and the Making of Modern Conservatism* (Princeton, NJ: Princeton University Press, 2005); Jefferson Cowie, *Stayin' Alive: The 1970s and the Last Days of the Working Class* (New York: New Press, 2010).

5   Morgan v. Hennigan, 379 F. Supp. 410 (D.Mass.1974).

6   Legally this strategy worked. Six months later the US Court of Appeals ruled, "In light of the ample factual record and the precedents of the Supreme Court, we do not see how the court could have reached any other decision" (Lukas, *Common Ground*, 238–39).

7   The architect of the state plan, Charles Glenn explained, "We simply took a large map and started moving across the city in a big arc from northwest to southeast, dividing it into districts so that each school would include the right proportions of black and white kids" (Lukas, *Common Ground*, 239).

8   Massachusetts Advisory Committee to the US Commission on Civil Rights and Massachusetts Commission Against Discrimination, *Route 128: Boston's Road to Segregation* (Washington, DC: US Commission on Civil Rights, 1975), xi.

9   Someone Who Just Wants to Be Equal to Judge W. Arthur Garrity, box 49, folder, WAG.

10   "Wellesley Garrity," September 1974, box 49, folder 4, WAG.

11   In the years following his decision Garrity received thousands of letters, demonstrating the range of frustration that Bostonians felt over the desegregation order. Garrity meticulously organized and saved all these letters, which he preserved in chronological order as part of the W. Arthur Garrity Jr. Papers on the Boston Schools Desegregation Case. To protect people's privacy, Garrity stipulated that only a single initial for each author could be published.

12   Anonymous father to Judge Garrity, June 23, 1974, box 49, folder 1, WAG; "Life and Death Drama," September 1974, WAG.

13   Tom Mulligan, "Wellesley Protest," *South Middlesex News*, October 5, 1974; Lukas, *Common Ground*, 244–45.

14   For more about Garrity's background and judicial philosophy, see Lukas, *Common Ground*, 222–25.

15   Lukas, *Common Ground*, 222–51.

16   "A Suggested Letter from Wendell to Southie," February 5, 1975, box 50, folder 19, WAG.

17   Formisano, *Boston against Busing*, 56, 189–90.

18   Robert Reinhold, "More Segregated Than Ever," *New York Times*, September 30, 1973; Boston School Committee, "Proceedings of the School Committee," January 15, 1974.

19   For example, a Roslindale couple who called themselves "United States citizens, lifetime residents of Boston, homeowners in Roslindale, hardworking taxpayers and parents," wrote to Garrity that they "would like our tax money spent for quality education and teachers and not for buses, fuel, police and helicopters and motorcycles around our homes and community constantly." T and M to Judge Garrity, October 8, 1974, box 49, folder 6, WAG.

20   "To Whom It May Concern," September 23, 1974, box 49, folder 5, WAG; Johanne Tallent to the editor, *Boston Herald American*, September 23, 1976.

21   Nick King, "For Metco, It's Been a Topsy-turvy Year," *Boston Globe*, April 24, 1975.

22   In 1973, Kevin White called for equalizing state aid to schools, building magnet schools to attract suburbanites, and significantly expanding the student body and METCO's funding. See Kevin White "Achieving Equal Education in Boston," April 10, 1973, box 4, FWS; Lupo, *Liberty's Chosen Home*, 159–61. In May, 1974, Francis Sargent suggested that instead of mandatory two-way busing, the state should adopt a "freedom of choice" plan for minority children by doubling the size of METCO, increasing the program's budget, creating magnet schools, and giving black parents the option of either an imbalanced

neighborhood school or integrated school elsewhere in the city. See "Sargent's Televised Message on the Racial Imbalance Act," *Boston Globe*, May 11, 1974. Michael Dukakis proposed dividing the city into a dozen equally populated community districts of sixty thousand people each along "historical, geographical and natural boundaries" in order to further the goal of offering integrated learning, and also suggested the expansion of METCO. Michael Dukakis, "Statement on Racial Imbalance and the Boston Schools," May 14, 1974, box 20, folder 649, JHB.

23 Alen Jehlen, "Kathleen Sullivan Unafraid to Speak Mind," *Patriot Ledger*, May 15, 1975.

24 Alan Eisner, "NAACP Lawyer Doubtful about Suburban Busing," *Boston Herald-American*, October 18, 1974.

25 Lassiter, *Silent Majority*, 314–15.

26 "Garrity Broadens Final Plan Options," *Boston Globe*, October 17, 1974; Muriel Cohen, "Metco Expansion—The Choice Is Up to the Suburbs," *Boston Globe*, October 28, 1974.

27 Mark A. Michelson to W. Arthur Garrity, November 5, 1974, box 39, folder 2, METCO-NUSC.

28 Metropolitan Council for Educational Opportunity, "Annual Report 1973–1974 to the Board of Directors," box 1, folder 11, METCO-NUSC; Jean McGuire to Mr. John Taylor, January 21, 1974, box 12, folder 22, METCO-NUSC.

29 METCO's lawyer carefully read Garrity's entire Phase II decision, released in the spring of 1975, and found only one reference to the program in a footnote related to a handbook distributed to Boston parents. The reference read, "Footnote 3: METCO, EdCo or similar programs shall not be offered as options, but the booklet shall inform readers of the nature of such programs and shall provide an opportunity for the parent or student to request further information about the programs." See Mark A. Michelson to Stephen E. Shaw, May 16, 1975, box 29, folder 2, METCO-NUSC.

30 The METCO leadership led the campaign to successfully defeat the Daly-Sullivan bill. See Memorandum from Stephen E. Shaw to Jean McGuire, Arnold Vanderhoop, Subject: Legislative Agenda, January 16, 1975, box 19, folder 38, METCO-NUSC; METCO, "Minutes—METCO Staff Meeting," box 10, folder 39, METCO-NUSC.

31 Lupo, *Liberty's Chosen Home*, 310. See also Marjorie Arons, "Liberal Task Force Fears Hub Racist Triumph," *Newton Times*, October 16, 1974; Marjorie Arons, "Suburbanites Support Desegregated Schools," *Newton Times*, November 8, 1974.

32 "What Can Suburbs Do about Busing and Boston in Crisis?" *Wayland Town Crier*, October 24, 1974; Citizens for Participation in Political Action, "CPPAX Backs Boston Integration: Urge Suburban Support for the Garrity Ruling," October 10, 1974, box 57, folder 2402, FH; Citizens for Participation in Political Action, "Statement from the CPPAX Force on Racial Justice," October 10, 1974, box 57, folder 2402, FH.

33 "What Can Suburbs Do about Busing and Boston in Crisis?"

34 The rates of participation closely correlated with the geography of liberal politics and economic affluence. In 1973–74, Newton hosted 350 students, Lexington had 280, Brookline had 245, Wellesley and Weston hosted 161 each, Framingham had 144, and Lincoln had 120, which remained the largest concentrations of METCO children in any communities. Metropolitan Council for Educational Opportunity, "Annual Report to Board of Directors, 1973–1974," box 1, folder 11, METCO-NUSC.

35 "METCO Enrollment Increase," January 1975, box 27, folder 66, METCO-NUSC.

36 Amy Lamson to the editor, *Newton Graphic*, October 24, 1974.

37 For instance, even prior to Garrity's ruling, a group of suburban residents responded to a *Globe* opinion poll by a 51 to 38 percent margin that they supported the transportation of black students to their communities, but rejected by a 64 to 27 percent margin the busing of their own children. See "Busing: Races Split on the Issue," *Boston Globe*, May 14, 1974. See also Ian Menzies, "Symbols of Fear," *Boston Globe*, April 21, 1974.

38 See, for example, Carol Fielke to the editor, *Winchester Star*, November 21, 1974; Carolyn Roundey to the editor, *Winchester Star*, November 28, 1974; Catherine Fallon, "Town Needs Diversity," *Winchester Star*, December 5, 1974.

39 Ann-Mary Currier, "7 More Towns May Soon Take Metco Students," *Boston Globe*, November 25, 1974.

40 Alan Eisner, "Suburbs May Be Ordered to Aid in Desegregation in Boston," *Boston Herald American*, October 31, 1974; Muriel Cohen, "Anrig Bids Suburbs Supply 1,000 More METCO Seats," *Boston Globe*, October 31, 1974; WEEI news radio, "Metco," editorial, November 8, 1974, box 8, folder 66, METCO-NUSC.

41 Metropolitan Council for Educational Opportunity, "Annual Report to Board of Directors, 1974–1975," box 1, folder 11, METCO-NUSC; Metropolitan Council for Educational Opportunity, "Executive Board Minutes," February 1973, box 5, folder 29, METCO-NUSC; Currier, "7 More Towns May Soon Take Metco Students."

42 Arthur J. Hewis Jr. to the editor, *Winchester Star*, November 21, 1974.

43 Ross and Berg, *I Respectfully Disagree*, 449.

44 Nick King, "First Suburban Antibusing Center Opens in Dedham," *Boston Globe*, April 1, 1975.

45 Burdick, "Suburban Foes Fight Metropolitanization Plan."

46 "Dedham Rallies against Busing," *Dedham Daily Transcript*, January 25, 1975.

47 King, "First Suburban Antibusing Center Opens in Dedham."

48 Avi Nelson, "We've Allowed Our Government to Slip Away from Us," *Norfolk County Press*, April 2, 1975.

49 Glenon R. Suprenant to the editor, *Winchester Star*, February 6, 1975; "Vote NO! on Question 3," ca. 1975, box 40, folder 32, METCO-NUSC. See also "Similar Anti-METCO Campaigns, No Accident, Says Opponent," *Winchester Star*, April 3, 1975.

50 For more on changes in federal taxes in the 1970s, see Molly C. Michelmore, *Tax and Spend: The Welfare State, Tax Politics, and the Limits of American Liberalism* (Philadelphia: University of Pennsylvania Press, 2012), especially 118–19.

51 Robert W. Eisenmenger, Alicia Munnell, and Joan T. Poskanzer, "Options for Fiscal Structure in Massachusetts, Federal Reserve Bank of Boston Research Report," March 1975, unprocessed papers, ASN.

52 Memorandum from Ed Moscovitch to Governor-Elect, Secretary Designate Buckley, Subject: Overview of State Finances, November 11, 1974, box 36, folder 1284, JHB.

53 Saul Braun and Ziva Kwitney, "Downstairs, but Not a Comedown," *New York Times*, March 7, 1976.

54 Paula Leventman, *Professionals Out of Work* (New York: Free Press, 1981), 77.

55 "Suburban Schools: The Hardest Lesson Is Raising the Money," *Boston Globe*, September 14, 1975.

56 "Suburban Schools: The Hardest Lesson Is Raising the Money."

57 "State Acts to Save METCO in Face of Funds Reduction," *Boston Herald American*, August 27, 1975.

58 Memorandum from Stephen E. Shaw to Representative Doris Bunte, September 9, 1975, Subject: Rise in Amounts of Financial Support Requests for METCO, box 2, folder 78, METCO-NUSC.

59 Paul Parks to METCO Communities, August 25, 1975, box 11, folder 33, METCO-NUSC; Memorandum from Gregory R. Anrig to METCO Superintendents, September 2, 1975, box 22, folder 11, METCO-NUSC.

60 "State Acts to Save METCO in Face of Funds Reduction."

61 Michael S. Dukakis to Marilyn E. Barbour, May 19, 1976, box 43, METCO-NUSC; John Fuerbringer and Muriel Cohen, "Anrig Says Metco Budget $500,000 Short of Need," *Boston Globe*, March 31, 1976.

62 Parks privately discussed the "implications" if the state simply withdrew its support of METCO. See Memorandum from Richard Ames to Paul Parks, Subject: METCO, September 23, 1975, box 35, folder 3, METCO-NUSC.

63 Tonnie Katz, "Suburbs Cooling to Metco as Funds Fade," *Boston Globe*, April 15, 1976; "METCO, Money, and Race," *Boston Globe*, April 16, 1976; Mike Barnicle, "The Crisis At METCO," *Boston Globe*, September 22, 1975; Ian Menzies, "Is METCO Effort Dying in the Suburbs?" *Boston Globe*, September 27, 1976.

64 "METCO, Money, and Race."

65 Katz, "Suburbs Cooling to Metco as Funds Fade."

66 Peggy Brown, "Group Organizes to Oppose METCO," *Beverly Times*, March 17, 1975.

67 Katz, "Suburbs Cooling to Metco as Funds Fade."

68 "METCO Enrollment Increase," January 1975, box 27, folder 66, METCO-NUSC.

69 Katz, "Suburbs Cooling to Metco as Funds Fade."

70 Paul Brooks, *The View from Lincoln Hill: Man and the Land in a New England Town* (Boston: Houghton Mifflin, 1976), 262–63.

71 Paul Parks to the editor, *Boston Globe*, April 18, 1976.

72 William H. Herbert, "Suburban Schools Retreating from Cooperation with Cities," *Allston-Brighton Citizen*, April 15, 1976.

73 Marjorie Arons, "Where Are Liberals Going?" *Newton Times*, April 30, 1975.

74 Richard Alpert, "Professionalism, Policy Innovation, and Conflict: School Politics in Newton, Massachusetts" (master's thesis, Harvard University, March 1971).

75 Tonnie Katz, "Suburbs Growing Reluctant to Pay for Expensive Education," *Boston Globe*, March 7, 1976.

76 V. Nivola, "METCO Fares Well in Newton—for Now," *Newton Times*, December 10, 1975.

77 "Newton Board Votes to Add 100 More Metco Pupils from Boston," *Boston Globe*, November 26, 1974. Superintendent Aaron Fink provided a detailed proposal for how the system could accommodate this increase. See Memorandum from Aaron Fink to Members of the School Committee, re: A Proposal to Increase Our METCO Enrollment, November 7, 1974, box 20, folder 650, JHB.

78 Elizabeth McKinn, "Tax Hike Likely $10," *Newton Graphic*, August 28, 1975.

79 Kenneth E. Hartford to the editor, *Newton Times*, March 3, 1976.

80 Elizabeth McKinnon, "VOICE Makes Itself Heard," *Newton Graphic*, August 7, 1975.

81 "Cohen Scores Opponent for Lack of Concern for Newton Taxpayers," *Waltham News-Tribune*, September 11, 1975.

82 Katz, "Suburbs Growing Reluctant to Pay for Expensive Education."

83 William R. Torbert, "The Metropairways Pilot Year Evaluation: A Collaborative Inquiry into Voluntary Metropolitan Desegregation," June 30, 1976, box 25, folder 48, METCO-NUSC; Muriel Cohen and James Worsham, "13 Programs Tie Suburb, City Students," *Boston Globe*, January 20, 1974.

84 The curriculum varied by grade, and included courses called "Me, Myself, and I" that explored the similarities and differences between humans and animals, "Ethnicity" and "Then and Now." See Torbert, "The Metropairways Pilot Year Evaluation."

85 Kathy Jones, "The Newton School Committee 'On the Record,'" ca. 1976, box 4, folder 4, PMR.

86 Jones, "The Newton School Committee 'On the Record.'"

87 "Newton School Board Chairman Raps Area Proposal," March 12, 1976, box 57, folder 8, METCO-NUSC.

88 Louise E. Riley to the editor, *Boston Globe*, March 21, 1976.

89 Benjamin Taylor, "School Struggle in the Suburbs," *Boston Globe*, March 21, 1976.

90 "Angier's Connection to Roxbury Is Severed by the School Committee," *Newton Times*, March 10, 1976.

91   Carole Fischberg, "Angier Tie to Roxbury Threatened," *Newton Times*, March 3, 1976.

92   Carol Surkin, "Newton Faces School Battle," *Boston Globe*, March 2, 1976.

93   "A Public Message to the Newton School Committee," 1976, CPPAX-UMB.

94   Dan Ahern, "An Era Ends in Newton," n.d., box 57, folder 6, METCO-NUSC.

95   Lee Bolman to the editor, *Newton Times*, March 17, 1976; Nicholas Elliott to the editor, *Newton Times*, March 17, 1976; William F. Beckett to the editor, *Newton Times*, March 31, 1976.

96   Marjorie Arons, "Roxbury Rep Calls Action Racist," *Newton Times*, March 17, 1976.

97   Taylor, "School Struggle in the Suburbs."

98   "Suburbs Hit on METCO," *Boston Herald*, March 30, 1976.

99   League of Women Voters, "METCO in Newton," ca. 1978, NPL.

100   "Suburbs Hit on METCO"; "Weston Given $1,350 per Pupil for METCO plus Busing Costs," *Waltham News-Tribune*, April 22, 1976.

101   Alvin Mandell to Michael Dukakis, *Newton Graphic*, May 12, 1976; "Dukakis challenged on METCO," *Waltham News-Tribune*, May 5, 1976.

102   Joyce Morrissey Beatty to the editor, *Newton Times*, July 7, 1976.

103   George Poirer to the editor, *Waltham News-Tribune*, July 22, 1976.

104   "Disorderly Meeting in Newton Struggles over Cuts in METCO," *Waltham News-Tribune*, June 29, 1976.

105   See, for instance, Robert H. Goldman, chair, Newton Human Rights Commission, to Governor Michael Dukakis, April 15, 1976, box 43, folder "Legislative Funding Propose Cutbacks, 1976–1977," METCO-NUSC.

106   Robert C. Hayden, Press Statement: Newton School Committee Action on METCO and Voluntary Urban-Suburban Educational Programs, Newton, Mass., July 7, 1976, box 45, folder 23, METCO-NUSC; H. Darfour Anderson, "Action on METCO Condemned in Newton," *Bay State Banner*, July 15, 1976.

107   "METCO Is Less Costly Than No Metco at All," *Newton Times*, July 28, 1976; "METCO," *Newton Graphic*, July 8, 1976.

108   Metropolitan Council for Educational Opportunity, untitled flyer, May 11, 1976, box 2, folder 78, METCO-NUSC.

109   Eugene L. Notkin to the editor, *Dedham Daily Transcript*, December 16, 1975.

110   Carole Fischberg "SchoolCom Boycotts Metco Meeting," *Newton Times*, July 14, 1976.

111   Carole Fischberg, "Newton May Lose Metco over $37,000 Deadlock," *Newton Times*, August 4, 1976.

112   Alvin Mandell to Karl R. Fuller, July 22, 1976, JHB.

113   Adrian Birkett, "Black, White Pupils Evaluate Newton METCO," *Boston Evening Globe*, July 12, 1976.

114   Birkett, "Black, White Pupils Evaluate Newton METCO."

115   Fischberg, "SchoolCom Boycotts Metco Meeting."

116   Fischberg, "SchoolCom Boycotts Metco Meeting."

117   "Sen. Edward W. Brooke, Rep. Robert F. Drinan, and Rep. Michael J. Harrington to Newton School Committee," *Newton Graphic*, July 15, 1976.

118   Lois Pines, Governor Announces Restoration of State METCO Funds at Pines Fundraiser," press release, August 30, 1976, box 22, folder "Press Releases," addenda, LGP; "Dukakis Shifting $150,000 to Keep Newton in METCO," *Patriot Ledger*, August 28, 1976.

119   Evelyn Kaye, "METCO in Newton . . . a Family's Views," *Boston Globe*, August 30, 1976.

120   Menzies, "Is METCO Effort Dying in the Suburbs?"

121   Memorandum, from Charles Glenn to Gregory Anrig re: Interim Report on METCO Funding for FY'78, December 3, 1976, box 37, folder 24, METCO-NUSC.

122   Massachusetts Department of Elementary & Secondary Education, "Metco Program: FY14 Metco Districts and Grant Allocations," December 19, 2013, http://www.doe.mass

.edu/metco/funding.html; Deirdre Fernandes, "Answering Some Questions on the Proposed Newton Tax Hike," *Boston Globe*, March 10, 2013.

123 Tracy Jan, "METCO Fears for Its Future," *Boston Globe*, July 26, 2007.

124 Regents of the University of California v. Bakke, 438 U.S. 265 (1978); Thomas J. Sugrue, *Sweet Land of Liberty: The Forgotten Struggle for Civil Rights in the North* (New York: Random House, 2008), 507–8.

125 For one of the earliest and most controversial critiques of affirmative action as a symbolic measure that did not address structural issues, see William Julius Wilson, *The Declining Significance of Race: Blacks and Changing American Institutions* (Chicago: University of Chicago Press, 1978).

9 No One Home to Answer the Phone

1 Jean Dietz, "Equal Rights Rally Disrupted by Busing Foes," *Boston Globe*, April 10, 1975.

2 Dietz, "Equal Rights Rally Disrupted by Busing Foes."

3 See, for example, Steve Fraser and Gary Gerstle, *The Rise and Fall of the New Deal Order, 1930–1980* (Princeton, NJ: Princeton University Press, 1989); Jefferson Cowie, *Stayin' Alive: The 1970s and the Last Days of the Working Class* (New York: New Press, 2010), 235–36; Judith Stein, *Pivotal Decade: How the United States Traded Factories for Finance in the Seventies* (New Haven, CT: Yale University Press, 2010), xi. For a sharp contrast and critique of these interpretations, see Marisa Chappell, *The War on Welfare: Family, Poverty and Politics in Modern America* (Philadelphia: University of Pennsylvania Press, 2010), especially 17, 106–55; Robert O. Self, *All in the Family: The Realignment of the American Democracy since the 1960s* (New York: Hill and Wang, 2012).

4 Rickie Solinger, *Beggars and Choosers: How the Politics of Choice Shapes Adoption, Abortion, and Welfare in the United States* (New York: Hill and Wang, 2001), 224.

5 For more on the white middle-class focus of second-wave feminism and its impact on coalition building, see Becky Thompson, "Multiracial Feminism: Recasting the Chronology of Second Wave Feminism," *Feminist Studies* (Summer 2002): 337–60; Chappell, *The War on Welfare*; Marisa Chappell, "Rethinking Women's Politics in the 1970s: The League of Women Voters and the National Organization for Women Confront Poverty," *Journal of Women's History* 13, no. 4 (Winter 2002): 55–79; Stephanie Gilmore, ed., *Feminist Coalitions: Historical Perspectives on Second-Wave Feminism in the United States* (Champaign: University of Illinois Press, 2008); Stephanie Gilmore and Elizabeth Kaminski, "A Part and Apart: Lesbian and Straight Activists Negotiate Identity in a Second Wave-Organization," *Journal of the History of Sexuality* (January 2007): 95–113; Felicia Kornbluh, *The Battle Over Welfare Rights: Poverty and Politics in Modern American* (Philadelphia: University of Pennsylvania Press, 2007); Premilla Nadasen, *Welfare Warriors: The Welfare Rights Movement in the United States* (New York: Routledge, 2005); Jennifer Nelson, *Women of Color and the Reproductive Rights Movement* (New York: New York University Press, 2003); Self, *All in the Family*, 103–85.

6 Ellen Goodman, "The Unmarrying of Pat and Alan," *Boston Globe*, February 27, 1972.

7 Robert M. Blade, "Don't Call Her Mrs—More to a Woman Than a Man," *Patriot Ledger*, March 6, 1971.

8 Blade, "Don't Call Her Mrs."

9 Goodman, "The Unmarrying of Pat and Alan."

10 Bonnie Jones, interview by Norma McGavern-Norland, December 3, 1991, LOHP.

11 Jones interview.

12 Susan Auerbach, "Peace Warriors Break Rank," *Newton Times*, July 30, 1975. For examples of this trend, see Barbara Smith Silvers, "Lexington Woman Shows She Can Get Education

While Raising Family, "*Minute-Man Supplement*, February 1, 1973; "Lexington Woman on School Com. Balances Many Responsibilities," *Minute-Man Supplement*, October 11, 1973.

13   Town of Lexington, "Lexington Demographic Information, Human Needs Assessment," 1978, LPL.

14   Matthew D. Lassiter, "Inventing Family Values," in *Rightward Bound: Making America Conservative in the 1970s*, ed. Bruce J. Schulman and Julian E. Zelizer (Cambridge, MA: Harvard University Press, 2008), 14–15; Nancy Rubin, *The New Suburban Woman: Beyond Myth and Motherhood* (New York: Coward, McCann and Geoghegan, 1982), 75–78.

15   Berkeley Rice, "Down and Out Along Route 128," *New York Times*, November 1, 1970; Paula Leventman, *Professionals Out of Work* (New York: Free Press, 1981), 133–35, 157–61.

16   "More Working Wives in Lexington, " *Lexington Minute-Man*, August 22, 1973.

17   Town of Lexington, "Lexington Demographic Information."

18   See Voice of Women–New England, "30 Years Later: Voice of Women Questionnaires," box 1, folder 51, VOW-SL. Many of the women described how they divorced in the early 1970s and then pursued employment. See also Muriel K. Weinstein to Margaret Heckler, April 8, 1973, box 2, folder 76, NOW-Boston. For more on divorce in the 1970s, see Self, *All in the Family*, 328–30.

19   Jane O'Reilly, "In Massachusetts: Divorced Kids," *Time*, June 11, 1979.

20   Lucy Caldwell-Stair, "Peace Workers Active 15 Years Later," *Newton Times*, December 15, 1976.

21   For more on the founding of NOW, see Ruth Rosen, *The World Split Open: How the Modern Women's Movement Changed America* (New York: Viking, 2000), 74–93.

22   Eastern Massachusetts NOW Chapter, newsletter, June 1972, box 11, NOW-Newsletters.

23   Eastern Massachusetts NOW Chapter, newsletter, January 1971, box 11, NOW-Newsletters; Barbara Burgess, "Women's Liberation Movement in Boston," October 1970, box 2, folder 62, NOW-Boston.

24   Diane White, "Liberation Movement Seeks to Build Self-Respect," *Boston Globe*, February 23, 1970; Burgess, "Women's Liberation Movement in Boston."

25   Elizabeth W. Hogan to Jane Pollack, Nancy Valliant, and Barbara Zilber, August 5, 1970, box 1, folder 15, NOW-Boston; White, "Liberation Movement Seeks to Build Self-Respect."

26   NOW North Shore Unit, "Minutes," May 26, 1970, box 19, folder 683, NOW-Boston.

27   NOW Concord Unit, July 1, 1970, box 1, folder 14, NOW-Boston; Naomi Gernes et al. to the editor, *Lexington Minute-Man*, March 4, 1971; "A Look at Women's Lib in Suburbia: The Emphasis Is Different," *New York Times*, April 7, 1971"; Marilyn Smith Freifeld to Gregory Anrig, August 23, 1973, box 2, folder 77, NOW-Boston; Eleanor Tatosian, "Sex Stereotyping: Does It Occur in Our Schools?" *Bedford Minuteman*, December 20, 1973; NOW, "Checklist to Determine If Your School Violates Chapter 622, a Law That Prohibits Sex Discrimination in Public Schools," n.d., box 16, folder 575, NOW-Boston.

28   Public Schools Task Force, "A Case of Sex Discrimination," May 20, 1973, box 16, folder 562, NOW-Boston.

29   Lexington NOW Chapter, newsletter, August 1972, box 12, NOW-Newsletters.

30   "Women's Role in History Supplemental, Says NOW," *Lexington Minute-Man*, March 14, 1974; Citizens' Advisory Committee on Educational Opportunities for Girls and Boys, "Sex Inequality in Lexington's Schools, 1973–1974," January 17, 1975, LPL.

31   Diane Lund and Erik Lund to the editor, *Lexington Minute-Man*, June 28, 1973.

32   Jane Bachner, "NOW Attacks Schools System," *Newton Times*, June 13, 1973.

33   Lexington NOW Chapter, newsletter, February 1976, box 12, NOW-Newsletters.

34   Richard Kollen, *Lexington: From Liberty's Birthplace to Progressive Suburb* (Charleston, SC: Arcadia Publishing, 2004), 149.

35   Eastern Massachusetts NOW Chapter, newsletter, January 1972, box 11, NOW-Newsletters.

36   Eastern Massachusetts NOW Chapter, newsletter, January 1972.

37   For more on consciousness-raising, see Rosen, *World Split Open*, 196–201; Kathie Sara-child, "Consciousness-Raising: A Radical Weapon," in *Feminist Revolution*, ed. Redstock-ings (New York: Random House, 1978), 144–50. For a theoretical examination of the method and its political implications, see Catherine A. MacKinnon, *Toward a Feminist Theory of the State* (Cambridge, MA: Harvard University Press, 1989), 83–105. For its growth in the suburbs, see Linda Greenhouse, "Feminist Effort Grows in Croton," *New York Times*, April 5, 1970; "A Look at Women's Lib in Suburbia"; Linda Greenhouse, "These Wives Found Cure to Some of the Ills of Suburban Life," *New York Times*, October 1, 1971.

38   Judith Hole and Ellen Levine, *Rebirth of Feminism* (New York: Quadrangle Books, 1971), 126.

39   Naomi Garnes et al. to the editor, *Lexington Minute-Man*, March 4, 1971; Lexington NOW Chapter, newsletter, August 1972, box 12, NOW-Newsletters; Lexington NOW Chapter, newsletter, November 1975, box 12, NOW-Newsletters.

40   See, for instance, Westchester Radical Feminists, "Statement of Purpose, May, 1972," quoted in MacKinnon, *Toward a Feminist Theory of the State*, 92–93.

41   Elizabeth Hogan to Jane Pollack, Nancy Vailliant, and Barbara Ziller, August 5, 1970, box 1, folder 15, NOW-Boston. A Lexington consciousness-raising group did hold a few meetings with a "homogeneous" group of women from Cambridge in their twenties, which highlighted some basic similarities and differences in the two groups, whose "life-styles are so different." See Lexington NOW Chapter, newsletter, August 1972, box 12, NOW-Newsletters; Lexington NOW Chapter, newsletter, November 1972, box 12, NOW-Newsletters.

42   Jane Hilburt Davis, Margaret Dickerman, Bonnie Jones, and Patience Sampson, "A Study of Women's Liberation in a Suburban Community: Distinguishing Characteristics of Joiners of the Women's Liberation Movement" (master's thesis, Boston University, 1974).

43   For an overview of this critique and debate, see Thompson, "Multiracial Feminism," 337–60.

44   For more on the history of the ERA, see Nancy F. Cott, *The Grounding of Modern Feminism* (New Haven, CT: Yale University Press, 1987). For more on the battle over the federal ERA, see Jane J. Mansbridge, *Why We Lost the ERA* (Chicago: University of Chicago Press, 1986); Donald G. Matthews and Jane S. De Hart, *Sex, Gender, and the Politics of ERA: A State and the Nation* (New York: Oxford University Press, 1990).

45   Governor's Commission on the Status Women, newsletter 1, no. 2 (April 1975), SLM.

46   J. Anthony Lukas, *Common Ground: A Turbulent Decade in the Lives of Three American Families* (New York: Knopf, 1986), 269–71.

47   Some NOW members expressed sympathy with the antibusers and urged NOW to think about changing its priorities. See Boston NOW Chapter, *NOW News*, February 1, 1975, box 11, NOW-Newsletters.

48   Ellen Goodman, "Danger: Men at Work," *Boston Globe*, May 16, 1975.

49   William A. Henry III, "Foe Sees ERA Hurting Family Life," *Boston Globe*, May 7, 1975.

50   Alan Lupo, untitled column, *Boston Evening Globe*, March 25, 1976.

51   Stop ERA, "Beware of the Equal Rights Amendment," flyer, box 1, folder 6, CRMERA.

52   Lupo, untitled column.

53   Carol Mueller and Thomas Dimieri, "The Structure of Belief Systems among Contend-ing ERA Activists," *Social Forces* (March 1982): 667.

54   Susan Barron, "Women Do Better without Equal Rights," *Newton Times*, January 14, 1976; Manli Ho, "Atty. Mahoney's Breathless Race against the ERA," *Boston Globe*, October 10, 1976.

55   Mueller and Dimieri, "Structure of Belief Systems," 665.

56   Samuel Maddox, "Mass. Vote on ERA May Affect the Nation," *Lexington Minuteman Supplement*, September 30, 1976.

57   Pat Caplan, "Final Push Begins for State ERA Vote," *Monitor* (July 1976), box 1, folder 28, CRMERA; Committee to Ratify, "Suggestions for Mass. ERA Workers," 1976, box 1, folder 17, CRMERA.

58   Committee to Ratify the Massachusetts Equal Rights Amendment, news, no. 2 (July 1976), box 1, folder 30, CRMERA.

59   Committee to Ratify, "ERA Truthmobile," ca. 1976, box 2, folder 78, CRMERA.

60   Massachusetts Coalition to Ratify the State Equal Rights Amendment, press release, 1975, box 1, folder 11, CRMERA.

61   May Ellen Corbett, "Feminist Q&A," *Boston Herald Advertiser*, April 4, 1976.

62   Nancy Adler to the editor, *Lexington Minute-Man*, October 28, 1976.

63   Betsy Showstack, "Committees Organizing behind State ERA," *Patriot Ledger*, July 7, 1976.

64   Lisa E. Noble to the editor, *Boston Globe*, June 29, 1975.

65   Lupo, untitled column.

66   Ruth Kramer Baden, "What, a Man Stumping for ERA?" *Boston Herald American*, October 13, 1976.

67   "Survey Finds Bay State Voters Heavily Favor . . . ," *Boston Evening Globe*, October 7, 1976.

68   "Referenda Choices Spur Hottest Ballot Debates," *Lexington Minute-Man Supplement*, October 28, 1976.

69   Katherine P. Healy, "Massachusetts Citizens for Life Has during 1977 . . . ," ca. 1977, box 8, folder 208, NOW-Boston.

70   Christopher Lydon, "Abortion Foe Has Solid Core of Support," *New York Times*, March 2, 1976.

71   For a more comprehensive discussion of the Edelin case and its implications, see Sara Dubow, *Ourselves Unborn: A History of the Fetus in Modern America* (New York: Oxford University Press, 2010), 67–111; Kenneth C. Edelin, *Broken Justice: A True Story of Race Sex and Revenge in a Boston Courtroom* (Martha's Vineyard: Pondview Press, 2007); Ray Flynn, press release, ca. 1974, box 8, folder 269, NOW-Boston.

72   "Abortion: The Edelin Shock Wave," *Time*, March 3, 1975.

73   For more on this campaign, see Solinger, *Beggars and Choosers*, 8–20.

74   Massachusetts Organization for Repeal of Abortion Laws, "Background Information on the Supreme Court and Legislative Action," box 6, folder "ODU," MORAL-SL.

75   See Maher v. Roe, 432 U.S. 464 (1977); Beal v. Doe, 423 U.S. 438 (1977); Poelker v. Doe 432 U.S. 519 (1977). For Blackmun's dissent, see Beal v. Doe, 462 U.S. 438 (1977).

76   "Bill Would Forbid State to Pay for Abortion," *Boston Globe*, June 22, 1977.

77   "Bill Would Forbid State to Pay for Abortion."

78   Allen Rossiter, "Most Legislators against Abortion, but Favor Funding for the Poor," *Lexington Minute-Man Supplement*, August 18, 1977.

79   Norman Lockman, "House Votes Fund Cutoff for Medicaid Abortions," *Boston Globe*, August 10, 1977.

80   Dave O'Brian, "Pro-Life, Pro-Choice, and Déjà vu," *Boston Phoenix*, n.d., box 1, folder "Abortion-General," LGP.

81   "Abortion Lobbyists Jockey for Votes," *Boston Globe*, September 19, 1977.

82   Massachusetts Citizens for Life, "Arguments in Support of H6327," 1977, box 1, folder 24, AAC-NUSC.

83   Josephine Di Gregorio to legislator, August 8, 1977, box 37, folder 1328, JHB; Katherine Keefe to Senator Backman, August 4, 1977, box 37, folder 1328, JHB; Jane Crimlisk to Jack Backman, August 6, 1977, box 37, folder 1328, JHB.

84 Maria Karaganis, "Abortion Issue Flares in Massachusetts," n.d., *Boston Globe*, in Boston NOW, "The Right to Choose Is under Drastic Attack," flyer, July 1977, box 8, folder 273, NOW-Boston.

85 Marjorie Arons, "Abortion Factions Pin Hopes on Senate Vote," *Newton Times*, n.d. box 38, folder "Women's Issues, Press Releases," LGP.

86 Boston NOW, "The Right to Choose Is Under Drastic Attack."

87 NOW Boston, "Medicaid and Abortions Costs: A Fact Sheet," ca. 1977, box 8, folder 273, NOW-Boston.

88 "Should Tax Money Fund Abortions?" *Lexington Minuteman*, August 11, 1977.

89 Michael Dukakis to the Honorable Senate and House of Representatives, September 13, 1977, box 2, folder 121, AAC-NUSC; Lawrence Coluns, "Senators Reject Antiabortion Riders," *Boston Globe*, May 31, 1978; Abortion Action Coalition, "Fact Sheet: Abortion Legislation in Massachusetts," May 1978, box 1, folder 64, AAC-NUSC; Massachusetts Organization for Repeal of Abortion Laws, "Your Choice: Keep Abortion Safe and Legal"; Massachusetts Organization for Repeal of Abortion Laws, "Constitutional Defense Project," Summer 1978, box 2, folder 166, AAC-NUSC.

90 Maria Karagianis, "Abortion Law Signed by King," *Boston Globe*, June 13, 1979.

91 The Supreme Court heard cases related to the Massachusetts consent law twice during the 1970s. See Bellotti v. Baird, 428 U.S. 132 (1976); Bellotti v. Baird, 443 U.S. 622 (1979).

92 Although the US Supreme Court upheld the constitutionality of the Hyde Amendment in 1980, the Massachusetts Supreme Court in 1981 eased the limits on the public financing of abortion, instructing the state to pay for all "medically necessary" procedures even when a life was not in danger. Likewise, a federal court of appeals upheld the consent law, but struck down the stipulations requiring pregnant women to read the form outlining fetus gestation. Michael Knight, "U.S Court Suspends Massachusetts Abortion Law," *New York Times*, September 14, 1980; "Court Rejects Curb on Abortion Funds," *New York Times*, February 19, 1981; Walter Isaacson, "The Battle Over Abortion," *Time*, April 6, 1981.

93 Clark University News, "Large Majority Feels Abortion Is a Private Matter," July 1978, box 2, folder 130, AAC-NUSC. The polls showed that religion played a larger factor among state representatives than their constituents, as 80 percent of Catholics polled deemed abortion a private decision.

94 Clark University News, "Large Majority Feels Abortion Is a Private Matter."

95 Massachusetts Organization for Repeal of Abortion Laws, "MORAL Goes·Door-to-Door in Campaign for Abortion Rights," reprinted from Action Alliance, "Women's Agenda," ca. 1978, box 2, folder 166, AAC-NUSC.

96 Massachusetts Organization for Repeal of Abortion Laws, *Your Choice* (Spring 1979), box 1, folder "MORAL," NARAL-Newsletters.

97 Suzanne Staggenborg, *The Pro-Choice Movement: Organization and Activism in the Abortion Conflict* (New York: Oxford University Press, 1991), 94–95.

98 Massachusetts Organization for Repeal of Abortion Laws, "MORAL: An Overview of Our Growth," box 7, folder "Board and Budget," MORAL-SL.

99 Massachusetts Organization for Repeal of Abortion Laws, *Your Choice* (Spring 1979).

100 Massachusetts Organization for Repeal of Abortion Laws, "MORAL: An Overview of Our Growth."

101 Massachusetts Organization for Repeal of Abortion Laws, *Your Choice* (Summer 1978), box 1, folder "MORAL," NARAL-Newsletters.

102 Solinger, *Beggars and Choosers*, 5.

103 For more on the roots of this strategy, see Self, *All in the Family*, 136–37, 329–30, 377–78.

104 Leslie Cagan and Marla Erlien to Reproductive Rights National Network and Friends, January 30, 1980, box 1, folder 8, AAC-NUSC.

105   Massachusetts Organization for Repeal of Abortion Laws, "MORAL Plays a Key Role in the Pro-Choice Community," December 1978, box 6, folder "Press Releases," MORAL-SL; Staggenborg, *The Pro-Choice Movement*, 95.

106   Massachusetts Organization for Repeal of Abortion Laws, *Your Choice* (Spring 1979); Michael Knight, "Drive for Abortion Rights Begins," *New York Times*, January 23, 1980.

107   Massachusetts Organization for Repeal of Abortion Laws, *Your Choice* (Spring 1979).

108   Massachusetts Organization for Repeal of Abortion Laws, *Your Choice* (November 1979), box 1, folder "MORAL," NARAL-Newsletters.

109   Judy McDermott, "Pro-Abortion Activist Hopes Tactic Will Arouse 'Silent Majority,'" *Oregonian*, September 29, 1979, box 2, folder 166, AAC-NUSC.

110   For more on the defensive posture of the pro-choice movement, see Self, *All in the Family*, 367–78.

111   Memorandum from Jean Weinberg to 1981 Board of Directors, re: MORAL—Past, Present, and Future, 1981, box 7, folder "Board and Budget," MORAL-SL; Staggenborg, *The Pro-Choice Movement*, 93–109.

112   William Saletan, "Electoral Politics and Abortion: Narrowing the Political Message," in *Abortion Wars: A Half Century of Struggle*, ed. Rickie Solinger (Berkeley: University of California Press, 1998), 112–13.

113   For more on the relationship between the pro-choice movement and politicians in the 1980s, see Saletan, "Electoral Politics and Abortion: Narrowing the Political Message," 111–23.

10 From Taxachusetts to the Massachusetts Miracle

1   Massachusetts High Technology Council, *High Tech News* 5, no. 9 (December 1982).

2   For an excellent recent critique of the periodization of the last forty years, especially those studies that rely too heavily on Reagan's political career, see Daniel T. Rodgers, *The Age of Fracture* (Cambridge, MA: Harvard University Press, 2011), 3–4.

3   For more on the political mobilization of corporate and business groups, especially in the 1970s, see Kim Phillips-Fein, *Invisible Hands: The Making of the Conservative Movement from the New Deal to Reagan* (New York: W. W. Norton, 2009); Benjamin C. Waterhouse, *Lobbying America: The Politics of Business from Nixon to NAFTA* (Princeton, NJ: Princeton University Press, 2013).

4   Fox Butterfield, "Dukakis," *New York Times*, May 8, 1988.

5   Mike Dukakis for Governor, "Introducing Mike Dukakis," 1974, box 4, folder 221, MSD.

6   Edgar Litt, *The Political Cultures of Massachusetts* (Cambridge, MA: MIT Press, 1965), 151–72.

7   Michael S. Dukakis, "Announcement of Candidacy," October 1, 1973, box 35, folder 1254, JHB.

8   Richard Gaines and Michael Segal, *Dukakis and the Reform Impulse* (Boston: Quinlan Press, 1987), 99.

9   Ken Hartnett, "Gov. Sargent Blames 'Price of Hamburg,'" *Boston Globe*, November 6, 1974.

10   William A. Henry III, "Dukakis Seeking Voters' Mandate," *Boston Globe*, November 1, 1974.

11   Hartnett, "Gov. Sargent Blames 'Price of Hamburg'"; "1974 Massachusetts Election," *Boston Globe*, November 6, 1974.

12   The Dukakis Committee, "Mike Dukakis Looks at the Issues," 1974, box 35, folder 1254, JHB; Dukakis, "Announcement of Candidacy."

13 Joseph Kraft, "Democrats on the Hook; Parties' Image Erodes," *Los Angeles Times*, November 10, 1973.

14 William A. Henry III, "Dukakis Seeking Voters' Mandate," *Boston Globe*, November 1, 1974.

15 Bennett Harrison, "A Critique of the Economic 'Posture of the Dukakis Administration,'" November 19, 1975, box 2, folder 46, PMR.

16 Marjorie Arons, "Masses Protest Cuts in Welfare," *Newton Times*, October 1, 1975.

17 "Massachusetts: Working on Welfare," *Time*, June 27, 1977.

18 Michael Kenney, "Welfare Job Law Pushed," *Boston Globe*, March 31, 1976; Nick King, "Dukakis to Push 'Workfare' at US Hearing on Welfare," *Boston Globe*, March 31, 1977; Kirk Scharfenberg, "Lopping 'Workfare' off Welfare," *Boston Globe*, August 13, 1977.

19 "Some Questions and Answers about the Work Experience Program," box 13, folder 466, NOW-Boston; "Backman: Forced Work Programs ... Cruel Hoax," March 11, 1977, box 3, folder 94, JHB; Gaines and Segal, *Dukakis and the Reform Impulse*, 146.

20 Scharfenberg, "Lopping 'Workfare' off Welfare." For more on Carter's welfare policy, see Marisa Chappell, *The War on Welfare: Family, Poverty, and Politics in Modern America* (Philadelphia: University of Pennsylvania Press, 2010), 156–98.

21 For more on Clinton's welfare reform, see Jason DeParle, *American Dream: Three Women, Ten Kids, and a Nation's Drive to End Welfare* (New York: Viking, 2004), 101–54; R. Kent Weaver, *Welfare as We Knew It* (Washington, DC: Brookings Institute Press, 2000); Gwendolyn Mink, *Welfare's End* (Ithaca, NY: Cornell University Press, 2000).

22 Fantus Company, "Massachusetts Means Business: An Evaluation of Massachusetts' Changing Attitude Toward Industry," Commonwealth of Massachusetts Department of Business and Development, May 1978.

23 AnnaLee Saxenian, *Regional Advantage: Culture and Competition in Silicon Valley and Route 128* (Cambridge, MA: Harvard University Press, 1996), 8–9, 17–19.

24 Robert Healy, "The Real Dukakis Is a Manager," *Boston Globe*, January 13, 1978; Nick King, "Bay State's Economy Recovering—Dukakis," *Boston Globe*, September 3, 1978.

25 Barry Bluestone and Bennett Harrison, *The Deindustrialization of America: Plant Closings, Community Abandonment, and the Dismantling of Basic Industry* (New York: Basic Books, 1982), 93.

26 John K. White, "All in the Family: The 1978 Massachusetts Democratic Gubernatorial Primary," *Polity* (Summer 1982): 647.

27 For articles addressing the immediate impact of Proposition 13, see "All Aboard the Bandwagon!" *Time*, June 26, 1978; "The Big Tax Revolt," *Newsweek*, June 19, 1978.

28 Marjorie Arons, "Jarvis Brings Taxpayer Revolt to Newton," *Newton Times*, October 18, 1978.

29 Michael Knight, "Tax Revolt Ripple Sway Massachusetts," *New York Times*, June 27, 1978.

30 Jonathan Feuerbringer, "Proposition 13 in Bay State Would Cut Property Taxes 77%," *Boston Globe*, June 8, 1978.

31 Edward Quill and Paul Lagner, "Municipal Officials Feel Caught in the Middle, " *Boston Globe*, June 11, 1978.

32 "Voters Favor 45% Property Tax Cut," *Boston Globe*, June 16, 1978.

33 Nick King, "Style: Plodding ... Policy: Work—Edward J. King," *Boston Globe*, September 4, 1978.

34 Nick King, "King—Simple Issues," *Boston Evening Globe*, September 20, 1978.

35 Laurence Collins, "Dukakis Challengers Want Spending Controls," *Boston Globe*, June 11, 1978; Warren T. Brookes, "It Might Well Bring Us an Economic Revival," *Boston Herald American*, June 8, 1978.

36 White, "All in the Family," 652–53.

37   David B. Wilson, "'He Means What He Says, Says What He Means,'" *Boston Globe*, October 20, 1978.

38   White, "All in the Family," 653.

39   Warren T. Brookes, "Property Taxes Were the Key to Gov. Dukakis' Loss to King," *Boston Herald American*, September 28, 1978.

40   Jack W. Germond and Jules Witcover, "Dukakis Victim of National Trend," *Boston Globe*, September 23, 1978.

41   Jerry Taylor, "Why Some Bostonians Voted as They Did," *Boston Globe*, September 20, 1978.

42   Robert Healy, "Conservatives Prevail," *Boston Globe*, November 8, 1978.

43   Michael Hillard and James Parrolt, "The Massachusetts High Technology Council: An Assessment of Its Public Policy Agenda," draft, September 1981, SLM.

44   Hillard and Parrolt, "The Massachusetts High Technology Council."

45   Massachusetts High Technology Council, "Progress Report 1980," box 58, folder "Massachusetts High Technology Council, Proposal," Office of the Provost Records, Special Collections, Northeastern University, Boston.

46   Hillard and Parrolt, "The Massachusetts High Technology Council."

47   Phillips-Fein, *Invisible Hands*, 179–84; Rodgers, *The Age of Fracture*, 69–74.

48   Michael Knight, "Taxes Hurt Massachusetts Jobs," *New York Times*, March 29, 1979; Massachusetts High Technology Council, "Progress Report 1980."

49   Knight, "Taxes Hurt Massachusetts Jobs." See also Herbert Roth to Andrew Natsios, April 19, 1979, box 19, folder "Tax Cap," ASN.

50   Tracy Kidder, *Soul of a New Machine* (Boston: Little, Brown, 1981), 37.

51   "Data General Plans a New Computer Plant—in North Carolina," *Boston Globe*, September 18, 1979.

52   Knight, "Taxes Hurt Massachusetts Jobs."

53   Kidder, *Soul of a New Machine*, 72–73.

54   Paula Leventman, *Professionals Out of Work* (New York: Free Press, 1981), 192.

55   Gaines and Segal, *Dukakis and the Reform Impulse*, 181.

56   Hillard and Parrolt, "The Massachusetts High Technology Council."

57   Massachusetts High Technology Council, "Public Affairs Bulletin," 1979, box 19, folder "Taxation, 1979," ASN. See also Massachusetts High Technology Council, "A New Social Contract for Massachusetts," in *Massachusetts Miracle: High Technology and Economic Revitalization*, ed. David Lampe (Cambridge, MA: MIT Press, 1988), 155–68.

58   W. F. Allen, to All Employees, Stone and Webster Engineering Corporation, May 23, 1979, box 19, folder "Taxation," ASN; Massachusetts High Technology Council, "Public Affairs Bulletin."

59   Herbert Roth to Andrew Natsios, April 17, 1979, box 19, folder "Taxation," ASN.

60   See, for instance, Edward J. King, "The First Step: Property Tax Relief," February 9, 1979, box 36, folder 1302, JHB; Massachusetts Fair Share, press statement, February 12, 1979, box 36, folder 1302, JHB; Campaign for Tax Cuts Jobs and Services, "Questions and Answers About Taxbreaker," box 36, folder 1288, JHB; William G. Robinson, "Tax Relief Proposals," March 13, 1980, ASN.

61   Committee on Taxation, "Proposition 2½," box 30, folder 1315, LRA; Robert L. Turner, "Outrageous Proposition," *Boston Globe*, February 14, 1980.

62   Sherry Tvedt Davis, "A Brief History of Proposition 2½," in *Proposition 2½: Its Impact on Massachusetts*, ed. Lawrence E. Susskind (Cambridge, MA: Oelgeshlager, Gunn and Hain, 1983), 3–9.

63   Walter V. Robinson, "Proposition 2½: Budget Trimming or Fiscal Wipe Out?" *Boston Globe*, August 25, 1980.

64   George Briggs, "$77M at Risk in Hub, Prop 2½ Foes Claim," *Boston Herald American*, October 22, 1980.

65   Jonathan Robbins, "2½: A Disaster Either Way?" *Newton Graphic*, October 23, 1980.

66   "Does Mass Need Prop 2½: Q & A with Rep. Cohen, Chairman of the Tax Panel," *Boston Globe*, July 20, 1980.

67   Walter V. Robinson, "Prop 2½," *Boston Globe*, November 5, 1980.

68   Renee Loth, "For Tax Opponent, Same War, New Front," *Boston Globe*, July 23, 1989.

69   Nathan Cobb, "Barbara Anderson's Time Has Come," *Boston Globe*, January 14, 1990.

70   Robbins, "2½: A Disaster Either Way?"

71   Daniel A. Smith, *Tax Crusaders and the Politics of Direct Democracy* (New York: Routledge, 1998), 92.

72   Hillard and Parrolt, "The Massachusetts High Technology Council."

73   Smith, *Tax Crusaders*, 123–24.

74   Smith, *Tax Crusaders*, 10.

75   Loth, "For Tax Opponent, Same War, New Front."

76   Davis, "A Brief History of Proposition 2½," 3–9.

77   "Prop 2 ½ Alluring, Confusing," *Boston Globe*, October 13, 1980.

78   Arnold Adelman to the editor, *Newton Graphic*, October 23, 1980.

79   Peter Cowen, "Why? . . . Taxes . . . Services . . . the Urge to Get Out of the Voting Booth," *Boston Globe*, November 5, 1980.

80   Leventman, *Professionals Out of Work*, 192; Helen F. Ladd and Julie Boatwright Wilson, "Who Supports Tax Limitations: Evidence from Massachusetts' Proposition 2½," *Journal of Policy Analysis and Management* (Winter 1983): 267.

81   Richard A. Bumstead, "One Massachusetts School System Adapts to Proposition 21½," *Phi Delta Kappan* (June 1981): 721.

82   League of Women Voters of Massachusetts, "Questions We've Been Asked—And Answers," September 23, 1980, box 9, folder 383, JWO; Robert L. Turner, "King Hoping to Slip Past the Liberals," *Boston Globe*, September 6, 1977.

83   Bonnie Armor to the editor, *Newton Graphic*, October 9, 1980.

84   Mary Prince, "Panel Pans Prop. 2½," *Lexington Minute-Man*, September 25, 1980.

85   Bob Jeltsch, "How Will Lexington Vote on Proposition 2½," *Lexington Minute-Man*, October 30, 1980.

86   James Ring Adams, *Secrets of the Tax Revolt* (New York: Harcourt Brace, 1985), 328.

87   Robert L. Turner, "'The Haves' Were Winners," *Boston Globe*, November 11, 1980.

88   Anne Beaton, "Liberals Stay on the Sidelines," *Boston Herald American*, September 6, 1980.

89   Massachusetts High Technology Council, *High Tech News* 6, no. 3 (February 3, 1983).

90   Al Larkin, "Charlestown: Choices Based on Fear," *Boston Globe*, November 5, 1980.

91   Turner, "'The Haves' Were Winners"; "City/Town Vote for President, Proposition 2 ½," *Boston Globe*, November 6, 1980.

92   Ladd and Wilson, "Who Supports Tax Limitations," 268–69.

93   Muriel Cohen and Marvin Pave, "2½ Feeds Interest in Private Schools," *Boston Globe*, December 15, 1980. See also Muriel Cohen, "Private Schools: Alluring," *Boston Globe*, October 23, 1981.

94   Laurence Auros to Andrew Natsios, February 8, 1981, box 7, folder "Proposition 2½," ASN.

95   Cohen and Pave, "2½ Feeds Interest in Private Schools."

96   "Prop 2½ and a Democratic Society," *Boston Globe*, December 16, 1980.

97   See, for instance, Mary Prince, "Town Gets Set for 2½," *Lexington Minute-Man*, November 13, 1980; Steven Burke, "Mann Asks King to Act," *Newton Graphic*, November 13, 1980.

98   Prince, "Town Gets Set for 2½"; Burke, "Mann Asks King to Act," *Newton Graphic*. See, for instance, Michael E. Cam to Andrew Natsios, May 5, 1981, box 7, folder "Proposition 2½," ASN; Ruth C. Henry to Andrew Natsios, April 13, 1981, box 7, folder "Proposition 2½," ASN. Even the MHTC suggested that the state government should provide aid in order to offset the loss in necessary services. See Massachusetts High Tech Council, "Massachusetts

High Tech Council Endorses More Gradual 2½ Phase-Down and Increased Local Aid," April 24, 1981, box 29, folder 1311, LRA.

99   Hillard and Parrolt, "The Massachusetts High Technology Council."

100   Massachusetts High Technology Council, *High Tech News* 4, no. 5 (June 1981).

101   Lawrence Susskind and Cynthia Horan, "Understanding How and Why the Most Drastic Cuts Were Avoided," in *Proposition 2½: Its Impact on Massachusetts*, ed. Lawrence E. Susskind (Cambridge, MA: Oelgeshlager, Gunn and Hain, 1983), 276. Many suburbs had routinely not valued property at full market price and decided to change this practice, which enabled them to increase the tax base while still adhering to the law.

102   Black, "No Surgery for These Towns"; Andrew Laing "Wayland: Dealing with Uncertainty," in *Proposition 2½: Its Impact on Massachusetts*, ed. Lawrence E. Susskind (Cambridge, MA: Oelgeshlager, Gunn and Hain, 1983), 253–60; Jerome Rubin, "Quincy Schools Take a Big Cut," in *Proposition 2½: Its Impact on Massachusetts*, ed. Lawrence E. Susskind (Cambridge, MA: Oelgeshlager, Gunn and Hain, 1983), 209–10.

103   Town of Brookline, "Brookline to Debate Proposition 2½ at Town Meeting Wednesday," 1980, box 3, folder 102, JHB.

104   Patricia Nealon, "Attempt to Override Prop 2½ Reach New Heights," *Boston Globe*, April 2, 1989.

105   Lawrence E. Susskind, *Proposition 2½: Its Impact on Massachusetts* (Cambridge, MA: Oelgeshlager, Gunn and Hain, 1983).

106   Bruce J. Schulman, *The Seventies: The Great Shift in American Culture, Society, and Politics* (New York: Da Capo Press, 2001), 214–15.

107   Charles Kenney, "Massachusetts Makes a Comeback: What Is Responsible for the State's Amazing Comeback? Would You Believe Proposition 2½?" *Boston Globe*, May 18, 1986.

108   Citizens for Participation in Political Action, "Governor Edward J. King Report Card," 1979, CPPAX-UMB.

109   Tom Ashbrook, "What Kind of Governor Does One Want?" *Boston Globe*, September 12, 1982.

110   Norman Lockman, "Campaign '82: Democrats Engaged in Class Warfare?" *Boston Globe*, August 22, 1982.

111   For more on "Reagan Democrats," see Stanley B. Greenberg, *Middle-Class Dreams: The Politics and Power of the New American Majority* (New Haven, CT: Yale University Press, 1996).

112   "Governors: Different Democratic Styles," *Time*, September 27, 1982.

113   Wayne Woodlief, "Dukakis Endorsed," *Boston Herald American*, November 22, 1981.

114   Mike Dukakis for Governor, "Dukakis Proposes Action Plan for Jobs," May 18, 1982, box 35, folder 1254, JHB; Michael Dukakis, "Statement to the Honeywell Political Action Committee," August 23, 1982, box 7, folder 385, MSD.

115   Mike Dukakis for Governor, "The Dukakis Program," ca. 1982, box 4, folder 236, MSD; Mike Dukakis/John Kerry, "Economic Prosperity and Jobs for Our People," ca. 1982, box 7, folder 385, MSD; Laurence Collins, "The Feeling Is for Dukakis in Newton," *Boston Globe*, September 9, 1982.

116   Lockman, "Campaign '82"; Chris Black, "Issue of Corruption Hurt King, Polls Show," *Boston Globe*, September 15, 1982.

117   "Governors: Different Democratic Styles," *Time*, September 27, 1982.

118   "Democrat for Governor: The City and Town Primary Votes, Incumbent 1982," *Boston Globe*, September 16, 1982; Walter V. Robinson, "Dukakis Ousts Gov. King; Sears Is GOP Nominee," *Boston Globe*, September 15, 1982.

119   Laurence Collins, "Massachusetts: Dukakis," *Boston Globe*, September 15, 1982.

120   Richard Stengel, "A Tale of Two States," *Time*, May 26, 1986. See David Lampe, "Introduction: The Making of a Miracle," in *Massachusetts Miracle: High Technology and Economic*

Revitalization, ed. David Lampe (Cambridge, MA: MIT Press, 1988), 1–18; Kenney, "Massachusetts Makes a Comeback"; Warren T. Brookes, "Proposition 2½ Is Massachusetts 'Dirty Little Secret,'" *Wall Street Journal*, July 15, 1986; Massachusetts High Technology Council, *Mass High Tech*, March 30–April 12, 1987, box 23, folder 1221, MSD.

121   Lynn E. Browne and John S. Hekman, "New England's Economy in the 1980s," Federal Reserve Bank of Boston, January 1981, in *Massachusetts Miracle: High Technology and Economic Revitalization*, ed. David Lampe (Cambridge, MA: MIT Press, 1988), 169.

122   "High Technology/The Market," *New York Times*, March 27, 1983.

123   Massachusetts High Technology Council, *High Tech News 5*.

124   Massachusetts High Technology Council, *High Tech News 6*.

125   Massachusetts High Technology Council, *High Tech News 5*.

126   Leslie Wayne, "Designing a New Economics for the Atari Democrats," *New York Times*, September 26, 1982; John Herbers, "New Democratic Governors Seek Blend of Right and Left," *New York Times*, June 9, 1985.

127   The administration distributed loans through the Massachusetts Industrial Finance Agency to diversify the state's economy by encouraging the development of biotechnology, genetic engineering, photovoltaic, and other emerging technologies. See Thomas J. Lueck, "Boston Looks Past Computers," *New York Times*, July 29, 1985; Michael S. Dukakis, "Creating the Future: Opportunity, Innovation, and Growth in the Massachusetts Economy," Governor's Office of Economic Development, Boston, 1987, box 4, folder 235, MSD.

128   David L. Birch, "The Role of Small Business in New England," in *Massachusetts Miracle: High Technology and Economic Revitalization*, ed. David Lampe (Cambridge, MA: MIT Press, 1988), 225–39.

129   Stengel, "A Tale of Two States."

130   Wayne, "Designing a New Economics for the Atari Democrats"; Robert Lekachman, "Atari Democrats," *New York Times*, October 10, 1982; "1984 Campaign Rhetoric Is Yielding Few Memorable Terms," *New York Times*, September 1, 1984; Randall Rothenberg, *The Neoliberals: Creating the New American Politics* (New York: Simon and Schuster, 1984), 79–91.

131   E. J. Dionne Jr., "Greening of Democrats: An 80's Mix of Idealism and Shrewd Politics," *New York Times*, June 14, 1989.

132   Paul Tsongas, *The Road from Here: Liberalism and Realities in the 1980s* (New York: Knopf, 1981); John B. Judis and Ruy Teixeira, *The Emerging Democratic Majority* (New York: Scribner, 2002), 132; Rothenberg, *The Neoliberals*, 40–47.

133   Bluestone and Harrison, *Deindustrialization of America*, 92–98; David E. Sanger, "High Technology: Narrow Sector of the Economy That Affects Many American Industries," *New York Times*, October 14, 1984.

134   Rothenberg, *The Neoliberals*, 90.

135   Neal Peirce and Carol Steinbach, "Massachusetts, After Going from Rags to Riches, Looks to Spread the Wealth," *National Journal*, May 25, 1985; "A Survey of New England," *The Economist*, August 8, 1987.

136   Jerry Ackerman, "The Suburbs Gain the Edge: Rapid Job Growth Outside Boston Has Led to a Shift in the Demand for Office Space," *Boston Globe*, July 18, 1993; Susan Diesenhouse, "Cisco Is Building Corporate Campus Outside Boston," *New York Times*, March 18, 2001; Alan R. Earls, "Route 495 Commercial, Industrial Market Picks Up," *Boston Globe*, November 25, 2006.

137   Bruce Katz, "Welcome to the 'Exit Ramp' Economy," *Boston Globe*, May 13, 2001.

138   Cindy Rodriguez, "Along I-495, a Concrete Ribbon of Growth—Once Rural Towns Are Now Suburbs," *Boston Globe*, April 9, 2001.

139   Lowell, which a decade earlier had one of the highest unemployment rates in the country, became "a model of high tech revitalization," and by 1987 high-tech companies employed 24 percent of Lowell workers—a rate 20 percent higher than the national average.

See Patricia M. Flynn, "Lowell: A High Tech Success Story," in *Massachusetts Miracle: High Technology and Economic Revitalization*, ed. David Lampe (Cambridge, MA: MIT Press, 1988), 276; Dukakis, "Creating the Future"; "A Survey of New England."

140 Peirce and Steinbach, "Massachusetts, After Going from Rags to Riches."

141 Dionne, "Greening of Democrats."

142 Fox Butterfield, "Law on Plant Closings Is Signed in Massachusetts," *New York Times*, July 14, 1984.

143 Steven V. Roberts, "President Decides Not to Veto Bill Requiring Notice of Plant Closings," *New York Times*, August 3, 1988.

144 Michael S. Dukakis and Rosabeth Moss Kanter, *Creating the Future: The Massachusetts Comeback and Its Promise for America* (New York: Summit Books, 1988), 111.

145 "Dukakis Touts ET Program, Says 8,000 Off Welfare," *Boston Globe*, August 29, 1987.

146 John Herbers, "Job Training Efforts in Massachusetts and Michigan Move Poor Off Welfare," *New York Times*, March 30, 1987.

147 Matthew Wald, "Joblessness in Massachusetts Drops and, with Help, So Do the Welfare Rolls," *New York Times*, November 17, 1985.

148 David Osborne, *Laboratories of Democracy: New Breed of Governor Creates Models for National Growth* (Cambridge, MA: Harvard Business School Press, 1988), 205; Dukakis and Kanter, *Creating the Future*, 107–20.

149 Charles Kenney and Robert L. Turner, *Dukakis: An American Odyssey* (Boston: Houghton Mifflin, 1988), 191.

150 Osborne, *Laboratories of Democracy*, 205.

151 "Dukakis Touts ET Program, Says 8,000 Off Welfare."

152 Douglas Foster, "An Interview with Michael Dukakis," *Mother Jones*, December 1987.

153 Herbers, "New Democratic Governors Seek Blend of Right and Left."

154 Shawn Doherty, "The Duke Turns Things around in 'Taxachusetts,'" *Newsweek*, March 24, 1986, box 23, folder 1218, MSD.

155 Fox Butterfield, "Massachusetts Tax Success Seen as a Boon to Dukakis," *New York Times*, January 19, 1986.

156 Herbers, "New Democratic Governors Seek Blend of Right and Left."

157 Michael Grunwald, "Dig the Big Dig," *Washington Post*, August 6, 2006. For more on Central Artery Project, see Alan A. Altshuler and David E. Luberoff, *Mega-Projects: The Changing Politics of Urban Public Investment* (Washington, DC: Brookings Institute Press, 2003), 76–122.

158 Andrea Lamberti, "Dukakis Outlines Economic Strategy," *Tech* 109, no. 51 (November 17, 1989).

159 John A. Farrell, *Tip O'Neill and the Democratic Century: A Biography* (Boston: Little, Brown, 2001), 666–68.

160 "How the Governors See It: A Newsweek Poll," *Newsweek*, March 24, 1986; Matthew Wald, "Dukakis Turns Eye to White House," *New York Times*, December 28, 1986; Charles Kenney, "Why Not the Duke?" *Boston Globe*, January 4, 1987; Stengel, "A Tale of Two States."

161 Matthew L. Wald, "Dukakis Opens Presidential Quest," *New York Times*, April 30, 1987.

162 Walter Shapiro, "The Duke of Economic Uplift," *Time*, July 27, 1987; Peter T. Kilborn, "In State's Success, Dukakis Seeks His Own," *New York Times*, August 5, 1987; Bob Drogin, "'There's a Method to His Dullness': Voters Lured by Dukakis' Consistency," April 21, 1988.

163 E. J. Dionne Jr., "The Democrats in Atlanta," *New York Times*, July 22, 1988.

164 Osborne, *Laboratories of Democracy*, 209.

165 For more on Dukakis's use of his ethnic identity, see Matthew Frye Jacobson, *Roots Two: White Ethnic Revival in Post–Civil Rights America* (Cambridge, MA: Harvard University

Press, 2006), 324–35; E. J. Dionne Jr., *Why Americans Hate Politics* (New York: Simon and Schuster, 1991), 310.

166   Jacobson, *Roots Two*, 328.

167   Butterfield, "Dukakis."

168   George J. Church, "Battling Over the Big Three," *Time*, September 12, 1988.

169   Church, "Battling Over the Big Three."

170   Marie Cocce, "Candidates Woe Suburban Votes," *Newsday*, September 4, 1988.

171   Bruce Nussbaum, "The Business Guru behind Dukakis," *Business Week*, May 30, 1988.

172   E. J. Dionne Jr., "Labor Federation Endorses Dukakis, Citing Union Issues," *New York Times*, August 25, 1988.

173   Thomas Geoghegan, *Which Side Are You On? Trying to Be for Labor When It's Flat on Its Back* (New York: New Press, 1991), 7, 277–84.

174   Nussbaum, "The Business Guru Behind Dukakis."

175   Thomas Oliphant, "Holding Back the Counterpunch, Dukakis Ignores Repeated Bush Attacks—for Now," *Boston Globe*, June 19, 1988; Walter V. Robinson, "Bush Strategy: Bash Dukakis Aim Is Replay of '84," *Boston Globe*, May 6, 1988; Jonathan Alter, "How Liberal Is Dukakis?" *Newsweek*, July 4, 1988; E. J. Dionne Jr., "Many Split Tickets," *New York Times*, November 9, 1988.

176   Robinson, "Bush Strategy: Bash Dukakis Aim Is Replay of '84"; Alter, "How Liberal Is Dukakis?"

177   Dionne, *Why Americans Hate Politics*, 301–2.

178   For more about the Willie Horton controversy, see Jacobson, *Roots Two*, 331–34.

179   Dukakis for President, "Background on Mandatory Minimum Sentences," ca. 1988, box 4, folder 242, MSD; Eric Fehnstrom, "Dukakis Cuts Back on Commutations for Cons," *Boston Herald*, May 18, 1988.

180   Dukakis for President, "Background on Furloughs," flyer, ca. 1988, box 4, folder 241, MSD.

181   Dionne, *Why Americans Hate Politics*, 80.

182   E. J. Dionne Jr., "Many Split Tickets," *New York Times*, November 9, 1988.

183   Mark Muro, "Knocking Massachusetts Off Its Pedestal, the Election Became a Referendum on—and Repudiation—of the Bay State," *Boston Globe*, November 13, 1988.

184   Muro, "Knocking Massachusetts Off Its Pedestal."

185   William Galston and Elaine Kamarck, "The Politics of Evasion: Democrats and the Presidency," Progressive Policy Institute, www.dlc.org/documents/Politics_ogf_Evasion.pdf. See also Kenneth S. Baer, *Reinventing the Democrats: The Politics of Liberalism from Reagan to Clinton* (Lawrence: University of Kansas Press, 2000).

186   Democratic Leadership Council, "New Orleans Declaration," March 1, 1990, http://www.dlc.org/ndol_ci.cfm?contentid=878&kaid=128&subid=174; Baer, *Reinventing the Democrats*, 118–92.

187   Will Marshall and Martin Schram, eds., *Mandate for Change* (New York: Berkeley Books, 1992), xvi–xvii; Doug Ross, "Enterprise Economics on the Front Lines: Empowering Firms and Workers to Win," in *Mandate for Change*, ed. Will Marshall and Martin Schram (New York: Berkeley Books, 1992), 51–80. For more on the tense relationship between the DLC and organized labor movement, see Democratic Leadership Council, "Why America Needs a New Labor," *New Democrat*, March 1, 1998, http://www.dlc.org/ndol_ci4e05.html?kaid=107&subid=297&contentid=1603.

188   Gwen Ifill, "Clinton: Promising a Changed Party," *New York Times*, October 10, 1988.

189   Henry Weinstein, "1988 Democratic National Convention: Restores Focus on 'Apostle of Hope': Clinton Talk Lauds Virtues of Dukakis," *Los Angeles Times*, July 21, 1988.

190   Jeff Faux, "The Myth of the New Democrats," *American Prospect*, September 21, 1993.

191   Robert L. Turner, "The State We're in Massachusetts Still Gets Labeled 'Liberal', but the Truth Is More Complicated," *Boston Globe*, October 18, 1998; Joanna Weiss, "Political Clout Moves to Bay State Suburbs," *Boston Globe*, November 16, 2002.

192   Michael Kranish and Scott Helman, *The Real Romney* (New York: Harper, 2012), 224–60.

Epilogue

1   Barack Obama, keynote address, Democratic National Convention, Boston, July 27, 2004, available online by Gerhard Peters and John T. Woolley, *The American Presidency Project*, http://www.presidency.ucsb.edu/ws/?pid=76988.

2   Richard Florida, *The Rise of the Creative Class, Revisited* (New York: Basic Books, 2012), xvi–xvii.

3   Ernest Luning, "Re-energized Romney Campaigns in Jeffco," *Colorado Statesman*, September 28, 2012; Colleen McCain Nelson, "President's Populist Pitch Divides Suburban Voters," *Wall Street Journal*, July 17, 2012; Kent Hoover, "Mitt Romney Tells NVTC That Obama Is Discouraging Innovation," *Washington Business Journal*, February 20, 2012; White House, Office of the Press Secretary, "President Obama Signs America Invents Act, Overhauling the Patent System to Stimulate Economic Growth, and Announces New Steps to Help Entrepreneurs Create Jobs," September 16, 2011, http://www.whitehouse.gov/the-press-office/2011/09/16/president-obama-signs-america-invents-act-over hauling-patent-system-stim.

4   Nate Silver, "In Silicon Valley, Technology Talent Gap Threatens G.O.P Campaigns," *New York Times*, November 29, 2012; Nate Cohn, "Bankers—Abandoned Obama, but the Rest of the Rich Hold Surprisingly Strong," *New Republic Online*, November 14, 2012; George Packer, "Change the World," *New Yorker*, May 27, 2013.

5   Irene Sege, "Moving Out and Moving Up: Asian-Americans Establish Growing Presence in the Suburbs," *Boston Globe*, May 19, 1991. Beginning in the late 1990s, the Boston area experienced a particularly large influx of engineers and other white-collar professionals from India. See Kimberly Blanton, "Out of India Computer Pioneers from Bombay to Delhi Are Flocking to Greater Boston to Pursue a High-Tech Version of the American Dream," *Boston Globe*, September 30, 2001; Cindy Rodriguez, "A High-Tech Home for Indians," *Boston Globe*, July 22, 2000.

6   Lexington Demographic Change Task Force, "Report of the Demographic Change Task Force—Final," March 19, 2010, http://www.lexingtonma.gov/committees/2020/DCTFre port3-19-2010.pdf.

7   Blanton, "Out of India."

8   Sege, "Moving Out and Moving Up."

9   Linda Wertheimer, "Culture Shift," *Boston Globe*, December 4, 2011; Kathleen Burge, "Town in Transition," *Boston Globe*, July 8, 2010; Christine McConville, "Small Town Sees World of Change—Immigrants Bring Greater Diversity to Public Schools," *Boston Globe*, November 10, 2002.

10   US Census Bureau, *American Factfinder, 2010 Census*, http://factfinder2.census.gov.

11   Barry Bluestone and Mary Huff Stevenson, *The Boston Renaissance: Race, Space, and Economic Change in an American Metropolis* (New York: Russell Sage, 2002), 126; Guy Stuart, "Segregation in the Boston Metropolitan Area at the End of the 20th Century" (Cambridge, MA: Civil Rights Project at Harvard University, February 2000).

12   US Census Bureau, "2010 Census Quick Facts for Lawrence Massachusetts, http://quick facts.census.gov/qfd/states/25; US Census Bureau, "2010 Census Quick Facts for Chelsea, Massachusetts," http://quickfacts.census.gov/qfd/states/25; Massachusetts Department of

Elementary and Secondary Education, "2012–13 Selected Populations Report (District)," http://profiles.doe.mass.edu/state_report/selectedpopulations.aspx.

13 US Census Bureau, *2010 Census: Population and Housing Data*, https://www.census.gov /prod/www/decennial.html; Jennifer B. Ayscue, Alyssa Greenberg, et al., "Losing Ground: School Segregation in Massachusetts," UCLA Civil Rights Project, May 2013.

14 Kimberly Atkins, "Mapping the Quiet Divide," *Boston Globe*, March 9, 2003.

15 Rhonda Stewart, "Towns Seek New Housing Strategies—Affordable Rate of 10% Still Far Off," *Boston Globe*, May 9, 2004; "No Quarter for Snob Zoning," *Boston Globe*, July 27, 2007.

16 Debra Goldman, "Supporting METCO program," *Wayland Town Crier*, October 21, 2012.

17 James Vaznis, "METCO in a Budget Squeeze," *Boston Globe*, April 27, 2009.

18 Tracy Jan, "METCO Fears for Its Future," *Boston Globe*, July 26, 2007; Laura J. Nelson, "Metco Students on 'Positive Track,'" *Boston Globe*, June 16, 2011.

19 Gary Orfield, Jennifer Arenson, Tara Jackson, Christine Bohrer, Dawn Gavin, Emily Kalejs, et al., "City-Suburban Desegregation: Parent and Student Perspectives in Metropolitan Boston" (Cambridge, MA: Civil Rights Project at Harvard University, September 1997).

20 Bluestone and Stevenson, *The Boston Renaissance*, 11, 24.

21 Massachusetts Department of Elementary and Secondary Education, "METCO Program Frequently Asked Questions," www.doe.mass.edu/metco/faq.html. These figures include the 145 students in the Springfield program.

22 Susan E. Eaton, *The Other Boston Busing Story: What's Won and Lost Across the Boundary Line* (New Haven, CT: Yale University Press, 2001), 3, 197–217.

23 Nancy McArdle, Theresa Osypuk, and Dolores Acevedo-García, "Prospects for Equity in Boston Public Schools' School Assignment Plans," issue brief, September 2010, Diversity Data.Org, http://diversitydata.sph.harvard.edu/Publications/Prospects_for_Equity_in%20 _Boston_Schools.pdf.

24 Noah Bierman, "Patrick Targets Local Aid to Cover Budget Gap," *Boston Globe*, December 5, 2012.

25 Boston School Choice, "Quality, Close to Home: The Home-Based School Choice Plan," http://bostonschoolchoice.org/.

26 Allison Kilkenny, "As Boston Ends Desegregation Busing, Students Face New Inequities," *Nation*, April 8, 2013; Dana Goldstein, "Bostonians Committed to School Diversity Haven't Given Up on Busing," *Atlantic Cities*, October 10, 2012.

27 Katharine Q. Seelye, "No Division Required in This School Problem," *New York Times*, March 12, 2013; James Vaznis, "Boston Adopts New School Assignment Plan," *Boston Globe*, March 13, 2013.

28 William H. Frey, "Demographic Reversal: Cities Thrive, Suburbs Sputter," Brookings Institute, June 29, 2012, www.brookings.edu/research/opinions/2012/06/29-cities-suburbs -frey; Alan Berube, "Where the Grads Are: Degree Attainment in Metro Areas," Brookings Institute, May 31, 2012, http://www.brookings.edu/blogs/the-avenue/posts/2012/05/31 -educational-attainment-berube.

29 For a discussion of the desire to live near "like-minded" people, see Bill Bishop, *The Big Sort: Why the Clustering of Like-Minded America Is Tearing Us Apart* (Boston: Houghton Mifflin Harcourt, 2008).

30 For examples of how these qualities have been translated into market terms, see Florida, *Rise of the Creative Class, Revisited*, 183–265; Edward Glaeser, *The Triumph of the City: How Our Greatest Invention Makes Us Richer, Smarter, Greener, Healthier, and Happier* (New York: Penguin Books, 2011).

31 Elizabeth Kneebone and Alan Berube, *Confronting Suburban Poverty in America* (Washington, DC: Brookings Institution Press, 2013).

Index

Note: pages in *italics* refer to illustrations.